FORD CORSAIR V4

Owner's Workshop Manual

by J.H.Haynes

Associate Member of the Guild of Motoring Writers

and D.H.Stead

Models Covered

1663 c.c.	De - Luxe Saloon	September 1965 to October 1970
1996 c.c.	GT	September 1967 to January 1967
	Estate Car GT	March 1966 to January 1967
	2000E	January 1967 to October 1970
	2000 Saloon, Estate Car	March 1967 to October 1970

SBN 900550 23 6

© J.H. HAYNES & CO. LTD. 1971

22-26 Lower Odcombe, Yeovil, Somerset

Tel. West Coker 406

Acknowledgements

Thanks are due to the Ford Motor Company Ltd., for their assistance with regard to the use of technical material and illustrations; to Castrol Ltd., for lubrication chart information; to the 'Autocar' for permission to use the cutaway illustration on the cover; and to Champion Ltd., for the sparking plug photographs.

Thanks are especially due to R.T. Grainger for his assistance when working on the engine and to Lt. Col. F.T. Nicholson for advice on the text.

Whilst every care is taken to ensure that the information in this manual is correct bearing in mind the changes in design and specification which are a continuous process, even within a model range, no liability can be accepted by the authors and publishers for any loss, damage or injury caused by any errors or omissions in the information given.

Photographic Captions & Cross References

The book is divided into twelve chapters. Each chapter is divided into numbered sections which are headed in bold type between horizontal lines. Each section consists of serially numbered paragraphs.

There are two types of illustration. (1) Figures which are numbered according to Chapter and sequence of occurrence in that chapter and having an individual caption to each figure. (2) Photographs which have a reference number in the bottom left hand corner. All photographs apply to the chapter in which they occur so that the reference figures pinpoint the pertinent section and paragraph numbers.

Procedures, once described in the text, are not normally repeated. If it is necessary to refer to another chapter the reference will be given in chapter number and section number thus:- Chapter 1/6.

If it is considered necessary to refer to a particular paragraph in another chapter the reference is 'Chapter 1/6:5'. Cross references given without use of the word 'Chapter' apply to sections and/or paragraphs in the same chapter, e.g., 'see section 8' means also 'in this chapter'.

When the left or right hand side of a car is mentioned it is as if one was looking in the forward direction of travel.

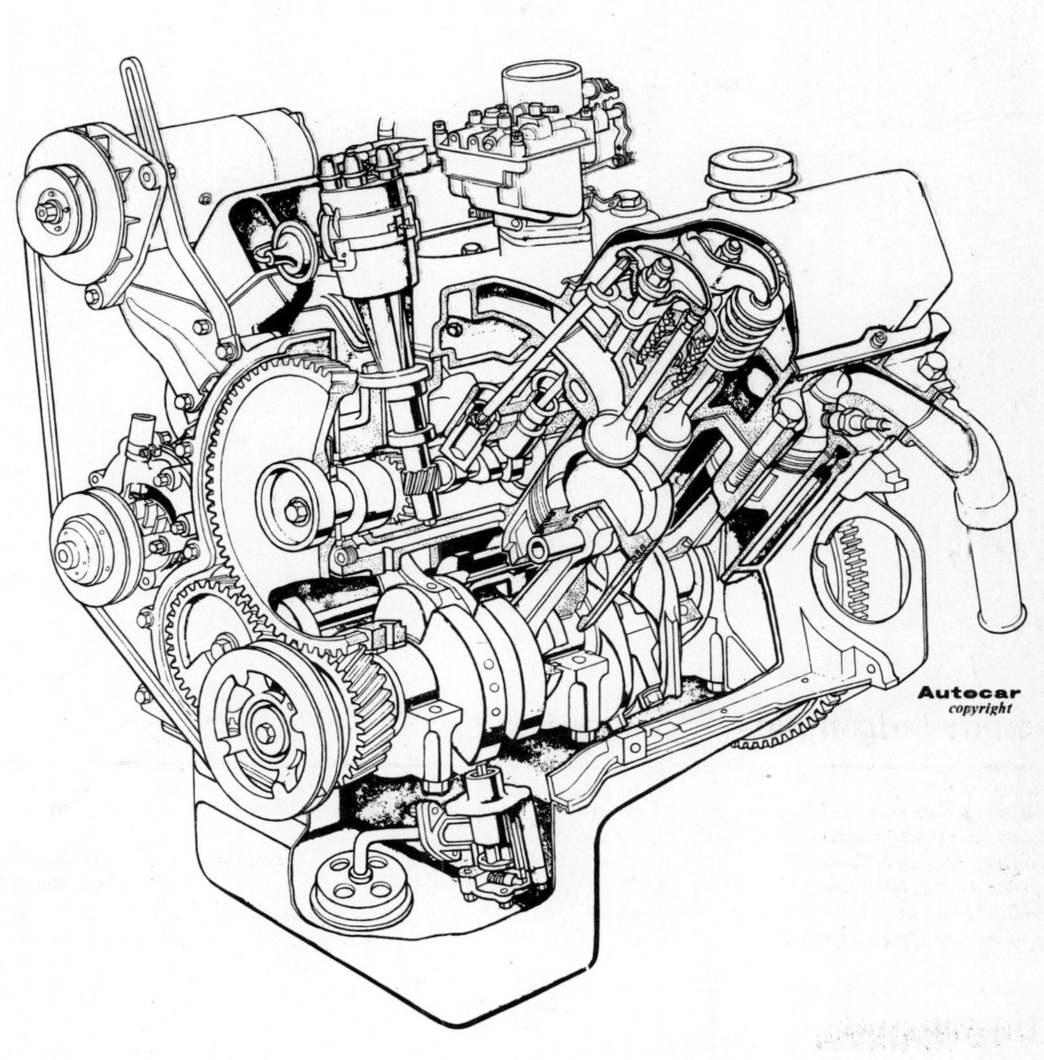

THE V4 IS A ROBUST ENGINE WITH GOOD TORQUE CHARACTERISTICS
FOR ITS COMPACT SIZE

Introduction

This manual is intended for those who wish to find out more about the Corsair V4, which they may own, and to show them also how to carry out the maintenance and repairs necessary to keep it performing safely and economically.

The older a car gets the more attention it will need as normal wear and tear takes it toll. Thus the buyer of a cheaper, older model is faced with the need for more attention to his vehicle in order to enable it to run safely and pass the tests required by law every 12 months. As the purchase of a cheaper car is usually due to economic necessity it follows that garage bills are equally to be avoided.

This manual is the **only** one written which is based on the author's personal experiences. The hands in most of the photographs are those of the person who has written the book. Manufacturers' own official workshop manuals are all very well for those whose knowledge on certain basic terminology and methods is assumed. For the rest, this manual provides clear illustrations and descriptions of the order and method for the jobs to be done, step by step.

It must be assumed that a range of tools is available to the do-it-yourself owner. The accumulation of good tools is normally done over a period of time and this is the one expense that the do-it-yourself man must be prepared for. Never buy cheap tools. Be discreet in borrowing tools and do not be annoyed if someone refuses to lend them. Appreciate how much they cost if lost or damaged.

Certain jobs require specialised tools and where these are essential this manual will say so. Otherwise alternative means are given. Much of the work involved in looking after a car and carrying out repairs depends on accurate diagnosis in the first place. Where possible therefore a methodical and progressive way of diagnosis is presented. The time that can be wasted in hopping from one possible source of trouble to another suggested at random quite often by self styled 'experts' must have been experienced by many people. It is best to say at the start therefore, 'This could be one of several things - let's get the book out'.

Contents

Routine Maintenance

Maintenance should be regarded as essential for ensuring safety and desirable for the purpose of obtaining economy and performance from the car. By far the largest element of the maintenance routine is visual examination. Each chapter of the manual gives details of the routine maintenance requirements. In the summary given here the safety items are shown in **bold type.** These **must** be attended to regularly in the interests of preventing accidents and possible loss of life.

Neglect of other items results in unreliability, overall increased running costs and more rapid depreciation of the value of the car.

---

500 miles

EVERY 500 MILES (or weekly)

ENGINE
Check the oil level in the sump and top up as required.
Check the radiator coolant level and top up as required.
Check the battery electrolyte level and top up as required.

STEERING
Check the tyre pressures.
Examine tyres for wear or damage.
Is the steering still smooth and accurate?

BRAKES
Check the hydraulic fluid reservoir level. If a significant drop is apparent examine the system for leaks immediately.
Is there any reduction in braking efficiency?
Try an emergency stop. Is adjustment necessary?

LIGHTS
Do all bulbs work at the front and rear?
Are the headlight beams correctly aligned?

Fan belt adjustment

5,000 miles

EVERY 5,000 miles (or every six months if 5,000 miles are not exceeded) or if indications are that safety items in particular are not performing correctly.

ENGINE
Drain the sump of oil when hot, renew the oil filter element and refill the sump with fresh oil.
Check the valve clearances and adjust as necessary.
Check the distributor contact breaker points and adjust as necessary.
Check the tension of the fan belt.
Clean the fuel pump filter.
Check the sparking plug electrode gaps.
Lubricate the distributor.
Lubricate the generator rear end bush.

CLUTCH
Check the hydraulic reservoir level. If there is a significant drop examine for leaks.

STEERING
Is there free play between the steering wheel and road wheels?
Examine all steering linkage rods, joints and bushes for signs of wear or damage.
Check the front wheel hub bearings and adjust if necessary.
Check the oil level in the steering box and top up as required.

BRAKES
Examine the disc pads and drum shoes to determine the amount of friction material remaining. Renew as necessary.
Examine all hydraulic pipes, cylinders and unions for signs of chafing, corrosion, dents or any other form of deterioration or leaks.

SUSPENSION
Examine all bolts and shackles securing the suspension units and springs and tighten as necessary.
Check for play in the rubber bushes.

10,000 miles

EVERY 10,000 miles (or annually if 10,000 miles are not exceeded) or if indications are that safety items in particular are not performing correctly.

ENGINE
Fit new distributor contact breaker points.
Fit new sparking plugs.
Fit a new carburettor air cleaner element.
Flush out the cooling system.

GEARBOX
Check the oil level and top up as required.

REAR AXLE
Check the oil level and top up as required.

STEERING
Remove front wheel hub bearings, flush, inspect and repack with grease.

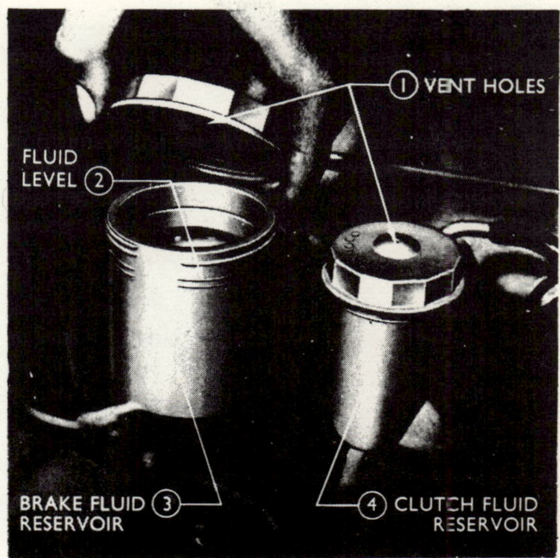

The brake and clutch hydraulic fluid reservoirs

Fitting the air cleaner cover

BODYFRAME
Examine for rust where suspension is attached.

30,000 miles

GEARBOX
Drain and replenish the oil.

REAR AXLE
Drain and replenish the oil.

Additionally the following items should be attended to as time can be spared:-

CLEANING
Examination of components requires that they be cleaned. The same applies to the body of the car, inside and out, in order that deterioration due to rust or unknown damage may be detected. Certain parts of the body frame, if rusted badly, can result in the vehicle being declared unsafe and it will not pass the annual test for roadworthiness.

EXHAUST SYSTEM
An exhaust system must be leakproof, and the noise level below a certain minimum. Excessive leaks may cause carbon monoxide fumes to enter the passenger compartment. Excessive noise consistutes a public nuisance. Both these faults may cause the vehicle to be kept off the road. Repair or replace defective sections when symptoms are apparent.

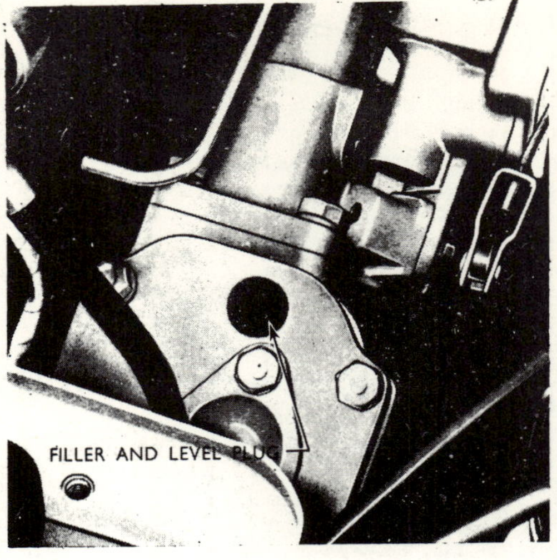

The steering box filler and level plug

The rear axle filler and level plug

LUBRICATION CHART

CASTROL GTX
An ultra high performance motor oil approved for use in the engine in summer and winter.

CASTROL HYPOY LIGHT GEAR OIL
A powerful, extreme pressure lubricant recommended for the transmission and steering gear.

CASTROL HYPOY GEAR OIL
A powerful, extreme pressure gear oil essential for the lubrication of the hypoid rear axle.

CASTROL LM GREASE
Recommended for the wheel bearings. May also be used for chassis lubrication.

DAILY

ENGINE
Check oil level and, if necessary, top up to the "Full" mark on the dipstick with **Castrol GTX.**

EVERY 15,000 MILES
Including daily and 5,000 mile services

FRONT WHEEL BEARING
Clean out old grease and repack with fresh **Castrol LM Grease.** This operation should be carried out by your Dealer.

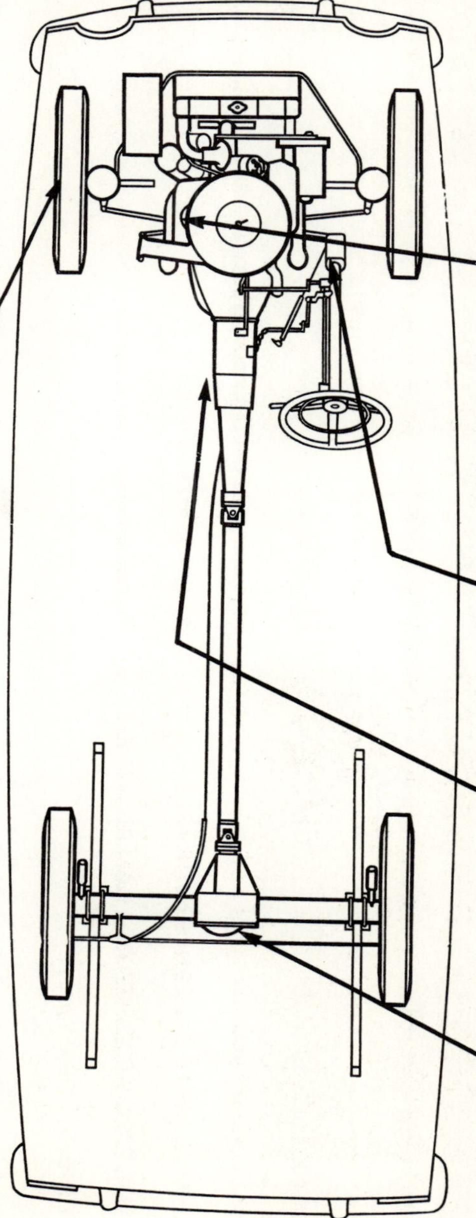

EVERY 5,000 MILES
Including daily service

ENGINE
Every 5,000 miles drain off the old oil while warm and refill with fresh **Castrol GTX.** At the same time, renew oil filter element and rubber sealing ring.

Note: It is necessary to drain and refill more frequently when driving under adverse conditions such as stop/start motoring, cold weather operation where appreciable engine idling is experienced, or driving under dusty conditions: in these circumstances the oil and oil filter element should be changed more frequently.

Capacity:—6 pints plus 1½ pints for filter.

OVERSEAS
Air temperature
Above −23°C (−10°F) **Castrol GTX**
Below −23°C (−10°F) **Castrol Super 10W/40**

STEERING BOX
After the first 500 miles, thereafter every 5,000 miles, check oil level and, if necessary, replenish to the bottom of the filler plug hole with **Castrol Hypoy Gear Oil.**

GEARBOX
After the first 500 miles, check oil level and, if necessary, top up with **Castrol Hypoy Light Gear Oil.** After the the first 5,000 miles, drain off the old oil while warm and refill with fresh **Castrol Hypoy Light Gear Oil.** At subsequent 5,000 mile intervals it is only necessary to check and maintain the oil level.
Capacity:—1¾ pints
2¼ pints (approx.) 2000E

OVERSEAS
Castrol Hypoy Light Gear Oil is recommended for all climatic conditions

REAR AXLE
After the first 500 miles, thereafter every 5,000 miles, check level by means of combined filler and level plug and top up if necessary with **Castrol Hypoy Gear Oil.**
Capacity . .—2 pints

OVERSEAS
Air temperature
Below −23°C (−10°F) **Castrol Hypoy Light Gear Oil**

Recommended Lubricants

COMPONENT	TYPE OF LUBRICANT OR FLUID	CASTROL PRODUCT
ENGINE	Multigrade engine oil	Castrol G.T.X.
GEARBOX	S.A.E. 80 E.P.	Castrol S.T. gear oil
REAR AXLE	S.A.E. 90 E.P.	Castrol 'Hypoy'
STEERING BOX	S.A.E. 90 E.P.	
FRONT WHEEL BEARINGS	Medium grade multi-purpose grease	Castrol L.M. grease
DISTRIBUTOR, STARTER & GENERATOR BUSHES	Engine or light oil	Castrol G.T.X. or Castrolite
DISTRIBUTOR CONTACT BREAKER CAM & BATTERY	Petroleum jelly	
UPPER CYLINDER LUBRICANT		'Castrollo'
HYDRAULIC PISTONS	Rubber grease	Castrol rubber grease
BRAKE MASTER CYLINDER FLUID RESERVOIR	Hydraulic fluid	Castrol/Girling 'Crimson'

Additionally Castrol 'Everyman' oil can be used to lubricate door, boot and bonnet hinges, and locks, pivots, etc.

Ordering Spare Parts

Buy genuine Fo Mo Co spare parts from a Ford dealer direct, or through a local garage. If you go to an authorised dealer the correctly fitting genuine parts can usually be supplied from stock which, of course, is a greatly added convenience.

Always have details of the car's serial number available when obtaining parts. If you can take along the part to be renewed as well it is helpful. Modifications are a continuing and unpublicized process in car manufacture, apart from all the variations of model types. If a storeman says he cannot guarantee that the part he supplies is correct, because the engine number is not known, he is perfectly justified. Variations can occur from month to month.

The vehicle identification plate is mounted on the right hand mudguard apron inside the engine compartment. It is not a bad idea to write down the details in your diary or pocket book.

DRIVE	1 R.H.D. or 2 L.H.D.
ENGINE	Denoting capacity and compression ratio. The figures 1, 2 and 3 refer to the 1498 c.c. engine. The V4 engine is covered by letters:- A 1700 c.c. H.C. C 2000 c.c. H.C. B 1700 c.c. L.C. D 2000 c.c. L.C.
TRANSMISSION	Denotes type of gearbox. 1 Floor gear change A Floor change 2 Steering column change B Steering column change 3 Automatic C Automatic 4 Floor change G.T.
AXLE	Denotes axle ratio:- S 3.777:1
TRIM	Indicates the colour and types of trim used.
S.V.C.	Used by an assembly plant when manufactured parts are shipped elsewhere.
VEHICLE NUMBER	A code, which is explained at the front of every parts list denoting country and plant of manufacture, body style, year and month of manufacture, and serial number.
PAINT CODE	Consists of letters indicating colours and type of original paint.

Chapter 1/Engine

Contents

Specifications

Engine Specifications and Data 1664 cc and 1996 cc (September, 1965 onwards)

Engine - General

Type	4 cylinder 60°Vee pushrod operated OHV
Weight	336 lbs. approx. 399 lbs. with gearbox (approx.)
Bore	3.6878 in. (93.67 mm)
Stroke - 1.7 litre	2.376 in. (60.35 mm)
- 2 litre	2.851 in. (72.42 mm)
Cubic capacity - 1.7 litre	1664 cc
- 2 litre	1996 cc
Compression ratio - 1.7 litre H.C.	9.1:1
- 2 litre H.C.	8.9:1
- Both - Low compression	7.7:1
Compression pressure:	
Low compression	140-160 lbs/in.^{2} (9.843-11.25 kg/cm^2) at 300 r.p.m.
High compression	160-180 lbs/in.^{2} (11.25-12.66 kg/cm^2) at 300 r.p.m.

Maximum B.H.P. - 1.7 litre H.C. ... ...   81.5 (gross) at 4750 r.p.m.
              - 1.7 litre L.C. ... ...   73.5 (gross) at 4750 r.p.m.
              - 2 litre H.C. ... ...   93.0 (gross) at 4750 r.p.m.
              - 2 litre L.C. ... ...   88.0 (gross) at 4750 r.p.m.
Maximum torque - 1.7 litre H.C. ... ...   99.5 lbs/ft. (13.2 Kg/m) gross at 3000 r.p.m.
              - 1.7 litre L.C. ... ...   94.0 lbs/ft. (12.4 Kg/m) gross at 3000 r.p.m.
              - 2 litre H.C. ... ...   123.5 lbs/ft. (16.4 Kg/m) gross at 2750 r.p.m.
              - 2 litre L.C. ... ...   117.5 lbs/ft. (15.6 Kg/m) gross at 2750 r.p.m.
Location of No. 1 cylinder ... ...   Right hand bank next to radiator
Idling speed ... ...   580 to 620 r.p.m.
Firing order ... ...   1 (R), 3 (L), 4 (L), 2 (R)
Engine mountings... ... ...   3. One each side of engine and one beneath the gearbox
                                                           extension

Camshaft & Camshaft Bearings

Camshaft drive ... ...   Fibre gearwheel from crankshaft
Camshaft bearings ... ...   3 steel back, white metal bushes
Bearing oversize available ... ...   .020 in. (0.51 mm) oversize on O.D. Standard I.D.
Camshaft journal diameter - front ... ...   1.8737 to 1.8745 in. (47.59 to 47.67 mm)
                          - intermediate ... ...   1.8137 to 1.8145 in. (46.07 to 46.15 mm)
                          - rear ... ...   1.7537 to 1.7545 in. (44.54 to 44.56 mm)
Camshaft bearing I.D. - front ... ...   1.8753 to 1.8763 in. (47.63 to 47.66 mm)
                      - intermediate ... ...   1.8153 to 1.8163 in. (46.36 to 46.39 mm)
                      - rear ... ...   1.7553 to 1.7563 in. (44.58 to 44.60 mm)
Diametrical bearing clearance ... ...   .0008 to .0026 in. (.023 to .066 mm)
End float ... ...   .003 to .007 in. (.076 to .178 mm)
Thrust plate thickness ... ...   .180 to .182 in. (4.572 to 4.623 mm)
Maximum cam lift - inlet ... ...   .25465 in. (6.4681 mm)
                 - exhaust ... ...   .26065 in. (6.6205 mm)
Cam heel to toe dimension - inlet ... ...   1.3372 to 1.3462 in. (33.96 to 34.19 mm)
                          - exhaust ... ...   1.3432 to 1.3522 in. (34.12 to 34.35 mm)
Backlash - crankshaft to camshaft gear ... ...   .002 to .004 in. (.05 to .10 mm)

Balance Shaft and Balance Shaft Bearings

Balance shaft drive ... ...   steel gear from crankshaft
Balance shaft bearings ... ...   2 steel back, white metal bushes
Bearing oversize available ... ...   .020 in. (0.51 mm) oversize on O.D. Standard I.D.
Journal diameter - front ... ...   2.625 to 2.6258 in. (66.675 - 66.695 mm)
                 - rear ... ...   2.250 to 2.2508 in. (57.150 - 57.170 mm)
Bearing I.D. - front ... ...   2.6276 to 2.6283 in. (66.741 - 66.759 mm)
             - rear ... ...   2.2526 to 2.2533 in. (57.216 - 57.234 mm)
Diametrical bearing clearance ... ...   .0018 to .0033 (.046 to .0584 mm)
End float ... ...   .010 to .015 in. (.25 to .38 mm)
Thrust plate thickness ... ...   .180 to .182 in. (4.57 to 4.623 mm)

Connecting Rods and Big and Small End Bearings

Connecting Rod type ... ...   'H' section steel forging
Length between centres ... ...   5.641 to 5.643 in. (143.28 to 143.32 mm)
Big end bearings - material & type... ... ...   Steel back copper/lead or aluminium/tin liners - shells
Big end diameter ... ...   2.521 to 2.5215 in. (143.28 to 143.32 mm)
Bearing liner wall thickness ... ...   .07145 to .0717 in. (1.8149 to 1.8212 mm)
Undersize bearings obtainable ... ...   .002, .010, .020, .030, 040 in.)
                                                           .051, .254, .508, .76, 1.02 mm) I.D.

Crankpin to bearing clearance ... ...   .0012 to .003 in. (.030 to .08 mm)
Crankpin end float ... ...   .004 to .010 in. (.102 to .254 mm)
Small end diameter ... ...   .9358 to .9362 in. (23.769 to 23.779 mm)

Crankshaft and main bearings

Number of bearings   3
Main bearing journal diameter - BLUE ... ...   2.5006 to 2.5010 in. (63.515 to 63.525 mm)
                                RED... ... ...   2.5010 to 2.5014 in. (63.525 to 63.536 mm)
                                GREEN... ... ...   2.4906 to 2.4910 in. (63.261 to 63.271 mm)
                                YELLOW ... ...   2.4910 to 2.4914 in. (63.271 to 63.282 mm)
Regrind diameters:
     .010 in. (.25 mm) U/S RED ... ...   2.4902 to 2.4906 in. (63.251 to 63.261 mm)
                        BLUE ... ...   2.4906 to 2.4910 in. (63.261 to 63.271 mm)
     .020 in. (.51 mm) U/S RED, YELLOW ... ...   2.4802 to 2.4806 in. (62.997 to 63.007 mm)
                        BLUE, GREEN ... ...   2.4806 to 2.4810 in. (63.007 to 63.017 mm)
     .030 in. (.76 mm) RED, YELLOW ... ...   2.4702 to 2.4706 in. (62.743 to 62.753 mm)
                        BLUE, GREEN ... ...   2.4706 to 2.4710 in. (62.753 to 62.763 mm)
     .040 in. (1.02 mm) RED ... ...   2.4602 to 2.4606 in. (62.489 to 62.499 mm)

.040 in. (1.02 mm) BLUE	2.4606 to 2.4610 in. (62.499 to 62.509 mm)
Main journal length - Front	.95 to 1.00 in. (24.13 to 25.40 mm)
Centre	1.059 to 1.061 in. (26.90 to 26.95 mm)
Rear	1.06 to 1.09 in. (26.9 to 27.7 mm)
Crankshaft end thrust	Taken by steel back copper/lead or aluminium/tin split washers at the centre main bearing.
Crankshaft end float	.003 to .011in. (.08 to .28 mm)
Main bearing material	Steel back copper/lead or aluminium/tin
Undersize bearings available (Std. O.D.)	.010, .020, .030, .040 in. (.25, .51, .76, .102 mm)
Undersize bearings available [.0˙5 in. (.381 mm) u/s on O.D.]	Std. I.D.) Graded .010 (.25 mm)) .020 (.51 mm) .030 (.76 mm)
Main bearing liner wall thickness - RED	.08135 to .08160 (2.0714 to 2.0777 mm)
BLUE	.0817 to .08200 in. (2.0816 to 2.0879 mm)
YELLOW	.09405 to .09430 in. (2.3889 to 2.3952 mm)
GREEN	.09445 to .09470 (2.3991 to 2.4054 mm)
Crankpin journal diameter	2.3756 to 2.3764 in. (60.340 to 60.361 mm)
Crankpin journal length	.838 to .842 in. (2.128 to 2.139 mm)
Crankpin journal fillet radius	.080 to .094 in. (2.03 to 2.39 mm)
Thrust washer thickness	.091 to .093 in. (2.31 to 2.36 mm)
Oversize thrust washer available	.0025, .005, .0075, .010 in. (.064, .13, .191, .25 mm)
Spigot bearing bore	1.3766 to 1.3778 in. (34.966 to 34.996 mm)

Cylinder Block

Type	Cylinder cast integral with top half of crankcase
Water jackets	Full length
Vee angle	60º
Cylinder bore diameters	Graded
Grade 1	3.6869 to 3.6872 in. (93.647 to 93.655 mm)
Grade 2	3.6872 to 3.6875 in. (93.655 to 93.663 mm)
Grade 3	3.6875 to 3.6878 in. (93.663 to 93.670 mm)
Grade 4	3.6878 to 3.6881 in. (93.670 to 93.678 mm)
Grade 5	3.6881 to 3.6884 in. (93.678 to 93.686 mm)
Grade 6	3.6884 to 3.6887 in. (93.686 to 93.693 mm)
Grading point	1.875 in. (47.63 mm) from block face on thrust plane
Cylinder liners available	Std. and .020 (.51 mm) o/s on O.D.
Cylinder liner I.D.	3.652 to 3.657 in. (92.761 to 2.888 mm)
O.D. (Std.)	3.8345 to 3.8355 in. (97.396 to 97.412 mm)
Bore for liners (Std.)	3.8315 to 3.8325 in. (97.320 to 97.34 mm)
Bore for balance shaft bushes - Front	2.8128 to 2.8137 in. (71.438 to 71.468 mm)
- Rear	2.4375 to 2.4387 in. (61.913 to 61.943 mm)
Bore for camshaft bushes - Front	2.040 to 2.0416 in. (51.816 to 51.857 mm)
- Centre	1.9800 to 1.9816 in. (50.292 to 50.333 mm)
- Rear	1.9200 to 1.9216 in. (48.768 to 48.809 mm)
Bore for main bearing liners - RED	2.6654 to 2.6658 in. (67.701 to 67.711 mm)
- BLUE	2.6658 to 2.6662 in. (67.711 to 67.721 mm)
- YELLOW	2.6804 to 2.6808 in. (68.082 to 68.092 mm)
- GREEN	2.6808 to 2.6 812 in. (68.092 to 68.102 mm)

Cylinder Heads

Type	Cast iron with vertical valves
Port arrangement	Inlet and exhaust ports separate on opposite sides
Number of inlet ports	4
Number of exhaust ports	4

Gudgeon Pin

Type	Semi-floating, interference fit into connecting rod
Material	Machined seamless steel tubing
Length	2.93 to 2.95 in. (74.42 to 74.93 mm)
Outside diameter	.9370 to .9373 in. (23.793 to 23.906 mm)
Fit in piston	.0003 to .0005 in. (.0076 to .0127 mm) selective

Lubrication System

Type	Wet sump - pressure and spray
Oil filter	Full flow with replaceable element
Oil filter capacity	1½ pints Imp. (1.8 pints U.S., .85 litre)
Sump capacity (less filter)	6 pints Imp. (7.2 pints U.S., 3.4 litres)

Oil pump type	Eccentric bi-rotor or sliding vane
Oil pressure	50 lbs/in.^{2} (3.52 Kg/cm^2)

Oil Pump - Eccentric Bi-rotor Type

Capacity	10 Imp. gallons (12 U.S. galls. 45.425 litres) per minute at 2,500 r.p.m.
Body bore diameter	.50 to .501 in. (12.7 to 12.725 mm)
Drive shaft diameter	.498 to .4985 in. (12.649 to 12.662 mm)
Clearance - shaft to body	.0015 to .003 in. (.038 to .076 mm)
Inner and outer rotor clearance	.006 in. (.152 mm) max.
Outer rotor and housing clearance	.010 in. (.254 mm) max.
Inner and outer rotor end float	.005 in. (.127 mm) max.

Oil Pump - Sliding Vane Type

Capacity	10 Imp. gallons (12 U.S. galls. 45.425 litres) per minute at 2,500 r.p.m.
Body bore diameter	.50 to .501 in. (12.7 to 12.725 mm)
Drive shaft diameter	.498 to .4985 in. (12.649 to 12.662 mm)
Shaft to body clearance	.0015 to .003 in. (.038 to .076 mm)
Vane clearance in rotor	.005 in. (0.127 mm) max.
Rotor and vane end float	.005 in. (0.127 mm) max.

Pistons

Type	Cut away skirt with combustion chamber in crown
Material	Aluminium alloy - tin-plated
Clearance in cylinder...	.002 to .0026 in. (.51 to .066 mm)
Number of rings	3. Two compression, one oil control
Width of ring grooves:	
Compression rings...	.080 to .081 in. (2.032 to 2.057 mm)
Oil control ring...	.1885 to .1875 in. (4.787 to 4.762 mm)
Gudgeon pin bore	Graded
Grade - Red	.9374 to .9375 in. (23.810 to 23.813 mm)
- Yellow	.9375 to .9376 in. (23.813 to 23.815 mm)
- Blue	.9376 to .9377 in. (23.815 to 23.818 mm)
Gudgeon pin bore offset	.06 in. (1.5 mm) towards thrust face
Piston oversizes available	.0025, .005, .015, .030, .045, .060 in. (.0635, .127, .381, .872, 1.14, 1.52 mm)

Piston Rings

Top compression ring	Barrel face cast iron - chrome plated
Top ring width	.077 to .078 in. (1.96 to 1.98 mm)
Top ring fitted gap	.010 to .020 in. (.254 to .508 mm)
Lower compression ring...	Internal bevel, cast iron, molybdenum coated
Lower ring width	.077 to .078 in. (1.956 to 1.981 mm)
Lower ring fitted gap	.010 to .020 in. (.254 to .508 mm)
Upper & lower ring groove clearance	.002 to .004 in. (.0508 to .1016 mm)
Oil control ring	'Micro-land' cast iron slotted scraper
Oil control ring width	.1855 to .1865 in. (4.711 to 4.73 mm)
Oil control ring fitted gap	.010 to .015 in. (.254 to .381 mm)
Groove clearance	.001 to .003 in. (.0254 to .0762 mm)
Oversize oil control rings available	.0025, .005, .015, .030, .045, .060 in. (.0635, .127, .381, .762, 1.14, 1.52 mm)

Tappets

Type	Cylindrical flat based
Diameter	.8740 to .8745 in. (22.2 to 22.21 mm)
Length	2.00 in. (50.8 mm)

Pushrods and Rockers

Type	Hollow tube, hemispherical ends
Diameter	.312 to .314 in. (7.925 to 7.976 mm)
Length	5.87 in. (149.1 mm)
Rocker ratio	1.4754:1

Valves

Head diameter - Inlet...	1.592 to 1.602 in. (40.34 to 40.69 mm)
- Exhaust	1.428 to 1.438 in. (36.27 to 36.52 mm)
Seat angle	45º to 45º 15'
Stem diameter - Inlet	.3095 to .3105 in. (7.861 to 7.887 mm)
- Exhaust	.3086 to .3096 in. (7.838 to 7.864 mm)
Stem to guide clearance - Inlet	.0008 to .003 in. (.020 to .076 mm)
- Exhaust	.0017 to .0039 in. (.043 to .099 mm)

Oversize stems available	.003, .015, .030 in. (.076, .38, .76 mm)
Valve lift - both	.366 in. (9.3 mm)
Valve stem to rocker arm clearance:	
Hot - Inlet	.010 in. (.25 mm)
- Exhaust	.018 in. (.46 mm)
Cold - Inlet	.012 in. (.30 mm)
- Exhaust	.020 in. (.51 mm)

Valve Guides

Type	Machined in cylinder head. Insert bushes available.
Bore for insert guide bushes	.4383 to .4391 in. (11.133 to 11.153 mm)
Guide inside diameter	.3115 to .3125 in. (7.907 to 7.938 mm)
Valve timing	(nominal clearances .018 in. inlet, .026 in. exhaust)
Inlet valve: Opens	20º B.T.D.C.
Closes	56º A.B.D.C.
Exhaust valve: Opens	62º B.B.D.C.
Closes	17º A.T.D.C.
Timing marks	Dimples on crankshaft, camshaft and balance shaft gear wheels

Valve Springs

Type	Single coil spring
Free length	2.028 in. (51.51 mm)
Load at fitted length	(1.60 ins., 40.64 mm) valve closed 59.75 to 69.75 lbs. (27.1 to 31.64 Kgs.)
Load at fitted length	(1.223 in., 31.06 mm) valve open 130 to 144 lbs (58.97 to 65.32 Kgs.)
Total number of coils	6.75

Torque Wrench Settings

Big end bolts	25 to 30 lbs/ft. (3.46 to 4.15 Kg/m)
Camshaft gear bolt	24 to 28 lbs/ft. (3.32 to 3.87 Kg/m)
Crankshaft pulley bolt	24 to 28 lbs/ft. (3.32 to 3.87 Kg/m)
Cylinder head bolts	65 to 70 lbs/ft. (8.98 to 9.67 Kg/m)
Timing gear cover bolts	11 to 13 lbs/ft. (1.52 to 1.80 Kg/m)
Flywheel to crankshaft bolts	45 to 50 lbs/ft. (6.22 to 6.91 Kg/m)
Main bearing bolts	55 to 60 lbs/ft. (7.60 to 8.29 Kg/m)
Inlet manifold bolts	13 to 16 lbs/ft. (1.80 to 2.21 Kg/m)
Oil pump to block	12 to 15 lbs/ft. (1.66 to 2.07 Kg/m)
Rear oil seal retainer bolts	11 to 13 lbs/ft. (1.52 to 1.80 Kg/m)
Rocker cover	2½ to 3½ lbs/ft. (.34 to .42 Kg/m)
Sump	6 to 8 lbs/ft. (.83 to 1.11 Kg/m)
Sump drain plug	20 to 25 lbs/ft. (2.76 to 3.45 Kg/m)
Balance shaft gear bolt	24 to 28 lbs/ft. (3.32 to 3.87 Kg/m)
Carburettor attaching nuts	15 to 18 lbs/ft. (2.07 to 2.49 Kg/m)

1. General Description

The engine is a 4-cylinder unit with the cylinders arranged in a 60º vee formation to give two cylinders in each bank. There are two versions of the engine - the 1664 c.c. and 1996 c.c. with 9.1:1 and 8.9:1 compression ratios respectively. Alternative cylinder heads are available to provide a low compression ratio for both versions of 7.7:1.

Both engines use the same block and bores - the additional capacity being obtained by increasing the stroke. This is done by a larger-throw crankshaft and lower crowned pistons.

The bores are machined directly into the block which has full length water jacketry and three main bearings with removable caps for the crankshaft.

The crankshaft, of cast iron, runs in three large diameter bearings which have renewable shell liners of steel backed aluminium/tin or copper/lead. Endfloat is controlled by thrust washers on each side of the centre bearing. The rear oil seal runs on the crankshaft flange whereas the front one is mounted in the front cover and bears on the crankshaft pulley hub.

The camshaft is mounted centrally in the vee above the crankshaft and is driven at half engine speed by a large fibre helical gear in direct mesh with the crankshaft gear. The camshaft runs in three white metal steel backed bushes.

A skew gear is machined into the camshaft just behind the front bearing and this drives the distributor which is mounted centrally above the camshaft in the vee.

This, indirectly, also drives the oil pump which is connected by a long, hexagonal-section shaft which fits into a recess in the bottom of the distributor drive shaft. The camshaft thrust is taken by a plate bolted to the front block face.

The valves are mounted overhead and are pushrod operated from the camshaft via rockers. The rockers are each mounted on a stud and pivot on a hemispherical fulcrum seat which is located on the stud.

The height of this seat is adjusted by a self locking nut and this provides the means of adjusting the valve to rocker

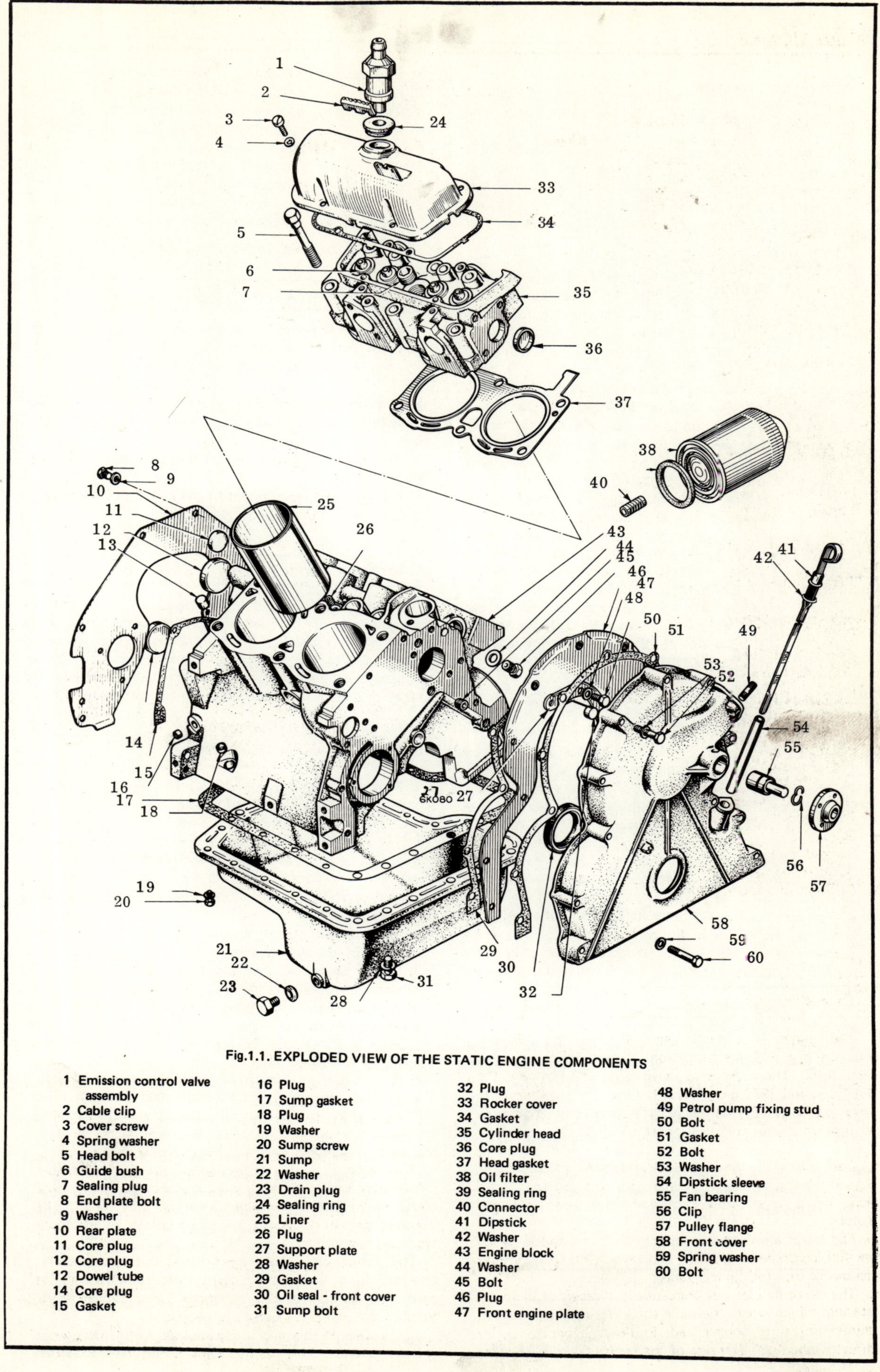

Fig.1.1. EXPLODED VIEW OF THE STATIC ENGINE COMPONENTS

1 Emission control valve assembly	16 Plug	32 Plug	48 Washer
2 Cable clip	17 Sump gasket	33 Rocker cover	49 Petrol pump fixing stud
3 Cover screw	18 Plug	34 Gasket	50 Bolt
4 Spring washer	19 Washer	35 Cylinder head	51 Gasket
5 Head bolt	20 Sump screw	36 Core plug	52 Bolt
6 Guide bush	21 Sump	37 Head gasket	53 Washer
7 Sealing plug	22 Washer	38 Oil filter	54 Dipstick sleeve
8 End plate bolt	23 Drain plug	39 Sealing ring	55 Fan bearing
9 Washer	24 Sealing ring	40 Connector	56 Clip
10 Rear plate	25 Liner	41 Dipstick	57 Pulley flange
11 Core plug	26 Plug	42 Washer	58 Front cover
12 Core plug	27 Support plate	43 Engine block	59 Spring washer
12 Dowel tube	28 Washer	44 Washer	60 Bolt
14 Core plug	29 Gasket	45 Bolt	
15 Gasket	30 Oil seal - front cover	46 Plug	
	31 Sump bolt	47 Front engine plate	

clearances.

The pistons are made of aluminium alloy, tin plated, and have the combustion chambers machined in the crown. The skirts are cut away.

The gudgeon pins are semifloating, being a shrink fit in the connecting rods. The connecting rods are made of forged steel and are of 'H' section with detachable big end caps located by hollow dowel pins. The bearing liners are renewable shells of steel backed aluminium/tin or copper/lead.

Each piston has two compression rings and an oil control ring. The top compression ring is barrel faced and chromium plated on its cylinder wall surface. The lower compression ring is internally chamfered on the top face and molybdenum coated on its cylinder wall face.

As the engine is a 60° Vee configuration the rotating and recipricating parts are inherently out of balance. To compensate for this imbalance the crankshaft pulley, crankshaft and flywheel all have counter balances built in and in addition a separate counterbalance shaft is installed, driven at engine speed, by gear directly from the crankshaft.

The oil pump is either of the bi-rotor or sliding vane type of exceptionally high capacity. Oil pressure is maintained at 50 lbs/in^2 to the main, big end, camshaft, and balance shaft bearings and also to the tappets where oil flow is controlled to run up the inside of the hollow pushrods to lubricate the rocker gear. Cylinder bores are lubricated by a small jet of oil once every revolution from a fine hole in the connecting rod web. Gudgeon pins are lubricated by oil mist in the crankcase, and oil scraped from the cylinder walls which passes through the scraper ring groove. Oil circulates at 10 gallons per minute at an engine speed of 2,500 r.p.m.

2. Routine Maintenance

1. At weekly intervals (or every 300 miles) check the oil level in the sump by removing the dipstick, wiping it clean, replacing it and noting the level on withdrawing it again. The 'fill' mark is the absolute minimum to which the level must be allowed to fall and to regain the 'full' mark 1½ pints of oil will be required. If oil consumption exceeds 1 pint per 300 miles then there is either a leak or the cylinder bores or rings are very worn. Do not overfill with oil as it is simply a waste.
2. At intervals of 5,000 miles (8,000 kms.) the engine oil should be changed. Run the engine until it is hot, place a container of 8 pints capacity under the drain plug in the sump and undo the drain plug. Let the oil drain for at least 10 minutes.
3. At the same time unscrew the filter unit from the left side of the block and fit a new one.
4. Clean the sump drain plug and washer and replace and tighten them. Refill the engine with 7½ pints of the recommended oil, run the engine, and check that the level is correct.
5. At 5,000 miles the valve rocker clearances should be checked and adjusted if necessary, as described in Section 48.2.
6. Check also and clean the oil filler cap and crankcase emission valve in the left and right rocker covers respectively. (See Section 27 for details.)

3. Major Operations with Engine in Place

The following major operations may be carried out without taking the engine from the car:-

1) Removal and replacement of the cylinder heads.
2) Removal and replacement of the sump.
3) Removal and replacement of the big end bearings.
4) Removal and replacement of the pistons and connecting rods.
5) Removal and replacement of the timing gear.
6) Removal and replacement of the oil pump.
7) Removal and replacement of the front engine mountings.
8) Removal and replacement of the engine-gearbox rear mounting.

4. Major Operations with the Engine Removed

Although it would be possible to carry out some of the following operations with the engine in the car if the gearbox and clutch were removed it is deemed inadvisable:-

1) Removal and replacement of the flywheel.
2) Removal and replacement of the rear main bearing oil seal.
3) Removal and replacement of the crankshaft and crankshaft bearings.
4) Removal and replacement of the camshaft and camshaft bushes.

5. Method of Engine Removal

The engine may be lifted out together with the gearbox or separated from the gearbox and lifted out by itself. If the gearbox is left attached the disadvantage is that the engine has to be tilted to a very steep angle to get it out. Unless both the engine and gearbox are being repaired or overhauled together there is little reason for removing them as a unit.

6. Engine Removal without Gearbox

1. A do-it-yourself owner should be able to remove the engine from the car in about 3 hours. It is essential to have a good hoist. If an inspection pit is not available, two support stands will also be required. In the later stages, when the engine is being separated from the gearbox and lifted, the assistance of another person is most useful to help guide the engine and prevent it from swaying about and possibly causing damage.
2. Remove the bonnet as described in Chapter 12/16 ., followed by the battery as described in Chapter 10.
3. Obtain two suitable receptacles to collect the engine oil and cooling water. Rather than use the washing up bowls from the kitchen, it is better to find an empty gallon oil can and cut one side out to use as a container for the oil. If the coolant is to be kept because of anti-freeze a 2 gallon container will be required.
4. Drain the cooling system and remove the radiator as described in Chapter 2/7.
5. Detach the heater hose at the back of the water pump (photo).
6. Unclip the same hose from the side of the engine block under the right hand exhaust manifold (photo).
7. Detach the heater hose from the 'T' piece in the back of the inlet manifold by undoing the pipe clip (photo). Disconnect the valve cable if fitted.
8. Remove the air cleaner assembly from the carburettor as described in Chapter 3/3.3.
9. In view of the way it projects, it is advisable to remove the dynamo complete with its mounting brackets by first removing the fan belt as described in Chapter 2/12 and detaching the two Lucar connectors from the dynamo.

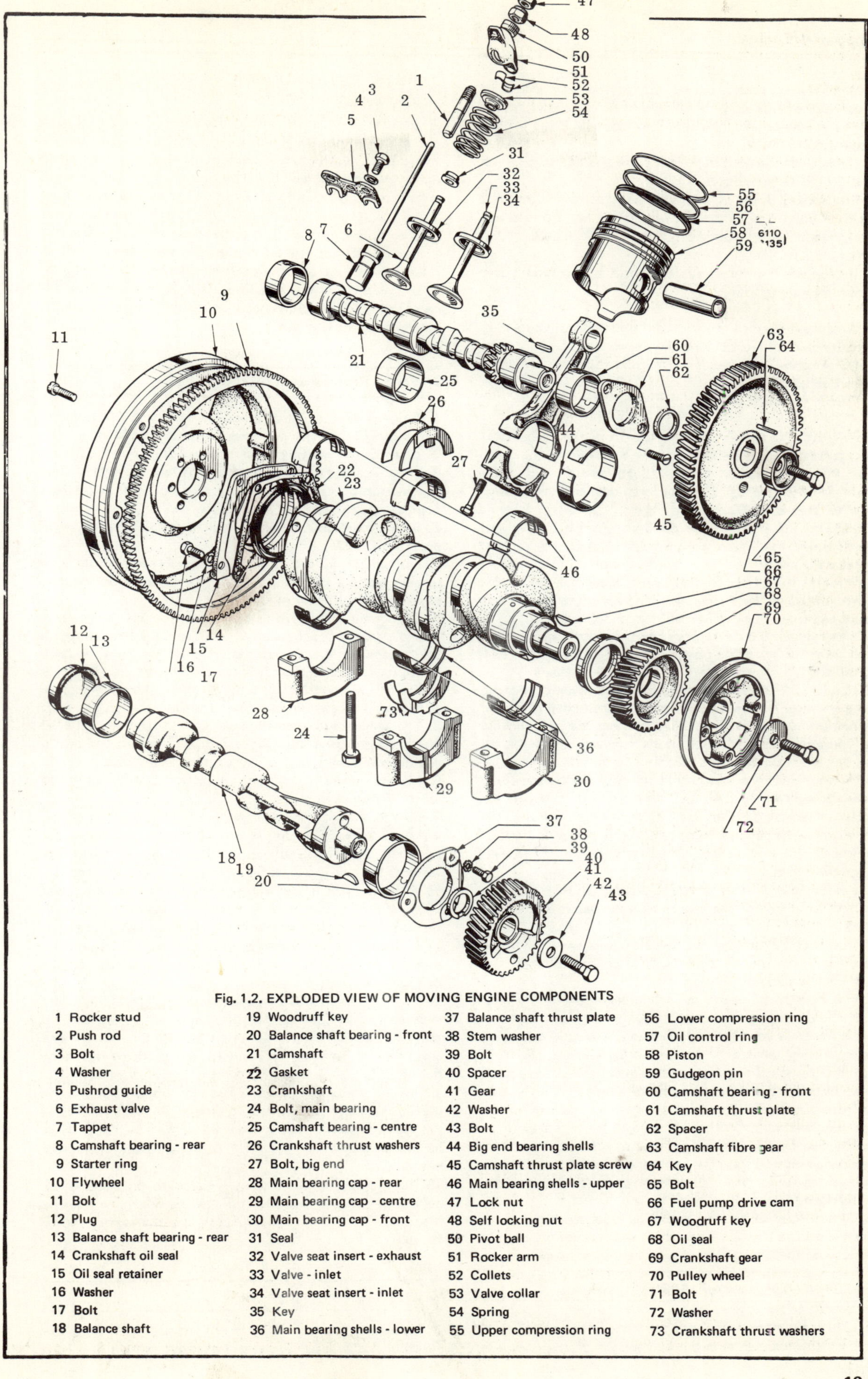

Fig. 1.2. EXPLODED VIEW OF MOVING ENGINE COMPONENTS

1 Rocker stud	19 Woodruff key	37 Balance shaft thrust plate	56 Lower compression ring
2 Push rod	20 Balance shaft bearing - front	38 Stem washer	57 Oil control ring
3 Bolt	21 Camshaft	39 Bolt	58 Piston
4 Washer	22 Gasket	40 Spacer	59 Gudgeon pin
5 Pushrod guide	23 Crankshaft	41 Gear	60 Camshaft bearing - front
6 Exhaust valve	24 Bolt, main bearing	42 Washer	61 Camshaft thrust plate
7 Tappet	25 Camshaft bearing - centre	43 Bolt	62 Spacer
8 Camshaft bearing - rear	26 Crankshaft thrust washers	44 Big end bearing shells	63 Camshaft fibre gear
9 Starter ring	27 Bolt, big end	45 Camshaft thrust plate screw	64 Key
10 Flywheel	28 Main bearing cap - rear	46 Main bearing shells - upper	65 Bolt
11 Bolt	29 Main bearing cap - centre	47 Lock nut	66 Fuel pump drive cam
12 Plug	30 Main bearing cap - front	48 Self locking nut	67 Woodruff key
13 Balance shaft bearing - rear	31 Seal	50 Pivot ball	68 Oil seal
14 Crankshaft oil seal	32 Valve seat insert - exhaust	51 Rocker arm	69 Crankshaft gear
15 Oil seal retainer	33 Valve - inlet	52 Collets	70 Pulley wheel
16 Washer	34 Valve seat insert - inlet	53 Valve collar	71 Bolt
17 Bolt	35 Key	54 Spring	72 Washer
18 Balance shaft	36 Main bearing shells - lower	55 Upper compression ring	73 Crankshaft thrust washers

10 With the generator swung out of the way the bolts attaching the brackets to the block may be removed (photo).

11 The generator and brackets may then be lifted off the block (photo).

12 Detach the starter motor lead from the solenoid switch by undoing the nut (photo).

13 Seal the cap of the clutch hydraulic fluid reservoir with a piece of polythene to prevent loss of fluid and disconnect the hydraulic pipe from the clutch cylinder as described in Chapter 5/4.

14 Detach all the necessary leads held by push-on Lucar connectors, these being:-

a) Water temperature gauge sender unit (photo) situated in the inlet manifold just behind the distributor.
b) Oil pressure gauge sender unit situated on the left of the block behind the coil.
c) The '+' (SW) coil lead.

15 Pull off the two adjustable rods from the carburettor linkage cross-shaft and then undo the bolt holding the cross-shaft mounting bracket to the engine (photo). The cross-shaft may then be removed. For more details of the linkage refer to Chapter 3/10.

16 Jack up the front of the car and support it on proper stands under the frame side members. Detach the exhaust manifold pipes from the exhaust system by undoing the clamps which are held by two bolts. These clamps are low down relative to the engine and can be reached from either above or below. For details see Chapter 3, Section 20.

17 From under the car remove the bolts holding the sheet steel cover plate to the bottom section of the clutch bell-housing.

18 Place a jack under the bellhousing and support it under the front edge (from where the cover has just been removed) with a piece of wooden packing between the jack and the bellhousing. This will support the forward weight of the gearbox when the engine is eventually removed.

19 Remove the bolts which hold the engine and upper bellhousing together (photo) and take out the starter motor bolts and remove the starter at the same time. Although the photograph shows them being removed with the unit out of the car they are, of course, accessible with the engine/gearbox unit in 'situ'.

20 Remove the oil filter cartridge situated under the coil on the left hand side of the engine by unscrewing it from the block.

21 With the oil filter removed, the left hand engine mounting becomes accessible and the nut on the bracket locating stud may now be removed (photo).

22 The right hand engine mounting bracket with a similar nut on the locating stud is under the water pump and this nut is removed next (photo). The engine is now resting on its mountings located by the mounting studs at the front and the gearbox input shaft in the clutch and is ready to be lifted out. Using a strong rope make a looped sling so that the rope passes right under the engine to the rear of the mounting brackets. On the right side of the engine the loop should also pass inside the exhaust manifold between the two flange mountings. (The left hand manifold is offset to the rear too far for this - it would tend to tilt the engine too far forward.)

23 Tie the loop above the engine as close to the block as possible using a bowline knot which will not slip or jam.

24 Hook in the lifting gear whether cantilever beam or hoist and then take some strain and see that the sling will not bend or damage anything when completely tight with the full weight of the engine on it.

25 Take some more strain until the front of the car starts to rise, which indicates that the full weight of the engine is held by the sling. It must then be lifted clear of the two mounting studs.

26 The engine must be pulled forward to disengage it from the splined end of the gearbox input shaft. This may call for two people and a certain amount of sideways rocking to disengage it completely. It will be free when the gap between engine and bellhousing is about 3 inches (75 mm). Care should be taken at this point as the rear of the engine will tend to drop down when it comes clear of the gearbox and it is essential that at least two people are available, one to steady the engine and the other to operate the lifting gear. It is unwise to hurry this final stage of engine removal as damage and accidents can occur unless the engine is watched carefully all the way out.

7. Engine Removal with Gearbox

1. Proceed exactly as outlined in Section 6 up as far as paragraph 16 inclusive and then continue as follows.

2. Unscrew the gearbox drain plug and drain out the oil.

3. From inside the car remove completely the gear change lever remote control assembly and housing from the gearbox as described in detail in Chapter 6/3.

4. Support the gearbox with a jack in the vicinity of the oil drain plug.

5. Disconnect the cables from the handbrake fulcrum lever underneath the car by unbolting the cable ends from the clevises (photo) (early models only).

6. Then remove the centre bolt which locates the gearbox into the rear support member, this being the item to which the handbrake fulcrum lever is attached (on early models). Then, making sure that the gearbox support jack is firmly in position, remove the four bolts attaching the crossmember to the body frame. Remove the crossmember.

7. The speedometer cable is held into the gearbox by a 'U' plate secured by a small bolt. Remove the bolt and clamp and draw the speedometer cable from the gearbox.

8. Now continue as described in Section 6 from paragraph 20 to 25 inclusive.

9. Due to the fact that the gearbox is attached, the engine will have to be lifted out at a much steeper angle than for removing the engine above. As the weight is now more towards the rear it will be fairly easy to achieve this angle.

10 With the jack under the gearbox still in position start lifting and at the same time move the engine forward until the propeller shaft is nearly ready to come out of the gearbox. Do not let the propeller shaft drop to the ground but support it until clear and then lower it and rest it on a suitable pad.

11 Continue to raise the engine and move it forwards at the necessary angle (photo). At this stage the forward edge of the bellhousing is likely to catch against the front frame crossmember and the tail end of the gearbox will need raising until the whole unit is forward and clear of it.

12 Finally the whole unit will rise clear (photo) and if the maximum height of the lifting tackle has been reached it will be necessary to swing the unit so that the tail end can be lifted clear whilst the hoist is moved away or the car pushed clear.

13 The whole unit should be lowered to the ground (or bench) as soon as possible and the gearbox may then be separated from the engine (photo) and the starter motor removed at the same time.

8. Engine Dismantling - General

1. Ideally, the engine is mounted on a proper stand for overhaul but it is anticipated that most owners will have

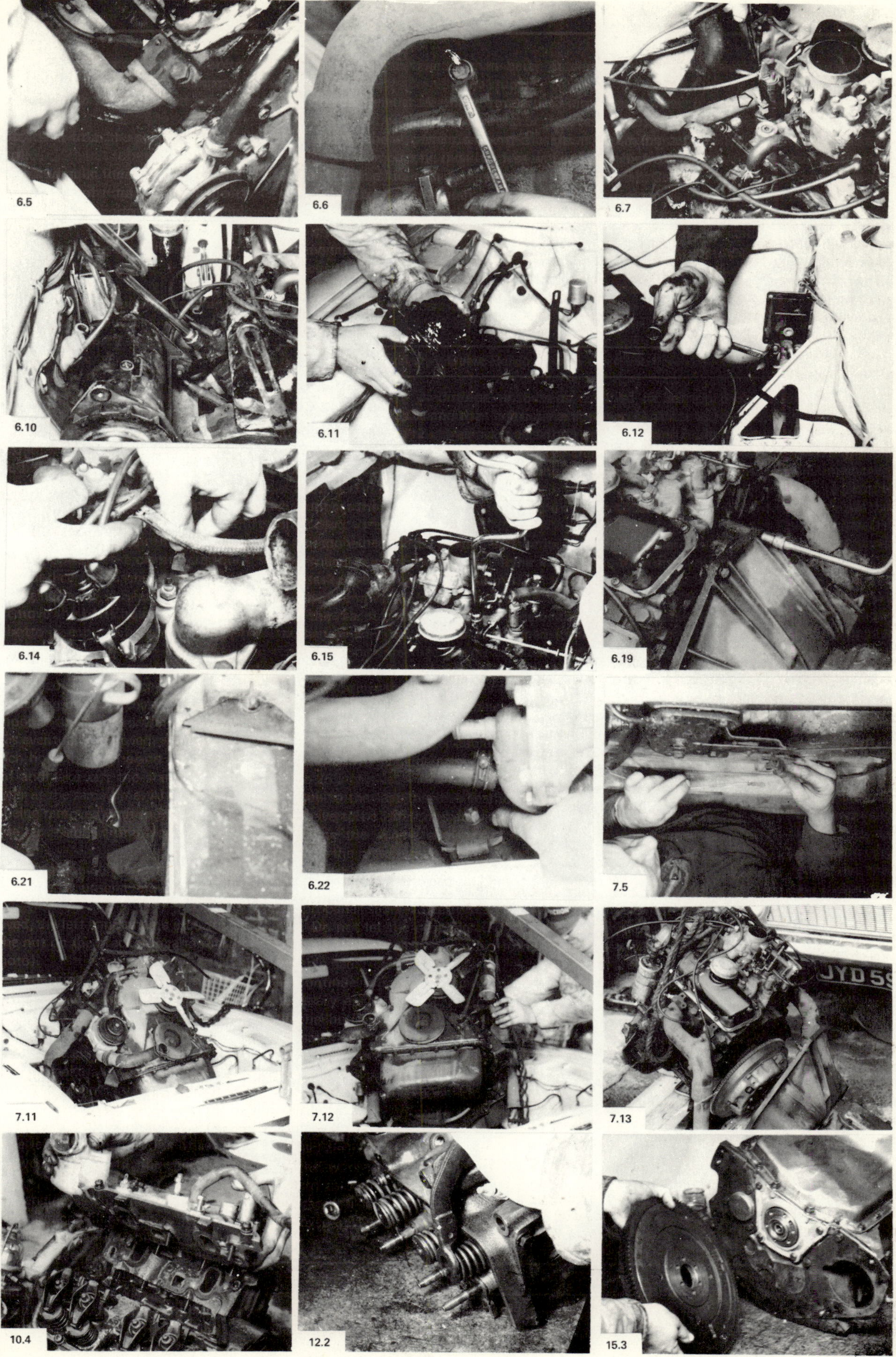

6.5

6.6

6.7

6.10

6.11

6.12

6.14

6.15

6.19

6.21

6.22

7.5

7.11

7.12

7.13

10.4

12.2

15.3

a strong bench on which to place it. If a sufficiently large strong bench is not available then the work can be done at ground level. It is essential, however, that some form of substantial wooden surface is available. Timber should be at least ¾ inch thick, otherwise the weight of the engine will cause projections to punch holes straight through it.

2. It will save a great deal of time later if the engine is thoroughly cleaned down on the exterior before any dismantling begins. This can be done by using paraffin and a stiff brush or more easily, probably, by the use of a proprietary solvent such as 'Gunk' which can be brushed on and then the dirt swilled off with a water jet. This will dispose of all the heavy muck and grit once and for all so that later cleaning of individual components will be a relatively clean process and the paraffin bath will not become contaminated with abrasive material.

3. As the engine is stripped down, clean each part as it comes off. Try to avoid immersing parts with oilways in paraffin as pockets of liquid could remain and cause oil dilution in the critical first few revolutions after reassembly. Clean oilways with pipe cleaners or, preferably, an air jet.

4. Where possible, avoid damaging gaskets on removal, especially if new ones have not been obtained. They can be used as patterns if new ones have to be specially cut.

5. It is helpful to obtain a few blocks of wood to support the engine whilst it is in the process of dismantling. Start dismantling at the top of the engine and then turn the block over and deal with the sump and crankshaft etc., afterwards.

6. Nuts and bolts should be replaced in their locations where possible to avoid confusion later. As an alternative keep each group of nuts and bolts (all the timing gear cover bolts for example) together in a jar or tin.

7. Many items dismantled must be replaced in the same position, if they are not being renewed. These include valves, rocker arms, tappets, pistons, pushrods, bearings and connecting rods. Some of these are marked on assembly to avoid any possibility of mixing them up during overhaul. Others are not, and it is a great help if adequate preparation is made in advance to classify these parts. Suitably labelled tins or jars and, for small items, egg trays, tobacco tins and so on, can be used. The time spent in this preparation will be amply repaid later.

9. Engine Ancillaries - Removal

1. Before beginning a complete overhaul or if the engine is being exchanged for a works reconditioned unit the following items should be removed:-

Fuel system components:
   Carburettor
   Inlet manifold
   Exhaust manifolds
   Fuel pump
   Fuel lines

Ignition system components:
   Sparking plugs
   Distributor
   Coil

Electrical system components:
   Generator and mounting brackets
   Starter motor

Cooling system components:
   Fan
   Fan pulley

Water pump
Thermostat housing and thermostat
Water temperature sender unit

Engine:
   Crankcase ventilation tube
   Oil filter element
   Oil pressure sender unit
   Oil level dipstick
   Oil filler cap
   Engine mounting brackets

Clutch:
   Clutch pressure plate assembly
   Clutch friction plate assembly
All nuts and bolts associated with the foregoing

Some of these items have to be removed for individual servicing or renewal periodically and details can be found under the appropriate Chapter.

10. Cylinder Heads - Removal with Engine Out

1. Remove the two valve rocker covers by undoing the four screws holding each one to its respective cylinder head.

2. Remove the distributor (Chapter 4/7) and plug leads.

3. Remove the carburettor (Chapter 3/11).

4. Remove the inlet manifold by slackening first the two bolts holding the centre section and then the other four at the corners. The manifold casting may stick to the heads at the joint in which case tap it on the ends in the centre with a soft mallet to dislodge it. Then lift it off (photo).

5. Taking each cylinder head in turn, remove the six holding down bolts. As the bolts are slackened off the pressure of the springs on any open valves should force the head away from the block.

6. When the head is sufficiently clear remove the four pushrods and note which valve they came from and which way up. Keep them in order and the right way up by pushing them through a piece of stiff paper or cardboard with the valve numbers marked and the top and bottom ends identified.

7. On occasions the heads stick to the block in which case they should be struck smartly with a block of wood and hammer or soft mallet in order to break the joint. However, the exhaust manifold should provide sufficient grip to provide the necessary lifting force required. Do not try and prise them off with a blade of any description or damage will be caused to the faces of the head or block or both. As a last resort in stubborn cases revolve the engine and the piston compression should lift the heads (make sure the sparking plugs are in place!).

8. Lift the heads off carefully. Note which side each head comes from as they are identical and it is preferable to replace them on the same bank of cylinders. Place them where they cannot be damaged. Undo the bolts holding the exhaust manifold to each head.

11. Cylinder Heads - Removal with Engine in Car

1. The procedure described in Section 10 should be followed exactly except that the following should be done first:-

a) Disconnect the battery leads (Chapter 10/2).

b) Drain the cooling system (Chapter 2/3).

c) Remove the top hose from the thermostat housing and the heater hose connection from the inlet manifold. Remove also the by-pass hose connection at the thermostat (Chapter

2).

d) Remove the fan belt and generator (Chapter 10). The generator brackets may also be removed but this is not essential.

e) Disconnect the exhaust manifolds from the exhaust pipes by removing the clamping rings (Section 6/16).

f) Disconnect the water temperature sender unit lead (Section 6/14).

g) Remove the coil from the front of the left hand head by undoing the securing bolt.

h) Remove the accelerator linkage cross-shaft (Section 6/15)

12. Cylinder Heads - Dismantling of Rocker Gear, Valves and Springs

1. With the cylinder head on the bench undo the nut from each rocker stud in the centre of the rocker arm. Lift out the hemispherical rocker pivot and then lift off the rocker arm.

2. Lay the cylinder head on its side and using a proper valve spring compressor tool place the 'U' shaped end over the valve collar (photo) and the screw on the valve head and compress the spring. Sometimes the valve collar sticks, in which case the end of the compressor over the spring should be tapped with a hammer to release the collar from the valve.

3. As the spring is pressed down the valve stem two tapered split collars (collets) will be revealed and these should be taken from the recess in the valve stem.

4. When the compressor is released the spring may be removed from the valve. Pull off the seal cap from the valve stem and then push the valve out of the head.

5. It is essential that the valves, springs, rocker arms and nuts are all kept in order so that they may be replaced in their original positions.

13. Tappets - Removal

1. The tappets may now be removed from the cylinder block by pushing them up from the camshaft (which can be revolved if necessary to raise the tappets) and lifting them out.

2. If necessary the pushrod bearing cups in each tappet can be taken out by first extracting the retaining circlip.

3. Make sure that all the tappets are kept in order so that they may be replaced in the location they came from.

14. Crankshaft Pulley Wheel - Removal

1. Remove the bolt and washer locating the pulley to the front of the crankshaft. The pulley is keyed to the crankshaft and must be drawn off with a proper sprocket puller. Attempts to lever it off with long bladed articles such as screwdrivers or tyre levers are not suitable in this case because the timing cover behind the pulley is a light and relatively fragile casting. Any pressure against it could certainly crack it and possibly break a hole in it.

2. The pulley may be removed with the engine in the car but it may be necessary to remove the radiator, depending on the type of pulley extractor used and the clearance it allows.

15. Flywheel - Removal

1. Remove the clutch assembly as described in Chapter 5/7.

2. The flywheel is held in position to the crankshaft by six bolts. One of these bolts is spaced unevenly so that the flywheel will only fit in one position.

3. Remove the six bolts, taking care to support the weight of the flywheel as they are slackened off in case it slips off the flange. Secure it carefully, taking care not to damage the mating surfaces on the crankshaft and flywheel (photo).

16. Sump - Removal

1. The sump may be removed with the engine in the car by undoing the bolts which hold it to the crankcase and timing cover at the front. With the engine out of the car, first invert the engine and then remove the bolts.

2. The sump may be stuck quite firmly to the engine if sealing compound has been used on the gasket. It is in order to lever it off in this case. The gasket should be removed anyway.

17. Timing Gear and Cover - Removal

1. Remove the sump and crankshaft pulley wheel.

2. Take out the fixing bolts and lift off the cover (complete with fan). If the engine is in the car the fuel pump and fan belt will first need removal also.

3. The camshaft timing drive mechanism consists of a helical gear on the crankshaft and a large fibre gear on the camshaft. There is also another gear in mesh with the crankshaft which drives the balance shaft.

4. Remove the camshaft and balance shaft gears by removing the bolts and washers and drawing them off. They should not require the services of a puller to come off. Be careful with the large fibre gear as this can be damaged very easily if mishandled. The crankshaft gear should be left in position as this is not normally detached. On the front of the fibre gear there is an eccentric boss held also by the locating bolt and this operates the fuel pump actuating lever.

18. Camshaft - Removal

1. The camshaft cannot be conveniently removed with the engine in the car as the tappets will jam it in position and therefore the valve rocker gear, pushrods and tappets all need to be removed in addition to the radiator, timing cover and gear.

2. With the timing cover and gear removed, undo the bolts holding the front cover backplate. Note the pressure plate underneath the three bolts.

3. The camshaft thrust plate is held to the block by two countersunk cross-head screws and these will need removing with an impact screwdriver.

4. The camshaft may then be withdrawn. Take great care to avoid hitting the three bearing bushes with the cam lobes as this could damage them. If the tappets have not been removed the camshaft may also need rotating to avoid them.

19. Oil Pump - Removal

1. Remove the sump.

2. Undo the two mounting bolts holding the pump to the crankcase and lift it out (photo). This operation may be carried out with the engine in the car. Note that the long hexagonal-section driveshaft will come out with the pump. This is driven in turn from the distributor shaft.

20. Pistons, Connecting Rods and Big End Bearings - Removal

1. Pistons and connecting rods may be removed with the engine in the car, provided the sump and cylinder heads are first removed. The bearing shells may be removed with the heads on.

2. Slacken the two bolts holding each bearing cap to the connecting rod. Use a good quality socket spanner for this work. A ring spanner may be used for removal only - not replacement which calls for a special torque spanner. Having slackened the bolts two or three turns tap the bolt heads to dislodge the caps from the connecting rods. Hollow dowel pegs locate the caps in position. When the caps are free of the pegs they can be easily lifted off after the bolts are completely removed.

3. Each bearing cap normally has the cylinder number etched on one end as does the connecting rod. However, this must be verified and if in doubt the cap should be marked with a dab of paint or punch mark to ensure that its relationship with the connecting rod is not altered.

4. The piston and connecting rod may then be pushed out of the top of each cylinder (photo).

5. The big end bearing shells can be removed from the connecting rod and cap by sliding them round in the direction of the notch at the end of the shell and lifting them out. If they are not being renewed it is vital that they are not interchanged - either between pistons or between cap and connecting rod.

21. Piston Rings - Removal

1. Remove the pistons from the engine.

2. The rings come off over the top of the piston. Starting with the top one, lift one end of the ring out of the groove and gradually ease it out all the way round. With the second and third rings an old feeler blade is useful for sliding them over the other grooves. However, as rings are only normally removed if they are going to be renewed it should not matter if breakages occur.

22. Gudgeon Pins - Removal

1. The gudgeon pins need removing if the pistons are being removed. New pistons are supplied with new pins for fitting to the existing connecting rods. The gudgeon pin is semi-floating - that is it is a tight shrink fit with the connecting rod and a moving fit in the piston. To press it out requires considerable force and under usual circumstances a proper press and special tools are essential. Otherwise piston damage will occur. If damage to the pistons does not matter, then the pins may be pressed out using suitable diameter pieces of rod and tube between the jaws of a vice. However, this is not recommended as the connecting rod might be damaged also. It is recommended that gudgeon pins and pistons are removed from, and refitted to, connecting rods by Ford dealers with the necessary facilities.

23. Crankshaft Rear Oil Seal - Removal

1. The rear oil seal comprises a spring inset type flexible ring fitted in a separate carrier plate. This plate is bolted to the crankcase and the seal bears directly onto the crankshaft flange.

2. The engine rear plate may first be removed by undoing the bolts (photo A) and lifting it away (photo B). Although this is not essential it is a simple operation and prevents the plate from becoming bent when the engine is being moved about.

3. Undo the four bolts holding the oil seal retainer plate to the engine and lift the plate away.

24. Main Bearings and Crankshaft - Removal

1. The engine should be taken from the car and the sump, cylinder heads, timing gears and pistons removed.

2. With a good quality socket spanner undo the six bolts holding the three main bearing caps in position.

3. When all the bolts are removed lift out the caps. If they should be tight tap the sides gently with a piece of wood or soft mallet to dislodge them.

4. Lift out the crankshaft (photo).

5. Slide out the bearing shells from the caps and also from the crankcase seats. Also take away the thrust washers on each side of the centre main bearing. The half which is on each side of the centre bearing cap is fitted with a tang to prevent rotation.

25. Balance Shaft - Removal

1. If it is wished to remove the balance shaft the engine need not be out of the car but the timing cover, radiator and grille should first be removed.

2. Remove the balance shaft gear as described in Section 17/3. The key and spacer collar may be left in position on the shaft.

3. Undo the three bolts holding the thrust plate to the face of the block.

4. Withdraw the balance shaft carefully so as not to damage the bearing bushes in which it runs (photo).

26. Lubrication and Crankcase Ventilation System - Description

1. A general description of the oil circulation system is given in Section 1 of this Chapter.

2. The oil pump may be of two types - the by-rotor or sliding vane. Both types were fitted throughout the life of the V4 Corsair range and are interchangeable.

3. The oil is drawn through a gauze screen and tube which is below the oil level in the well of the sump. It is then pumped via the full flow oil filter to the system of oil galleries in the block as previously described. The oil filter cartridge is mounted externally on the left hand side of the block.

4. The crankcase is positively ventilated. Air enters through the oil filler cap in the left hand rocker cover which is fitted with a washable gauze filter. Air enters directly under the rim of the cap or as in the closed system, the cap is connected to the carburettor air filter by a pipe so that filtration of the air is done by the existing air filter.

5. Air passes through the pushrod and oil drain channels in the tappet chamber and up the right hand bank of the block to the right hand rocker cover. The right hand rocker cover is fitted with an outlet connected by a pipe to the engine intake manifold. A tapered valve in the rocker cover outlet controls the outlet of fumes so that when manifold depression is high the valve closes partially, thus reducing the flow proportionately.

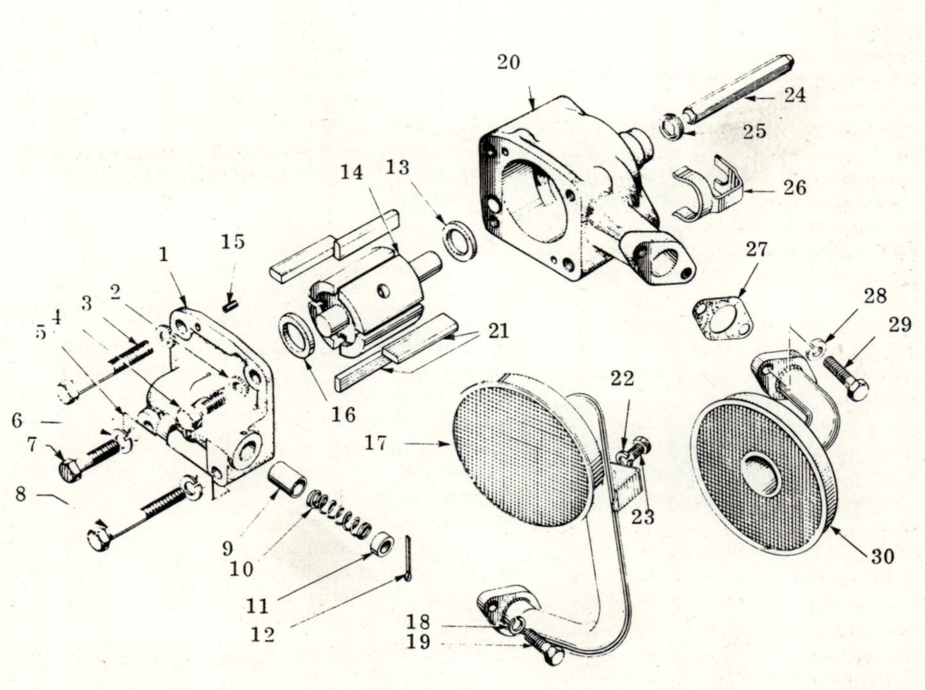

Fig. 1.3. VANE TYPE OIL PUMP FITTED PRIOR TO OCTOBER, 1968

1 Bottom cover	9 Relief valve plunger	17 Screen	25 Circlip
2 Spring washers	10 Spring	18 Spring washer	26 Retaining clip
3 Holding bolt	11 Spring seat	19 Bolt	27 Gasket
4 Cover bolt	12 Split pin	20 Body	28 Spring washer
5 Keep plate	13 Spacer	21 Vanes	29 Bolt
6 Spring washer	14 Rotor	22 Spring washer	30 Screen
7 Lower bolt	15 Dowel pin	23 Bolt	
8 Holding bolt	16 Spacer	24 Drive shaft	

27. Crankcase Ventilation System - Routine Maintenance

1. Every 5,000 miles, or when changing the oil, remove the oil filler cap (if fitted with the gauze filter) and wash the whole unit thoroughly in petrol. Blow dry and apply a little clean engine oil to the gauze filter.
2. Clean the emission control valve. First remove the hose and then pull the valve out of the grommet in the right hand rocker cover. Dismantle the valve by removing the circlip and taking out the valve seal, valve and spring. Wash thoroughly in petrol, reassemble and replace.
3. Do not try and run the engine with any part of the emission vlave or pipe disconnected as this will completely upset the fuel mixture due to the inlet manifold being opened to atmospheric pressure. It should also be born in mind that malfunctioning of the emission control valve may affect the fuel mixture to the engine.

28. Oil Pumps - Overhaul

1. The oil pump maintains a pressure of around 50 lbs. in.^{2} but any drop in this is not notified until it gets as low as 5 to 7 lbs. in.^{2} when the warning light comes on. If an oil pressure gauge is fitted earlier warning is given of falling oil pressures due either to overheating, pump or bearing wear.
2. At a major engine overhaul it is as well to check the pump and exchange it for a reconditioned unit if necessary. The efficient operation of the oil pump depends on the finely machined tolerances between the moving parts of the rotor (or vanes) and the body and reconditioning of these is generally not within the competence of the non-specialist owner.
3. To dismantle the pump first remove it from the engine as described in Section 19.
4. Remove the two bolts holding the end cover to the body and remove the cover and relief valve parts which will be released (except in early vane type pumps).
5. The necessary clearances may now be checked using a machined straight edge (a good steel rule) and a feeler gauge.
6. On bi-rotor type pumps the critical clearances are between the lobes of the centre rotor and convex faces of the outer rotor, between the outer rotor and the pump body, and between both rotors and the end cover plate.
7. The rotor lobe clearances may be checked as shown in Fig. 1/4. The clearances should not exceed .006 in. (.152 mm) at points 1 in the figure. The clearance between the outer rotor and pump body (3 and 4) should not exceed .010 in. (.254 mm).
8. The endfloat clearance can be measured by placing a steel straight edge across the end of the pump and measuring the gap between the rotors and the straight edge as shown in Fig. 1/5. The gap on either rotor should not exceed .005 in. (.127 mm).
9. For vane type pumps check the end clearance of both the rotor and vanes as shown in Fig. 1/6. which should not exceed .005 in. (.127 mm).
10 The clearances between vane and rotor, rotor and body, and vane and body must be checked with the rotor positioned as in Fig. 1/7. The gap between vane and rotor groove and rotor and body should not exceed .005 in. (.127 mm). A maximum of .011 in. (.279 mm) is permissible between the end of the vane and the pump body.
11 If the only excessive clearances are endfloat it is possible to reduce them by removing the rotors and vanes from the pump body and lapping away the face of the body on a flat bed until the necessary clearances are obtained. It must be emphasised, however, that the face of the body must remain

perfectly flat and square to the axis of the rotor spindle otherwise the clearances will not be equal and the end cover will not be a pressure tight fit to the body. It is worth trying, of course, if the pump is in need of renewal any way but unless done properly it could seriously jeopardise the rest of an overhaul. Any variations in the other clearances should be overcome with an exchange unit.
12 When reassembling the pump and refitting the end cover make sure that the interior is scrupulously clean and that the pressure relief valve parts are assembled in the correct positions as indicated in the exploded drawings.

29. Oil Filter - Removal and Replacement

The oil filter is a complete throwaway cartridge screwed into the left hand side of the engine block (photo). Simply unscrew the old unit, clean the seating on the block, and screw the new one in, taking care not to cross the thread. Continue until the sealing ring just touches the block face. Then tighten one half turn. Always run the engine and check for signs of leaks after installation.

30. Engine Components - Examination for Wear

When the engine has been stripped down and all parts properly cleaned decisions have to be made as to what needs renewal and the following sections tell the examiner what to look for. In any border line case it is always best to decide in favour of a new part. Even if a part may still be serviceable its life will have been reduced by wear and the degree of trouble needed to replace it in the future must be taken into consideration. However, these things are relative and it depends on whether a quick 'survival' job is being done or whether the car as a whole is being regarded as having many thousands of miles of useful and economical life remaining.

31. Crankshaft - Examination and Renovation

1. Look at the three main bearing journals and the four crankpins and if there are any scratches or score marks then the shaft will need regrinding. Such conditions will nearly always be accompanied by similar deterioration in the matching bearing shells.
2. Each bearing journal should also be round and can be checked with a micrometer or caliper gauge around the periphery at several points. If there is more than .001 in. of ovality regrinding is necessary.
3. A main Ford agent or motor engineering specialist will be able to decide to what extent regrinding is necessary and also supply the special under-size shell bearings to match whatever may need grinding off.
4. Before taking the crankshaft for regrinding check also the cylinder bores and pistons as it may be advantageous to have the whole engine done together.

32. Crankshaft (Main) Bearings and Big End (Connecting Rod) Bearings - Examination and Renovation

1. With careful servicing and regular oil and filter changes bearings will last for a very long time but they can still fail for unforeseen reasons. With big end bearings the indications are regular rhythmic loud knocking from the crankcase, the frequency depending on engine speed. It is particularly noticeable when the engine is under load. This symptom is accompanied by a fall in oil pressure although this is not

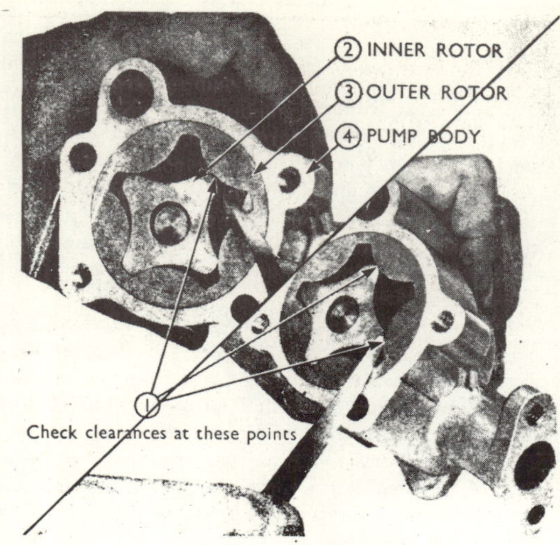

Fig. 1.4. Checking rotor type oil pump lobe clearances

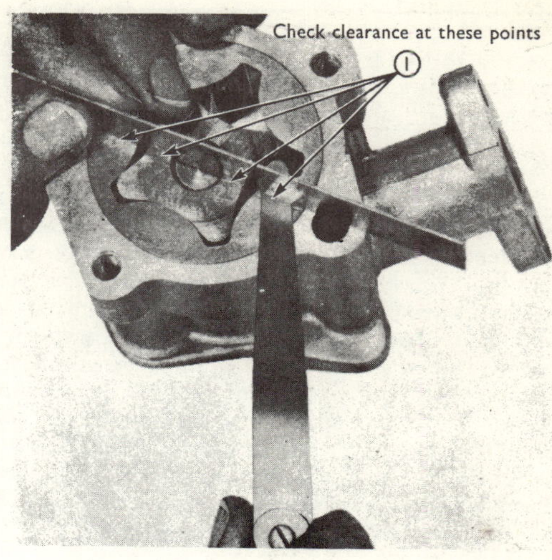

Fig. 1.5. Checking rotor type oil pump end float clearances

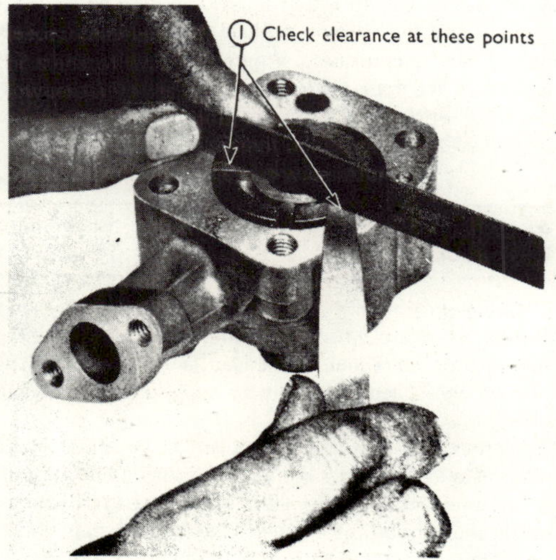

Fig. 1.6. Checking vane type oil pump end float clearances

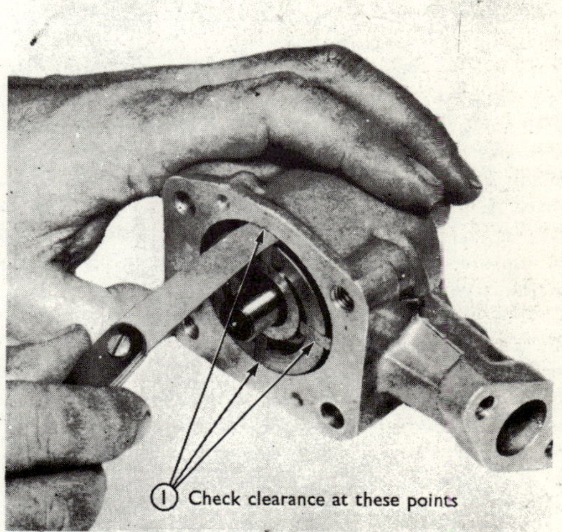

Fig. 1.7. Checking vane type oil pump rotor and vane clearances

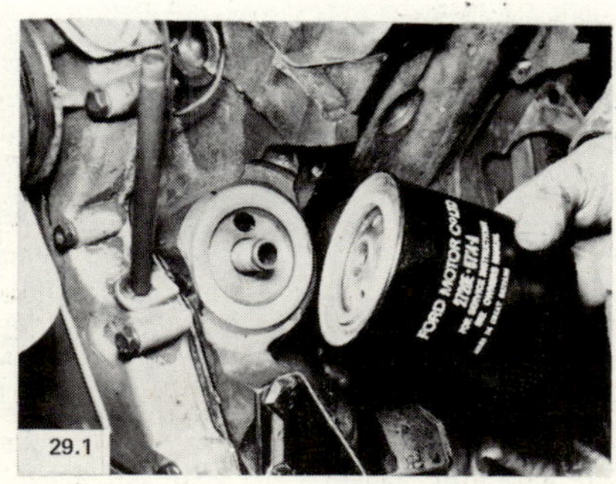

normally noticeable unless an oil pressure gauge is fitted. Main bearing failure is usually indicated by serious vibration, particularly at higher engine revolutions, accompanied by a more significant drop in oil pressure and a 'rumbling' noise.

2. In the section on big end bearing removal it was mentioned that this could be done with the engine still in the car. If the failure is sudden and the engine has a low mileage since new or overhaul this is possibly worth doing. Bearing shells in good condition have bearing surfaces with a smooth, even, matt silver/grey colour all over. Worn bearings will show patches of a different colour where the bearing metal has worn away and exposed the underlay. Damaged bearings will be pitted or scored. It is nearly always well worthwhile fitting new shells as their cost is relatively low. If the crankshaft is in good condition it is merely a question of obtaining another set of standard size. A reground crankshaft will need new bearing shells as a matter of course.

33. Cylinder Bores - Examination and Renovation

1. A new cylinder is perfectly round and the walls parallel throughout its length. The action of the piston tends to wear the walls at right angles to the gudgeon pin due to side thrust. This wear takes place principally on that section of the cylinder swept by the piston rings.

2. It is possible to get an indication of bore wear by removing the cylinder heads with the engine still in the car. With the piston down in the bore first signs of wear can be seen and felt just below the top of the bore where the top piston ring reaches and there will be a noticeable lip. If there is no lip it is fairly reasonable to expect that bore wear is not severe and any lack of compression or excessive oil consumption is due to worn or broken piston rings or pistons (see next section).

3. If it is possible to obtain a bore measuring micrometer measure the bore in the thrust plane below the lip and again at the bottom of the cylinder in the same plane. If the difference is more than .003 in. then a rebore is necessary. Similarly, a difference of .003 in. or more across the bore diameter is a sign of ovality calling for a rebore.

4. Any bore which is significantly scratched or scored will need reboring. This symptom usually indicates that the piston or rings are damaged also in that cylinder. In the event of only one cylinder being in need of reboring it will still be necessary for all four to be bored and fitted with new oversize pistons and rings. Your Ford agent or local motor engineering specialist will be able to rebore and obtain the necessary matched pistons. If the crankshaft is undergoing regrinding also it is a good idea to let the same firm renovate and reassemble the crankshaft and pistons to the block. A reputable firm normally gives a guarantee for such work. In cases where engines have been rebored already to their maximum new cylinder liners are available which may be fitted. In such cases the same reboring processes have to be followed and the services of a specialist engineering firm are required.

34. Pistons and Piston Rings - Examination and Renovation

1. Worn pistons and rings can usually be diagnosed when the symptoms of excessive oil consumption and low compression occur and are sometimes, though not always, associated with worn cylinder bores. Compression testers that fit into the sparking plug holes are available and these can indicate where low compression is occuring. Wear usually accelerates the more it is left so when the symptoms occur early action can possibly save the expense of a rebore.

2. Another symptom of piston wear is piston slap - a knocking noise from the crankcase not to be confused with big end bearing failure. It can be heard clearly at low engine speed when there is no load (idling for example) and is much less audible when the engine speed increases. Piston wear usually occurs in the skirt or lower end of the piston and is indicated by vertical streaks in the worn area which is always on the thrust side. It can also be seen where the skirt thickness is different.

3. Piston ring wear can be checked by first removing the rings from the pistons as described in Section 19. Then place the rings in the cylinder bores from the top, pushing them down about 1½ inches with the head of a piston (from which the rings have been removed) so that they rest square in the cylinder. Then measure the gap at the ends of the ring with a feeler gauge. If it exceeds .020 in. for the two top compression rings, or .015 in. for the oil control ring then they need renewal.

4. The grooves in which the rings locate in the piston can also become enlarged in use. The clearance between ring and piston, in the groove, should not exceed .004 in. for the top two compression rings and .003 in. for the lower oil control ring.

5. However, it is rare that a piston is only worn in the ring grooves and the need to replace them for this fault alone is hardly ever encountered. Wherever pistons are renewed the weight of the four piston/connecting rod assemblies should be kept within the limit variation of 8 gms. to maintain engine balance.

35. Connecting Rods and Gudgeon Pins - Examination and Renovation

1. Gudgeon pins are a shrink fit into the connecting rods. Neither of these would normally need replacement unless the pistons were being changed, in which case the new pistons would automatically be supplied with new gudgeon pins.

2. Connecting rods are not subject to wear but in extreme circumstances such as engine seizure they could be distorted. Such conditions may be visually apparent but where doubt exists they should be changed. The bearing caps should also be examined for indications of filing down which may have been attempted in the mistaken idea that bearing slackness could be remedied in this way. If there are such signs then the connecting rods should be replaced.

36. Camshaft and Camshaft Bearings - Examination and Renovation

1. The camshaft bearing bushes should be examined for signs of scoring and pitting. If they need renewal they will have to be dealt with professionally as although it may be relatively easy to remove the old bushes, the correct fitting of new ones requires special tools. If they are not fitted evenly and square from the very start they can be distorted thus causing localized wear in a very short time. See your Ford dealer or local engineering specialist for this work.

2. The camshaft itself may show signs of wear on the bearing journals, cam lobes or the skew gear. The main decision to take is what degree of wear justifies replacement, which is costly. Any signs of scoring or damage to the bearing journals must be rectified and as undersize bearing bushes are not supplied the journals cannot be reground. Renewal of the whole camshaft is the only solution. Similarly, excessive wear on the skew gear which can be seen where the distributor driveshaft teeth mesh will mean

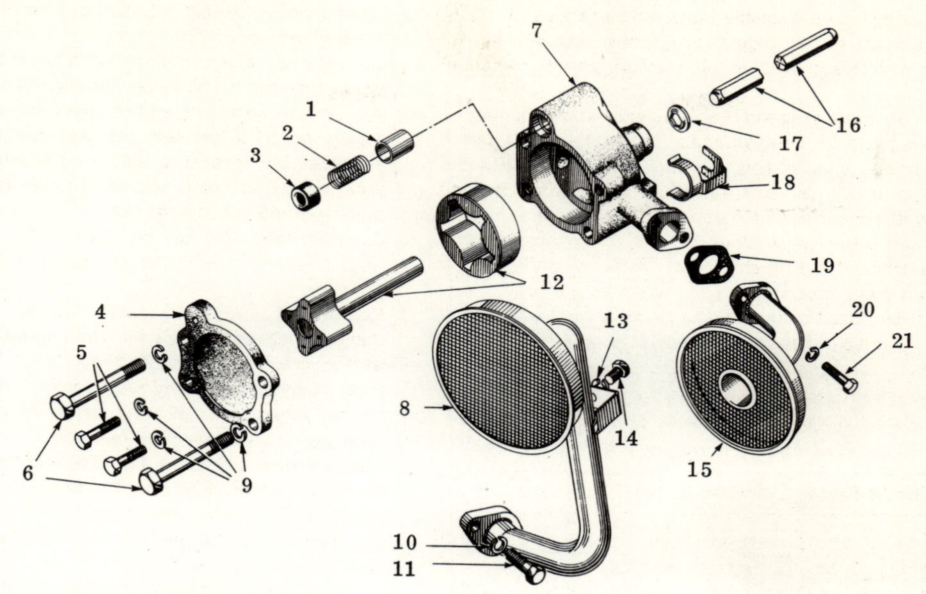

Fig. 1.8. ROTOR TYPE OIL PUMP FITTED PRIOR TO OCTOBER, 1968

1 Relief valve plunger	7 Body	13 Spring washer	19 Gasket
2 Spring	8 Screen	14 Bolt	20 Spring washer
3 Plug	9 Spring washers	15 Screen	21 Bolt
4 Bottom cover	10 Spring washer	16 Drive shaft	
5 Cover bolts	11 Bolt	17 Circlip	
6 Mounting bolts	12 Rotor assemblies	18 Retaining clip	

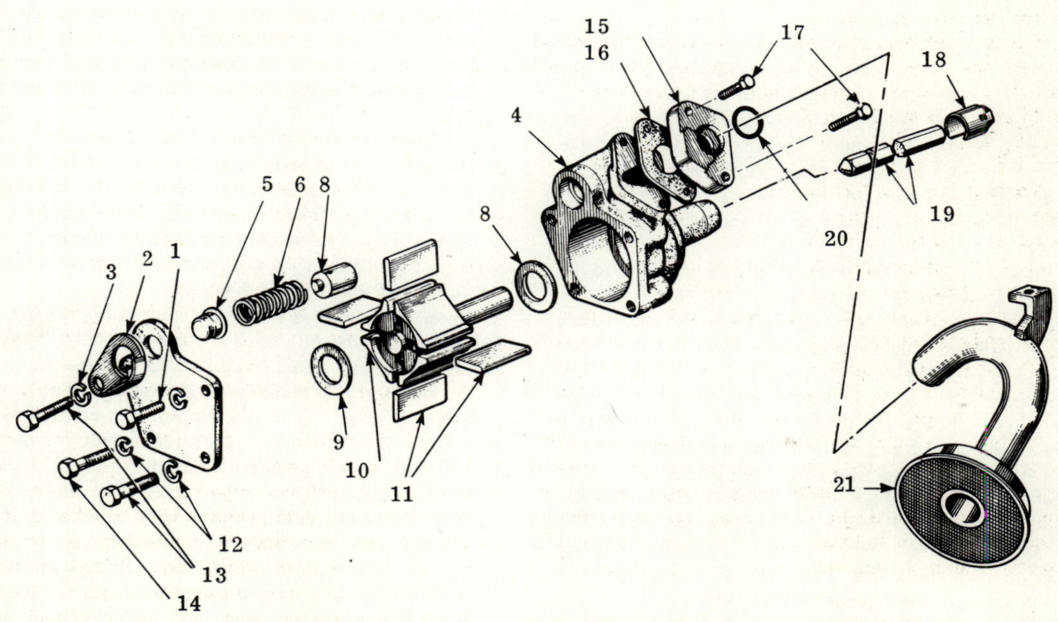

Fig. 1.9. VANE TYPE OIL PUMP FITTED AFTER OCTOBER, 1968

1 Bolt	6 Spring	11 Vanes	16 Gasket
2 Baffle plate	7 Relief valve plunger	12 Spring washers	17 Bolts
3 Spring washer	8 Spacer	13 Bolts	18 Clip
4 Body	9 Spacer	14 Bolt	19 Drive shaft
5 Spring seat	10 Rotor	15 Adaptor - pump to inlet pipe	20 'O' ring

renewal of the whole camshaft.

3. The cam lobes themselves may show signs of ridging or pitting on the high points. If the ridging is light then it may be possible to smooth it out with fine emery. The cam lobes, however, are surface hardened and once this is penetrated wear will be very rapid thereafter. The cams are also offset and tapered to cause the tappets to rotate - thus ensuring that wear is even - so do not mistake this condition for wear.

37. Tappets - Examination and Renovation

1. The faces of the tappets which bear on the camshaft should show no signs of pitting, scoring or other forms of wear. They should also not be a loose fit in their housing. Wear is only normally encountered at very high mileages or in cases of neglected engine lubrication. Renew if necessary.

38. Valves and Valve Seats - Examination and Renovation

1. With the valves removed from the cylinder heads examine the heads for signs of cracking, burning away and pitting of the edge where it seats in the port. The seats of the valves in the cylinder head should also be examined for the same signs. Usually it is the valve that deteriorates first but if a bad valve is not rectified the seat will suffer and this is more difficult to repair.

2. Provided there are no obvious signs of serious pitting the valve should be ground with its seat. This may be done by placing a smear of carborundum paste on the edge of the valve and using a suction type valve holder, grinding the valve in situ. This is done with a semi-rotary action, twirling the handle of the valve holder between the hands and lifting it occasionally to re-distribute the traces of paste. Use a coarse paste to start with. As soon as a matt grey unbroken line appears on both the valve and seat the valve is 'ground in'. All traces of carbon should also be cleaned from the head and neck of the valve stem. A wire brush mounted in a power drill is a quick and effective way of doing this.

3. If the valve requires renewal it should be ground into the seat in the same way as an old valve.

4. Another form of valve wear can occur on the stem where it runs in the guide in the cylinder head. This can be detected by trying to rock the valve from side to side. If there is any movement at all it is an indication that the valve stem or guide is worn. Check the stem first with a micrometer at points all along and around its length and if they are not within the specified size new valves will probably solve the problem. If the guides are worn, however, they will need reboring for oversize valves or for fitting guide inserts. The valve seats will also need recutting to ensure they are concentric with the stems. This work should be given to your Ford dealer or local engineering works.

5. When valve seats are badly burnt or pitted, requiring replacement, inserts may be fitted - or replaced if already fitted once before - and once again this is a specialist task to be carried out by a suitable engineering firm.

6. When all valve grinding is completed it is essential that every trace of grinding paste is removed from the valves and ports in the cylinder head. This should be done with thorough washing in petrol or paraffin and blowing out with a jet of air. If particles of carborundum should work their way into the engine they would cause havoc with bearings or cylinder walls.

39. Timing Gears - Examination and Renovation

1. Any wear which takes place in the timing mechanism will be on the teeth of the fibre gear which is driven from the crankshaft gear. The backlash, which can be measured with a feeler gauge between the gear teeth, should not exceed .004 in. The balance shaft gear backlash should be the same but this is not so critical. If the crankshaft gear to camshaft gear backlash is excessive the fibre gear wheel should be renewed.

40. Flywheel Ring Gear - Examination and Renovation

1. If the ring gear is badly worn or has missing teeth it should be renewed. The old ring can be removed from the flywheel by cutting a notch between two teeth with a hacksaw and then splitting it with a cold chisel.

2. To fit a new ring gear requires heating the ring to 400ºF. (204ºC). This can be done by polishing four equally spaced sections of the gear, laying it on a suitable heat resistant surface (such as fire bricks) and heating it evenly with a blow lamp or torch until the polished areas turn a light yellow tint. Do not overheat or the hard wearing properties will be lost. The gear has a chamfered inner edge which should go against the shoulder when put on the flywheel. When hot enough place the gear in position quickly, tapping it home if necessary and let it cool naturally without quenching in any way.

41. Cylinder Heads and Piston Crowns - Decarbonisation

1. When cylinder heads are removed either in the course of an overhaul or for inspection of bores or valve condition when the engine is in the car it is normal to remove all carbon deposits from the piston crowns and heads.

2. This is best done with a cup shaped wire brush and an electric drill and is fairly straightforward when the engine is dismantled and the pistons removed. Sometimes hard spots of carbon are not easily removed except by a scraper. When cleaning the pistons with a scraper take care not to damage the surface of the piston in any way.

3. When the engine is in the car certain precautions must be taken when decarbonising the piston crowns in order to prevent dislodged pieces of carbon falling into the interior of the engine which could cause damage to cylinder bores, pistons and rings - or if allowed into the water passages - damage to the water pump. Turn the engine, therefore, so that the piston being worked on is at the top of its stroke and then mask off the adjacent cylinder bore and all surrounding water jacket orifices with paper and adhesive tape. Press grease into the gap all round the piston to keep carbon particles out and then scrape all carbon away by hand carefully. Do not use a power drill and wire brush when the engine is in the car as it will be virtually impossible to keep all the carbon dust clear of the engine. When completed carefully clear out the grease round the rim of the piston with a matchstick or something similar - bringing any carbon particles with it. Repeat the process on the other three piston crowns. It is not recommended that a ring of carbon is left round the edge of the piston on the theory that it will aid oil consumption. This was valid in the earlier days of long stroke low revving engines but modern engines, fuels and lubricants cause less carbon deposits any way and any left behind tends merely to cause hot-spots.

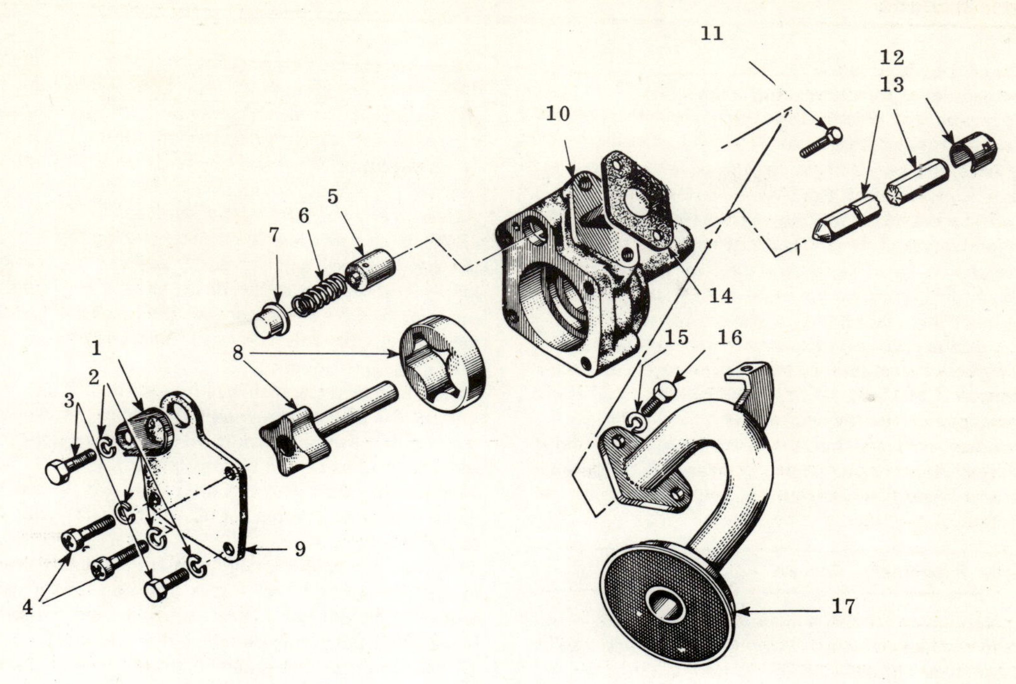

Fig. 1.10. ROTOR TYPE OIL PUMP FITTED AFTER OCTOBER, 1968

1 Baffle plate	6 Spring	11 Bolt	16 Bolt
2 Spring washers	7 Spring seat	12 Clip	17 Strainer
3 Mounting bolts	8 Rotor assembly	13 Drive shaft	
4 Set screws	9 End plate	14 Gasket	
5 Relief valve plunger	10 Body	15 Spring washer	

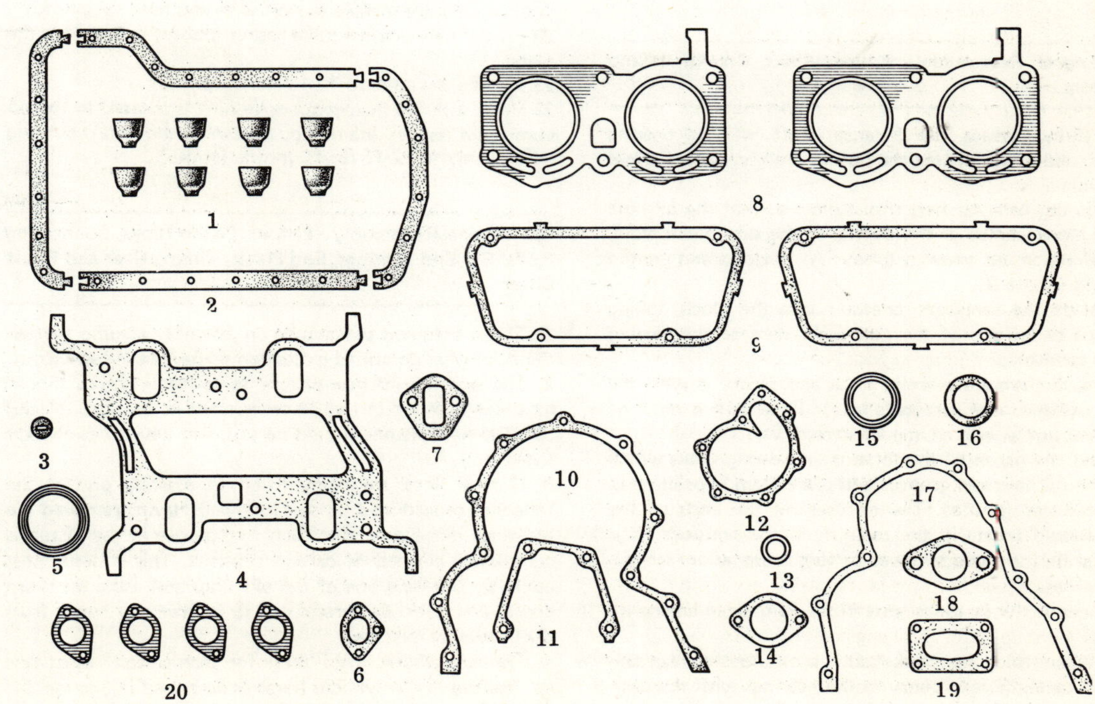

Fig. 1.11. COMPLETE ENGINE GASKET SET

1 Valve stem seals	6 Water pump to block	11 Crankshaft oil seal retainer	16 Crankshaft front bearing
2 Sump	7 Fuel pump to front cover	12 Water pump body	17 Front plate to block
3 Dipstick	8 Cylinder heads	13 Sump drain plug	18 Oil pump to inlet tube
4 Inlet manifold	9 Rocker covers	14 Thermostat elbow	19 Carburettor to manifold
5 Crankshaft rear oil seal	10 Front cover to engine	15 Balance shaft rear bearing	20 Exhaust manifolds

42. Rocker Gear - Examination and Renovation

1. The studs on which the rocker arms pivot are a press fit into the head and by placing a straight edge across the top of all four it can be seen if any have worked loose. If any have it will be necessary to have the hole bored out and an oversize stud fitted. This is a specialist task. The threads on the studs should be in good condition to ensure that the self-locking unit grips sufficiently tightly to prevent it working loose and altering the valve clearance.
2. If the torque required to turn any adjusting unit is less than 3 lbs/ft. on oiled threads the units should be replaced. If the torque is still inadequate it is possible to fit a second nut on the stud to lock the adjustment.
3. The rocker arms and fulcrum seats are matched and if either should show signs of ridging or pitting on the bearing surfaces both should be renewed.

43. Engine Reassembly - General

1. All components of the engine must be cleaned of oil sludge and old gaskets and the working area should also be cleared and clean. In addition to the normal range of good quality socket spanners and general tools which are essential, the following must be available before reassembly begins:-

1) Complete set of new gaskets.
2) Supply of clean rags.
3) Clean oil can full of clean engine oil.
4) Torque spanner.
5) All new spare parts as necessary.

44. Engine Reassembly - Balance Shaft, Crankshaft and Oil Pump

1. Carefully replace the balance shaft into its bearing bushes, and avoid hitting the bushes with any sharp edges (photo).
2. Refit the balance shaft thrust plate so that the oil hole in the block comes in the centre of the slot in the plate, both of which are arrowed (photo A). Replace and tighten the bolts (photo B).
3. Replace the camshaft carefully into the block, taking care not to let any of the cam lobes damage the bearing bushes (photo).
4. Refit the camshaft thrust plate and secure it with the two crosshead sunk screws (photo). These screws must be tightened firmly with an impact screwdriver.
5. Select the halves of the three main bearing shells which have the oil hole and grooves and place them in position in the crankcase (photo). The notches on the ends of the shells should locate in the cut-outs in the housings. It is essential that the two surfaces coming together are scrupulously clean.
6. Lubricate the bearings generously with clean engine oil (photo).
7. Make sure that the crankshaft is scrupulously clean and lower it carefully into place on the bearings with the gearwheel towards the front of the engine (photo).
8. Take the two halves of the thrust washers which do not have tags on and very carefully slide them into position round the side of the centre main bearing. The grooves in the washers should face outwards from the bearing (photo).
9. The end of the top half of the thrust washer can easily be pushed finally into position with a finger (photo).
10 Fit the plain halves of the main bearing shells into the caps with the notches in the shells corresponding with the grooves in the caps (photo).

11 The centre bearing cap has machined recesses on each side to accept the lower halves of the thrust washers which have the tags on them to prevent rotation (photo).
12 Hold the thrust washers in place while fitting the centre bearing cap (photo) and check that the grooves on the washer are facing away from the cap.
13 When the crankshaft and centre bearing cap is in position the endfloat may be checked by pushing the crankshaft as far as it will go in either direction and checking the gap between the thrust washer and the crankshaft web with a feeler gauge (photo). The gap should be between .003 and .011 in. (.08 to .28 mm).
14 The front and rear main bearing caps do not automatically line up for bolting down and it may be necessary to tap them with a hammer handle or other soft weight to enable the bolts to pick up the threads (photo).
15 Make sure that the bolts are clean, and tighten them all down evenly to a torque of 55 to 60 lbs/ft. (photo) with a torque spanner.
16 Although not absolutely necessary it is best to renew the rear crankshaft oil seal - it is provided in the gasket set anyhow. The old one can be removed from the seal carrier by carefully but firmly punching it out (photo).
17 Place the new seal squarely in position with the open lip facing away from the shoulder in the carrier bore (photo).
18 The seal can be tapped home squarely with a soft headed mallet (photo). It is important to make sure that the seal is driven in square from the very start, otherwise it will buckle; so if one side tends to go in too far to start with pull it out and start afresh until it is squarely and firmly 'started' all round.
19 Lubricate the crankshaft flange well so that the seal will not run on a dry surface to start with and heat up (photo).
20 Fit the new retainer plate gasket (photo) and replace the plate.
21 Tighten the bolts to 11-13 lbs/ft. (photo).
22 Make sure the hexagonal driveshaft is located in the oil pump and replace the pump, tightening the two mounting bolts evenly to 12-15 lbs/ft. torque (photo).

45. Engine Reassembly - Pistons, Piston Rings, Connecting Rods, Big End Bearings, End Plates, Timing Gear and Front Cover

1. The subsequent paragraphs on assembly assume that all the assemblies described in Section 44 have been carried out.
2. The assembly of new pistons to connecting rods should have been carried out as recommended in Sections 34 and 35. The new pistons should be supplied with rings already fitted.
3. If new rings are being fitted to existing pistons the following procedure should be followed. Having removed the old rings make sure that each ring groove in the piston is completely cleaned of carbon deposits. This is done most easily by breaking one of the old rings and using the sharp end as a scraper. Be careful not to remove any metal from the groove by mistake!
4. The new piston rings - three for each piston - must first be checked in the cylinder bores as described in Section 34: 3 and 4 It is assumed that the gap at the ends of the rings will not be too great. However, it is equally important that the gaps are not too small - otherwise the ends could meet when normal operating temperatures are reached and the rings would then break.
5. The minimum gap for all three rings is .010 in. (.25 mm). If the gap is too small, one end of the ring must be filed to increase the gap. To do this the ring should be gripped in a vice between two thin pieces of soft metal in such a way that

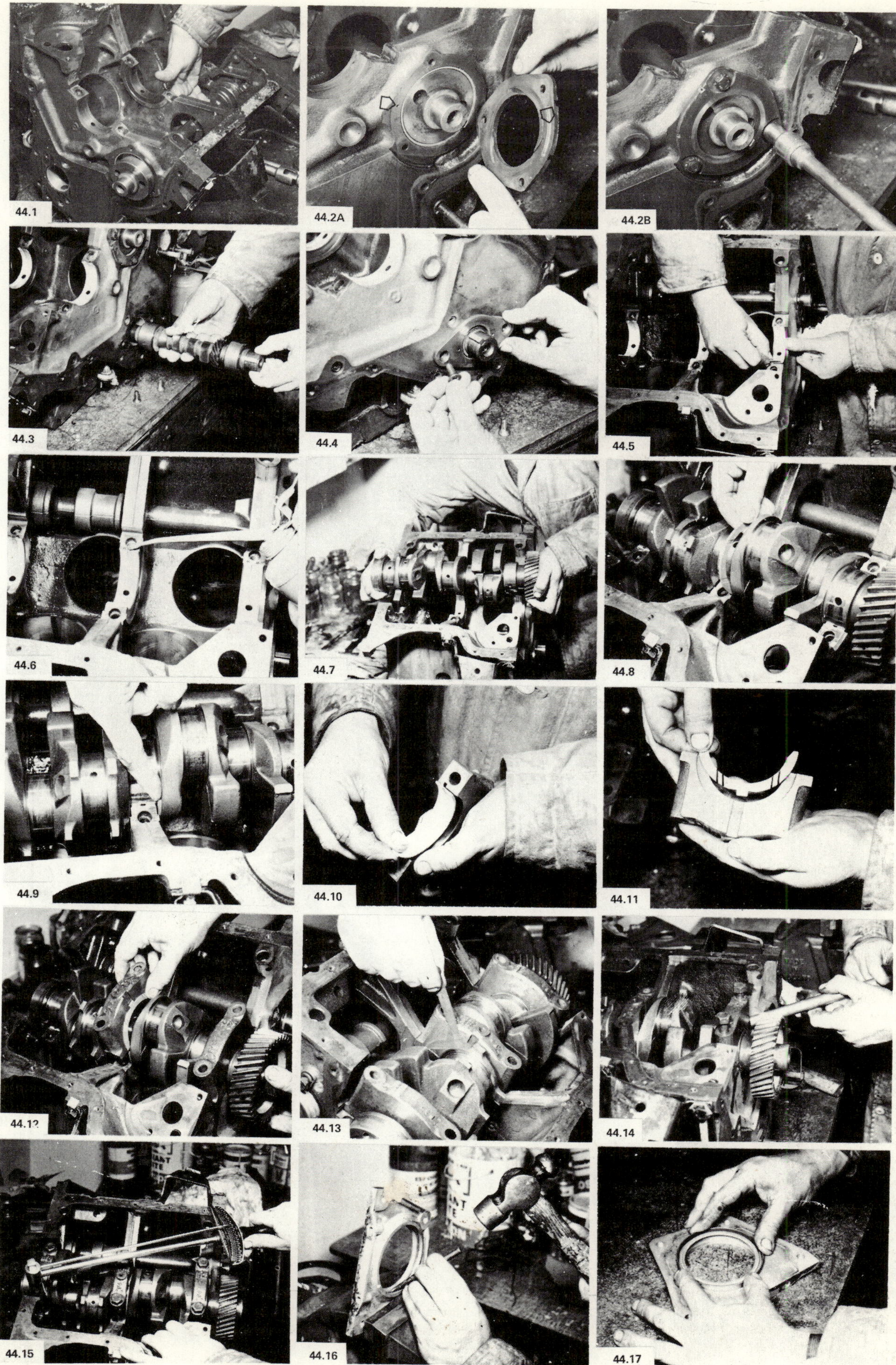

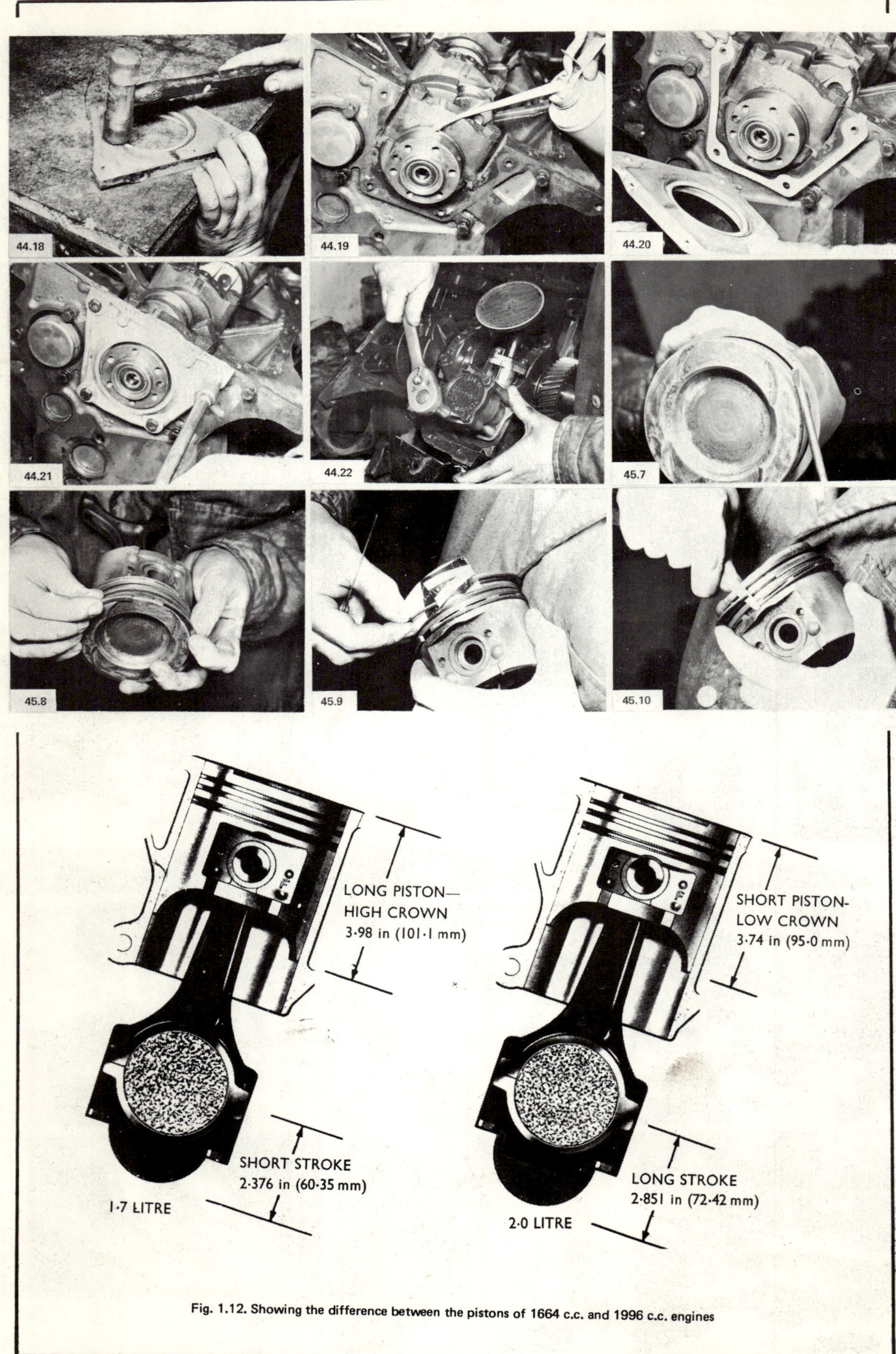

Fig. 1.12. Showing the difference between the pistons of 1664 c.c. and 1996 c.c. engines

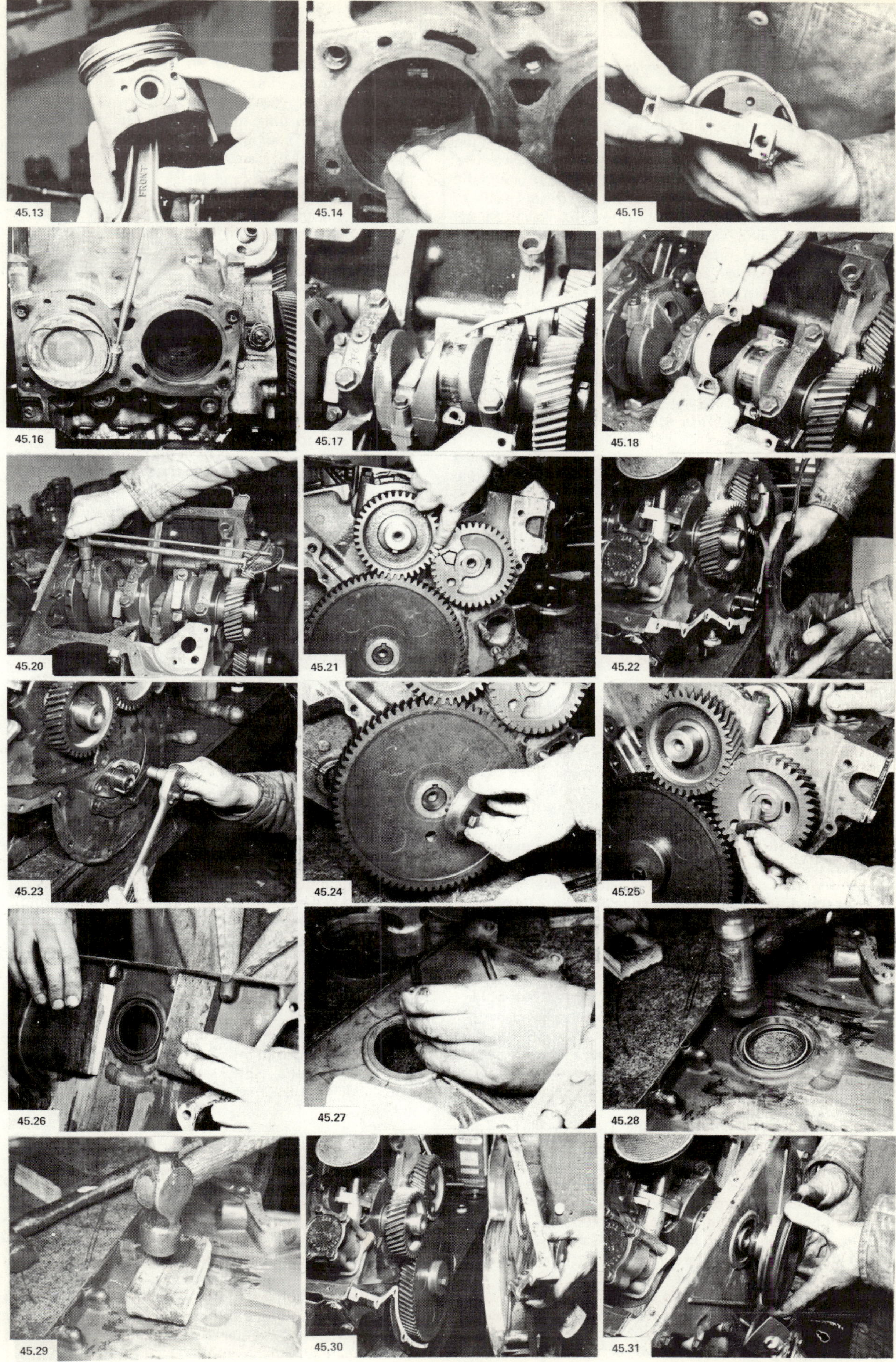

45.13

45.14

45.15

45.16

45.17

45.18

45.20

45.21

45.22

45.23

45.24

45.25

45.26

45.27

45.28

45.29

45.30

45.31

only the end to be filed is gripped and so that it only protrudes above the jaws of the vice a very small distance. This will eliminate the possibility of bending and breaking the ring while filing the end. Use a thin, fine file and proceed in easy stages - checking the gap by replacing the ring in the bore until the necessary minimum gap is obtained. This must be done with every ring - checking each one in the bore to which it will eventually be fitted. To avoid mistakes it is best to complete one set of rings at a time and replace the piston in the cylinder before proceeding to the next.

6. To replace the rings on to the pistons calls for patience and care if breakages are to be avoided. The three rings for each piston must all be fitted over the crown so obviously the first one to go on is the slotted oil control ring. Hold the ring over the top of the piston and spread the ends just enough to get it around the circumference. Then, with the fingers, ease it down, keeping it parallel to the ring grooves by 'walking' the ring ends alternately down the piston. Being wider than the compression rings no difficulty should be encountered in getting it over the first two grooves in the piston.

7. The lower compression ring, which goes on next, must only be fitted one way up. It is marked 'TOP' to indicate its upper face (photo).

8. Start fitting this ring by spreading the ends to get it located over the top of the piston (photo).

9. The lower compression ring has to be guided over the top ring groove and this can be done by using a suitably cut piece of tin which can be placed so as to cover the top groove under the ends of the ring (photo).

10 Alternatively, a feeler blade may be slid around under the ring to guide it into its groove (photo).

11 The top ring may be fitted either way up as it is barrel faced.

12 With the rings fitted the piston/connecting rod assembly is ready for replacement in the cylinder.

13 Each connecting rod and bearing cap should have been marked on removal (Section 20) but in any case the cylinder number is etched lightly on the end of the cap and connecting rod alongside. The piston and connecting rod are also marked to show which side faces the front of the engine (photo).

14 Start with No. 1 cylinder and remove the existing oil 'glaze' from the bore by rubbing it down with very fine emery. This will break down the hardened skin and permit the new piston rings to bed down more quickly (photo).

15 Fit a new shell bearing half into the connecting rod of No. 1 piston so that the notch in the bearing shell locates in the groove in the connecting rod (photo).

16 Place the piston in the cylinder bore the correct way round until the oil control ring abuts the face of the block. Then, using a large hose clip as a compressor (photo) contract each ring in turn and tap the piston into the cylinder. Take great care to be sure that the ring is not trapped on the top edge of the cylinder bore and when tapping the piston in do not use any force. If this is not done the rings could easily be broken.

17 When the piston has been fully located in the bore push it down so that the end of the connecting rod seats on the journal on the crankshaft. Make sure the journal is well lubricated with engine oil (photo).

18 Maintaining absolute cleanliness all the time fit the other shell bearing half into the cap, once again with the notches in the bearing and cap lined up. Lubricate it with engine oil and fit it onto the connecting rod so that the holes in the cap fit to the dowels in the connecting rod (photo).

19 Replace all pistons and connecting rods in a similar manner and do not make any mistakes locating the correct No. piston in the correct bore. Nos. 1 and 2 cylinders are front and rear respectively on the right hand bank and

Nos. 3 and 4 front and rear on the left hand bank. However, due to the Vee formation of the engine the big end journals on the crankshaft starting at the front run 1, 3, 2, 4. This is different again from the firing order so make sure you have it all clear in your mind to start with!

20 When all caps are correctly fitted tighten down the bolts to the correct torque of 25-30 lbs/ft. (photo).

21 The timing gears are easily fitted but care must be taken to ensure that the marks line up properly. Both the balance shaft and camshaft gears are keyed on to their respective shafts. The crankshaft gear has two countersunk dimples machined in its periphery. Both these must match up simultaneously with the single dimple in each of the other two gears. The photograph shows how this should be. An arrow points to the crankshaft/camshaft marks and the finger to the crankshaft/balance shaft marks (photo).

22 Before replacing the camshaft timing gear the front engine plate must be fitted back. Select the new gasket and coat the clean face of the block with suitable sealing compound (Hermetite, Wellseal) and stick the gasket to it in position. Then offer up the cover plate (photo).

23 Bolt the cover plate up tight to the block, not forgetting to fit the support plate behind the three centre bolts (Photo).

24 Fit the camshaft gear and balance shaft gears so that the timing marks line up. Replace the camshaft gear locking bolt together with the eccentric boss that drives the fuel pump. Tighten the bolt to 24-28 lbs/ft. There is no special position for the boss, although it was marked by a pencil on the fibre gear in this photo before removal (photo).

25 Replace and tighten the bolt and washer (photo) holding the balance shaft gear to 24-28 lbs/ft.

26 If the crankshaft pulley wheel oil seal is being replaced in the front cover it will be necessary to take care in driving out the old one as the cover is a light alloy casting which will not stand rough treatment. As the old seal must be driven out from the front it is essential to find two pieces of wood thicker than the depth of the cover so that the immediate area near the seal ring may be supported (photo).

27 With the cover firmly supported inside, it can be laid on the bench and the old seal driven out with a punch (photo).

28 Turn the cover over and carefully tap in the new seal evenly with the inner lip facing away from the shoulder in the bore (photo).

29 Tap the seal home finally with a block of wood (photo).

30 Select the front cover gasket and using a suitable sealing compound position it on the engine front plate and offer up the cover (photo).

31 Place the front cover bolts in position and screw them up loosely. Then fit the crankshaft pulley wheel onto the keyway of the crankshaft (photo). See that the boss of the pulley is lubricated where the oil seal runs.

32 The replacement of the crankshaft pulley, before tightening the cover bolts, centralises the seal to the pulley. The bolts holding the cover may then be tightened to 11-13 lbs/ft. (photo).

---

46. Engine Reassembly - Rear Plate, Crankshaft Pulley Wheel, Sump and Flywheel

---

1. If the engine rear plate has been removed it should now be replaced. Make sure that both metal faces are quite clean before refitting. No gasket is used.

2. Replace the bolt and washer which locate the crankshaft pulley wheel, block the crankshaft with a piece of wood against the side of the crankcase and tighten the bolt to a torque of 24-28 lbs/ft. (photo).

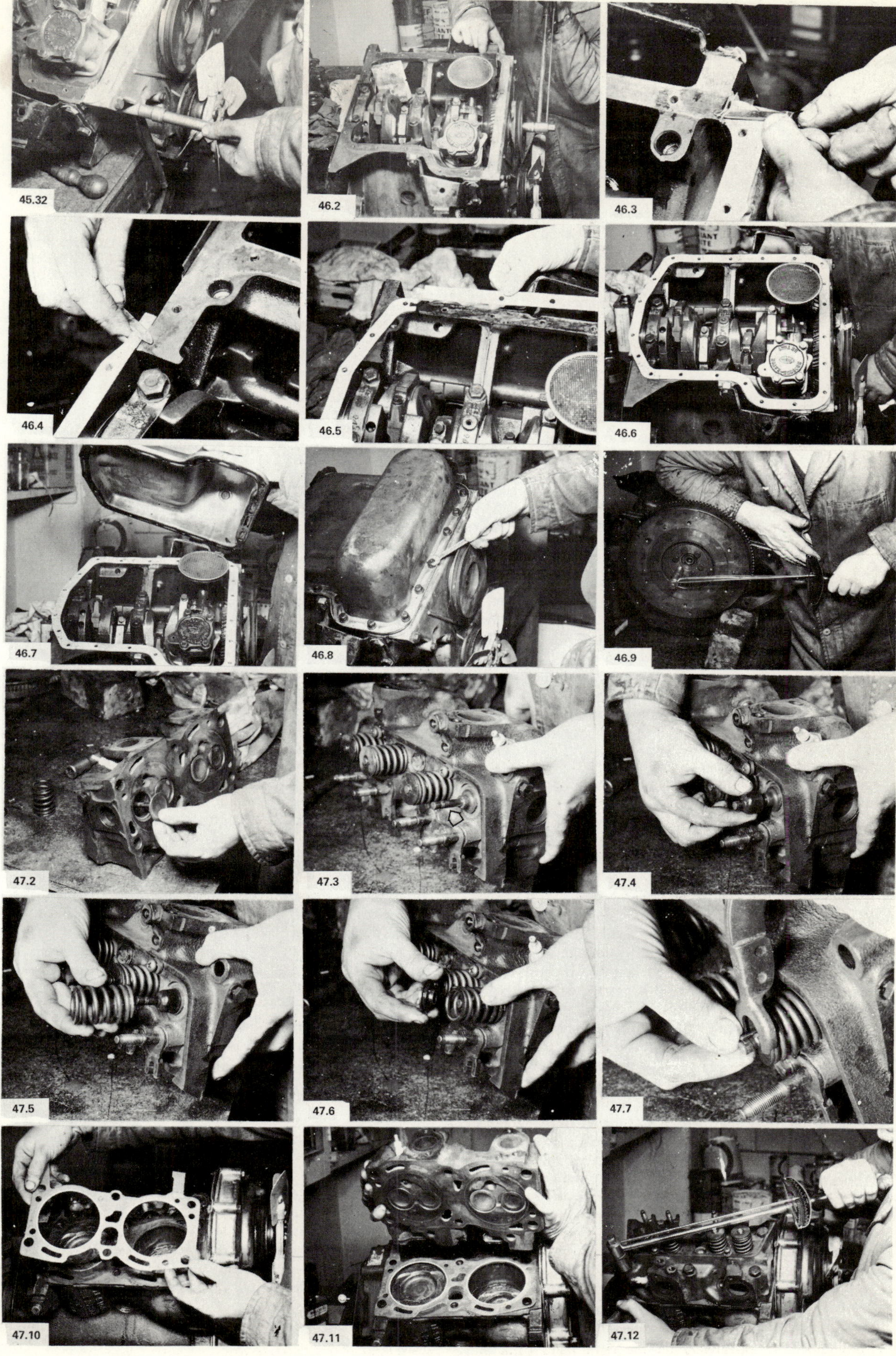

3. Trim the projecting pieces of the front cover and back-plate gaskets at the sump face of the block and front cover (photo).

4. Trim the projecting edge of the rear oil seal carrier on the sump face at the rear of the crankcase (photo).

5. Clean all traces of old gasket which may remain from the sump joint faces and cover the faces of both the crankcase and sump with sealing compound. The sump gasket is in four sections which dovetail together and these should be carefully positioned and the joints interlocked (photo).

6. The engine is then ready for the sump to be replaced (photo).

7. Clean the interior of the sump thoroughly, apply sealer to the joint edge and place it in position (photo).

8. Replace all the sump bolts and tighten them evenly to a final torque of 6-8 lbs/ft. (photo).

9. The flywheel may now be replaced. Make sure that the mating flanges are clean and free from burrs and line up the bolt holes correctly. They are so positioned that they will only line up in one position. Do not hammer the flywheel into position if it should be difficult to get it fully onto the flange. Support it squarely and replace the bolts, tightening them evenly so as to draw the flywheel squarely onto its seat. There are no washers and the bolts should be tightened evenly and progressively to a final torque of 45 to 50 lbs/ft. (photo).

47. Engine Reassembly - Valve Gear, Cylinder Heads, Inlet and Exhaust Manifolds

1. When the cylinder heads have been decarbonised and the valves ground in as described in Sections 38 and 41 the cylinder heads may be reassembled. If the valves have been removed as described in Section 12 there will be no confusion as to which valve belongs in which position.

2. Make sure all traces of carbon and grinding paste have been removed, lubricate the valve stem with engine oil and place it in the appropriate guide (photo).

3. It will then protrude through the top of the cylinder head (photo).

4. Fit a new seal cup over the valve stem (photo).

5. Place the valve spring over the valve stem with the close coils of the spring nearest the cylinder head (photo).

6. Fit the circular spring collar over the spring with the protruding centre boss of the collar downwards (photo).

7. Using a proper valve spring compressor tool, compress the spring down the valve stem sufficiently far to enable the two halves of the split collar (collets) to be fitted into the groove in the valve stem (photo). If necessary the collets should be smeared with grease to keep them in position. The spring compressor may then be released. Watch to ensure that the collets stay together in position as the spring collar comes past them. If the collar is a little off centre it may force one collet out of its groove in which case the spring must be re-compressed and the collet re-positioned. When the compressor is finally released tap the head of the valve stem with a soft mallet to make sure the valve assembly is securely held in position.

8. Stand the engine the right way up on the bench and replace the tappets if they have been removed from the block. If these have been kept in order on removal, as suggested, it will be a simple matter to replace them.

9. The two cylinder heads are identical so if they were marked left and right on removal they can be replaced on the same bank. If they have been muddled up no real harm will result but the pushrods will not be matched to their correct rocker arms. As these normally 'run in' together excessive wear could occur until such time as the two unfamiliar surfaces have bedded in again.

10 Select a new cylinder head gasket and place it in position on the block on one bank. These gaskets are identical and can fit either bank but they can only go on the bank one way - which is obvious from the way the bolt holes and cooling jacket holes line up (photo).

11 Locate the gasket over the protruding spigots in the block and then place the cylinder head in position (photo).

12 Make sure the cylinder head bolts are clean and lightly oiled and replace them. Nip them all down lightly and then tighten them in the sequence shown in Fig.1.13. The bolts should be tightened down to progressive torque loadings - all to 50 lbs/ft., then all to 60 lbs/ft. and finally to the specified requirement of 65-70 lbs/ft. (photo).

13 Now fit the pushrods into position, making sure that they are replaced the same way up as they came out and according to the original valve position. This will not be difficult if they have been kept in order as described in Sections 10 and 11. The pushrods are located at their upper ends in brackets bolted to the head (photo).

14 Locate the appropriate rocker arm over each stud so that the recessed end locates over the pushrod. Then place the fulcrum seat over the stud followed by the self locking nut (photo).

15 When both heads are replaced and fully tightened down the inlet manifold may be replaced. In view of the large area to be sealed for both air and water it is a safety measure - if not essential - to use a jointing compound such as 'Wellseal' in addition to the gasket (photo) on the mating surfaces.

16 Place the inlet manifold gasket in position in the Vee so that the single square hole (arrowed) is on the left hand cylinder head (photo). The gasket is obviously incorrect if put on any other way but this is a positive guide.

17 Apply jointing compound to the mating faces of the inlet manifold. Note the square port (arrowed) which matches the gasket hole and port in the left hand cylinder head (photo).

18 Place the manifold in position with the thermostat housing to the front (photo).

19 Replace the six manifold securing bolts, ensuring that the gasket is lined up to permit them to pick up the threads in the cylinder heads, and screw them up lightly (photo).

20 With a torque wrench (photo) tighten the bolts down evenly in the sequence shown in Fig. 1.14. to 13-16 lbs/ft. This tightening should be done in stages - all being tightened to 5 lbs/ft., then to 10 lbs/ft. before finally reaching the specified figure. Any uneven or excessive tightening may crack the manifold casting so take care.

48. Valve to Rocker Clearances - Adjustment

1. The valve stem to rocker clearance, which is in effect the mechanical free play between the camshaft and the end of the valve stem, is important to the correct operation and performance of the engine. If the clearance is too great the valve opening is reduced with consequent reduction in gas flow - and is also very noisy. If the clearance is too little the valve could open too much with the danger of it hitting the crown of the piston. The clearance is checked when the tappet is on the heel of the cam (opposite the highest point) and the valve therefore closed. This position coincides with certain other valves being fully open with their tappets on the high point of the cam. This can be seen easily when the valve spring is fully compressed.

2. The table below shows the relationship between the fully open valves and the closed valves which are to be checked. The diagram shows the valve numbering - Nos. 1-4 front to rear on the right hand bank and Nos. 5-8 front to rear on the left hand bank.

Fig. 1.13. Sequence for tightening the cylinder head bolts

Fig. 1.14. Sequence for tightening the inlet manifold bolts

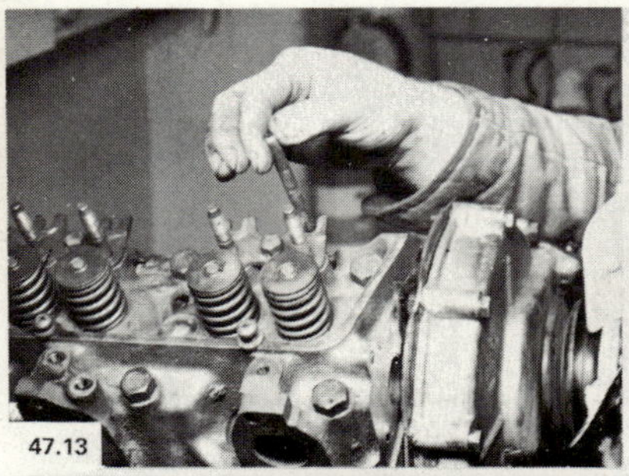

47.13

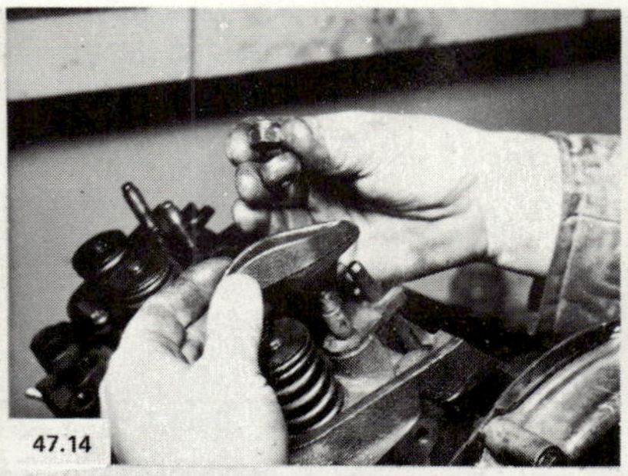

47.14

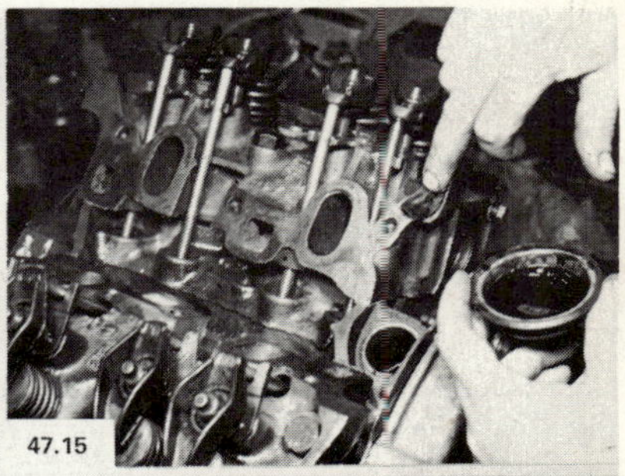

47.15

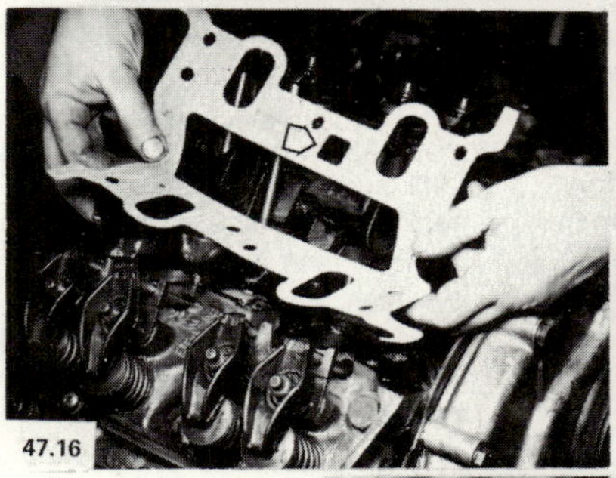

47.16

47.17

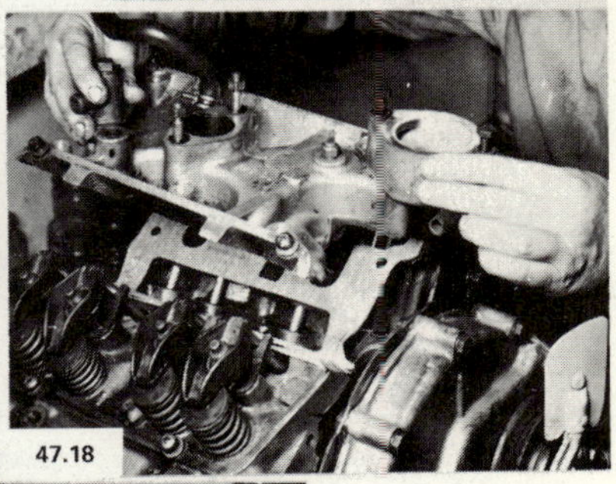

47.18

47.19

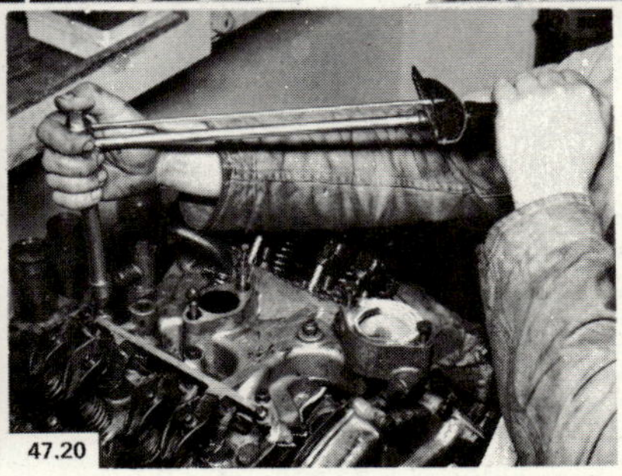

47.20

Valves open (together)	Adjust
Nos. 1 and 4	Nos. 5 (Inlet) and 8 (Exhaust)
Nos. 2 and 6	Nos. 3 (Exhaust) and 7 (Inlet)
Nos. 5 and 8	Nos. 1 (Exhaust) and 4 (Inlet)
Nos. 3 and 7	Nos. 2 (Inlet) and 6 (Exhaust)

Front of Engine	
L.H. Bank	R.H. Bank
5	1
6	2
7	3
8	4

The clearances after reassembly should be set at .012 in. (.3 mm) for the inlet valves and .020 in. (.51 mm) for the exhaust valves for a cold engine. They should be checked later when the engine has reached normal running temperature when they should be set at .010 in. (.25 mm) for inlet valves and .018 in. (.46 mm) for exhaust valves.

3. The actual adjustment procedure is straightforward. With the appropriate valve ready for checking place a feeler gauge of the required thickness (for exhaust or inlet valve) between the top of the valve stem and the rocker arm (photo). If it will not go the clearance is too small so slacken off the self-locking nut on the stud until it will go. If the clearance is too large the nut should be screwed down. The correct clearance is obtained when the feeler blade can be moved readily but a firm drag is felt.

4. It is a wise precaution to check each clearance measurement after the adjusting socket spanner has been removed from the nut. This is because the socket may possibly bind against the side of the rocker arm and tilt it, thus causing a false clearance measurement.

5. After the clearance adjustments are completed replace the rocker covers, each fitted with a new gasket (photo).

6. Tighten down the screws firmly and evenly (photo). NOTE: The rocker cover with the oil filler cap goes on the left hand bank. Rocker clearances should NOT be checked with a feeler gauge while the engine is running. In certain circumstances the valve could be forced against the crown of the piston causing serious damage. If one rocker is noisy it is possible to identify which one by removing the rocker cover and pressing a finger on each rocker in turn. The noisy one will be quiet when pressed.

49. Engine Reassembly - Final Ancillary Components

1. The exhaust manifolds are best replaced before putting the engine back into the car as they provide very useful holds if the engine has to be manhandled at all. Select the new gaskets and fit them the correct way, as they are not symmetrical (photo).

2. Replace each manifold and tighten the bolts evenly (photo).

3. The ancillary engine components must be replaced and the method of doing this is detailed in the appropriate Chapters. Section 9 of this Chapter gives a full list of the items involved. When this has been done the engine is ready to be put back in the car.

50. Engine Replacement - Without Gearbox

1. The engine must be positioned suitably so that the sling used to remove it can be easily refitted and the lifting tackle hooked on. Position the engine the right way round in front of the car and then raise it so that it may be brought into position over the car or the car rolled into position underneath it.

2. The gearbox should be jacked up to its approximately normal position.

3. Lower the engine steadily into the engine compartment, keeping all ancillary wires, pipes and cables well clear of the sides. It is best to have a second person guiding the engine while it is being lowered.

4. The tricky part is finally mating the engine to the gearbox, which involves locating the gearbox input shaft into the clutch housing and flywheel. Provided that the clutch friction plate has been centred correctly as described in Chapter 5, there should be little difficulty. Grease the splines of the gearbox input shaft first. It may be necessary to rock the engine from side to side in order to get the engine fully home. Under no circumstances let any strain be imparted onto the gearbox input shaft. This could occur if the shaft was not fully located and the engine was raised or lowered more than the amount required for very slight adjustment of position.

5. As soon as the engine is fully up to the gearbox bell-housing replace the bolts holding the two together.

6. The final positioning of the engine brackets onto the mountings requires some attention because the positioning bolts on the mounting are angled inwards and therefore do not exactly line up with the holes in the brackets. However, they are flexibly mounted so provided two people are doing the work they may be levered into position whilst the engine is lowered.

7. Replace all electrical connections and the generator, the fuel lines and carburettor linkages, cooling system hoses and radiator in the reverse order as described in Section 6.

8. Reconnect the exhaust pipes to the manifolds and replace the plate covering the lower section of the bell-housing. Remove the jack supporting if this has not already been done.

9. Refill the engine with new oil and replace the coolant liquid.

51. Engine Replacement - With Gearbox

1. The gearbox should be refitted to the engine, taking the same precautions as regards the input shaft as mentioned in Section 50.

2. The general principles of lifting the engine/gearbox assembly are the same as for the engine above but the gearbox will tilt everything to a much steeper angle as shown in the photos for Section 7. Replacement will certainly require the assistance of a second person.

3. Lift the gearbox end of the unit into the engine compartment (unless you are fortunate enough to have a hoist with a very high lift) and then lower and guide the unit down. One of the first things to be done is to reconnect the propeller shaft into the gearbox rear extension casing so someone should be ready to lift and guide the propeller shaft into position as soon as the gearbox is near enough. This cannot be done after the unit has been lowered to a certain position.

4. If a trolley jack is available this is the time to place it under the gearbox so that as the engine is lowered further the rear end can be supported and raised as necessary - at the same time being able to roll back as required. Without such a jack, support the rear in such a way that it can slide if possible. In any case the gearbox will have to be jacked and held up in position when the unit nears its final position.

5. Locate the front mounting brackets on the locating bolts as described in Section 50.

6. Refit the speedometer drive cable with the gearbox drive socket and refix the clamping plate and bolt. This MUST be done before the gearbox supporting crossmember

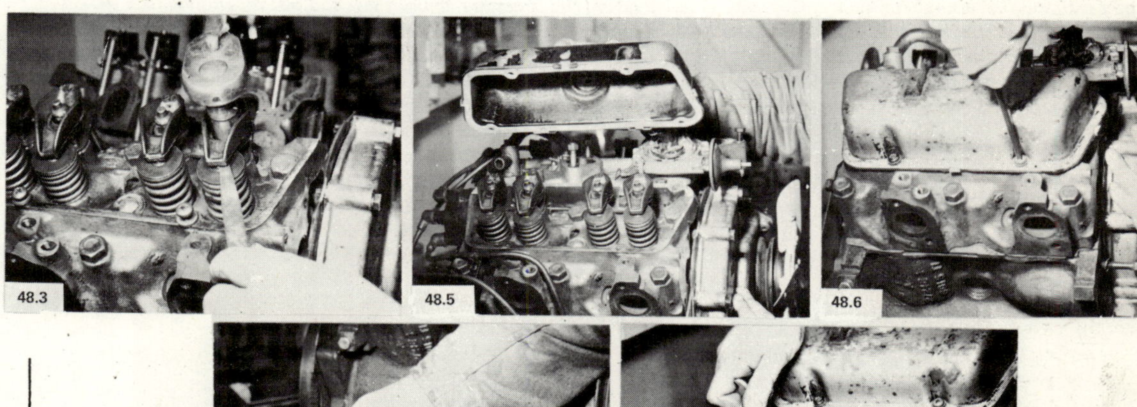

48.3

48.5

48.6

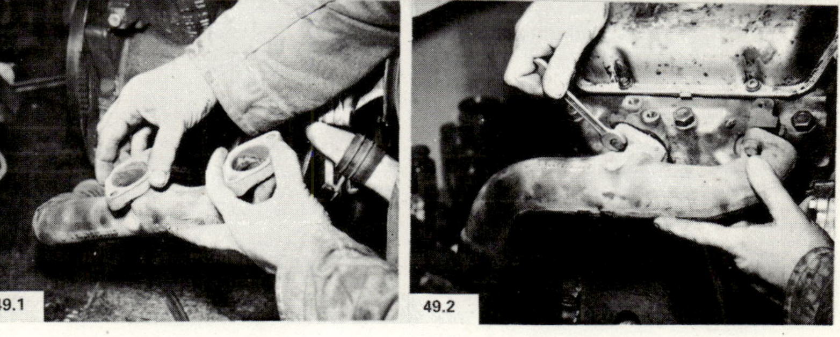

49.1

49.2

is replaced.

7. Fit the gearbox supporting plate to the gearbox and secure it with the bolt which goes through the centre of the plate. Make sure that the plate is fitted so that the hand-brake fulcrum lever is on the left ready to hook up the two cables.

8. Using the jack, position the crossmember up to the body frame and replace and tighten the four securing bolts. One of these also secures the earthing strap connected to the gearbox rear cover.

9. Replace the gearbox remote control change lever and housing as described in Chapter 6.

10 Reconnect the hydraulic pipe to the clutch slave cylinder and bleed the system as described in Chapter 5. The final connections should then be made to the engine as described in Section 50 and in addition to the engine lubricant and coolant the gearbox should also be refilled with fresh oil.

52. Engine - Initial Start Up After Overhaul or Major Repair

1. Make sure that the battery is fully charged and that all lubricants, coolants and fuel are replenished.

2. If the fuel system has been dismantled it will require several revolutions of the engine on the starter motor to get the petrol up to the carburettor. An initial 'prime' of about 1/3 of a cupful of petrol poured down the in tube of the carburettor will help the engine to fire quickly, thus relieving the load on the battery. Do not overdo this however, as flooding may result.

3. As soon as the engine fires and runs keep it going at a fast tickover only (no faster) and bring it up to normal working temperature.

4. As the engine warms up there will be odd smells and some smoke from parts getting hot and burning off oil deposits. The signs to look for are leaks of oil or water which will be obvious if serious. Check also the clamp connections of the exhaust pipes to the manifolds as these do not always 'find' their exact gas tight position until the warmth and vibration have acted on them and it is almost certain that they will need tightening further. This should be done of course with the engine stopped.

5. When running temperature has been reached adjust the idling speed as described in Chapter 3.

6. Stop the engine and wait a few minutes to see if any lubricants or coolant is dripping out when the engine is stationary.

7. Road test the car to check that the timing is correct and giving the necessary smoothness and power. Do not race the engine - if new bearings and/or pistons and rings have been fitted it should be treated as a new engine and run in at reduced revolutions for 500 miles.

Symptom	Reason/s	Remedy
Engine will not turn over when starter switch is operated	Flat battery. Bad battery connections. Bad connections at solenoid switch and/or starter motor.	Check that battery is fully charged and that all connections are clean and tight.
	Starter motor jammed.	Turn the square headed end of the starter motor shaft with a spanner to free it.
	Defective solenoid.	Bridge the main terminals of the solenoid switch with a piece of heavy duty cable in order to operate the starter.
	Starter motor defective.	Remove and overhaul starter motor.
Engine turns over normally but fails to fire and run	No spark at plugs.	Check ignition system according to procedures given in Chapter 4.
	No fuel reaching engine.	Check fuel system according to procedures given in Chapter 3.
	Too much fuel reaching the engine (flooding).	Check the fuel system as above.
Engine starts but runs unevenly and misfires	Ignition and/or fuel system faults.	Check the ignition and fuel systems as though the engine had failed to start.
	Incorrect valve clearances.	Check and reset clearances.
	Burnt out valves. Blown cylinder head gasket.	Remove cylinder heads and examine and overhaul as necessary.
	Worn out piston rings. Worn cylinder bores.	Remove cylinder heads and examine pistons and cylinder bores. Overhaul as necessary.
Lack of power	Ignition and/or fuel system faults.	Check the ignition and fuel systems for correct ignition timing and carburettor settings.
	Incorrect valve clearances.	Check and reset the clearances.
	Burnt out valves. Blown cylinder head gasket.	Remove cylinder heads and examine and overhaul as necessary.
	Worn out piston rings. Worn cylinder bores.	Remove cylinder heads and examine pistons and cylinder bores. Overhaul as necessary.
Excessive oil consumption	Oil leaks from crankshaft rear oil seal, timing cover gasket and oil seal, rocker cover gasket, oil filter gasket, sump gasket, sump plug washer.	Identify source of leak and renew seal as appropriate.
	Worn piston rings or cylinder bores resulting in oil being burnt by engine. Smoky exhaust is an indication.	Fit new rings or rebore cylinders and fit new pistons, depending on degree of wear.
	Worn valve guides and/or defective valve stem seals. Smoke blowing out from the rocker cover vents is an indication.	Remove cylinder heads and recondition valve stem bores and valves and seals as necessary.
Excessive mechanical noise from engine	Wrong valve to rocker clearances.	Adjust valve clearances.
	Worn crankshaft bearings. Worn cylinders (piston slap). Worn timing gears.	Inspect and overhaul where necessary.

NOTE: When investigating starting and uneven running faults do not be tempted into snap diagnosis. Start from the beginning of the check procedure and follow it through. It will take less time in the long run. Poor performance from an engine in terms of power and economy is not normally diagnosed quickly. In any event the ignition and fuel systems must be checked first before assuming any further investigation needs to be made.

Chapter 2/Cooling System

Contents

Specifications

Type of System	Pressurised, assisted by pump and fan.

Thermostat

Type	Wax
Location	Front end of cylinder block between the heads
Starts to open	185^{0} to 192^{0}F (85^{0} to 89^{0}C)
Fully open	210^{0} to 215^{0}F (99^{0} to 102^{0}C)
Radiator filler cap opening pressure	13 lbs/in.^{2} (.91 Kg/cm^{2})
Fan	2 or 4 blade 11 in. (27.9 cm) diameter
Fan belt and pulley	Tension ½ in. (12.7 mm) total free play. Pulley ratio 1.35 to 1
Water pump type	Centrifugal with volute chamber. Pulley ratio 1.406:1
Coolant capacity:	
1.7 litre with heater	13½ Imp. pints (16.2 U.S. pints, 7.5 litres)
1.7 litre without heater	12½ Imp. pints (15 U.S. pints, 6.9 litres)
2 litre with heater	15 Imp. pints (18 U.S. pints, 8.3 litres)
2 litre without heater	14 Imp. pints (16.8 U.S. pints, 7.7 litres)
Radiator type	Corrugated tin
Number of tubes - 1.7 litre engine...	56
- 2 litre engine	64

1. General Description

The engine cooling system is of the positive circulation pressurized type, the coolant liquid being passed round the system by an impeller pump driven by a V-belt from the crankshaft pulley. The same V-belt also drives the fan which is independently mounted on the engine front cover.

Water circulates from the bottom of the radiator to the pump and from there to the right hand bank of the cylinder block. It then passes to the left hand bank and from both banks passes up through the cylinder heads to the jacketing of the inlet manifold. The thermostat housing is an integral part of the inlet manifold and water passes through the thermostat to the top of the radiator or by-passes back to the pump when the thermostat is shut. It then passes down through the cooling tubes, through which air is drawn by the fan, and the cycle starts over again. The thermostat restricts circulation at low coolant temperatures. Water temperature is measured by an electro-sensitive plug fitted in the inlet manifold jacketing connected to a gauge in the car.

The cooling system also provides the heat for the heating system. The heater radiator is fed from a pipe connected to an outlet from the inlet manifold jacketing and the return is direct to the water pump. This ensures that the hottest water in the system goes directly to the heater under positive circulation.

2. Routine Maintenance

1. The coolant level should be checked at least weekly or more often in conditions of high mileages or exceptionally high temperatures. Coolant loss is normally negligible and any indications of excessive loss need to be investigated. Always top up with clean water, preferably soft; Rain water is perfect. When antifreeze has been added to the system make sure that topping up is done with a mixture similar in proportion to the contents of the radiator.

2. Check the fan belt tension (details in Section 12) at least every 5,000 miles and examine all hoses and connections for signs of deterioration or leaks.

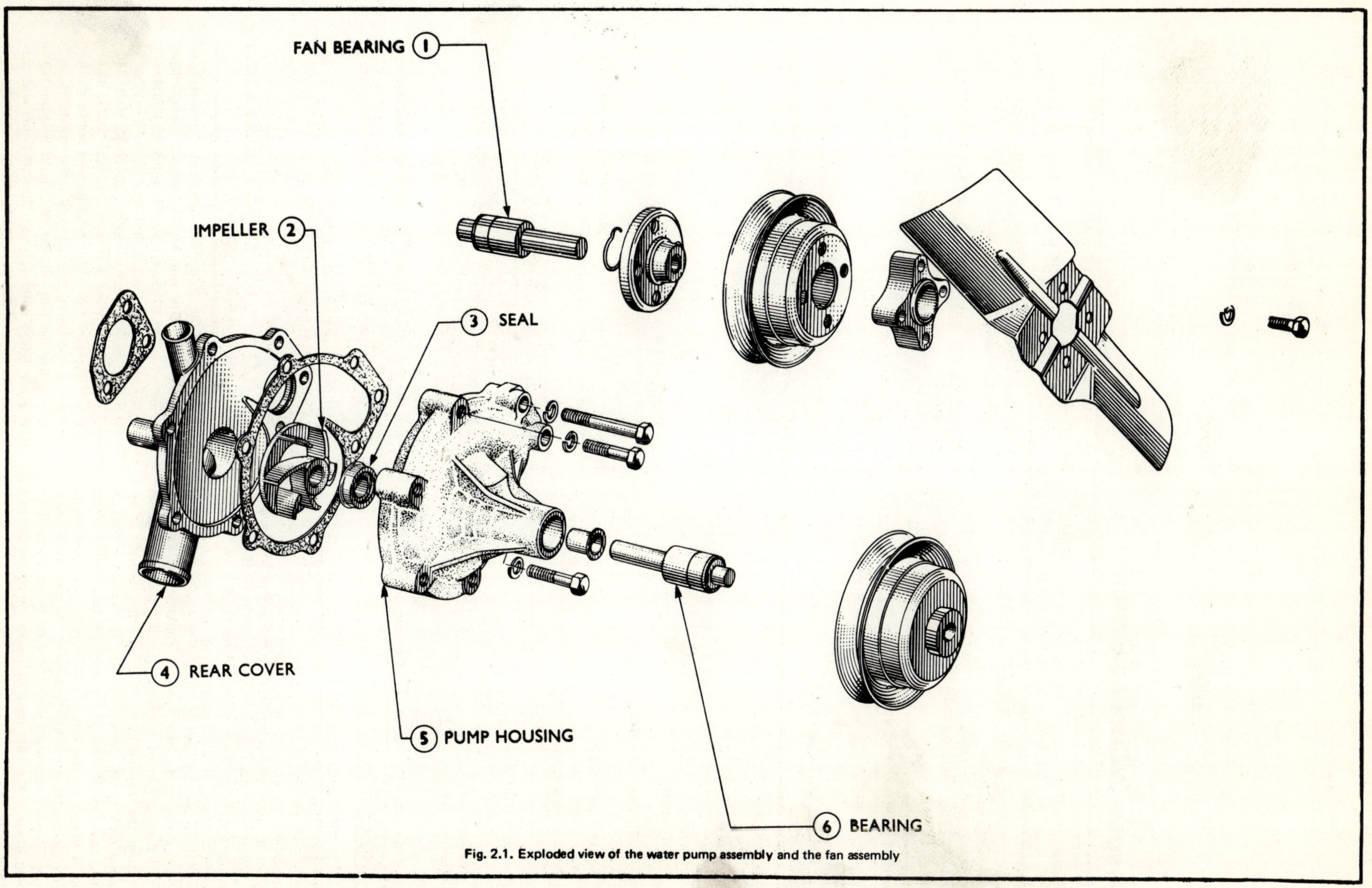

Fig. 2.1. Exploded view of the water pump assembly and the fan assembly

3. Cooling System - Draining

1. Place the car on a level surface and acquire a container of two gallons capacity which is shallow enough to get under the radiator if you wish to retain the coolant because of antifreeze.
2. Remove the radiator cap. If the coolant is hot be careful. Cover the cap with a cloth and remove it slowly. The system is under a pressure of anything up to 13 lbs/in^2 and unless care is taken there is a danger of being scalded when the water boils up under reduced pressure.
3. Unscrew the drain cock at the bottom of the radiator (photo). It is not necessary to take it right out but if the water is very dirty it is as well to do so. The orifice can then be probed to ensure all sludge is cleared from the bottom of the radiator.
4. To ensure that all liquid leaves the block the drain tap behind the oil filter should also be opened.

4. Cooling System - Flushing

1. With time, the radiator and the jacketing waterways in the engine may become restricted or even blocked with scale and sediment deposits so reducing the efficiency of the cooling system. This is when flushing is necessary.
2. With the system drained and taps removed run water from a hose through it for several minutes to clear loose deposits. It may be necessary to probe the drain outlets while this is going on.
3. Close the drain taps and refill the system with water and a proprietary chemical radiator cleaner. Replace the filler cap and run the engine for ten to fifteen minutes. Then drain out and flush thoroughly with clean water. If the scale deposits are particularly heavy a second treatment may be necessary. Under no circumstances, however, should the cleaning compound be left in the system.

5. Cooling System - Filling

1. Close both drain taps.
2. Fill the system slowly to avoid air locks and at the same time make sure the heater valve is open by moving the control lever to 'HOT'. Use soft water or rain water if possible. Use antifreeze as prescribed in Section 6.
3. Fill within ½ inch of the neck of the filler tube cap flange and replace the cap firmly, screwing it fully clockwise up to the stops.
4. Run the engine and recheck the level.

6. Antifreeze Mixture

1. In climatic conditions where the ambient temperature is likely to drop below freezing point the use of antifreeze is essential. If the coolant is permitted to freeze in the car serious damage can result.
2. Any good proprietary brand may be used of specification BS 3151 or 3152. Do not use one with an alcohol base as the evaporation rate is very high.
3. The quantity of antifreeze which should be used for various levels of protection is given in the table below, expressed as a percentage of the cooling system capacity.

Antifreeze volume	Protection to:	Spec. gravity
10%	-8ºC (17ºF)	1.017
15%	-13ºC (7ºF)	1.024
20%	-19ºC (-3ºF)	1.032
25%	-29ºC (-20ºF)	1.040

In all cases, however, the directions on the tin should be followed as variations occur between different manufacturers products.

7. Radiator - Removal, Inspection, Cleaning and Replacement

1. Drain the cooling system as described in Section 3.
2. Undo the clip securing the top hose to the radiator (or thermostat housing) (photo).
3. Remove the clip securing the lower hose to the radiator (photo).
4. Unscrew the cross-head self tapping screws holding the fibre fairing piece around the top of the radiator and take it off.
5. Remove the four bolts holding the radiator to the front panel (photo).
6. Lift out the radiator (photo).
7. If there are leaks these can usually be repaired by soldering, or with the use of one of the proprietary brands of resin based fillers such as 'Cataloy' that are generally available.
8. Make sure the honeycomb matrix is cleared of flies, etc., by hosing it with a strong water jet.
9. Flush out the radiator with clean water, inverting it to clear any deposits which may not otherwise be easy to clear from the header tank.
10 Inspect the hoses for signs of perishing and cracking, particularly near the clips and ensure that the clips are not distorted. Renew any doubtful items.
11 Examine the drain tap and tap seat for wear or damage which could cause leaking.
12 Replacement of the radiator is a reversal of the removal procedure. Always check carefully for leaks as soon as the system is refilled and has reached its normal running temperature.

8. Thermostat - Removal, Testing and Replacement

1. A faulty thermostat can cause overheating or failure of the engine to warm up quickly in cold weather. It will also affect the performance of the heater.
2. To remove it first draw off about four pints from the cooling system.
3. Undo the top radiator hose clip at the thermostat elbow (photo 7.2) and pull it off the elbow.
4. Undo the two bolts holding the elbow to the manifold (photo).
5. Lift off the elbow revealing the thermostat.
6. The thermostat is often stuck to the rim of the housing with sediment. To loosen it without damage tap it with a flat nosed punch right on the edge as if trying to rotate it in the housing. Be careful as the lip acts as a form of seal and although not critical it should not be damaged.
7. The loose thermostat may then be lifted out (photo).
8. To test whether the thermostat functions as it should, suspend it in a pan of water with a piece of string. Then, with a thermometer in the water (not touching the pan) note at what temperature it starts to open (it should be 185-192ºF (85º-89ºC)). Then note when it is fully open (.4 in.-10.3 in.) which should be at 210-215ºF (99º-102ºC). Check that the thermostat closes once again at the lower temperature (after cooling naturally). Should it fail on any of these checks it must be renewed. Note that the operation of the thermostat is not instantaneous so allow sufficient time when testing it. Should the thermostat have stuck open it

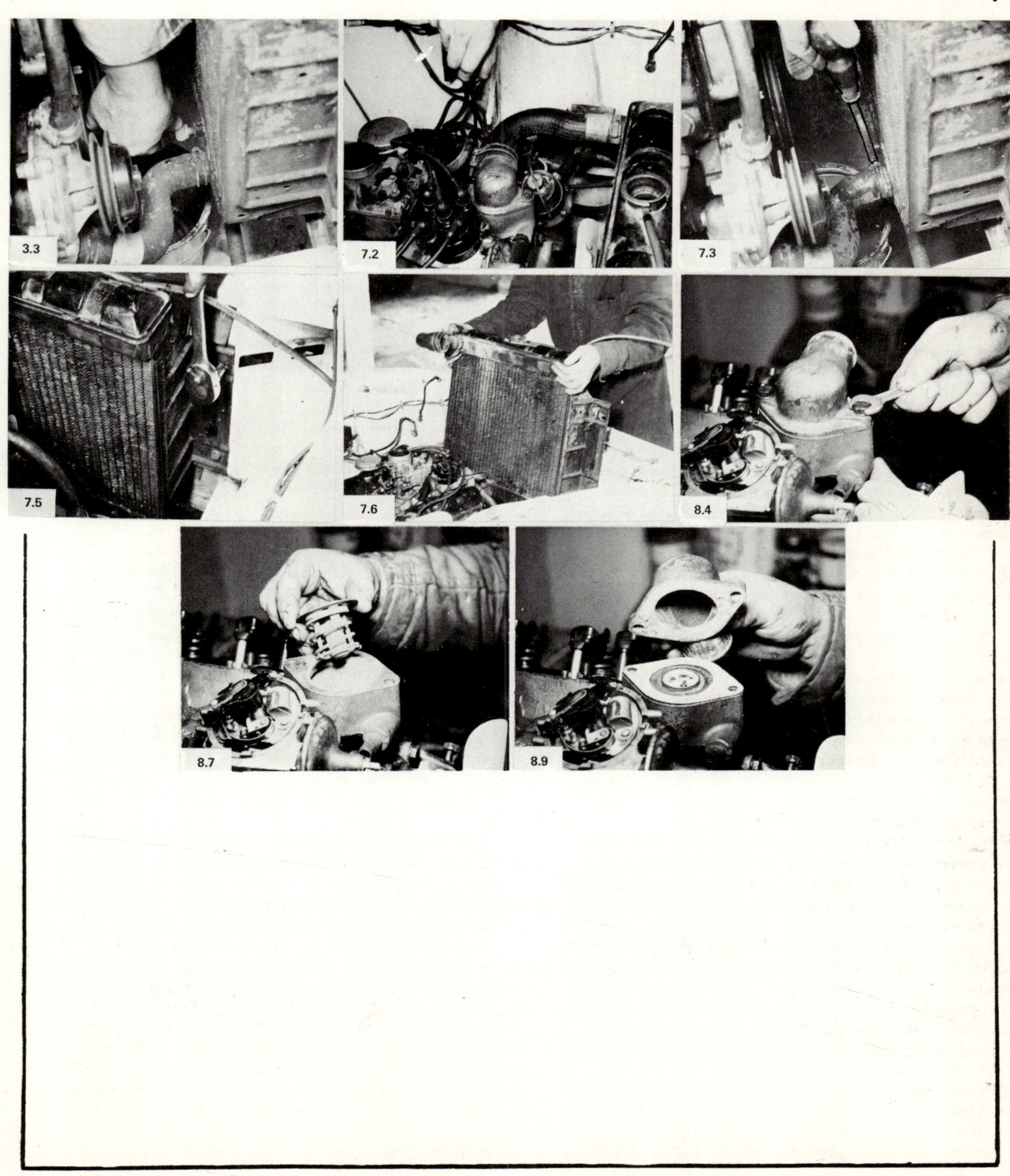

3.3

7.2

7.3

7.5

7.6

8.4

8.7

8.9

would have been apparent when the housing cover was removed.

9. Replacement of the thermostat is a reversal of the removal procedure. Ensure that the mating faces of the two flanges are clean and use a new gasket (photo). It is a sensible insurance to use a sealing compound also such as 'Hermetite'. If the elbow is very deeply corroded it should be renewed.

9. Water Pump - Removal and Replacement

1. Drain the cooling system as described in Section 3 and remove the fan belt as described in Section 12.
2. Slacken off the three clips and detach the three inlet hoses. It may be convenient to remove the bottom radiator hose at the radiator end and the by-pass hose at the thermostat housing in which case they can be lifted away with the pump in due course.
3 Remove the three bolts holding the pump to the face of the cylinder block (photo). (In the photo the engine is not in the car.) Lift the pump away from the engine.
4. Replacement is a reversal of the removal procedure. A new gasket should be fitted (photo A) and sealed with jointing compound before replacing the pump (photo B). Do not overtighten the bolts.

10. Water Pump - Dismantling and Reassembly

1. Remove the pump from the engine. One bolt will be 'trapped' by the pulley so cannot be removed from the body of the pump.
2. Remove the four bolts attaching the rear cover to the pump housing and take it off.
3. It must be appreciated that all the component parts are held together by press fit. Obviously these press fits are tight, otherwise the pump would simply fly apart in use so before proceeding any further it is essential that for pressing operations a wide opening vice at least and an assortment of drifts and hollow tubes for use as spacers is available. The use of hammers and blocks is possible but the force required is such that the likelihood of fracturing the pump body is very high.
4. Draw off the V-belt pulley from the shaft with a hub puller.
5. Next press the shaft and bearing assembly complete with impeller, seal and slinger out of the housing. One way to do this is to support the housing with a short piece cut from a cast-iron rainpipe and then placing the whole assembly in the vice jaws and pressing on the nose of the shaft. When the shaft is flush with the housing obtain a suitable piece of rod slightly smaller than the shaft in diameter and use this to press it right through.
6. No further dismantling is necessary as all the components of the shaft and bearing come together as a repair kit.
7. Using a suitable length of tube press the slinger onto the longer end of the new shaft and bearing assembly in the vice so that the slinger flange abuts the bearing.
8. Then press the shaft and bearing into the housing, short end first, so that the bearing race comes flush with the end of the housing. A suitable sleeve will be needed to go over the pulley end of the shaft and up against the housing during the final pressing operation.
9. Next press the pump seal into the housing with the carbon face away from the bearing.
10 With the flat face of the impeller supported by a piece of flat steel plate the shaft is now pressed into it. The correct distance is reached when the rear face of the housing has a 0 to .005 in. (0 to 0.13 mm) clearance from the plate

supporting the impeller. Any over-pressing will dislodge the position of the bearing in the housing.
11 Replace the trapped bolt into its correct hole and re-fit the pulley to the shaft, recessed side over the housing. When pressing the pulley on care must be taken to ensure that support is so arranged that the shaft is not dislodged in the housing. The pulley is in position when the centre line of the 'V' is 2.2 to 2.25 ins. (56 to 57 mm) from the rear face of the housing.
12 Clean off the faces of the pump body and rear cover, fit a new gasket and replace the rear cover, tightening down the four bolts evenly and not too tightly, bearing in mind that the housing and cover are made from aluminium alloy.

11. Fan - Removal, Overhaul and Replacement

1. Remove the fan belt (Section 12).
2. Remove the fan blades and pulley by unscrewing the four bolts and lockwashers holding them to the hub.
3. Remove the engine front cover (See Chapter 1/17.).
4. A circlip is located in a groove in the bearing and a corresponding groove in the housing. Remove this circlip and then press the shaft bearing and expansion plug together with the hub, out of the front cover. The shaft can then be pressed out of the hub.
5. The new shaft and bearing assembly is first pressed into the housing so that the circlip grooves are in alignment. The circlip is then refitted.
6. The hub is pressed in until the front face is $3\frac{3}{8}$ in. (85.8 mm) from the REAR face of the front cover.
7. Fit a new expansion plug to the shaft bore in the rear face of the bearing housing.
8. Replace the front cover and refit the pulley and fan blades.
9. Replace the fan belt and adjust as described in Section 12.

12. Fan Belt - Adjustment, Removal and Replacement

1. The tension of the fan belt is of considerable importance. If too tight the bearings in the water pump, generator and fan will be subjected to excessive strain - thus wearing them out, or if too slack it will slip, reducing the efficiency of the water pump and the output of the generator.
2. To adjust the tension it is necessary to move the generator. Slacken off the three bolts which hold the generator in position. Two of these are at each end of the generator body opposite each of them (the mounting bolts) and the third runs in a slotted bar (the adjusting bolt) (photo).
3. Pull the generator outwards to tighten the bolt and clamp the adjustment bolt, followed by the mounting bolts.
4. The tension should be such that there is ½ inch (12 mm) of free movement in the belt between the generator and fan (see Fig. 2.2.).
5. To remove the belt entirely, simply slacken it off by moving the generator inwards enough to enable the belt to be lifted over the pulley (photo). If the belt breaks it will be immediately apparent because the generator warning light will come on. In order to fit a new belt slacken off the generator mounting and adjusting bolts and proceed as for adjustment after fitting the new belt over the pulleys.
6. As the V.4 belt is comparatively long there is more stretch tendency so a new belt should be checked after a few hundred miles.

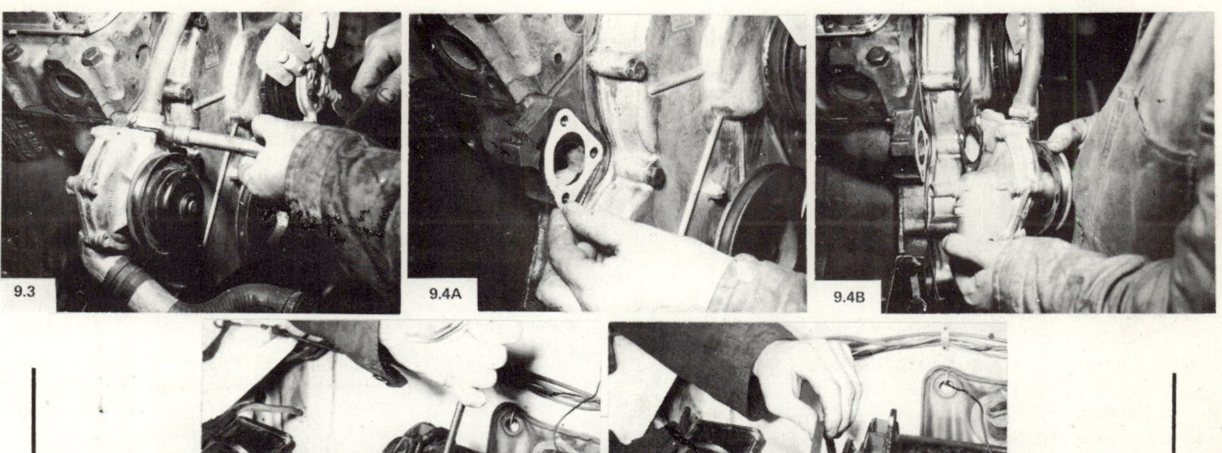

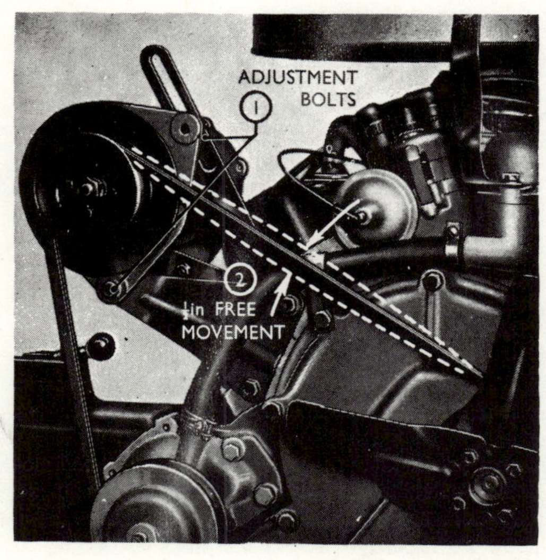

Fig. 2.2. Fan belt tension adjustment

13. Water Temperature Gauge - Fault Finding

1. Correct operation of the water temperature gauge is important as the engine could attain a considerable degree of overheating, unnoticed, without it.

2. To check the correct operation of the installation, first disconnect the 'Lucar' connector from the sender unit plug screwed into the top of the inlet manifold. With the ignition 'on' the gauge should be at the cold mark. Then earth the lead to the engine block when the needle should indicate hot, at the opposite end of the scale. This test shows that the gauge on the dash is functioning properly. If it is not then it will need renewal (see Chapter 10). If there is still a fault in the system with this check completed satisfactorily, there will be a fault in the sender unit or the wire leading from it to the gauge. Renew these as necessary.

3. If the fuel gauge should be showing signs of malfunctioning at the same time as the temperature gauge fault may lie in the instrument voltage regulator which should be checked as described in Chapter 10.

Symptom	Reason/s	Remedy
Loss of coolant	Leak in system.	Examine all hoses, hose connections, drain taps and the radiator and heater for signs of leakage when the engine is cold, then when hot and under pressure. Tighten clips, renew hoses and repair radiator. Examine gasket between inlet manifold and thermostat housing elbow for signs of leaks.
	Defective radiator pressure cap.	Examine cap for defective seal or spring and renew if necessary.
	Overheating causing rapid evaporation due to excessive pressure in system forcing vapour past radiator cap.	Check reasons for overheating.
	Blown cylinder head gasket, causing excess pressure in cooling system forcing coolant past radiator cap.	Remove suspect cylinder head (or heads) and renew gasket.
	Cracked block or head or inlet manifold due to freezing or careless reassembly.	Strip engine and examine. Repair as required.
Overheating	Insufficient coolant in system.	Top up.
	Water pump not turning properly due to slack fan belt.	Tighten fan belt.
	Kinked or collapsed water hoses causing restriction to circulation of coolant.	Renew hose as required.
	Faulty thermostat (not opening properly).	Fit new thermostat.
	Engine out of tune.	Check ignition setting and carburettor adjustments.
	Blocked radiator either internally or externally.	Flush out cooling system and clean out cooling fins.
	Cylinder head gasket blown, forcing coolant out of system.	Remove head (or heads) and renew gasket.
	New engine not run-in.	Adjust engine speed until run-in.
	Binding brakes causing excessive power load on engine.	Check and adjust brakes.
	Blocked or restricted exhaust system.	Examine exhaust system for kinks, dents or blockage.
Engine running too cool	Missing, faulty or wrong type of thermostat.	Fit new thermostat.

Chapter 3/Fuel System and Carburation

Contents

Specifications

All Models

Tank capacity ... ...   10 Imp gallons (12 U.S. gallons, 45.4 litres)

Fuel lines
Feed pipe O.D. ... ...   5/16 in. (7.94 mm)
Return pipe O.D. ... ...   1/4 in. (6.35 mm)
Return pipe restriction orifice ... ...   1.3 mm

1664 cc and 1994 cc models Sept. 1965 - Sept. 1966

Fuel pump
Type ... ...   Mechanical - driven from an eccentric in front of the camshaft gear.
Delivery pressure ... ...   2¾ - 4¼ lb/in.^{2} (.07 to .14 kg/cm^2)
Inlet vacuum ... ...   8.5 in mercury (21.6 cm)
Diaphragm spring test length ... ...   .625 in. (15.88 mm)
Diaphragm spring test pressure ... ...   7 to 7¾ lbs. (3.18 to 3.52 kg)
Securing nuts torque ... ...   15 to 18 lbs/ft. (2.07 to 2.49 kg/m)

Carburettor

Type ... ...   Zenith 36 IV single choke downdraught

	1664 cc	1996 cc
Colour code	white	green
Choke diameter	28 mm	29 mm
Main jet	92	102
Compensating jet	120	120
Idling jet		55
Part throttle air bleed		2.6
Full throttle air bleed		1.0
Idling jet air bleed		1.4
Accelerator pump jet		55

Fuel pump (Oct. 1966 on)
Type ... ...   Mechanical - driven from eccentric in front of the camshaft gear.
Delivery pressure ... ...   3½ to 5 lb/in.^{2} (.25 to .35 kg/cm^2)
Identification ... ...   Body retaining screws coloured GREEN

Inlet vacuum	8.5 in. (21.6 cm) Hg.
Diaphragm spring test length	.625 in. (15.88 mm)
Diaphragm spring test pressure	$9^{3}/8$ to 9¾ lb. (4.25 to 4.42 kg)
Securing nuts torque	15 to 18 lb/ft. (2.07 to 2.49 kg/m)

Carburettor (Oct. 1966 on)

Type...	Ford, single choke, downdraught
Idling speed	580 to 620 r.p.m.
Fast idle	950 to 1150 r.p.m.
Float setting (up)	1.12 to 1.14 in. (28.5 to 29.0 mm)
(down)	1.38 to 1.40 in. (35.0 to 35.5 mm)
Choke plate pull down	.14 to .16 in. (3.5 to 4.0 mm)
Accelerator pump stroke	.17 to .18 in. (4.3 to 4.6 mm)
Accelerator pump spring	RED
Throttle barrel diameter...	36 mm
Choke diameter	28 mm
Main jet	1.4 mm
Idling jet	.6 mm
Air correction jet	1.65 mm
Power jet	.8 mm
Accelerator pump jet	.55 mm
Accelerator pump lever (between centres)	.4 in. (10.2 mm)

Type	Weber 32-DIF-4
Choke diameter (primary)	26 mm
Choke diameter (secondary)	27 mm
Main jet (primary)	155
Main jet (secondary)	140
Idling jet (primary)	50
Idling jet (secondary)	45
Main air correction jet (both)	180
Emulsion tube (both)	F6
Accelerator pump jet	65
Needle valve	200
Fast idle setting (throttle plate gap)	1.2 mm
Choke plate pull-down	5 mm
Choke plate opening	7.5 to 8.5 mm with lever backed off 10 mm
Mounting nut torque	15 to 18 lbs.ft. (2.07 to 2.49 kg/m)

1. General Description

The fuel tank is mounted under the boot of the car and fuel is pumped from it by a mechanical pump mounted on the front left hand side of the engine and driven by an arm running on an eccentric in part of the camshaft timing gear. The pump feeds the carburettor float chamber and when this is full the needle valve closes and fuel is returned to the tank via a return pipe connected to the delivery pipe near the carburettor. The return pipe is of a smaller diameter bore to prevent possible fuel starvation. This recirculatory system ensures that the fuel is kept at an even temperature and helps to prevent vapour locks.

On early models (Sept. '65 - Sept. '66) the standard carburettor fitted was a single choke Zenith but thereafter it changed to Ford's own model. The early G.T. and later '2,000' Series were fitted with Weber 32 twin choke carburettors. On all models, air drawn into the carburettor is filtered through a paper element type filter. Some of the later air filter casings are fitted with a pipe connection to the cylinder head rocker cover for crankcase fumes to be vented back to the carburettor.

2. Routine Servicing

1. Every 5,000 miles lubricate the throttle linkage, clean the sediment from the fuel pump bowl as described in Section 7 and adjust the slow running if necessary as described in Sections, 10, 13 and 16.
2. Every 10,000 miles renew the air filter element in addition to the necessary 5,000 mile service items. See Section 3 for details.

3. Air Filter - Removal and Replacement

1. To renew the paper filter element unscrew the wing nut holding the cover plate in place (photo). Some models are held by bolts (Fig. 3.2.).
2. Lift off the cover plate to gain access to the filter element (photo).
3. Note that the element is placed off centre in relation to the pan and fits round a raised ridge which can be seen in the photo.
4. If the complete assembly is to be removed first undo the

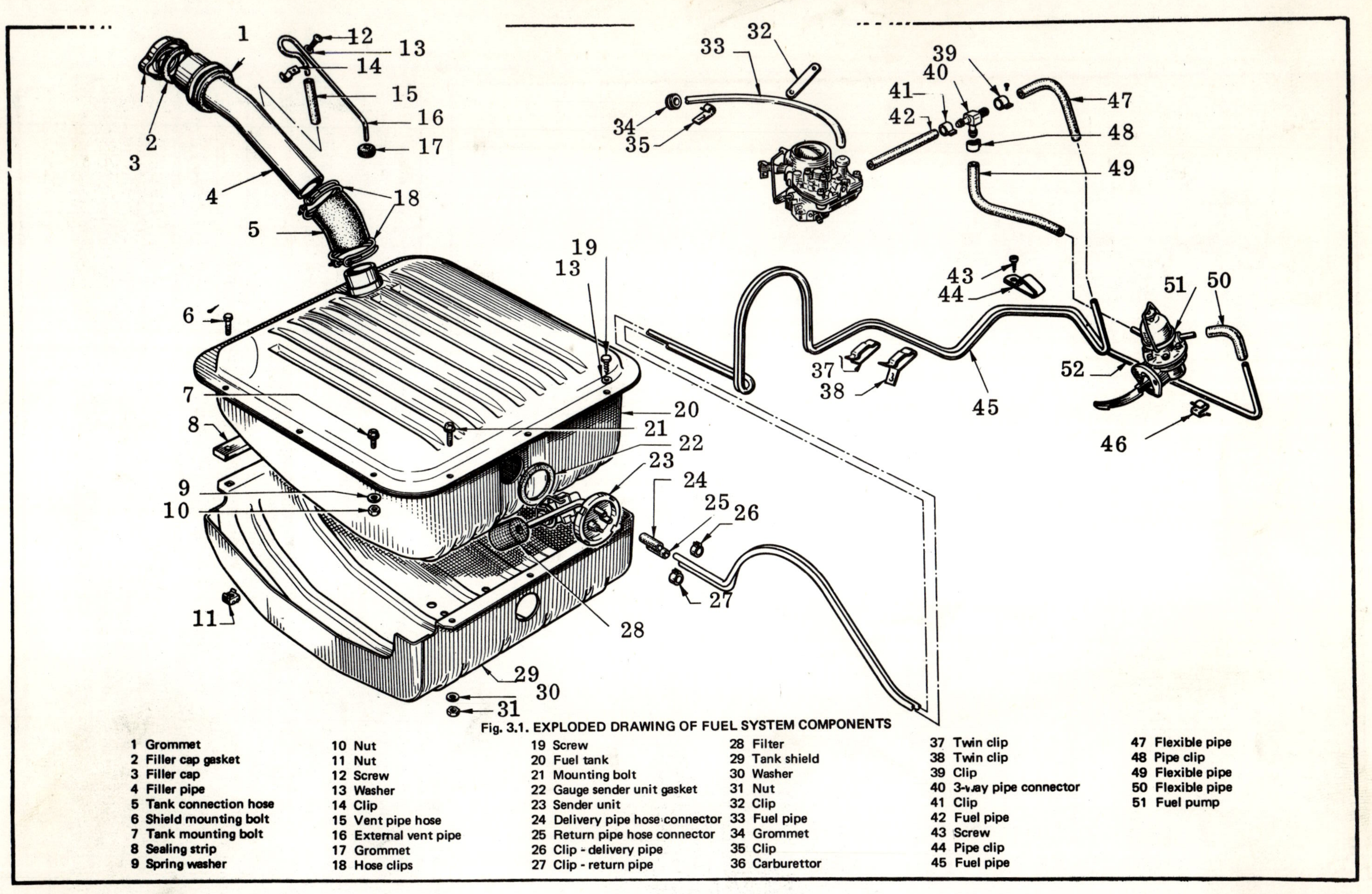

Fig. 3.1. EXPLODED DRAWING OF FUEL SYSTEM COMPONENTS

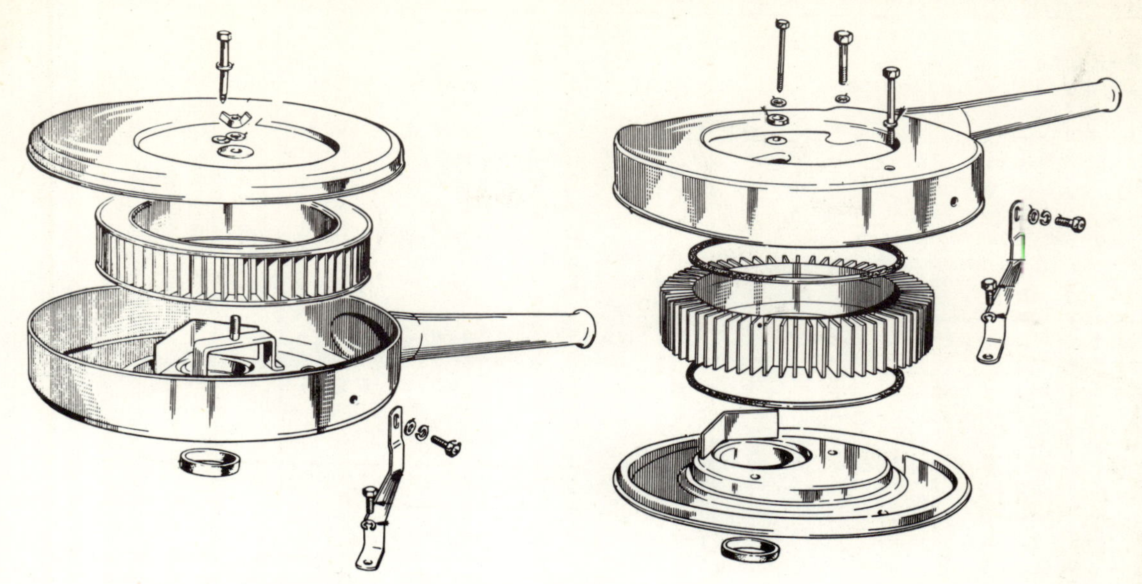

Fig. 3.2. Exploded view of 'Fram' and 'AC' air filters fitted to models with 1700 c.c. engines

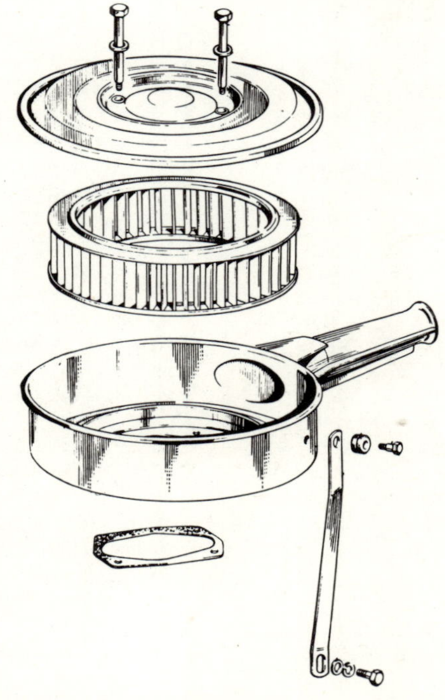

Fig. 3.3. Exploded view of the air filter fitted to Weber carburettors

bolt holding the stay (photo).

5. Slacken the bolt which holds the clamping ring onto the carburettor (photo).

6. Lift off the complete assembly (photo). N.B. Engines fitted with Weber carburettors have air cleaners which are fixed to studs on the carburettor. To remove these the cover and element should first be removed and the four nuts inside them taken off the studs (See Fig. 3.3.).

7. Replacement is a reversal of the removal procedure.

4. Fuel Tank - Removal and Replacement

1. If a fuel tank is damaged, leaks, or is suspected of containing quantities of sludge or water it will be necessary to remove it in order to effectively clean and repair it. Repairs to a tank using any form of heat must never be carried out unless the tank is removed, emptied and thoroughly steamed out and ventilated for a full 24 hours.

2. To remove the tank first drain it by feeding a piece of flexible pipe down the filler neck and siphoning the contents into a suitable container. It is obviously better to do this when the tank is nearly empty anyway.

3. At the front side of the tank, next pull off the two fuel line connections and detach the wire which is connected to the fuel gauge sender unit at the same place.

4. From inside the boot remove the floor covering and slacken off the two hose clips on the flexible pipe between the neck on the tank and the filler pipe. Slide the pipe off the tank neck.

5. Unscrew the self tapping bolts which hold the fuel tank to the boot floor and lift out the tank.

6. Flush out the tank with clean petrol to remove any sediment and/or water.

7. Most small repairs for leaks can be carried out using resin based filler pastes such as 'Cataloy'. Ensure they are fully hardened before the tank is replaced or filled for testing. If heat is used in repair work take the precautions detailed in the first paragraph of this section.

8. Replacement of the tank is a reversal of the removal procedure. Ensure the sealing strip between the tank flange and the boot floor is in good condition, otherwise water and mud from the road could come up into the boot. Rattles may also develop. When refitting the fuel pipes make sure they are connected correctly. This is not a problem as they are different sizes. Do not forget the wire to the gauge sender unit.

5. Fuel Gauge Sender Unit - Checking, Removal and Replacement

1. If the fuel gauge should not work properly first check the sender unit. (It is assumed that the water temperature gauge is working correctly - if not first check the instrument voltage regulator as described in Chapter 10.).

2. Detach the sender unit connector from the front of the fuel tank underneath the car. Then switch on the ignition and the gauge should read 'Empty'.

3. Next, short the end of the wire to earth on the frame of the car and the gauge should read 'Full'. Remember to wait a few seconds as the gauge needle does not move immediately into position.

4. Provided this test gives the required results the gauge is in order and the sender unit is faulty. If not, the gauge is certainly faulty so change that as described in Chapter 10. The sender unit may be faulty as well but this cannot be verified until a good gauge is fitted.

5. To remove the sender unit first drain the fuel tank and disconnect the fuel liner and sender unit wire as described in Section 4.

6. As a special tool is normally required to remove the locking ring which holds the sender unit to the tank it would be easier, if the tool cannot be readily obtained, to remove the tank from the car first.

7. Remove the locking ring from the sender unit by engaging a punch in one of the four cut-outs in the ring and tapping it round. Take off the sealing ring and lift out the unit.

8. Before replacing the unit ensure that the rheostat coils are in good condition and that the blade contact is actually touching the coil.

9. Replacement is a reversal of the removal procedure. The float on the arm should point to the right hand side of the tank and a new sealing ring should be fitted.

6. Fuel Pump - General Description

All figures refer to Fig. 3.4.

1. The fuel pump is mechanically driven by a rocker arm actuated from a cam mounted on the front of the camshaft gear. This in turn is attached to a rocker arm link (13) which is hooked into a loop on the pull rod of the diaphragm (12). When the centre of the diaphragm is pulled down by the pull rod, sufficient vacuum is created to draw fuel through the inlet port of the upper pump body (10), through the bowl (8) and filter (1) and the inlet valve (2 right) into the chamber above the diaphragm. When the rocker arm is released on the cam the diaphragm spring (3) pushes the diaphragm upwards. The one way inlet valve closes under pressure and the fuel is forced out of the outlet valve (2 left) to the carburettor. The rocker arm and link are split in effect at the pivot pin (15) so that the return action of the diaphragm is governed by the spring only. Any obstruction to the outlet flow would stop the diaphragm and the rocker arm would move independently. This is in effect what happens as the delivery capacity of the pump is always in excess of the carburettor requirements and, in this car, the return pipe flow capacity.

7. Fuel Pump, Testing, Cleaning, Removal and Replacement

1. If the fuel pump is suspected of not working it can be checked easily. Pull off the flexible fuel pipe from the carburettor which comes from the pump. Also pull the H.T. lead from the centre of the coil which is next to the fuel pump.

2. Place a container under the disconnected pipe and get someone to turn the engine over on the starter. A good spurt of petrol should come from the fuel pump every second revolution of the engine.

3. To clean the sediment bowl first unscrew the knurled nut over the glass bowl until the clip can be moved aside and the bowl lifted off. Lift out the gauze filter which may be cleaned in petrol if necessary and with a small brush remove any sediment that may be lying under the filter in the body of the pump.

4. Replace the glass bowl and clip, turning the screw no more than finger tight. Check the gasket under the bowl for leaks after refitting.

5. To remove the pump from the engine altogether, disconnect the two fuel hoses from the pump (photo).

6. Undo the retaining nuts (photo) and lift the pump off.

7. Replacement is a simple reversal but make sure that the pump is put back with a new gasket. The long curved rocker arm should also be put into the hole in the front cover in such a way that the end will rest on top of the operating cam on the front of the camshaft gear (photo). If

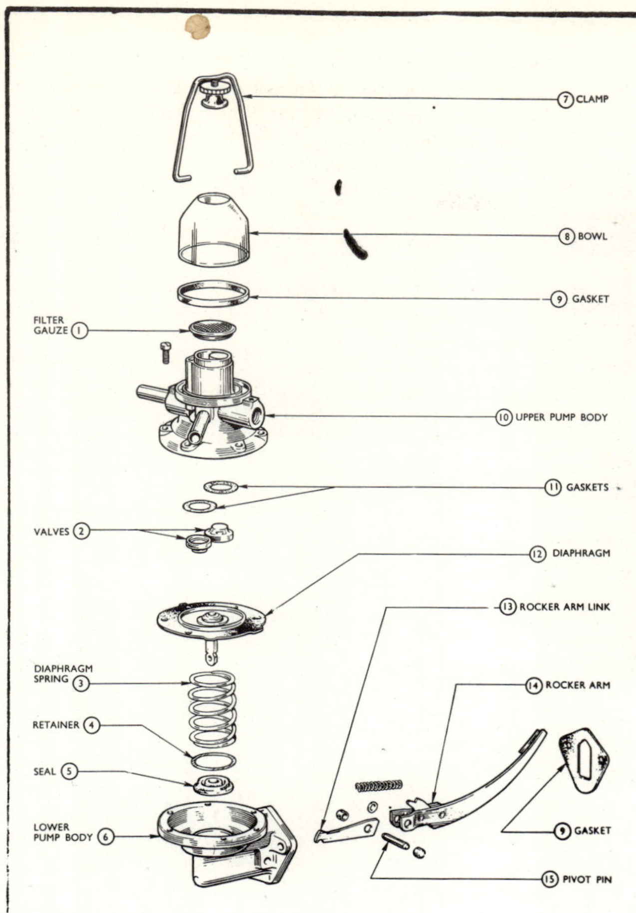

Fig. 3.4. Exploded view of the fuel pump

Fig. 3.5. Removal of glass bowl and filter gauze

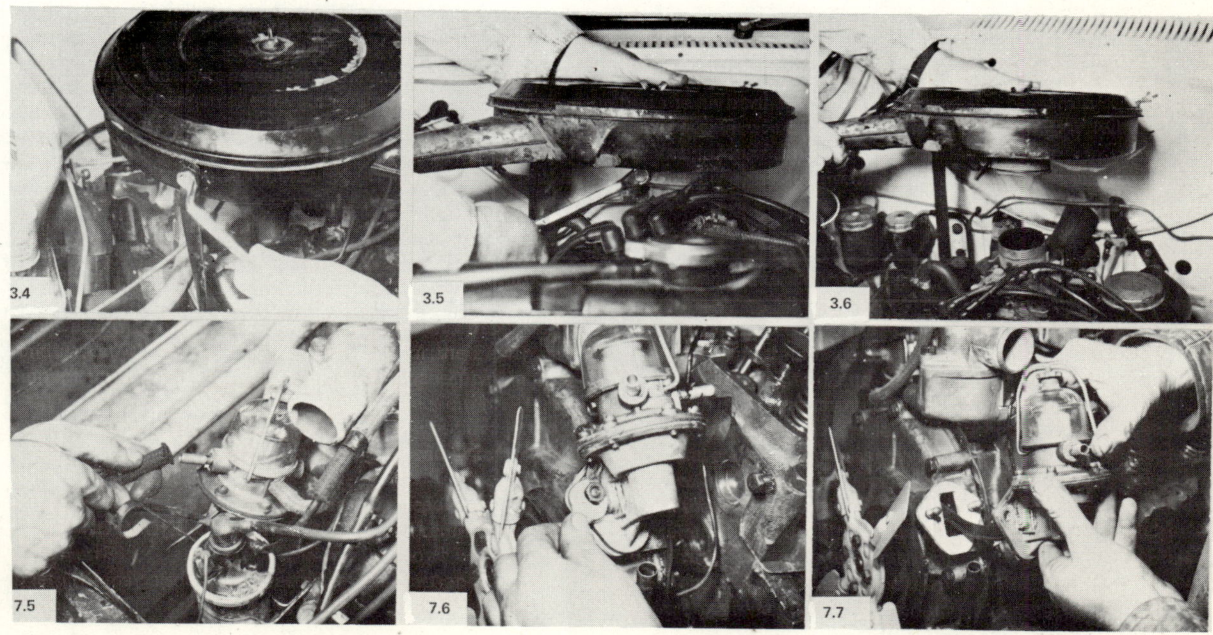

the arm is inadvertently caught UNDER the cam it will be impossible for the pump flange to mate up properly to the front cover.

8. Fuel Pump - Dismantling, Examination and Reassembly

All figures in the text refer to Fig. 3.4.

1. Remove the pump from the engine as described in Section 6. Slacken the knurled clamping nut (7), push the clip to one side and lift off the glass bowl (8). Remove the sealing washer (9) from the groove in the upper pump body (10).

2. Mark the upper and lower pump bodies (10, 6) so that they can be put together again the same way and then remove the six screws holding the two halves together.

3. To remove the diaphragm (12) from the lower pump body turn the body upside down and press the centre of the diaphragm in with the thumbs and then turn it through 90º. This will disengage the diaphragm rod from the hooked end of the rocker arm link (13). Carefully release the diaphragm and spring (3).

4. Examine the diaphragm carefully for signs of cracking or puncturing and renew it if necessary.

5. The lower seal and retainer may be hooked out of the base of the body if it is considered necessary to renew them.

6. The two valves (2) and gaskets (11) are fixed in the upper pump body by staking the sides of the recesses in the body where they locate. Unless it is certain that pump malfunctioning is due to these (and not the diaphragm) they should not be disturbed. If they are to be removed, carefully file off the stakes until the valves are free to fall out. Refit new valves and gaskets. Note that they will only seat correctly if they are put in their correct locations. When fully home they should be re-staked in position at six points equally spaced round the edge of each recess.

7. There is no need to dismantle the rocker arm (14) and link (13) from the lower pump body unless either one is badly worn or bent or there is a lot of play in the pivot pin which could mean renewal of the lower pump body if the pivot pin holes have become enlarged.

8. To dismantle the lower half drive out the pivot pin and it will all fall apart.

9. When reassembling first drive the pivot pin into the housing so that one end just protrudes on the inside.

10 Position the rocker arm link in the rocker arm with a washer on each side of the link. Line up the holes in the housing and push the pivot pin fully home. It is important that the hook on the link and the pad on the end of the rocker arm both face downwards.

11 Tap two new sealing cups over the ends of the pivot pin.

12 Replace the rocker arm spring so that the ends locate securely over the lugs on the arm and in the housing.

13 Fit a new seal and retainer in the lower body if necessary, place the diaphragm spring in position over it and carefully push the diaphragm rod through the seal. Line up the diaphragm so that when turned through 90º the SMALL tab corresponds with the mark on the lower body. Then press the diaphragm down with the thumbs, inverting the body to facilitate hooking the hole in the pushrod over the hook on the rocker arm link.

14 Aim up the screw holes in the diaphragm and the two halves of the body ensuring that the marks made line up. Replace the screws and tighten them down evenly.

15 Fit a new gasket into the upper body groove, replace the filter and glass bowl and tighten up the clamp.

16 Before replacing the pump operate the rocker arm and check that there are indications of suction and pressure over the inlet and outlet pipes.

9. Carburettors - General Description

Since the introduction of the V.4 engine into the Corsair the carburettors have all been of the fixed choke down-draught type. The first V4 standard engines were fitted with a Zenith which changed to Ford in September, 1966. The 1996 c.c. engines have had Weber twin-choke downdraught units with the inception of the G.T. version and later on the '2000' series.

The basic operating principles of all these carburettors are the same, the Weber units merely duplicating the principles by virtue of their twin choke design (though they have a single float chamber). The differences in performances are due to design detail differences rather than basic differences in principle.

The fuel is pumped to the carburettor where a chamber holds a small reservoir of fuel at a constant level controlled by a float valve. Depression at the choke (suction at the venturi) caused by the action of the engine, draws air through the choke and fuel through small holes - jets - into the inlet manifold in proportions according to the speed of the engine and demands made upon it. For example, at idling speeds there is a jet on the manifold side of the throttle flap which is nearly closed in such conditions. Also, in conditions calling for a rich mixture, such as when starting from cold, the strangler flap restricts the inflow of air so that a greater proportion of depression (suction) is applied to the fuel jets. For conditions of sudden acceleration a mechanical pump is incorporated which meters a jet of neat fuel into the choke tube when the accelerator pedal is depressed quickly. On the Zenith and Ford carburettors there is also an economy device fitted which automatically increases the air ratio under part load conditions (half-throttle) so preventing too rich a mixture when inlet manifold depression is high.

10. Zenith Carburettors - Maintenance and Adjustments

1. Before touching the carburettor, first check that the air filter is clean and correctly fitted (see Section 3), that the throttle linkage is lubricated and that the accelerator pedal is correctly set.

2. To set the accelerator pedal correctly a horizontal line through the pivot pin (to which the pad is fixed) should be 2.4 in. (60 mm) from another horizontal line drawn through the centre of the **brake** pedal pad. (On L.H.D. models this distance is 3 in. (75 mm)). The adjustment can be made on the pedal stop adjustment bolt (Item 9 in Fig. 3.6.).

3. To adjust the linkage first pull off the two adjustable connecting links between the pedal shaft/cross shaft and cross shaft/carburettor. (Items Nos. 19 and 25 in Fig. 3.6.). The respective length of these links is 3.3 in. and 3.0 in. (83 and 75 mm) when measured from the centres of the clevis eyes. These can be adjusted by slackening the locknut and rotating as required.

4. To adjust the idling speed first run the engine until it reaches normal working temperature. Then turn the throttle stop screw Fig. 3.7) until the engine is running at a fast idle speed.

5. Screw the volume control screw in until the engine noticeably slows down then screw it out until the fastest running speed is obtained.

6. Back off the throttle stop screw to normal idling speed. Final small adjustments may be made to the volume control screw to ascertain whether or not the fastest running setting has been obtained. If in fact the engine idle speed does increase as a result of further adjustment reduce the idle speed by backing off the throttle stop screw.

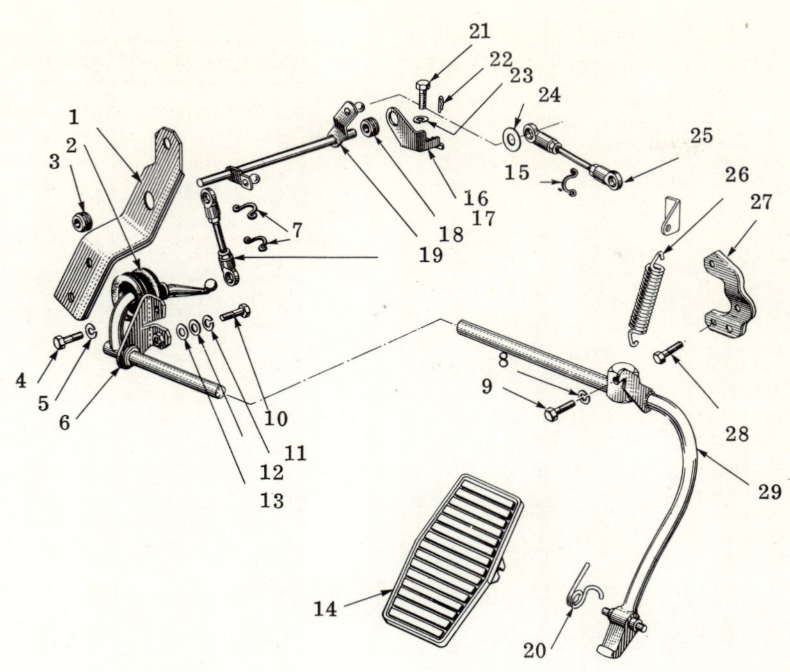

Fig. 3.6. ACCELERATOR CONTROL LINKAGE — EXPLODED VIEW

1 Mounting bracket	8 Spring washer	16 Lever	24 Washer
2 Grommet	9 Bolt	17 Bush	25 Adjustable link rod
3 Bush	10 Bolt	18 Cross link	26 Spring
4 Bolt	11 Spring washer	19 Adjustable link rod	27 Mounting bracket
5 Washer	12 Washer	20 Pedal clip	28 Bolt
6 Accelerator rod and bracket assembly	13 Washer	21 Bolt	29 Accelerator rod and bracket assembly
7 Clip	14 Foot pedal	22 Hair pin clip	
	15 Clip	23 Spring washer	

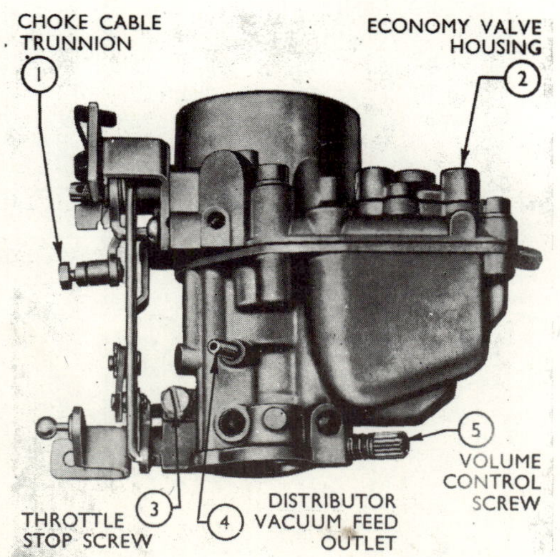

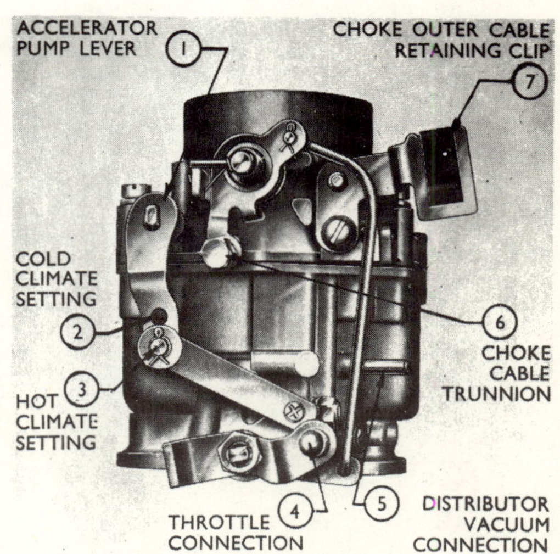

Fig. 3.7. Zenith 36 IV Carburettor adjustment screws and levers

7. The accelerator pump has two settings, for either hot or cold climate conditions. In Fig. 3.7. items 2 and 3 can be seen the two holes for the appropriate conditions. The colder setting provides a larger stroke on the pump piston thus delivering a larger quantity of fuel on the acceleration stroke. This setting does not affect constant speed running conditions at any engine speed from idle to full throttle.

11. Zenith Carburettors - Removal and Replacement

1. Before removing the carburettor to check any apparent faults make sure that the adjustments are correct and are not responsible as described in Section 10.
2. To remove the carburettor, first remove the air cleaner as described in Section 3.
3. Slacken the strangler cable clamp bolt (photo).
4. Remove the clip holding the strangler outer cable and pull the cable away from the choke spindle lever.
5. Pull the fuel pipe between the carburettor and the return pipe T-piece off the T-piece.
6. Detach the throttle cable link from the cross shaft (photo).
7. Remove the two holding down nuts (photo).
8. Lift off the carburettor (photo).
9. Replacement is a straightforward reversal of the removal procedure. It is generally a good idea to renew the insulating gasket between the carburettor and manifold (arrow in photo).
10 When refitting the choke cable clip engage the small loop in the slot in the bracket first and snap the clip over the top edge (photo).
11 Check that both throttle and choke flaps are vertical when fully open.

12. Zenith Carburettors - Dismantling and Reassembly

All bracketed numbers in the text refer to Fig. 3.8.
1. Disconnect the accelerator pump control arm from the operating lever by removing the split pin from the clevis pin and detaching it.
2. Remove the split pin from the choke link rod and detach it from the choke control lever.
3. Remove the four screws holding the two halves of the carburettor together and separate them. Take out the 'O' ring (18) from the choke tube.
4. Pull out the pivot pin from the bracket supporting the two floats (4) and lift out the float.
5. The needle valve (3) may now be taken out. Examine this for any sign of ridging on the needle taper and if there is any it must be renewed - and the seat also.
6. To detach the emulsion block (15) from the top half of the carburettor body first remove the needle valve housing and then the two screws, one each side of the choke tube.
7. The emulsion block and gasket (9) will now come away and the accelerator pump piston (13) and spring can be taken out.
8. The main jet (5), compensating jet (6), idling jet (7) and accelerator pump non-return valve (14) may now be removed using a screwdriver IN GOOD CONDITION. Any blade likely to slip should NOT be used as damage may be caused to the jet orifices. DO NOT POKE OUT ORIFICES WITH WIRE - USE A JET OF AIR.
9. The accelerator pump jet (16) may also be removed after first removing the plug in front of it.
10 The non-return inlet valve ball at the bottom of the accelerator pump cylinder bore can be removed if required by unhooking the circular wire spring clip. Do not damage the bore walls.

11 The economy valve assembly (10) may be dismantled by undoing the three screws holding the cover and lifting out the spring and diaphragm with its gaskets. Examine the diaphragm for signs of deterioration that could cause it to leak and renew it, together with the gaskets if necessary. The air bleed screw (8) may be removed from the underside if required.
12 Should the choke plate (11) and its spindle be damaged or sticking, requiring dismantling, undo the two screws retaining the choke plate to the spindle. Then withdraw the spindle together with the return spring parts from the carburettor body.
13 The accelerator pump operating lever (12) can be removed by unscrewing the brass nut and washer from the end of the shaft and taking the cam off. Then remove the circlip and withdraw the shaft and brass collar.
14 Remove the volume control screw (2) and spring. Examine the tapered needle for signs of wear and check that the condition of the spring is such that the screw cannot move under vibration. Renew both if necessary.
15 The throttle plate (19) may be removed by undoing the two screws holding it to the spindle and pulling out the spindle.
16 Reassembly is a reversal of the dismantling procedure, noting the following points in particular.
17 The larger flat on the throttle spindle must face the mounting flange when the throttle is closed. Lock the two screws with a blob of solder or a centre punch mark on the threads.
18 The accelerator pump operating cam should face the pump piston when assembled with the operating lever in the vertical position.
19 The choke spindle should be positioned so that the flat face is towards the air cleaner when the choke is closed.
20 On the economy valve assembly make sure that the air hole in the body lines up with the air holes in the diaphragm and gaskets and that the lug on the cover goes over the air hole.
21 Refit a new float chamber gasket (9) and a new 'O' ring (18).
22 When the choke is re-connected make sure that the throttle opens slightly when the choke is closed. If not it may be necessary to bend the link rod between the choke and throttle spindles a little.
23 The floats must be positioned so that when the upper half of the carburettor body is inverted the bottom of the float is 28-29 mm. from the mating face of the body (with the gasket in position). The centre tag which bears on the needle valve may be bent to achieve the required measurement.

13. Ford Carburettors - Maintenance and Adjustments

1. Maintenance and adjustment procedures are the same as for the Zenith carburettor, except that reference should be made to Fig. 3.9. for items referred to in the text of Section 10. The accelerator pump is also set differently, the pump link (Item 56) gooseneck being opened or closed by bending to decrease or increase the pump strokes respectively.
2. Provided that the fuel filters in the pump and above the needle valve are in good order the likelihood of blocked jets is remote. However, after prolonged use the float chamber bowl will accumulate a very fine sediment and the choke and throttle spindles may tend to stick as a result of petroleum deposits. It is not recommended that random adjustments to the choke and throttle settings are made without removing the carburettor from the car and making sure that all components are clean and intact. These adjustments are included, therefore, in Section 15 as it is con-

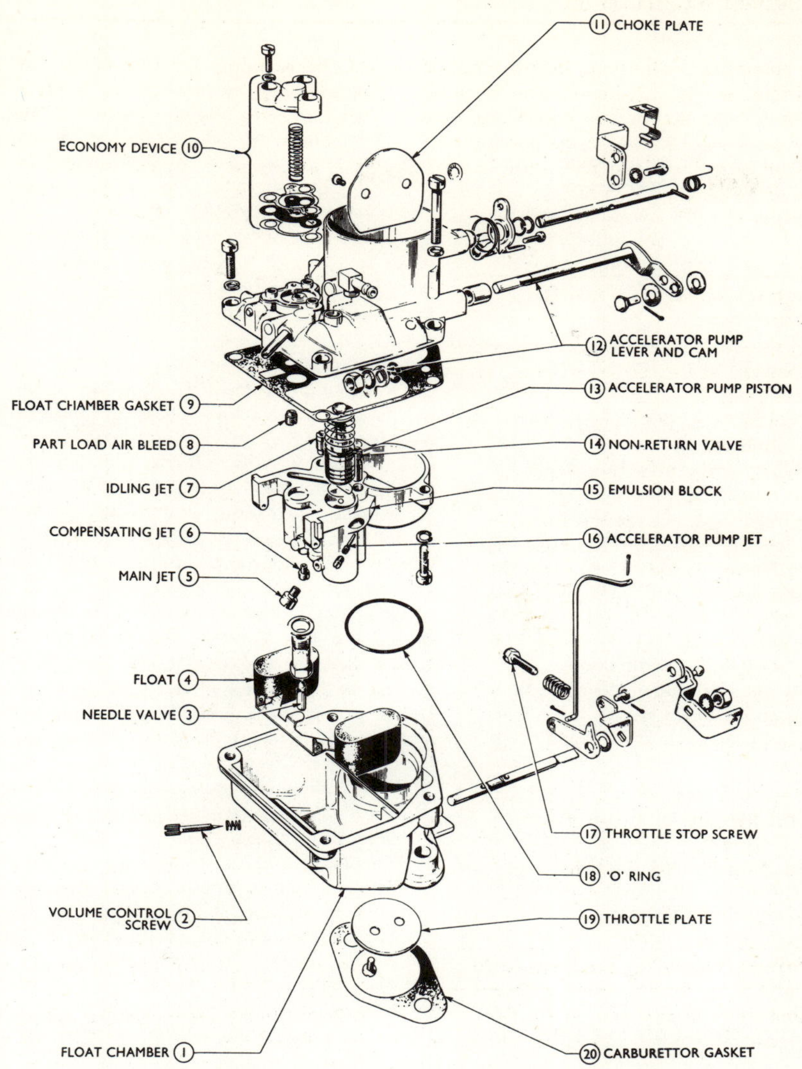

Fig. 3.8. Exploded view of the Zenith 36 IV Carburettor (Sept. 1965 to Sept. 1966)

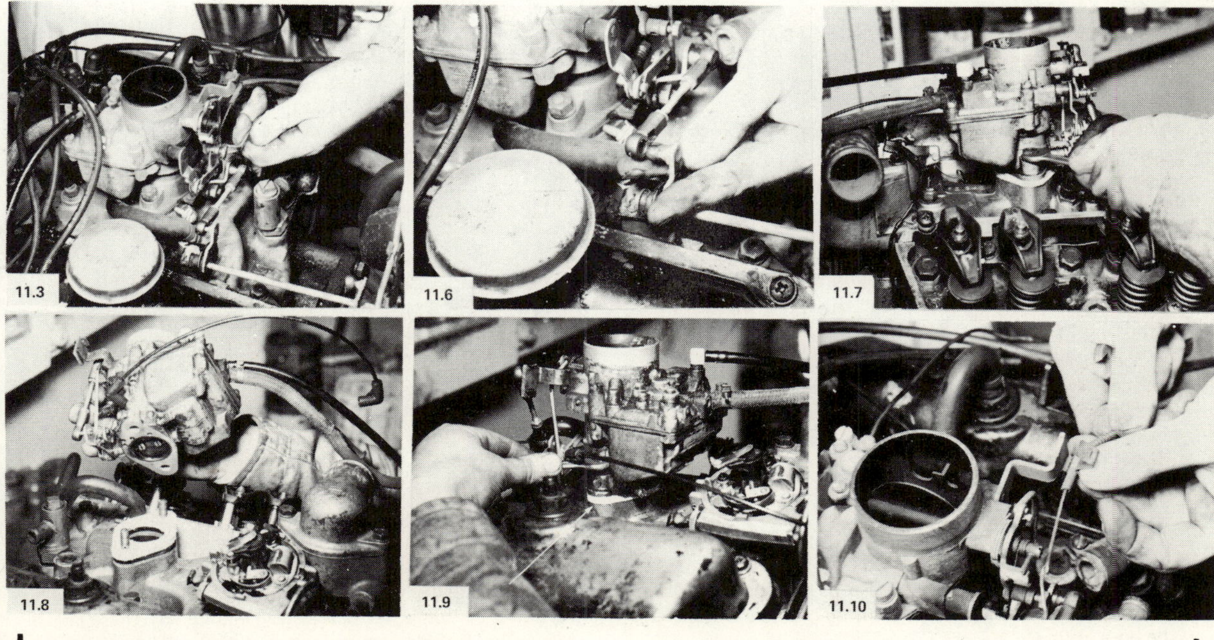

11.3

11.6

11.7

11.8

11.9

11.10

sidered that dismantling will be necessary, at least in part, and reassembly calls for these adjustments to be verified as a matter of course.

14. Ford Carburettors - Removal and Replacement

1. Proceed exactly as described for the Zenith carburettor in Section 11. Although the photographs show a Zenith carburettor, the connections to a Ford carburettor are the same.

15. Ford Carburettors - Dismantling and Reassembly

The bracketed numbers in the text refer to Fig. 3.9.

1. Having removed the carburettor, remove tne six screws and washers (33) which hold the carburettor top (35) to the main body (43).

2. Hold the carburettor upright and lift tne top from the main body very carefully. Still holding the carburettor the right way up detach the choke control rod and place the top half on one side. Then put one hand over the recess containing the weight (8) and ball valve (9) and invert the lower half of the carburettor so that they drop out. The gasket (34) should also come off with the top cover.

3. Pull out the float pivot pin (36) and remove the float (37). Examine the float to make sure it has no leaks in it. The needle valve and body (38) can be unscrewed and taken out, together with the gasket (31).

4. To remove the choke plate and spindle, first cut the heads off the pins (30) which hold the air cleaner mounting bracket (28). Remove the small screws holding the plate to the spindle and then draw the plate from the slot and pull out the spindle from the choke tube. It may be necessary to clean up the screw holes to remove the spindle.

5. The choke control lever (1) and spring (2) will be released from the spindle when it is drawn out.

6. Remove the main jet (35) from the top cover using a good screwdriver that will not slip and possibly damage the jet orifice. DO NOT USE WIRE TO CLEAN THE ORIFICE. USE AN AIR JET.

7. Undo the screw (39) which holds the pump control lever (19) to the throttle spindle (18) and detach them from the pump actuating lever (45) with the spring (25) and washer (26).

8. The four screws and washers (26) holding the cover may now be removed, releasing the cover, diaphragm (42) valve and springs (40). Be careful not to lose the small valve and spring on some models.

9. Inspect the diaphragm for signs of deterioration which may cause it to leak. If in doubt renew it.

10 To remove the throttle assembly, first undo the screw (13) holding the fast idle cam (12) and spring (11) and take them off.

11 Undo the two small screws holding the throttle plate (16) to the spindle (18) and take it out. Pull the spindle out of the carburettor, removing any rough spots if necessary to get it through the holes.

12 Remove the idle mixture adjustment screw (21) and spring (20). Examine the taper point of the needle for signs of damage or grooving and make sure the spring tension is sufficient to provide the necessary locking action on the screw. Renew the items if in doubt.

13 Reassembly is a reversal of the dismantling procedure, noting the following points.

14 When replacing the idle mixture adjustment screw close it fully home - lightly so as not to damage the needle or seat - and then back it off one turn to provide the initial setting.

14 When replacing the choke and throttle plates and spindles make sure that the spindles have the flats facing the air cleaner and manifold respectively when they are closed. The screws holding the plates into the spindles should be lightly staked or their threads punched as an anti-loosening precaution. Blobs of solder may also be used for this.

15 Fit a new gasket for the top cover.

16 When the float has been refitted to the upper body it must be checked to see that it operates in a way that maintains the fuel level correctly in the chamber. With the top cover held inverted so that the weight of the float closes the needle valve, the distance from the base of the float to the mating flange of the cover should be 1.12-1.14 in. (28.5-29.0 mm) (Fig. 3.10). The tab which bears on the needle valve may be bent to correct this as necessary. When held the right way up the float should fall so that the same measurement is 1.38-1.40 ins. (35-36.5 mm) (Fig. 3.11). If this is incorrect then the HINGE tabs may be bent accordingly. Be careful as the other setting may now be altered. Of the two settings the closed position of the needle valve is most important as this regulates the upper level of the fuel.

17 When fitting the two halves of the carburettor together engage the link between the choke and throttle levers, ensure the ball and weight are correctly located in the drilling in the lower half and hold the choke lever closed. Unless this latter is done the choke could be over-centred and jammed. Replace the screws and tighten them evenly. Check the free operation of all moving parts.

18 When completely reassembled ensure that the choke and throttle flaps open completely so that they are parallel with the sides of the choke tube.

19 The choke flap is spring loaded when in the closed position so that engine manifold depression will automatically partly open it to admit a small flow of air when the engine fires. The amount it opens is governed by the tab on the spindle. The distance is .14-.16 in. (3.5-4 mm) between the edge of the flap and the choke tube which can be measured with a suitable diameter rod such as a drill. If necessary, bend the stop tab so that the gap is correct (Fig. 3.12.).

20 When the choke flap is fully closed the control rod (Fig. 3.9., Item 12) moves the fast idle cam to open the throttle a small amount. The exact setting of this throttle opening cannot be made unless the carburettor is installed and the engine running. To start with, however, check that the throttle flap opens to leave a gap of 1-2 mm. between the throttle plate and the barrel. This can be adjusted by bending the tab which bears against the fast idle cam. When the carburettor is installed the same check should be made. The engine must be warm and the choke plate held open while the choke lever is rotated until stopped by the linkage (Fig. 3.14). Engine speed should then be 950 to 1150 r.p.m.

16. Weber 32 DIF 4 Carburettor - Maintenance and Adjustment

1. The maintenance and adjustments as described in Section 10 apply, with the following modifications.

2. Slow running adjustment will not be satisfactory if the throttle valve on the secondary throttle is not closing properly (the secondary of the two throttles is that furthest from the accelerator pump housing). The gap between the plate and the barrel wall can be adjusted by a screw in the main flange and it should be .0015 in. (.04 mm). On no account should the gap be too small or the throttle plate might jam.

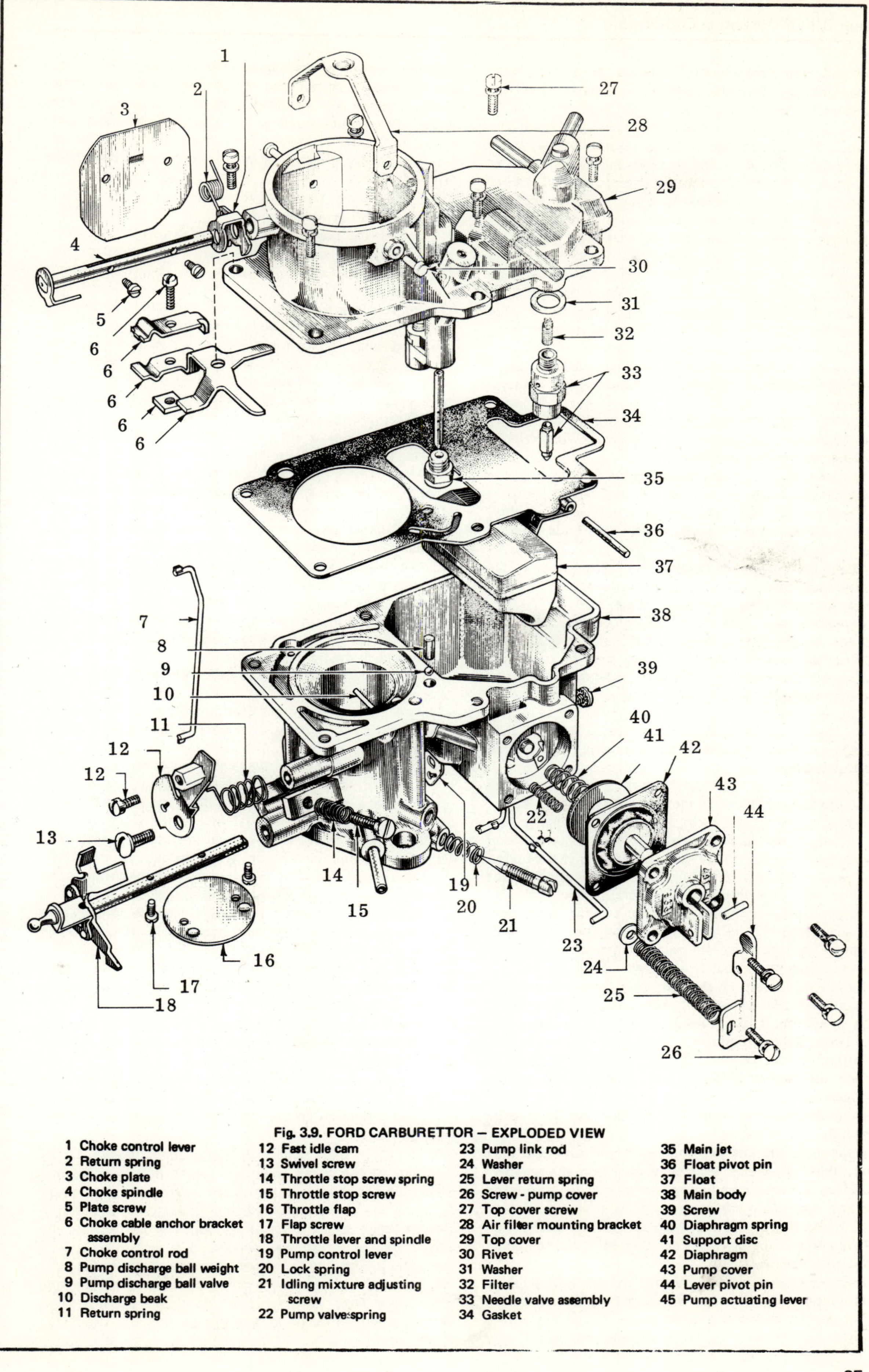

Fig. 3.9. FORD CARBURETTOR — EXPLODED VIEW

1 Choke control lever	12 Fast idle cam	23 Pump link rod	35 Main jet
2 Return spring	13 Swivel screw	24 Washer	36 Float pivot pin
3 Choke plate	14 Throttle stop screw spring	25 Lever return spring	37 Float
4 Choke spindle	15 Throttle stop screw	26 Screw - pump cover	38 Main body
5 Plate screw	16 Throttle flap	27 Top cover screw	39 Screw
6 Choke cable anchor bracket assembly	17 Flap screw	28 Air filter mounting bracket	40 Diaphragm spring
7 Choke control rod	18 Throttle lever and spindle	29 Top cover	41 Support disc
8 Pump discharge ball weight	19 Pump control lever	30 Rivet	42 Diaphragm
9 Pump discharge ball valve	20 Lock spring	31 Washer	43 Pump cover
10 Discharge beak	21 Idling mixture adjusting screw	32 Filter	44 Lever pivot pin
11 Return spring	22 Pump valve spring	33 Needle valve assembly	45 Pump actuating lever
		34 Gasket	

3. To alter the stroke of the accelerator pump the pin on which the pump lever (15) pivots can be put in one of two positions. These are numbered and the normal position is the lower, No. 2 hole. In very warm climates it may be moved to No. 1 hole (giving a short pump stroke) by driving out the pin from the plain end and refitting it in the other hole. When refitting put the plain end in first and drive it home so that the splines at the other end lock into the housing when finally tapped home.

4. Adjustments for choke and fast idle settings are best carried out, if necessary, with the carburettor removed from the engine when the choke and throttle plates are readily accessible. The risk of dropping measuring drills into the manifold is also reduced. These adjustments are described at the end of Section 18 after final reassembly.

17. Weber 32 DIF 4 Carburettors - Removal and Replacement

1. Remove the air cleaner cover as described in Section 3 and take out the filter element.

2. The four nuts and washers holding the filter body to the carburettor may then be removed and the body lifted off.

3. Disconnect the fuel pipe and vacuum pipe followed by the throttle and choke linkages as described under Section 11.

4. Undo the four nuts holding the carburettor to the manifold and take them off with the washers.

5. Lift the carburettor away with the gasket.

6. Replacement is a reversal of this procedure. Make sure that the flange gasket is renewed and the grommets round the studs are in good condition. Check that the choke and throttle linkages close and open their respective valve plates fully when the linkages are reconnected.

18. Weber 32 DIF 4 Carburettor - Dismantling, Inspection and Reassembly

All bracketed numbers in the text refer to Figure 3.20.
1. Having removed the carburettor from the engine, disconnect the choke operating rod (26) at the lower end and remove the five screws holding the cover plate to the body.

2. Take out the float pivot pin (33) and remove the float (5) followed by the needle valve (32) and carrier.

3. Remove the accelerator pump cover (15), diaphragm (16) and spring (17) by undoing the retaining screws (14). Examine the diaphragm for signs of deterioration which may cause leakage through it, and renew it if in doubt.

4. Remove the jets from their location, using a screwdriver in good condition so as not to risk slipping and damaging the orifices. Fig. 3.16. shows the position of the jets in the main body of the carburettor.

5. To remove the primary throttle spindle bend back the tab on the washer (58) and undo the nut (59) on the spindle.

6. Unhook the return spring (55) and draw off the throttle lever (69).

7. Disconnect the fast idle connecting rod (51), and then detach the bush, washer lever and washer from the spindle.

8. Detach the return spring on the spindle (61) from the stop lever (48) and remove them.

9. With the two screws (13) holding the plate (12) to the spindle undone, the plate can be taken out and the spindle withdrawn from the barrel.

10 Remove the secondary throttle spindle (10) by first undoing the nut (54) on the end of the spindle and taking off the washers and lever behind it.

1I Then remove the two screws holding the plate to the spindle, remove the plate and take out the spindle.

12 Remove the screw (50) and washer holding the choke operating lever (46) to the body, and then remove it and the return spring and toggle spring (42) from the relay lever (43).

13 Remove the split pin from the rod (26) and take off the relay lever.

14 Take the split pin from the other end of the rod, and take it off and extract the dust seal.

15 The choke plate screws (23) can now be removed, releasing the plates and spindle.

16 The fuel filter retaining plug may be unscrewed releasing the filter screen (3).

17 Before reassembly begins, wash all parts in methylated spirits which will remove any gummy petroleum deposits.

18 Jets should be blown out with an air jet and not poked with wire or hard metal under any circumstances. If the carburettor is old and suspected of faulty performance the jets should be renewed, as they may have worn, or the whole carburettor replaced.

19 Reassembly is a reversal of the dismantling process, bearing the following in mind.

20 When fitting the choke spindle and plates, make sure that the offset parts of the plates are to the rear and that the chamfers on the edges are parallel to the air intake when closed. The screws retaining the plates to the spindle should be staked or peened to lock them in position.

21 The throttle spindles should be located first of all with the slot parallel to the choke tube and the threaded holes inwards. The plates are fitted into the slots so that the face with the mark '78º' on it is below the spindle and facing outwards. This ensures that the chamfers on the plates face in the right direction.

22 Fit a new gasket beneath the accelerator pump jet assembly.

23 While tightening the accelerator pump cover screws, pull the operating lever away from the cam to the limit of the travel of the diaphragm.

24 Fit a new gasket under the needle valve housing.

25 After fitting the needle valve float and pivot pin it will be necessary to ensure that the float travel is correct to maintain the required level of fuel in the float chamber. With the needle valve in the closed position the bottom of the float should be 15 mm. from the face of the cover gasket (Fig. 3.17). This can be adjusted by bending the centre tag which rests against the needle valve.

26 When the reassembly is complete check that all the moving parts operate freely and return correctly under their respective springs.

27 With the carburettor still detached from the engine it is necessary now to check the setting of the choke plates and throttle plates.

28 The fast idle setting is checked with choke plates in the closed position when the gap between the edge of the primary throttle plate and the barrel should be 1.2 mm. (Fig. 3.18). The gap may be adjusted by bending the connecting rod but this must be done with great care as the slightest alteration on the rod has a considerable effect on the throttle.

29 The choke plate pull-down (that is the automatic partial opening of the choke when the engine fires after starting with the choke lever in the closed position) is checked by pushing the choke plates, when closed, against the section of the toggle spring as far as the stop. The gap between the plate and air intake wall should be 5 mm. This can be adjusted by bending the choke lever stop. (See Fig. 3.19).

29 The choke plate opening can be checked by first moving the choke lever 10 mm. from the closed position. This measurement is taken at the end of the arm where the cable fits (Fig. 3.19). At this position the gap between the

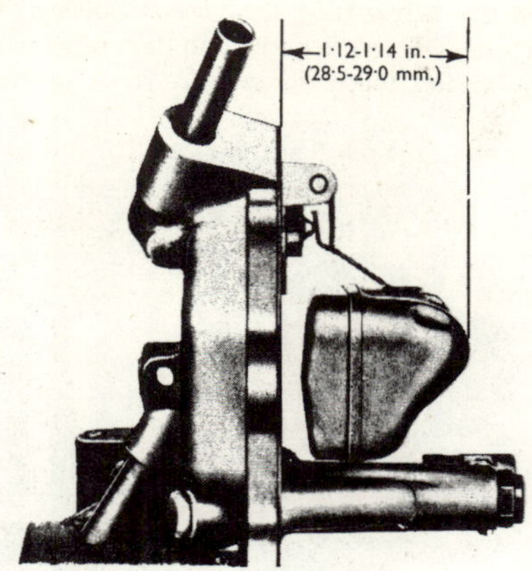

Fig. 3.10. Ford Carburettor - float setting - fully closed

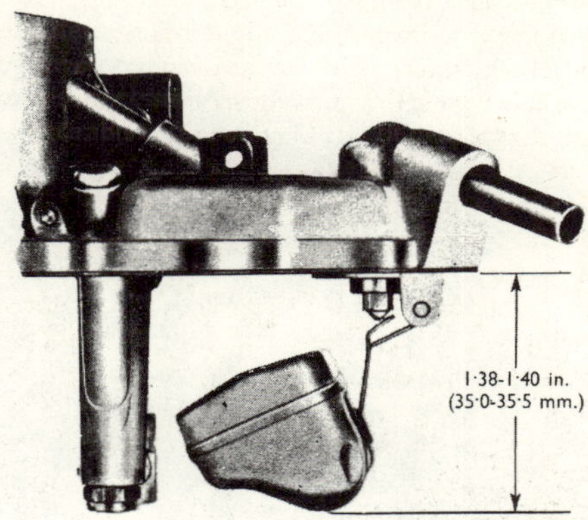

Fig. 3.11. Ford Carburettor - float setting - fully open

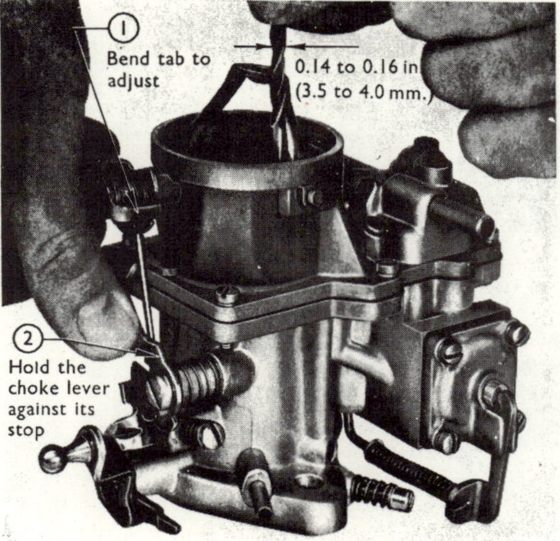

Fig. 3.12. Ford Carburettor - showing the use of a drill to measure choke pull - down gap and the tab to be bent as required in order to adjust it

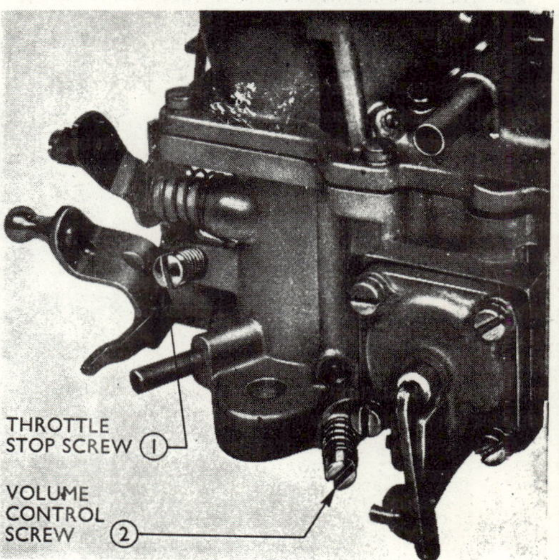

Fig. 3.13. Ford Carburettor - slow running adjustment screws

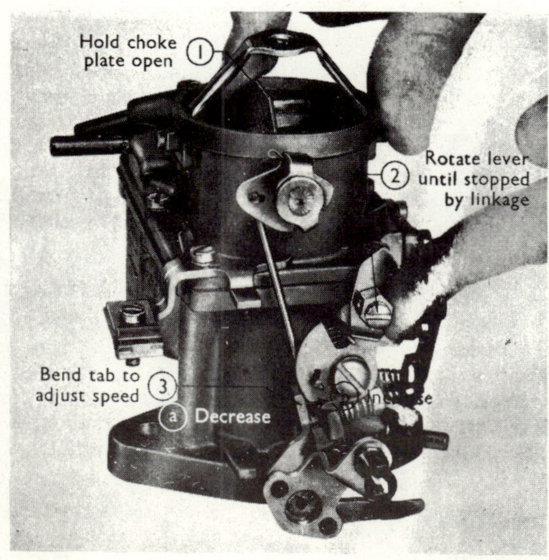

Fig. 3.14. Ford Carburettor - fast idle setting

Fig. 3.15. Weber 32 DIF 4 Carburettor - slow running adjustment screws

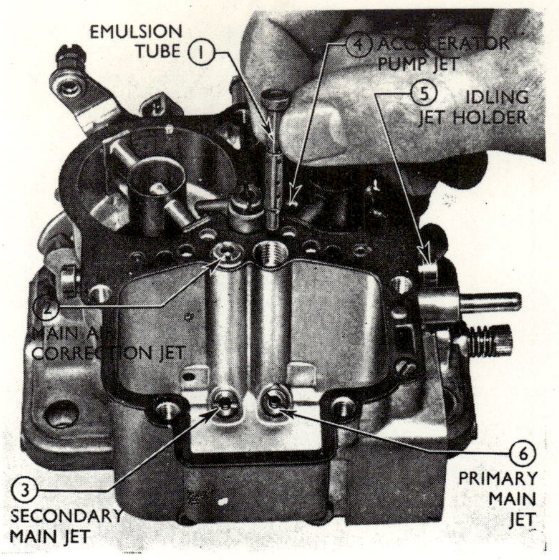

Fig. 3.16. Weber 32 DIF 4 Carburettor - location of jets

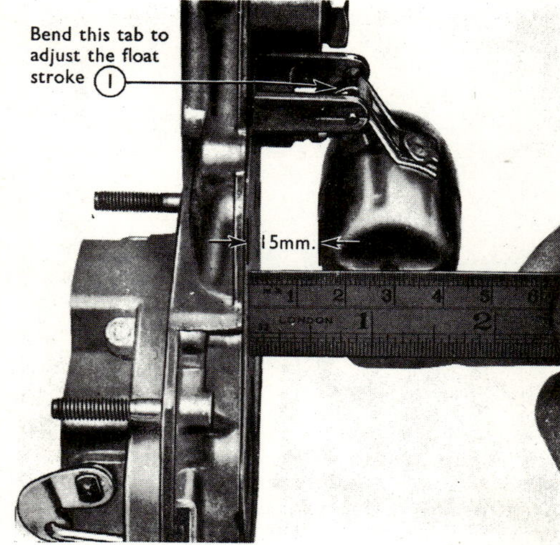

Fig. 3.17. Weber 32 DIF 4 Carburettor - needle valve float setting

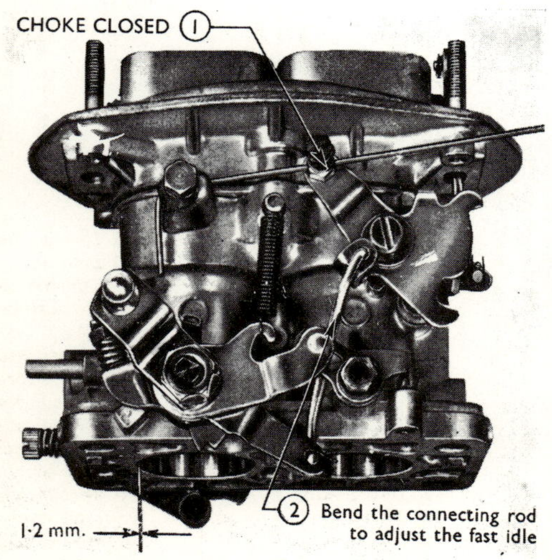

Fig. 3.18. Weber 32 DIF 4 Carburettor - fast idle setting

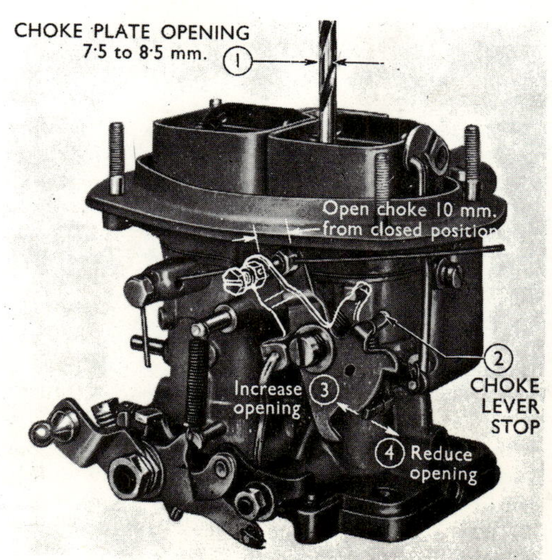

Fig. 3.19. Weber 32 DIF 4 Carburettor - choke opening setting and choke lever stop for choke plate pull-down adjustment

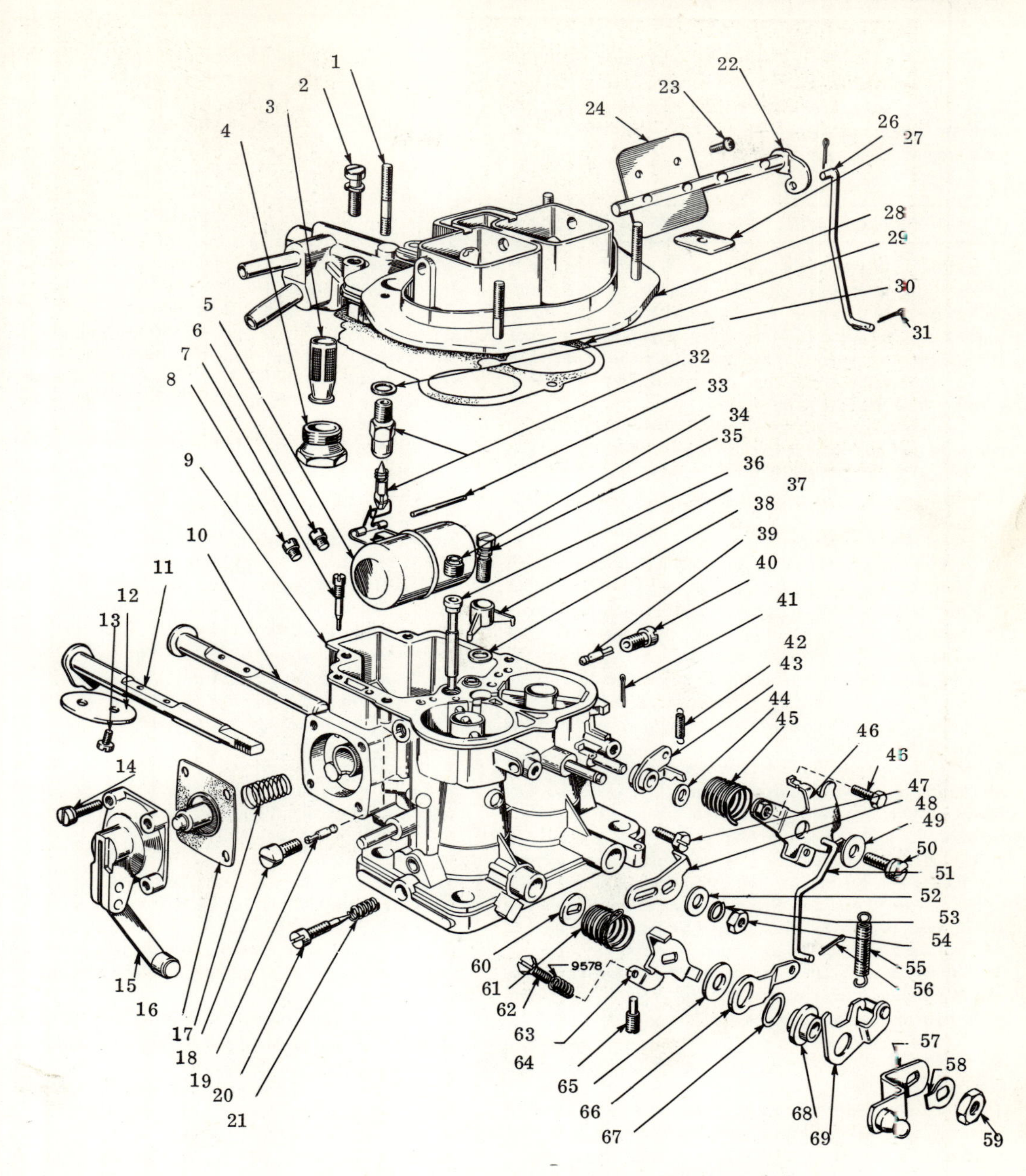

Fig. 3.20. WEBER 32 DIF 4 CARBURETTOR — EXPLODED DRAWING

1 Filter mounting stud	19 Idling jet - primary	37 Pump discharge nozzle	55 Spring - throttle stop
2 Cover screw	20 Volume control screw	38 Gasket	56 Split pin
3 Fuel filter	21 Spring	39 Idling jet - secondary	57 Thorttle operating lever
4 Retaining plug	22 Choke flap spindle	40 Idling jet holding screw	58 Tab washer
5 Float	23 Flap screw	41 Split pin	59 Nut
6 Main jet - secondary	24 Choke flap	42 Spring	60 Slotted washer
7 Pump needle	25 Split pin	43 Choke relay lever	61 Return spring
8 Main jet - primary	26 Choke actuating arm	44 Throttle stop lever	62 Idle adjusting screw
9 Main body	27 Dust seal	45 Piston spring	63 Idle adjusting lever
10 Throttle shaft - secondary	28 Top cover	46 Choke control lever	64 Adjuster screw
11 Throttle shaft - primary	29 Cover gasket	47 Cable fixing screw	65 Washer
12 Throttle plate	30 Washer	48 Throttle stop lever	66 Throttle/choke link fast
13 Screw	31 Split pin	49 Washer	idle lever
14 Pump cover screw	32 Needle valve	50 Screw	67 Washer
15 Pump cover assembly	33 Float pivot spindle	51 Fast idle link rod	68 Bush
16 Diaphragm	34 Starting air adjusting jet	52 Washer	69 Throttle control lever
17 Spring	35 Pump discharge valve	53 Spring washer	
18 Idling jet screw	36 Starting jet	54 Nut	

lower edge of the plates and the air intake wall should be 7½-8½ mm. To alter this the cam follower tag may be bent accordingly. Here again, great care is necessary as the slightest bending of the tag has a considerable effect on the measurement of the gap.

19. Fault Finding - Zenith, Ford and Weber Carburettors

1. Failure to start, difficulties in starting and noticeably uneven running or misfiring could be caused by carburettor faults. However, there is no doubt that the majority of such faults are caused by ignition faults or maladjustments. It must be emphasised that the ignition system must always be the first suspect and that the checks as described in Chapter 4 are the first to be made.
2. Having established that the ignition system is functioning correctly and that there is fuel in the tank which is reaching the petrol pump, the procedures as given below should be followed.

(a) Total failure to start:-
1) Remove the air cleaner, look into the air intake and get someone to depress the accelerator pedal quickly, once. The fuel delivered by the accelerator pump should normally be seen quite readily. If it IS seen, then the engine has probably been flooded by unnecessary 'pumping' of the accelerator pedal - which delivers more petrol at each depression. In such instances push the accelerator pedal right down to the floor, slowly, use no choke and turn the engine until it starts.
2) If it is seen that no fuel is being delivered by the accelerator pump disconnect the fuel line from the fuel pump at the carburettor. Turn the engine to check the delivery of fuel from the fuel pump (See Section 7). Assuming that the fuel pump is operating properly, then the fuel is not getting into the carburettor. The necessary operation to check the float chamber and needle valve should next be carried out followed by jet cleaning and so on until the fuel is being delivered as necessary.
3) If the ignition system and fuel systems are both in order, and the timing is correct and still the engine fails to start then there must be a major defect in the engine.

(b) Misfiring, jerky running, poor acceleration, surging and stopping.
1) Having checked the ignition system, it may be assumed that the engine is being either under supplied or over supplied with fuel.
2) Remove the air cleaner and check that it is not dirty and blocked. Verify that the choke plate opens fully when the control knob is pushed home and that the throttle plate (below the choke plate) opens fully when the accelerator pedal is fully depressed. Adjust if necessary.
3) Visually inspect the carburettor mounting flange and inlet manifold for obvious signs of looseness in the mounting nuts and bolts or any other reason which could cause an air leak - such as cracks.
4) Proceed as under the previous heading (a) and if on completion, the fault is not rectified check more thoroughly the possibility of air leaking into the system at the carburettor flange and inlet manifold gasket. If no leakage is found then there must be serious defects in the engine.

(c) Petrol odours while running (or stopped)
1) STOP (if running).
2) Switch off ignition, vacate car and detach fire extinguisher from bracket if fitted.
3) Open bonnet and stand back. If there is no sign of fire, disconnect the battery and investigate the source of smell

and repair the leak which is often simply a loose connection or stuck open float chamber needle. Do not drive with a knowingly leaking system as the risks of injury and total destruction of the vehicle by fire are very high.

(d) Excessive fuel consumption or rich mixture
1) Fuel consumption varies greatly depending on road and traffic conditions and the style of driving, maximum acceleration and high cruising speeds or prolonged crawling in traffic may result in 20-25% less miles per gallon than the manufacturers stated average.
2) Having checked that the ignition system and timing is in order and that there are no leaks in the fuel supply lines of the system, check that the air filter element is clean and the choke is opening fully. Then check that the carburettor settings are correct as detailed in the reassembly sections of this chapter.
3) Examine the exhaust tail pipe interior for tell-tale signs of a rich mixture which leaves black, dry sooty deposits, rather than the greyish brown one which indicates normal mixture. This visual check should only be regarded as significant after a reassembly lay run. Spark plug condition is also indicative (See Chapter 4/12).
4) With the engine warm and running at a fast tickover a bluish haze in the exhaust indicates an over rich mixture.
5) Dismantle the carburettor and examine the level of the float and condition of the needle valve. Renew the valve and re-set the float as necessary.
6) If all the foregoing checks yielded no improvements the excessive consumption must be due to wear in the engine, in either the piston rings, cylinder bores or valves. If the piston rings and bores are worn the exhaust smoke will have a greyish, smoky character and the deposit in the tail pipe will be slightly oily.

(e) Weak mixture
1) If fuel consumption is satisfactory but performance is not very sparkling it is possible that a weak mixture, caused by a restriction in the fuel flow in the carburettor is the reason. It is unusual, however, for any unwanted restriction not to affect the even running qualities of the engine to a more noticeable extent.
2) A whitish scaly deposit on the exhaust tail pipe interior is indicative of a weak mixture. Spark plug condition is also indicative (Chapter 4, Section 12).
3) Dismantle the carburettor for examination of the float level setting, cleanliness of filter and float chamber and blocked jets.
4) Check the carburettor mounting flange gasket and inlet manifold for signs of air leaks. To weaken the mixture without affecting the even running of the engine any such leaks would only be very small indeed and not easily apparent. Pour oil along the gasket joints when the engine is running to assist detection.
5) If all the foregoing checks do not overcome the problem, do not discount the possibility of a smaller main jet having been fitted to the carburettor by some previous owner obsessed with fuel economy. This intentional weakening of the mixture may improve consumption but will decrease performance, cause the engine to run hotter than normal and will burn out plugs and exhaust valves more quickly.

20. Exhaust System - Inspection, Removal and Replacement

1. Examination of the exhaust pipe and silencers at regular intervals is worthwhile as small defects may be repairable when, if left they will almost certainly require renewal of one of the sections of the system. Also, any leaks, apart from the noise factor, may cause poisonous exhaust gases

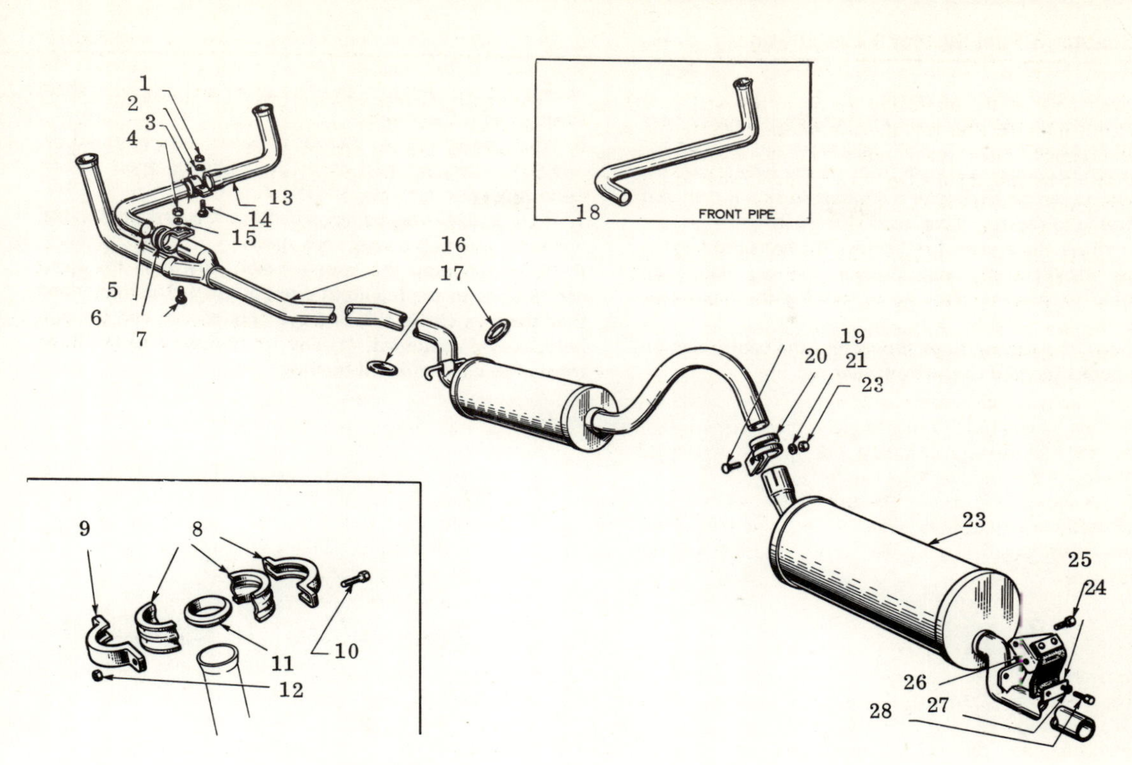

Fig. 3.21. EXHAUST SYSTEM — EXPLODED DRAWING

1 Nut	9 Clamp sleeve	17 Support rings	24 Hangar plate
2 Washer	10 Bolt	18 Front pipe R.H. (early	25 Bolt
3 Pipe clip	11 Sealing ring	models)	26 Flexible hangar
4 Nut	12 Nut	19 Bolt	27 Washer
5 Washer	13 Front pipe R.H.	20 Pipe clip	28 Bolt
6 Pipe, inner R.H.	14 Bolt	21 Washer	
7 Bolt	15 Washer	22 Nut	
8 Pipe clamp	16 Front pipe and silencer	23 Rear silencer	

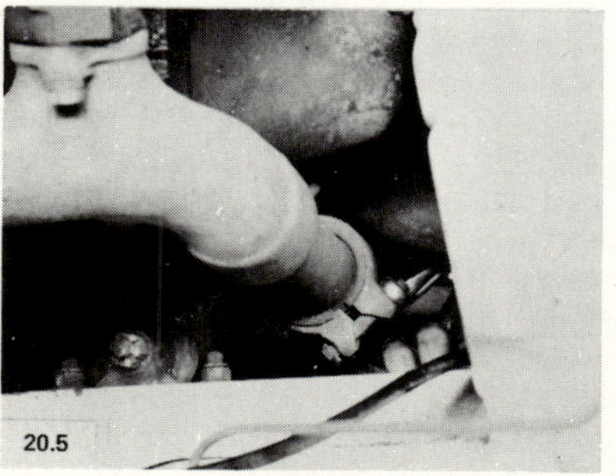

to get inside the car which can be unpleasant, to say the least, even in mild concentrations. Prolonged inhalation could cause sickness and giddiness.

2. As the sleeve connections and clamps are usually very difficult to separate it is quicker and easier in the long run to remove the complete system from the car when renewing a section. It can be expensive if another section is damaged when trying to separate a bad section from it.

3. To remove the system first remove the bolts holding the tail pipe bracket to the body. Support the rear silencer on something to prevent cracking or kinking the pipes elsewhere.

4. Unhook the rubber rings supporting the centre section on the hooks forward of the front silencer.

5. Disconnect the twin pipes from the exhaust manifolds at each side of the engine. This is done by slackening the clamps (photo) holding the two pipes and removing them together with the inserts.

6. When separating the damaged section to be renewed cut away the damaged part from the adjoining good section rather than risk damaging the latter.

7. If small repairs are being carried out it is best, if possible, not to try and pull the sections apart.

8. When replacing the system make sure that the front connections to the manifold pipes are seated correctly and that the two clamp halves are evenly spaced and the two bolts evenly tightened. It may be necessary to retighten them after a few miles of running.

Chapter 4/Ignition System

Contents

Specifications

Sparking Plugs

Size	14 mm
Type	Autolite AG 22
Gap	.023 to .028 ins. (.59 to .70 mm)

Coil

Type	12v. oil filled
Current consumption - stationary	3.9 amp.
- 2000 r.p.m.	1.4 amp.
Resistance at 20°C (68°F) Primary	4 to 4.4 ohms.
Secondary	7,000 to 8,000 ohms.

Distributor (up to August, 1966)

Type	Single pair contact breaker points
Drive	Skew gear from camshaft
Automatic advance	Centrifugal and vacuum controlled
	- Identification - HC - Natural Clear
	Cap clips
	- LC - Yellow cap clips
Contact points gap	.014 to .016 in. (.356 to .406 mm)
Contact points spring tension	18 to 24 oz. (510 to 680 gms.)
Dwell angle	57° to 63°
Rotation of rotor	Clockwise
Condenser capacity	.18 to .22 micro farads
Vacuum unit type	5 - 17 - 6

Octane rating, compression and static advance settings

1664 c.c. H.C.	100 octane	8° B.T.D.C.
	97 "	6° B.T.D.C.
	94 "	4° B.T.D.C.
1664 c.c. L.C.	89 "	8° B.T.D.C.
	86 "	4° B.T.D.C.
	80 "	0°
1996 c.c. H.C.	100 "	8° B.T.D.C.
	97 "	8° B.T.D.C.
	94 "	6° B.T.D.C.
1996 c.c. L.C.	89 "	6° B.T.D.C.
	86 "	4° B.T.D.C.
	80 "	2° A.T.D.C.

Centrifugal advance characteristics
H.C. engines:

    Advance starts ... ...   700 r.p.m. (crankshaft)
    3⁰ - 5⁰ advance   ... ...   1200 r.p.m.
    9⁰ - 11⁰ advance ... ...   2000 r.p.m.
    14⁰ - 16⁰ advance   ... ...   4000 r.p.m. (advance complete)

L.C. engines:

    Advance starts ... ...   950 r.p.m. (crankshaft)
    1⁰ - 3⁰ advance   ... ...   1200 r.p.m.
    7⁰ - 9⁰ advance   ... ...   2000 r.p.m.
    15⁰ - 17⁰ advance   ... ...   4100 r.p.m. (advance complete)

Vacuum advance characteristics
All engines:

Inches Hg.	Distributor advance
20	5⁰ - 7⁰ (maximum)
10	3⁰ - 5⁰
6	¼⁰ - 2½⁰
4	Nil

Distributor (Sept. 1966 onwards)

Type	Single pair contact breaker points
Drive	Skew gear from camshaft
Automatic advance	Centrifugal and vacuum controlled

Identification:

    2000 Series ... ...   C6CH - 12100 - C - Blue paint on vacuum plug
    H.C. 1.7, 2 litre V4 Series   ... ...   C6CH - 12100 - A - Red paint on vacuum plug
    L.C. 1.7, 2 litre V4 Series   ... ...   C6CH - 12100 -B - Green paint on vacuum plug

Contact points gap	.025 in. (.64 mm)
Contact points spring tension	17 to 21 oz. (481.9 to 567.0 gms.)
Dwell angle	38⁰ to 40⁰
Rotation of rotor	Clockwise
Condenser capacity	.21 to .25 micro farads

Octane rating, compression and static advance settings table:

V4 1664 cc:	H.C. 97 octane	8⁰ advance	L.C. 89 octane	6⁰ advance
	H.C. 94 octane	4⁰ advance	L.C. 86 octane	4⁰ advance
			L.C. 80 octane	0⁰ advance
V4 1996 cc:	H.C. 97 octane	8⁰ advance	L.C. 89 octane	6⁰ advance
	H.C. 94 octane	6⁰ advance	L.C. 86 octane	4⁰ advance
			L.C. 80 octane	0⁰ advance
2000 1996 cc:	97 octane	10⁰ advance		
	94 octane	6⁰ advance		

Centrifugal advance characteristics:

V4 1.7 and 2 litre H.C. engines:

    0.5⁰ to 2.5⁰   ... ...   1200 r.p.m. (crankshaft)
    10⁰ to 12⁰ ... ...   2400 r.p.m.
    14.5⁰ to 16.5⁰   ... ...   4200 r.p.m. (advance complete)

'2000' 1996 c.c. engines:

    2.5⁰ to 4.5⁰   ... ...   1200 r.p.m. (crankshaft)
    10.5⁰ to 12.5⁰   ... ...   2400 r.p.m.
    14.5⁰ to 16.5⁰... ... ...   4600 r.p.m. (advance complete)

'V4' 1664 c.c. and 1996 c.c. low compression:

    2⁰ to 4⁰   ... ...   1400 r.p.m. (crankshaft)
    9⁰ to 11⁰   ... ...   2400 r.p.m.
    14.5⁰ to 16.5⁰   ... ...   4000 r.p.m. (advance complete)

Vacuum advance characteristics

Inches Hg.	'2000'	Distributor advance H.C. 1.7 and 2 litre	L.C. 1.7 and 2 litre
7	—	—	1.5⁰ to 4.5⁰
8	1⁰ to 4⁰	1⁰ to 4⁰	
9			4.5⁰ to 7.5⁰
10	2.5⁰ to 5.5⁰		
11	3⁰ to 6⁰		7⁰ to 10⁰
12+	3.5⁰ to 6.5⁰ (max)		
13+			8⁰ to 11⁰ (max)
16+		5⁰ to 8⁰ (max)	

1. General Description

In order that the engine may run correctly it is necessary for an electrical spark to ignite the fuel/air mixture in the combustion chambers at exactly the right moment in relation to engine speed and loading. The ignition system is based on feeding low tension voltage from the battery to the coil where it is converted to high tension voltage. The high tension voltage is powerful enough to jump the gap between the electrodes of the sparking plugs in the cylinders many times a second under high compression, providing that the system is in good condition and all the adjustments are correct.

The system is divided into two circuits; the low tension and high tension.

The low tension (sometimes called primary) circuit consists of the battery, lead wire to the control box, lead from the control box to the ignition switch, lead from ignition switch to the coil low tension windings (SW or + terminal) and from the coil low tension windings (CB or — terminal) to the contact breaker points and condenser in the distributor.

The high tension circuit comprises the high tension or secondary windings in the coil, the heavily insulated lead from the coil to the distributor cap centre contact, the rotor arm, and the leads from the four distributor cap outer contacts (in turn) to the sparking plugs.

Low tension voltage is stepped up by the coil windings to high tension voltage intermittently by the operation of the contact points and the condenser in the low tension circuit. High tension voltage is then fed via the centre contact in the distributor cap to the rotor arm.

The rotor arm rotates clockwise at half engine revolutions inside the cap and each time it comes in line with one of the outer contacts in the cap the contact points open and the high voltage is discharged jumping the gap from rotor arm to contact and thence along the plug lead to the centre electrode of the plug where it jumps the other gap - sparking in the process - to the outer plug electrode and thence to earth.

The static timing of the spark is adjusted by revolving the outer body of the distributor in relation to the distributor shaft. This alters the position at which the points open in relation to the position of the crankshaft (and thus the pistons).

The timing is also altered automatically by a centrifugal device which further alters the position of the complete points mounting assembly in relation to the shaft when engine speed increases, and by a vacuum control working from the inlet manifold which varies the timing according to the position of the throttle and consequently load on the engine. Both of these automatic alterations advance the timing of the spark at light loads and higher speeds. The mechanical advance mechanism consists of two weights, which move out from the distributor shaft as engine speed rises due to centrifugal force. As they move out, so the cam rotates relative to the shaft and the contact breaker opening position is altered.

The degree to which the weights move out is controlled by springs, the tension of which significantly controls the extent of the advance to the timing.

The vacuum advance device is a diaphragm and connecting rod attached to the cam plate. When the diaphragm moves in either direction the cam plate is moved, thus altering the timing. The diaphragm is actuated by depression (vacuum) in the inlet manifold and is connected by a small bore pipe to the carburettor body above the throttle flap.

A knurled screw on the vacuum unit can be turned for manual adjustment of the static timing.

2. Routine Maintenance

1. Every 5,000 miles the contact breaker cam in the distributor should be lubricated with a light smear of petroleum jelly. The moving contact pivot bushing, cam spindle and governor weights should receive a few drops of engine oil. The spindle is oiled by removing the rotor arm and putting two drops in the centre. The governor weights can be reached through the apertures in the plate. On no account over lubricate as the points may be contaminated, causing arcing, and difficult starting.
2. Every 2,000 miles remove the sparking plugs and check the electrode gap which should be 023 ins. - 028 ins. (.59 - .70 mm). Examine the insulator and general condition (with reference to Page 84) and renew anyway after 10,000 miles.
3. Every 2,000 miles check the contact breaker points gap as described in Section 4 and reset as required.
4. In very damp weather examine the high tension leads and distributor cap for signs of condensation and wipe off any dampness with a dry cloth. Look inside the distributor cap as well to make sure it is dry. Dampness may cause short circuits and consequent misfiring or total stoppage of the engine.
5. Periodically examine both low tension and high tension wiring for signs of damage to insulation which may cause short circuits.

3. Firing Order and Plug Lead Positions

1. The piston firing order is 1, 3, 4, 2 and the rotor arm revolves clockwise. Figure 4.1. shows the piston numbering and H.T. lead connections to the distributor cap. The diagram follows the actual layout on the engine, with the distributor at the front.

4. Distributor (all types) Contact Breaker Points - Adjustment

1. Snap back the two spring clips which hold the distributor cap to the distributor and lift off the cap.
2. Pull the rotor arm off the spindle.
3. Put the car in gear and then move it so that any one of the four high points on the cam opens the breaker points. Make sure that the heel of the cam follower is on the highest point of the cam.
4. Slacken the locking screw (or screws in later models) holding the fixed contact bracket (Fig. 4.2.) and using the slot in the plate, move the bracket so that the gap between the points is .014-.016 ins. (.36-.41 mm) using a .015 in. feeler blade. Tighten the lock screw and check the gap once again. Make sure that when setting the gap the spring loaded contact point is not pushed back, thus giving a resulting gap which is too small. The contact on the feeler blade should be quite light.
5. If the surfaces of the contact points are deeply pitted and show signs of burning they may be removed and refaced with a fine stone AS A TEMPORARY MEASURE. It is best to replace them immediately but certainly as soon as possible. If signs of burning have occurred when checking for misfiring, or other ignition faults, then check the condenser also as described in Section 10.
6. Replace the rotor arm, making sure that it is fully located with the slot in the spindle lined up with the lug in the rotor and the lower face fully down on the edge of

the cam.

7. Refit the distributor cap so that the lugs and slots line up, and snap back the two spring leaf clips.

5. Distributor (up to Sept. 1966) Contact Breaker Points - Removal and Replacement

1. Remove the distributor cap and rotor arm and unscrew the small hexagonal nut from the top of the terminal post on the fixed contact.
2. Remove the flanged nylon bush from the terminal post and the two circular lead connectors. The moving breaker arm can then be lifted off and the two lower fibre washers on the terminal and pivot posts removed.
3. Unscrew the locking screw holding the fixed contact to the bearing plate and lift away the contact.
4. Some later types of contact sets are made with the two halves fixed together at the pivot post. With these the whole assembly is lifted away as soon as the two leads and the locking screw have been detached.
4. Replacement is a reversal of the removal procedure. Take care that the nylon bush on the terminal post goes through the two circular lead connectors before locating over the post inside the end loop of the breaker spring. Also make sure that both the fibre washers go over the terminal and pivot posts before fitting the breaker arm. If this is not done there will be no insulation between the two contacts when they are open. So no high tension will be produced and so no spark at the plugs.
5. Readjust the points gap as described in Section 4.

6. Distributor (Oct. 1966 on) Contact Breaker Points - Removal and Replacement

1. Remove the distributor cap and pull the rotor arm straight upwards off the spindle.
2. Slacken the screw holding the leads from the condenser and low tension and slide out the forked connectors.
3. Remove the two screws holding the contact breaker assembly to the breaker plate and lift it out.
4. Replacement is a reversal of the removal operations. Make sure that the two leads are not trapped between the contact assembly and plate.
5. Reset the points as described in Section 4.
6. Replace the rotor and distributor cap.

7. Distributor (all types) - Removal, Replacement and Ignition Timing

1. During the course of engine overhaul the distributor will normally be removed, it will also be removed for the purposes of renewal or rebuilding.
2. Remove the distributor cap and detach the lead from the coil which leads to the distributor.
3. Note carefully on a piece of paper the position of the distributor body and the rotor arm in relation to the body. Provided the engine is not turned and the distributor and rotor arm are replaced in the same relative positions, the ignition timing will not be altered.
4. The distributor is held to the engine by a single bolt which goes either through an elongated slot in a flange cast integral with the distributor body (up till Sept. 1966) or through a clamp and retainer plate which slides into grooves in the body (Oct. 1966 onwards).
5. The bolt is down in the Vee of the inlet manifold at the base of the distributor body and is somewhat difficult to get at. First of all mark the position of the bolt relative

to the lug with two scratch marks (early models) or the position of the distributor body relative to the clamp plate on later types. Ideally one would use a special socket with a flexible drive to undo the bolt. The universal connector or a conventional ½ inch square socket set is too big. However, if the socket is placed over the bolt head it is possible to undo the bolt with a broad bladed screwdriver set diagonally across the square of the socket (photo). The tightening torque required for this bolt is not great so no difficulties should be encountered with this method. If the bolt refuses to budge then the special tool (flexible socket drive) will be required. If the engine is being dismantled further wait until the inlet manifold is taken off. (This will mean grooving the side of the distributor body to allow the front right hand manifold bolt to come out - arrowed in photo 7/5).
6. With the bolt removed, gently ease the distributor upwards. Note that as it comes up, the rotor arm will move anti-clockwise due to the skew gear drive on the end of the spindle. This movement will have to be taken into account on replacement.
7. On later models it will be possible to draw out and remove the retainer plate and lift the distributor straight out but on the earlier type it will have to be turned slightly to enable the lug to clear the cylinder head.
8. Replacement is a reversal of the removal procedure but care must be taken to ensure that the skew gear on the spindle re-meshes in the same place as before.
9. Provided the precautions as described in paragraph 3 are taken no difficulty should be encountered. Before replacing the distributor set the rotor arm in a position approximately 30° anti-clockwise of the required installed position. As it goes down it will turn clockwise due to the spiral on the skew gear.
10 If for any reason the timing is lost the correct setting will have to be found as follows.
11 Turn the engine so that the timing groove on the crankshaft pulley lines up with one of the three positions on the front cover timing lug (photo) suitable for the particular engine as given in the specifications. The lower (anticlockwise) pointer is 8° before top dead centre (B.T.D.C.) and the right hand one is 4° B.T.D.C. The centre 'V' is, obviously, 6° B.T.D.C. The pulley must be set with No. 1 piston (front, right hand bank viewed from driving seat) on the compression stroke. This can be verified by removing the sparking plug and placing a finger over the hole while the engine is turned towards the timing mark. The only easy way to turn the engine is to engage top gear and move the car forwards. Removal of all the sparking plugs reduces the resistance of engine compression when doing this.
12 On early model distributors check that the scale on the vacuum advance mechanism is set so that the fourth line on the scale is in line with the edge of the distributor body. This can be achieved by turning the knurled adjustment screw. The adjustment is then centred so that the static timing may be finely adjusted in either direction when the distributor is finally fixed in position.
13 With the distributor out of the engine (and inverted) turn the spindle until the recessed end of the pin, locating the skew gear to the spindle, lines up with the notch in the bottom edge of the body. This will result in the rotor arm being in the position shown in the photo relative to the body of the distributor.
14 Place the bolt in the mounting hole at the base of the distributor and hold it in position while lowering the distributor into place (photo).
15 Push the distributor right home when the rotor arm will be in the position shown (photo). (This is adjacent to the No. 1 plug lead contact inside the distributor cap.)
16 If a mistake is made and the gear should have become

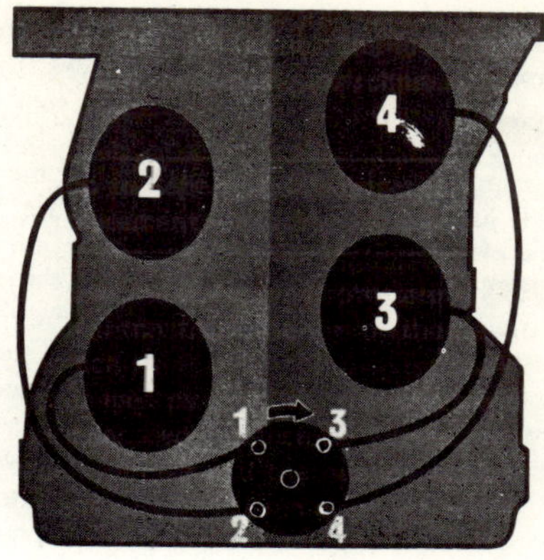

Fig. 4.1. Diagram showing the piston numbering and firing order connection of the H.T. leads to the distributor cap

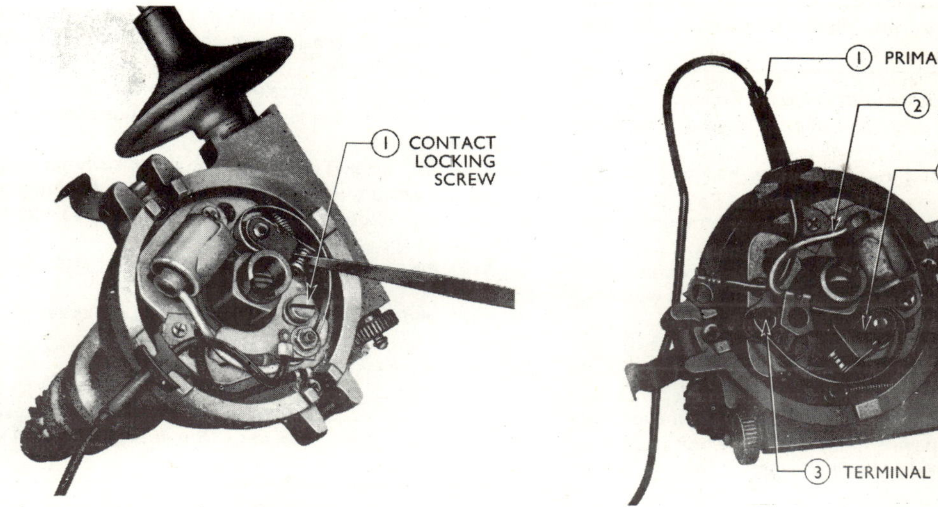

Fig. 4.2. Checking the contact breaker points with feeler blade in position

Fig. 4.3. Features of the contact breaker points and connections

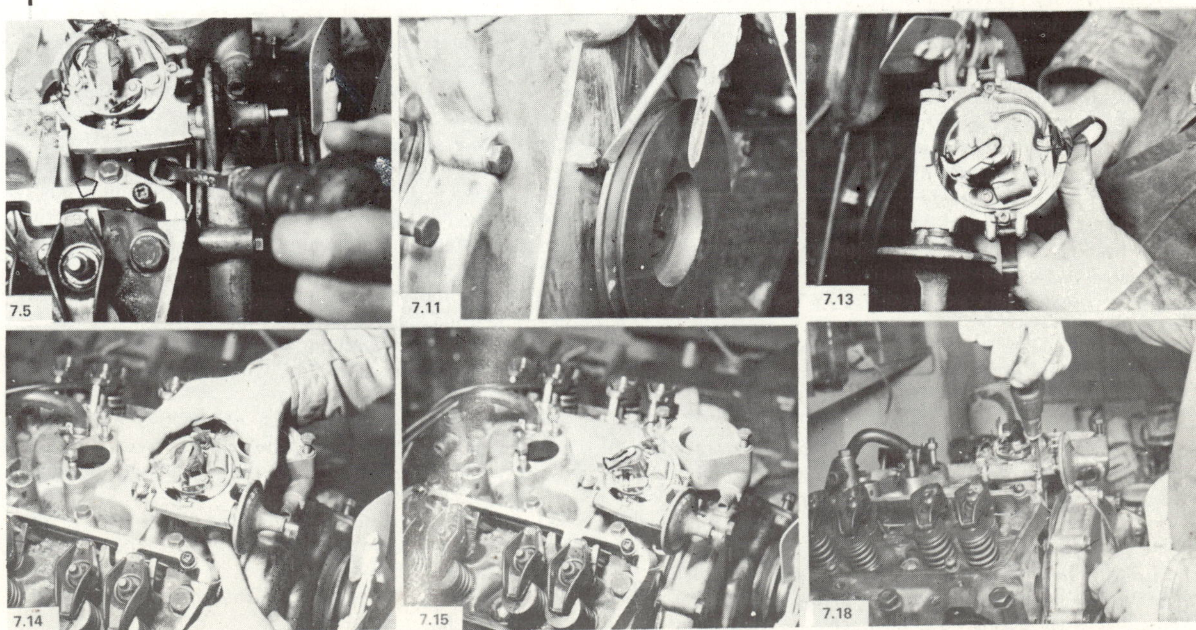

engaged one tooth amiss it will be very evident. There are only twelve teeth on the gear and this represents a variance of 30º in the position of the rotor arm.

17 Set the distributor body by turning it so that the contact points are just about to be opened by the cam. Remember that the rotor turns clockwise so that the 'just about to open position' of the breaker arm is on the clockwise side of the high point of the cam.

18 Clamp up the mounting bolt. On early models the static timing can be finely adjusted by the vernier screw but the later models must be carefully set by turning the distributor body before finally tightening the clamp bolt. Tighten the clamp bolt using a screwdriver in a socket as mentioned in paragraph 5 (photo).

19 Adjust the contact points gap (Section 3), replace the rotor arm and refit the distributor cap, making sure that the plug leads are securely connected in the correct locations (Section 3).

---

8. Distributor (Up to Sept. 1966) - Dismantling, Overhaul and Reassembly

---

1. Remove the distributor as described in Section 6.
2. Detach the cap, rotor and contact breaker points as described in Section 5.
3. Undo the condenser retaining screw and take off the condenser.
4. Unhook the vacuum unit spring from the mounting pin on the breaker plate assembly.
5. Remove the two screws holding the breaker plate assembly to the distributor sides. One of these screws also holds one end of the earth wire.
6. Pull up the rubber block from the side of the distributor body and take out the L.T. wire with it.
7. Lift out the breaker plate assembly.
8. Twist the breaker plate anti-clockwise until the locating peg is opposite the opening in the slot of the bearing plate.
9. Disengage the spring clip and separate the two plates (Fig. 4.5.).
10 Unhook the governor weight springs from the pegs on the cam plate.
11 Remove the screw holding the breaker cam to the spindle and lift the cam section clear of the governor weights.
12 Disconnect the springs from the pegs on the action plate and lift off the weights.
13 Should there be wear in the shaft bushes or excessive end float in the shaft then the skew gear retaining pin should be driven out and the gear and collar removed. The shaft, with the action plate can then be removed from the distributor body. Do not lose the nylon washer under the action plate.
14 The shaft bushes may be renewed by driving out the old ones with a suitable drift and carefully tapping in two new ones.
15 The vacuum advance unit may be removed by taking the locking pin out of the end of the screwed spindle and removing the knurled nut. The vacuum itself is a sealed unit and if defective must be renewed.
16 Reassembly is a reversal of the dismantling procedure. If the shaft end float is excessive renew the nylon washer under the action plate and the lower spacer washer above the skew gear. When refitting the skew gear use a new pin and peen over the end.
17 Fit the weight springs to the pegs on the action plate.
18 Replace the governor weights on the action plate with the flat sides against the fixed cam segments and the recessed edges around the spindle (Fig. 4.6.).
19 Fit the breaker cam over the spindle so that the two

lugs locate in the holes in the weights and replace the securing screw. Then fit the other ends of the springs to pegs on the cam plate. It is usually worthwhile renewing these springs but make sure that the correct type are obtained for the particular model of distributor. If the wrong ones are fitted the ignition timing in the higher engine revolution range will be completely upset. Turn the shaft to make sure it revolves smoothly with no trace of tightness. Lightly oil the cams and weights with engine oil. Make sure also that the action of the weights is smooth in the fully advanced position. This can be done by holding the skew gear and turning the cam clockwise to the limit.

20 Having checked the linkage, replace the vacuum unit. If a new unit is to be fitted it must be of the correct type. Others may physically fit but they are designed for different engines. The type number for the V4 engine is 5-17-6 and these numbers are stamped on the unit near the vacuum pipe union. When the unit is reassembled tighten it so that the fourth graduation line on the scale is in line with the distributor body.

21 Verify that the breaker plate is a snug fit on the bearing plate and that the breaker arm pivot is not bent or worn. Renew all if necessary.

22 When refitting the breaker plate to the bearing plate the latter should fit under the clip and horizontal lug as shown in Fig. 4.5.

23 Refit the breaker assembly to the distributor body, fitting the vacuum unit spring to the post on the lug of the breaker plate. Note that one securing screw also acts as a terminal for the earth wire.

24 Refit the condenser. It may be checked as described in Section 10.

25 Refit and adjust the breaker points as described in Sections 4 and 5.

26 Replace the rotor and distributor cap.

---

9. Distributor (Oct. 1966 on) - Dismantling, Overhaul and Reassembly

---

1. Remove the distributor from the car and take off the contact points as described in Sections 6 and 7.
2. Undo the screw retaining the condenser and lift it off.
3. Remove the small circlip from the post linking the upper and lower breaker plates and remove the plain and wave washers.
4. Remove the circlip from the vacuum unit connecting rod post.
5. Remove the upper breaker plate.
6. Undo the two crosshead screws securing the lower breaker plate to the distributor body and lift it out. Do not lose the small coil spring acting as an earth link between the two plates. Detach the grommet from the hole in the plate and remove the primary lead.
7. Take off the vacuum unit by removing first the two screws securing the bracket.
8. To dismantle the vacuum assembly hold the body in a vice and remove the end plug. Withdraw the shim, spring and vacuum stop.
9. Noting carefully the position of the two mechanical advance springs, which are not the same, remove them from the pivot posts on the cam and spring plate and from the grooved tabs on the action plate.
10 Lift out the felt oil wick from inside the bore of the breaker cam and then take out the circlip. The cam may then be pulled off the shaft.
11 Remove the circlips holding the governor weights in position on the action plate.
12 If the main shaft bushes are worn or the end float of the shaft is incorrect it will be necessary to remove the skew

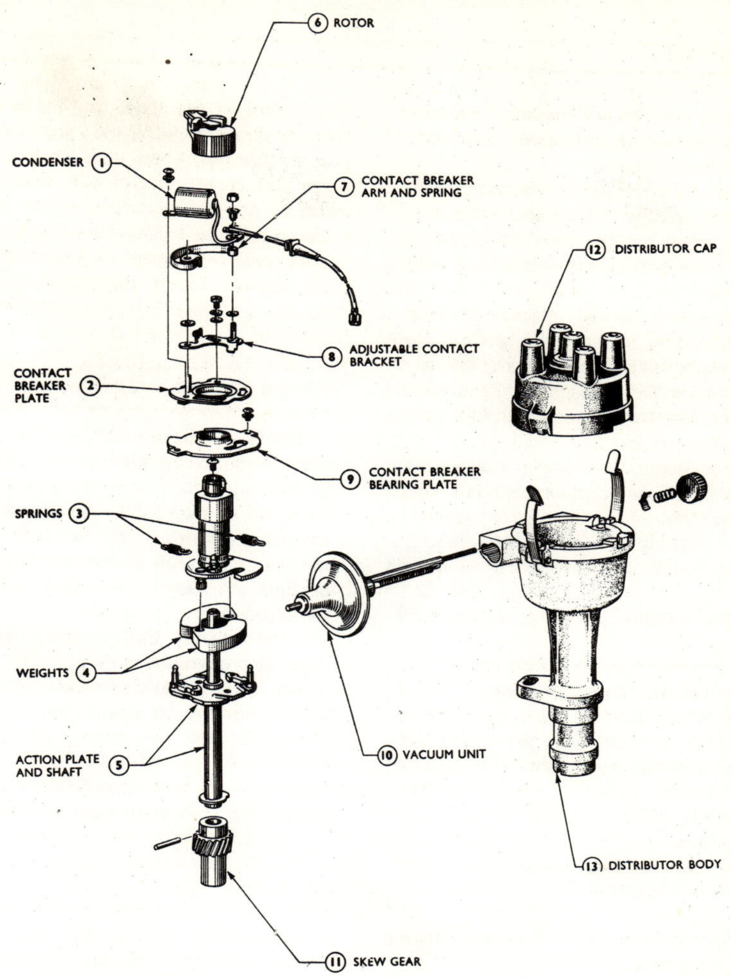

Fig. 4.4. Exploded view of the distributor fitted up to Sept. 1966

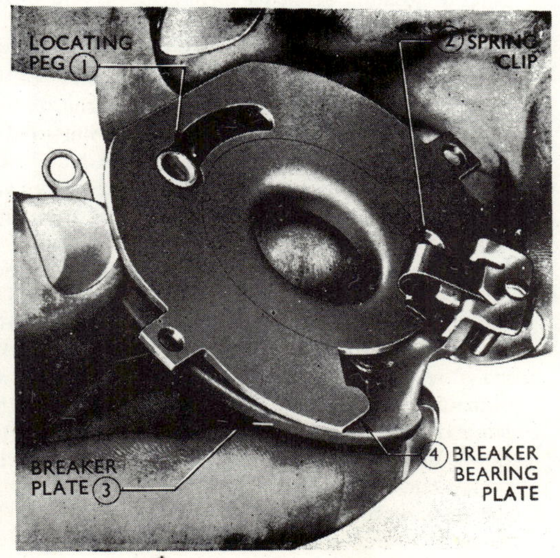

Fig. 4.5. Separating the breaker plate from the breaker bearing plate on pre September, 1966 distributors

Fig. 4.6. Location of weights on the action plate when reassembling pre September, 1966 distributors

gear so that the shaft can be taken out of the distributor body. This can be done by driving out the tubular retaining pin with a punch, thus allowing the gear to be pulled off and the shaft withdrawn.

13 New bushes may be carefully tapped into position after the old ones have been driven out with a punch or drift.

14 When replacing the shaft first refit a new washer between the action plate and distributor body and a new sealing ring and another new thrust washer at the lower end between the skew gear and body. To set the end float a piece of .004 in. shim (.1 mm) as shown in Fig. 4.7. should be placed behind the washer, and the skew gear placed on the shaft so that the pinhole is at right angles to the original in the shaft. The centre line of the rotor slot should also be in line with the top of any gear tooth.

15 Clamp the gear up to the body so that the shim is just held. Then drill a 1/8 in. (3.18 mm) hole in the shaft and fit a new pin. Take out the shim.

16 Reassembly of the distributor is a reversal of the dismantling procedure with particular attention to certain points.

17 Locate the governor weights correctly with the flat sides next to the shaft.

18 When refitting the cam and plate to the distributor shaft see that the advance stop on the action plate is located within the section marked '165R' (Fig. 4.8.).

19 Fit the primary and secondary springs correctly (Fig. 4.8).

20 The original parts of the vacuum unit should be replaced if it has been dismantled. Otherwise the timing advance will be altered (See Section 7.).

10. Condenser - Testing and Renewal

1. Faulty ignition resulting in misfiring and uneven running could be caused by a faulty condenser in the distributor.

2. If the contact breaker points (Section 4) show signs of excessive burning and pitting on the faces of the contacts it is an indication that the condenser has probably broken down and should be renewed.

3. To check the efficiency of the condenser remove the distributor cap and rotor arm. Then rotate the engine so that the points are closed - that is with the breaker arm resting between two high points on the cam.

4. Switch on the ignition and with a non-conductive article such as a splinter of wood, move the contacts open by levering on the spring of the moving breaker. If there is a severe flashing spark it indicates that the condenser has probably failed.

5. An additional test to confirm condenser failure is to open the points (this can be done by placing a piece of paper or postcard between the contacts) and disconnecting the condenser lead from the breaker terminal post. Then put a voltmeter or 12v bulb with two wander leads between the terminal post and the condenser lead. Switch on the ignition and if there is a reading or the bulb lights the condenser is faulty and must be replaced.

6. To renew the condenser, detach the wire from the screw or terminal post, whichever applies, remove the mounting screw and replace the old unit with a new one. Check that arcing has been virtually eliminated by testing as already described.

11. Vacuum and Mechanical Advance - Adjustments

1. The distributors fitted after September 1966 are so designed that the vacuum and mechanical advance characteristics may be altered.

2. Normally no adjustment is necessary and should not be attempted. However, if a new shaft is fitted, for example, the spring anchor tabs on the action plate may be in a relatively different position and thus could alter the tension on the springs. These tabs can be altered by bending them. This, however, is quite futile without specialist test and setting equipment so should not be attempted. Similarly, the vacuum advance setting can be altered by changing the thickness of the shims behind the plug. This should not be attempted without the specialised equipment needed to check the settings.

12. Sparking Plugs - Examination

1. Routine maintenance (Section 2) will normally be all that is required for satisfactory operation of sparking plugs.

2. In conjunction with the indications given on Page 84, the sparking plug can however, give a very useful indication of engine condition. It is not often that plugs of the wrong heat value are used so indications of 'too hot' or 'too cold' can indicate weak or rich mixtures requiring adjustments to the carburation.

3. Plugs with oily, black deposits can indicate worn cylinder bores or broken piston rings.

4. Do not try and counteract symptoms of weak or rich fuel mixtures by compensating with colder or hotter plugs. The basic fault will remain and cause other undesirable effects.

5. Do not try and economise by using plugs for a period longer than their normal useful life of 10,000 miles.

13. Fault Finding

1. Engine troubles normally associated with and usually caused by faults in the ignition system are:-

a) Failure to start when the engine is turned.

b) Uneven running caused by misfiring or mistiming.

c) Even running at low engine speed and misfiring when engine speeds up or is under the load of acceleration or hill-climbing.

d) Even running at higher engine speeds and misfiring or stoppage at slow speed.

a) First check that all wires are properly connected and dry. If the engine fails to catch when turned on the starter do not continue turning or the battery will be flattened and the problem made worse. Remove one spark plug lead from a plug and turn the engine again and see if a spark will jump from the end of the lead to the top of the plug or the engine block. It should jump a gap of ¼ inch with ease. If the spark is there, ensure that the static ignition timing is correct and then the fuel system. If there is no spark at the plug lead proceed further and remove the H.T. lead from the centre of the distributor which comes from the coil. Try again by turning the engine to see if a spark can be obtained from the end. If there is a spark the fault lies between the contact in the distributor cap and the plug. Check that the rotor arm is in good condition and making proper contact in the centre of the distributor cap and that the plug leads are properly attached to the cap. The four terminals inside the cap should be intact, clean and free from corrosion. If no spark comes from the coil H.T. lead, check next that the contact breaker points are clean and the gap is correct. If there is still no spark obtainable it may be assumed that the low tension circuit is at fault. To check the low tension circuit properly it is best to have a voltmeter handy or a 12v bulb in a holder with two wander leads attached. The procedure now given is arranged so that

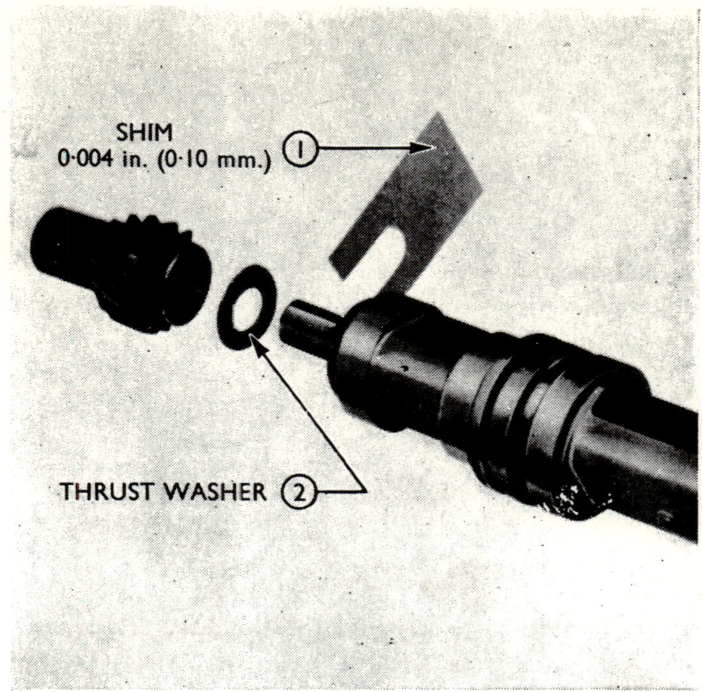

Fig. 4.7. Fitting a skew gear with the temporary shim to give the required end float on post October, 1966 distributors

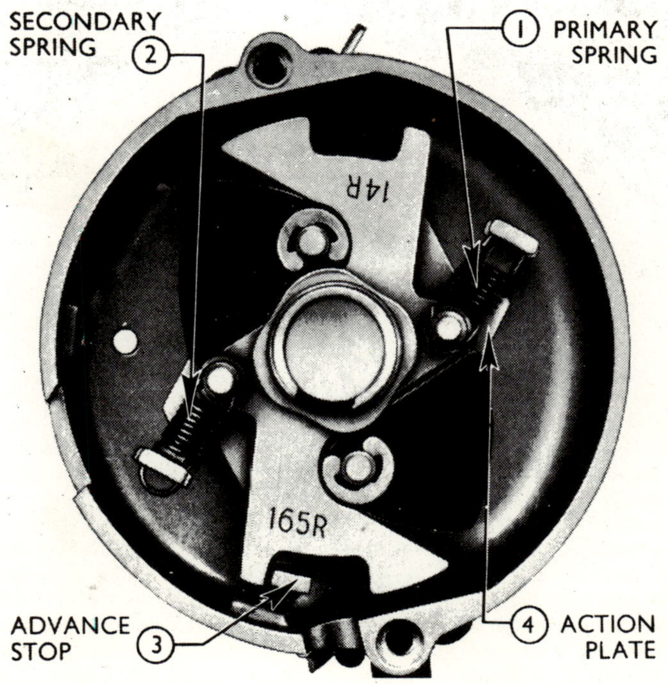

Fig. 4.8. Showing the correct locations of the governor springs, cam plate and advance stop on post 1966 distributors

the interruption in the circuit - if any - can be found. Starting at the distributor, put one of the two leads from the tester (be it lamp or voltmeter) to the moving contact terminal and the other to earth. A reading (or light) indicates that there is no break in the circuit between the ignition switch and the contact points. Check next that the condenser is ok as described in Section 10. If this is satisfactory it means that the coil is not delivering H.T. to the distributor and must therefore be renewed. If there is no L.T. reading on the first checkpoint repeat the test between the CB (–) terminal of the coil and earth. If a reading is now obtained there must be a break in the wire between the CB (–) terminal and the contact points. If there is no reading at this second checkpoint repeat the test between the SW (+) terminal of the coil and earth. If this produces a reading then the low tension post of the coil windings must be open-circuited and the coil must be renewed. If there is no reading at this third checkpoint there must be a break between the ignition switch and

the coil. If this is the case, a temporary lead between the + terminals of both coil and battery will provide the means to start the engine until the fault is traced.

b) Uneven running and misfiring should be checked first by ensuring that all H.T. wires are dry and properly connected. Ensure also that the leads are not short circuiting to earth against metal pipework or the engine itself. If this is happening an audible click can usually be heard from the place where the unwanted spark is being made.

c) If misfiring occurs at high speeds the points gap is too small or the sparking plugs need renewal due to failure under more severe operating pressures.

d) If misfiring is occuring at low engine speeds and the engine runs satisfactorily at high speed, the points gap is probably the cause - being too great.

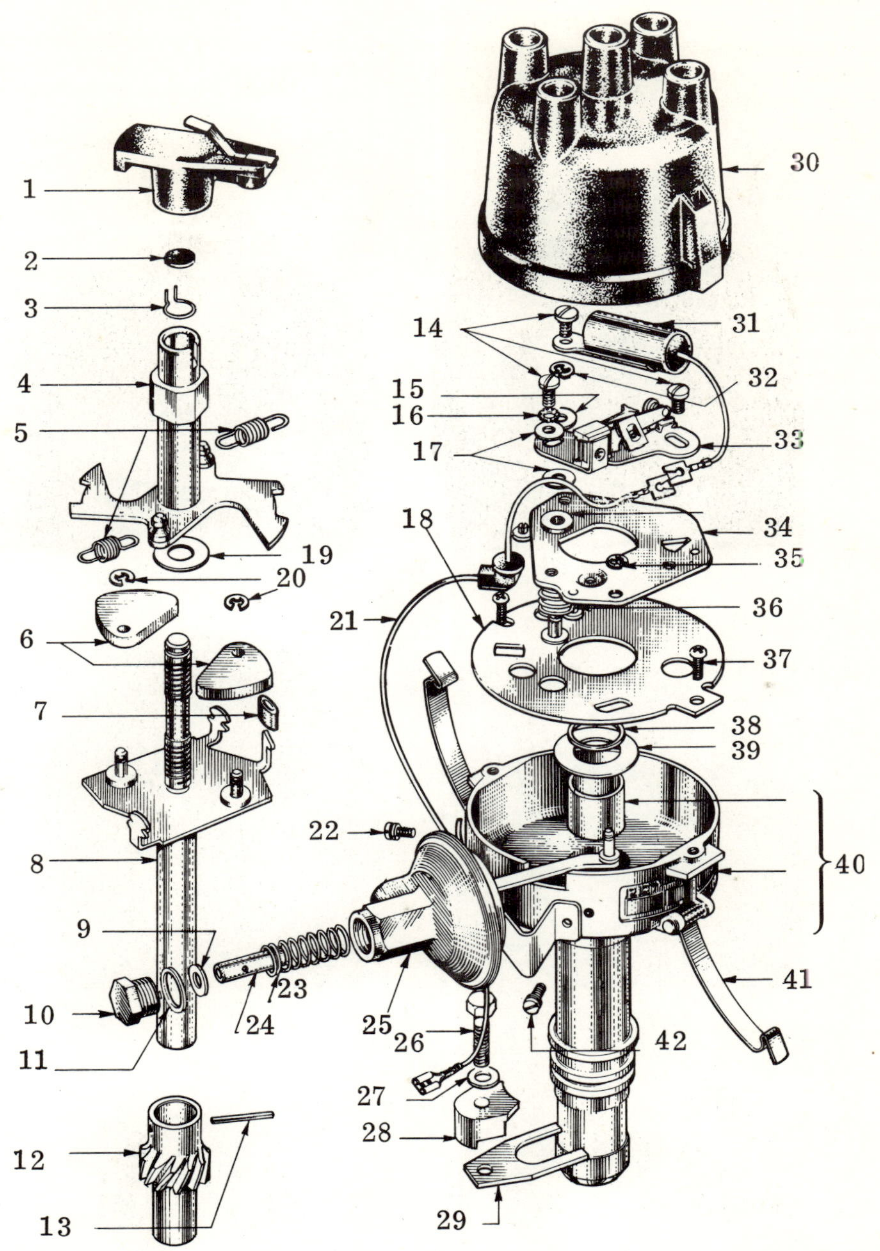

Fig. 4.9. DISTRIBUTOR FITTED FROM OCTOBER, 1966 ON — EXPLODED VIEW

1 Rotor arm	12 Drive gear	23 Vacuum advance spring	34 Upper plate
2 Lubricator wick	13 Pin	24 Vacuum advance stop	35 Circlip
3 Retainer clip (cam to shaft)	14 Screws	25 Vacuum advance unit	36 Earth spring
4 Cam	15 Washer	26 Clamp bolt	37 Screw - lower plate
5 Advance weight springs	16 Sten washer	27 Washer	38 Upper shaft washer
6 Advance weights	17 Washers	28 Clamp	39 Gear thrust washer
7 Sleeve	18 Lower plate	29 Retainer	40 Body and shaft bush
8 Distributor shaft	19 Thrust washer	30 Cap	41 Cap retaining clip
9 Shim	20 Circlips, weight retainers	31 Condenser	
10 Plug	21 Wire - contacts to coil	32 Circlip	
11 Gasket	22 Screw	33 Contact set	

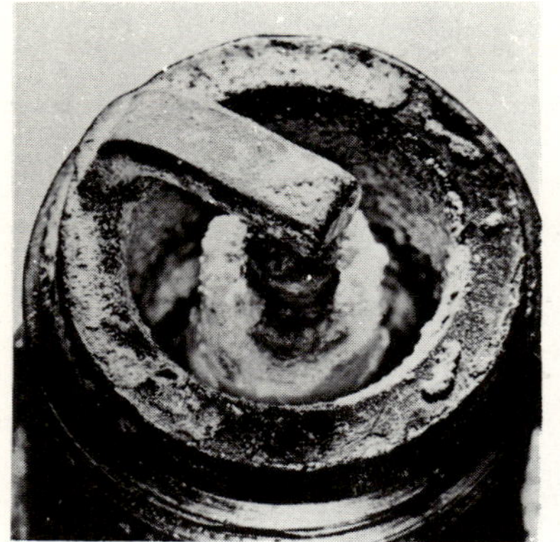

Chipped electrode

Too hot - white deposits

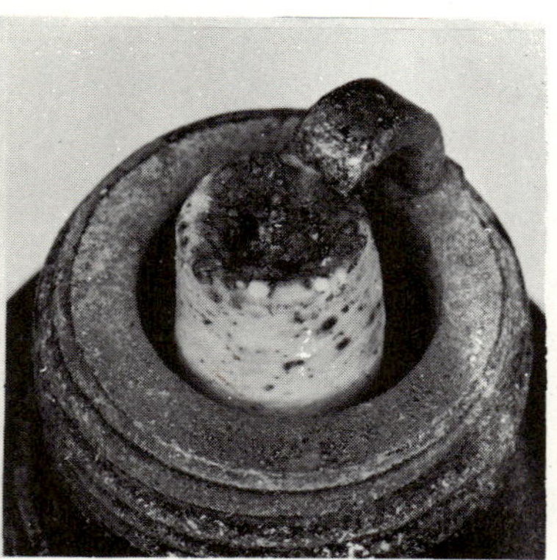

Pre-ignition damage

Too cold - dry, black fuel deposits

Badly burnt electrode

A normal clean plug with light deposits

Chapter 5/Clutch and Actuating Mechanism

Contents

Specifications

	1664 c.c.	1996 c.c.
Type	Single dry plate	
Operation	Hydraulic	
Master cylinder bore diameter	.75 in. (19 mm)	
Slave cylinder bore diameter	1.00 in. (25 mm)	
Friction lining diameter O.D.	7½ in. (198 mm)	8 in. (203 mm)
Friction lining diameter I.D.	5^{13}/16 in. (148 mm)	5¾ in. (146 mm)
Pressure plate diameter	7½ in. (198 mm)	8 in. (203 mm)

Torque Wrench Settings
Pressure plate to flywheel bolts   ... ...   12 to 15 lbs/ft. (1.6 to 2.0 Kg.m.)

1. General Description

1. Both the 1664 cc and 1996 cc models have diaphragm spring, single plate hydraulically operated clutches but the larger engine has an 8 inch diameter lining and pressure plate whereas the smaller has a 7½ inch diameter assembly. The unit comprises a steel cover which is dowelled and bolted to the rear face of the flywheel, and contains the pressure plate, pressure plate diaphragm spring, and fulcrum rings.

2. The clutch disc is free to slide along the splined first motion shaft and is held in position between the flywheel and the pressure plate by the pressure of the pressure plate spring. Friction lining material is riveted to the clutch disc and it has a spring cushioned hub to absorb transmission shocks and to help ensure a smooth take-off.

3. The circular diaphragm spring is mounted on shouldered pins and held in place in the cover by two fulcrum rings. The spring is also held to the pressure plate by three spring steel clips which are riveted in position.

4. The clutch is actuated hydraulically. The pendant clutch pedal is connected to the clutch master cylinder and hydraulic fluid reservoir by a short pushrod. The master cylinder and hydraulic reservoir are mounted on the engine side of the bulkhead in front of the driver.

5. Depressing the clutch pedal moves the piston in the master cylinder forwards, so forcing hydraulic fluid through the clutch hydraulic pipe to the slave cylinder.

6. The piston in the slave cylinder moves forward on the entry of the fluid and actuates the clutch release arm by means of a short pushrod.

7. The release arm pushes the release bearing forwards to bear against the release plate, so moving the centre of the diaphragm spring inwards. The spring is sandwiched between two annular rings which act as fulcrum points. As the centre of the spring is pushed in, the outside of the spring is pushed out, so moving the pressure plate backwards and disengaging the pressure plate from the clutch disc.

8. When the clutch pedal is released the diaphragm spring forces the pressure plate into contact with the high friction linings on the clutch disc and at the same time pushes the clutch disc a fraction of an inch forwards on its splines so engaging the clutch disc with the flywheel. The clutch disc is now firmly sandwiched between the pressure plate and the flywheel so the drive is taken up.

9. As the friction linings on the clutch disc wear the pressure plate automatically moves closer to the disc to compensate. There is therefore no need to periodically adjust the clutch.

2. Routine Maintenance

1. Routine maintenance consists of checking the level of the hydraulic fluid in the master cylinder every 5,000 miles.

2. If it is noted that the level of the liquid has fallen, then an immediate check should be made to determine the source of the leak.

3. Before checking the level of the fluid in the master cylinder reservoir, carefully clean the cap and body of the reservoir unit with clean rag so as to ensure that no dirt enters the system when the cap is removed. On no account should paraffin or any other cleaning solvent be used in case the hydraulic fluid becomes contaminated.

4. Check that the level of the hydraulic fluid is up to within ½ in. of the filler neck and that the vent hole in the cap is clear. Do not overfill.

5. Lubricate the pedal pivot bush with engine oil every 5,000 miles.

3. Hydraulic Clutch System - Bleeding

1. The hydraulic system needs bleeding whenever either of the cylinders or pipe is disconnected for any reason. It is NOT a remedy for any persistent malfunctioning of the clutch release mechanism. Its sole purpose is to dispose of any air that may be trapped in the system.

2. See that the level of hydraulic fluid in the reservoir is correct and then make sure that a jam jar, 1-2 ft. length of rubber tubing (3/16 in. bore diameter) and an additional quantity of new hydraulic fluid of the correct specification is available.

3. Remove the dust cap from the clutch cylinder bleed nipple and unscrew the nipple ¾ of a turn. Fit one end of the rubber tube over the nipple and place the other end in the jam jar (or similar container) which can be put on the ground or is better held by another person. The jar should have about one inch depth of hydraulic fluid in it and the end of the tube should be kept below the surface throughout the bleeding process.

4. The clutch pedal should now be depressed quickly and released slowly until air bubbles cease to emerge from the pipe. Quick depression ensures that air bubbles are carried along with the fluid rather than by-passed. Make sure that the reservoir level is kept up by topping up as necessary.

5. When the air bubbles stop emerging keep the pedal depressed and tighten the bleed nipple.

6. Check the operation of the clutch by depression of the pedal and observation of the clutch release arm.

7. Should the clutch fail to disengage properly due to insufficient movement of the release arm, it indicates that the seals in either the master cylinder or slave cylinder (or both) are defective and need renewal. As it is not practicable to decide which seals need renewal without first of all examining each cylinder it is best to plan for renewal of both sets of seals if one is defective.

4. Clutch Hydraulic Operating Cylinder - Removal, Dismantling, Reassembly and Replacement

1. The slave cylinder is located in the clutch bellhousing flange and is held in position by a circlip. Before dismantling anything, first remove the fluid reservoir cap and place a piece of thin plastic film over the reservoir and replace the cap. This will reduce any fluid loss when the system is open to atmosphere (photo).

2. Unscrew the lower end of the polythene pipe union from the slave cylinder and lift the pipe up out of the way (photo).

3. Remove the circlip holding the cylinder into the casting and then move the cylinder forward out of the locating hole, together with the pushrod which will come clear of the release arm.

4. Begin dismantling by pulling off the boot and pushrod and unscrewing the bleed nipple completely from the other end of the cylinder body.

5. Remove the circlip from inside the cylinder body and withdraw the piston, seal and spring. The spring and seal can then be pulled off the piston spigot.

6. Examine the seal for signs of swelling, feathering or any other deterioration. It is advisable to renew it if there is any doubt. Any scoring in the cylinder walls means that the cylinder should also be renewed.

7. Reassembly is a reversal of the dismantling procedure. Make sure the recessed side of the seal faces away from the piston and that the small coil end of the spring goes over the piston spigot.

8. All components should be perfectly clean and only new fluid, or meths, should be used in cleaning. Before reassembly coat the cylinder bore and piston and seal with clean hydraulic fluid.

9. Replace the assembly into the clutch housing and refit the circlip and rubber boot. Reconnect the fluid pipe and bleed the system as described in Section 3.

5. Clutch Hydraulic Master Cylinder - Removal, Dismantling, Reassembly and Replacement

1. The clutch master cylinder is mounted on the bulkhead in front of the driver and is connected to the clutch pedal by a pushrod. The reservoir is inside the engine compartment as shown in photo 4:1.

2. To remove the master cylinder first disconnect the pushrod from the pedal by undoing the nut and bolt and removing them and the associated washers. Do not lose the nylon bush in the pushrod.

3. Remove the two nuts and washers holding the mounting flange to the bulkhead studs.

4. Support the cylinder underneath with a piece of absorbent rag held in the hand and then unscrew the hydraulic pipe union and lift away the cylinder, avoiding spillage of fluid which will damage body paintwork.

5. Remove the reservoir cap and pour the contents into a clean container.

6. Begin dismantling by removing the rubber boot and withdrawing the circlip inside the cylinder.

7. Remove the pushrod and then pull out the piston and valve assembly complete.

8. The spring and valve assembly can next be removed from the spigot of the piston by prising up the tab in the retainer collar which locks it onto the piston (Fig. 5.4.).

9. The valve assembly can be dismantled next by compressing the spring so that the end of the valve stem can be disengaged via the slot in the retainer. Then slide the valve spacer and washer off the stem.

10 If the valve seal or piston seal need renewal pull each one off its respective location. When refitting these seals make sure that the lip on the valve seal faces away from the stem and that the lip of the piston seal faces away from the larger diameter of the piston. Make sure also that they are correctly located in their grooves.

11 Examine the cylinder bore for signs of wear or scoring and if there are any the cylinder should be renewed also.

12 Clean all parts thoroughly using only hydraulic fluid or meths. When ready to reassemble, coat the piston, seals and cylinder bore with clean fluid.

13 Reassembly is a reversal of the dismantling procedure. Make sure that the seals are properly located and that the spring retainer is positively located on the piston spigot. The convex face of the shim, or wave washer (which goes between the back of the valve seal and the valve spacer) should abut the flange in the valve stem.

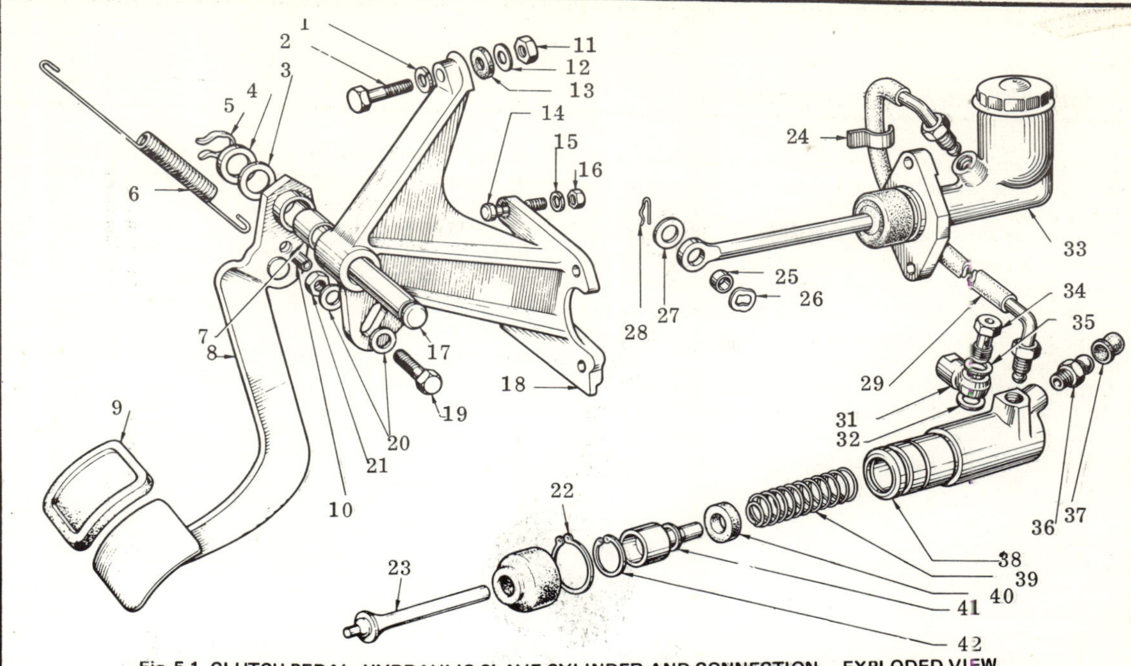

Fig. 5.1. CLUTCH PEDAL, HYDRAULIC SLAVE CYLINDER AND CONNECTION — EXPLODED VIEW

1 Spring washer	12 Washer	23 Push rod	34 Union connector
2 Bracket mounting bolt	13 Insulation	24 Pipe clip	35 Sealing washer
3 Washer	14 Mounting bolt	25 Bush	36 Bleed nipple
4 Spacer	15 Spring washer	26 Clip	37 Dust cover
5 Clip	16 Nut	27 Washer	38 Slave cylinder
6 Return spring	17 Pedal shaft	28 Hair pin clip	39 Spring
7 Bush	18 Mounting bracket	29 Pipe - master cylinder to slave cylinder	40 Piston seal
8 Pedal	19 Bolt		41 Piston
9 Pedal rubber	20 Washers	31 Pipe union	42 Circlip - internal
10 Spring bush	21 Nut	32 Sealing washer	
11 Nut	22 Circlip - external	33 Master cylinder	

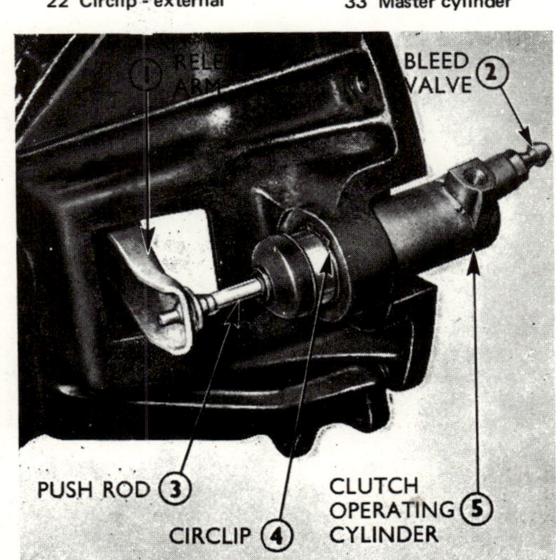

Fig. 5.2. Hydraulic clutch operating cylinder

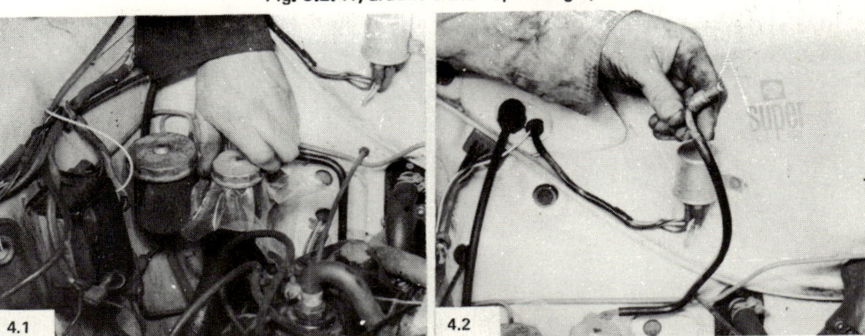

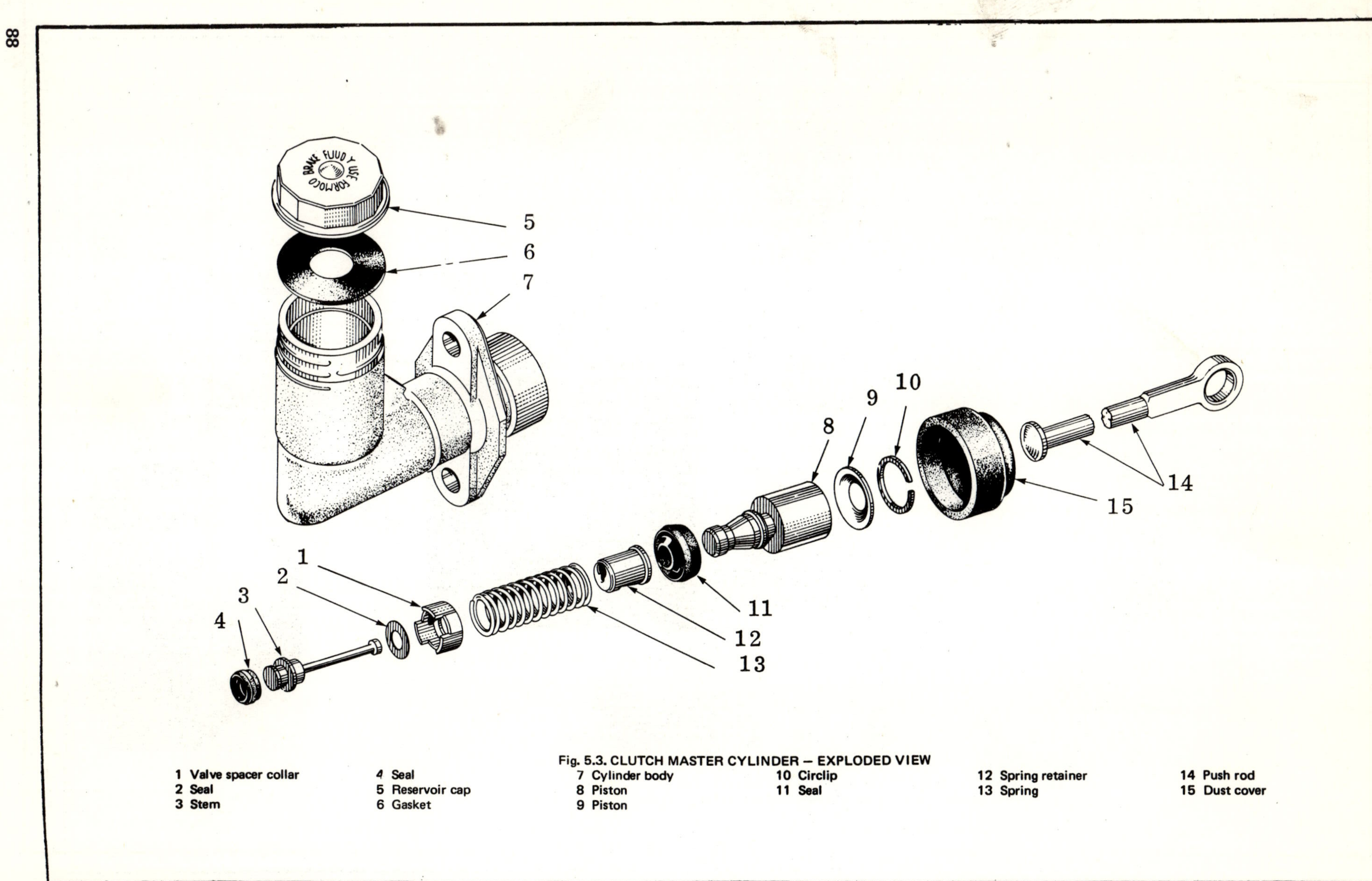

Fig. 5.3. CLUTCH MASTER CYLINDER — EXPLODED VIEW

1 Valve spacer collar	4 Seal	7 Cylinder body	10 Circlip
2 Seal	5 Reservoir cap	8 Piston	11 Seal
3 Stem	6 Gasket	9 Piston	

12 Spring retainer	14 Push rod
13 Spring	15 Dust cover

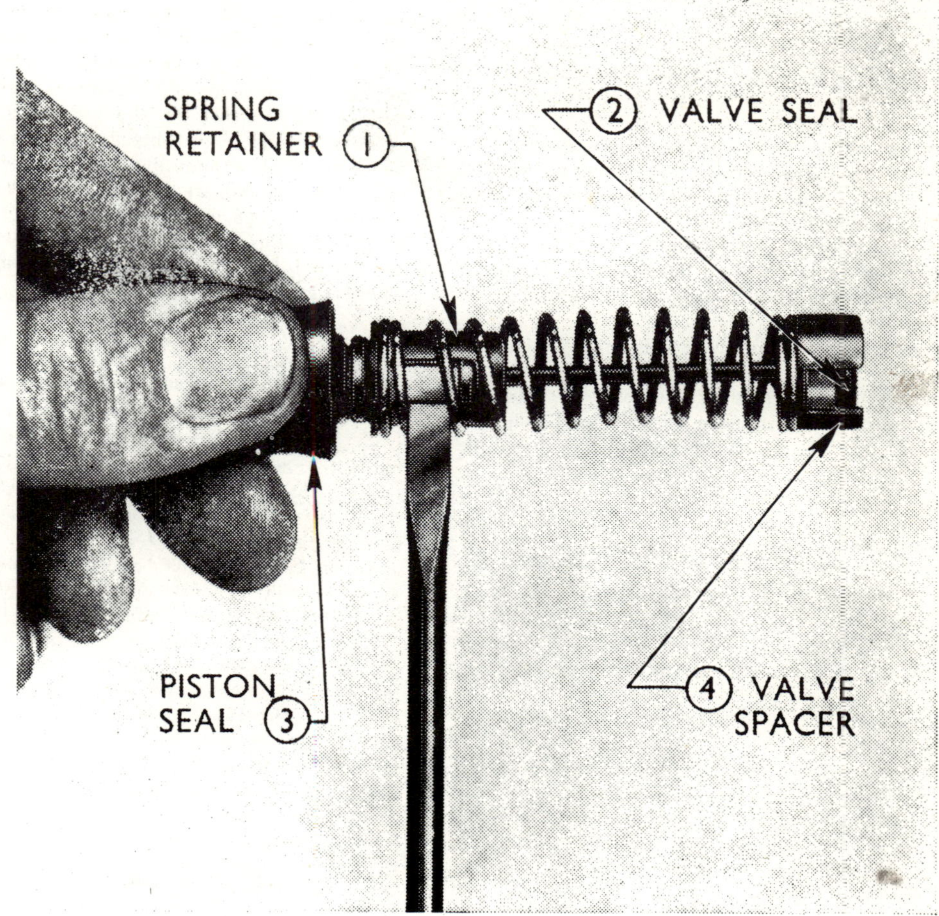

Fig. 5.4. Showing how to lift the locking tab on the master cylinder spring retainer which secures it to the piston spigot.

14 When replacing the piston assembly into the cylinder, care should be taken not to damage, or turn back, the lip of the seal.

15 Replace the assembly to the bulkhead and fit and tighten the two securing nuts and washers. Reconnect the hydraulic pipe union securely but do not overtighten them.

12 Reconnect the pushrod to the clutch pedal, not forgetting the nylon bush in the eye of the pushrod.

13 Refill the master cylinder reservoir with clean hydraulic fluid and bleed the system as described in Section 3.

6. Clutch Pedal - Removal and Replacement

1. It can happen that the clutch (and brake) pedals, which are both of the pendant type, become loose and sloppy in action due to wear on the pivot shaft. They are not adjustable.

2. To remove either of the pedals, first disconnect the pushrod from the master cylinder by undoing the nut and bolt. Do not lose the nylon bush, and if this is worn, causing some of the looseness, replace it.

3. Unhook the retractor spring from the pedal arm.

4. Remove the spring clip from the groove in the end of the pedal shaft, take off the plain and spring washer and slide off the pedal.

5. Examine the bronze bush in the pedal boss and renew it if worn.

6. Reassembly is a reversal of the removal procedure. Ensure the pedal pivot clips are correctly located in their grooves and that the bushes are lubricated with a little engine oil.

7. Clutch Assembly - Removal

1, Remove the gearbox as described in Chapter 6. This is not necessary if the engine has been removed from the car (without the gearbox). If the engine has been removed WITH the gearbox the two must be separated to gain access to the clutch.

2. Mark the position of the clutch assembly relative to the flywheel (photo).

3. Unscrew each of the six retaining bolts half a turn at a time until the pressure is relieved and the pressure plate assembly is loose (photo). The photo shows the assembly being removed with the engine out of the car but the bolts are quite accessible with the engine in the car, once the gearbox has been removed.

4. The pressure plate assembly is then removed from the locating dowels in the flywheel and the friction plate, which is no longer held, will fall free (photo).

8. Clutch - Inspection and Renovation

1. Due to the self adjusting nature of the clutch it is not always easy to decide when to go to the trouble of removing the gearbox in order to check the wear on the friction lining. The only positive indication that something needs doing is when it starts to slip or when squealing noises on engagement indicate that the friction lining has worn down to the rivets. In such instances it can only be hoped that the friction surfaces on the flywheel and pressure plate have not been badly worn or scored. A clutch will wear according to the way in which it is used. Much intentional slipping of the clutch while driving - rather than the correct selection of gears - will accelerate wear. It is best to assume, however, that the friction disc will need renewal every 35,000 miles at least and that it will be WORTH replacing it after

25,000 miles. The maintenance history of the car is obviously very useful in such cases.

2. Examine the surfaces of the pressure plate and flywheel for signs of scoring. If this is only light it may be left, but if very deep the pressure plate unit will have to be renewed. If the flywheel is deeply scored it should be taken off and advice sought from an engineering firm. Provided it may be machined completely across the face the overall balance of engine and flywheel should not be too severely upset. If renewal of the flywheel is necessary the new one will have to be balanced to match the original.

3. The friction plate lining surfaces should be at least $^1/_{32}$ in. (.8 mm) above the rivets, otherwise the disc is not worth putting back. If the lining material shows signs of breaking up or black areas where oil contamination has occurred it should also be renewed. If facilities are readily available for obtaining and fitting new friction pads to the existing disc this may be done but the saving is relatively small compared with obtaining a complete new disc assembly which ensures that the shock absorbing springs and the splined hub are renewed also. The same applies to the pressure plate assembly which cannot be readily dismantled and put back together without specialised riveting tools and balancing equipment. An allowance is usually given for exchange units.

9. Clutch - Replacement

1. If the original pressure plate assembly is being replaced, it should be lined up with the locating marks made before removal. Then hold it with the friction plate supported on a finger (photo). Note that the protruding boss (arrowed) of the friction plate faces the flywheel. (The other side of the plate can be seen in photo 7.4.).

2. Locate the pressure plate over the dowel pegs and replace all the bolts evenly finger tight - or until the friction plate is just held between the pressure plate and flywheel.

3. It is necessary to position the friction plate centrally, accurately, in relation to the pressure plate assembly so that the gearbox input shaft can locate right through the clutch into the spigot bearing recess in the flywheel when the gearbox and engine are put together. With the engine out of the car this can be done quite accurately enough by eye. The photos show the disc off centre (a) and correct (b). The friction plate can be moved about as required by levering the centre boss with a tommy-bar.

4. With the engine in the car it is a little more difficult as it is not possible to line up the centre boss by eye. It is worthwhile, therefore, spending a little time in acquiring pieces of rod/tube of the same diameter as the flywheel bearing bore and the friction disc bore. These can then be placed in the centre boss of the clutch and used to centralise the friction plate.

5. When the friction plate has been satisfactorily centralised the securing nuts should be tightened evenly in a diagonal sequence to the specified torque of 12 to 15 lbs/ft.

6. Check the condition of the clutch actuating mechanism (see Section 10) before replacing the gearbox.

7. Replace the gearbox as described in Chapter 6 and bleed the clutch hydraulic system.

10. Clutch Release Arm, Release Bearing and Associated Links and Springs - Dismantling and Reassembly

1. The operation of the clutch may be noisy, or in extreme cases, not fully effective due to the release bearing, which presses in the centre of the diaphragm spring of the pressure plate, being badly worn. If the wear is extreme it will not

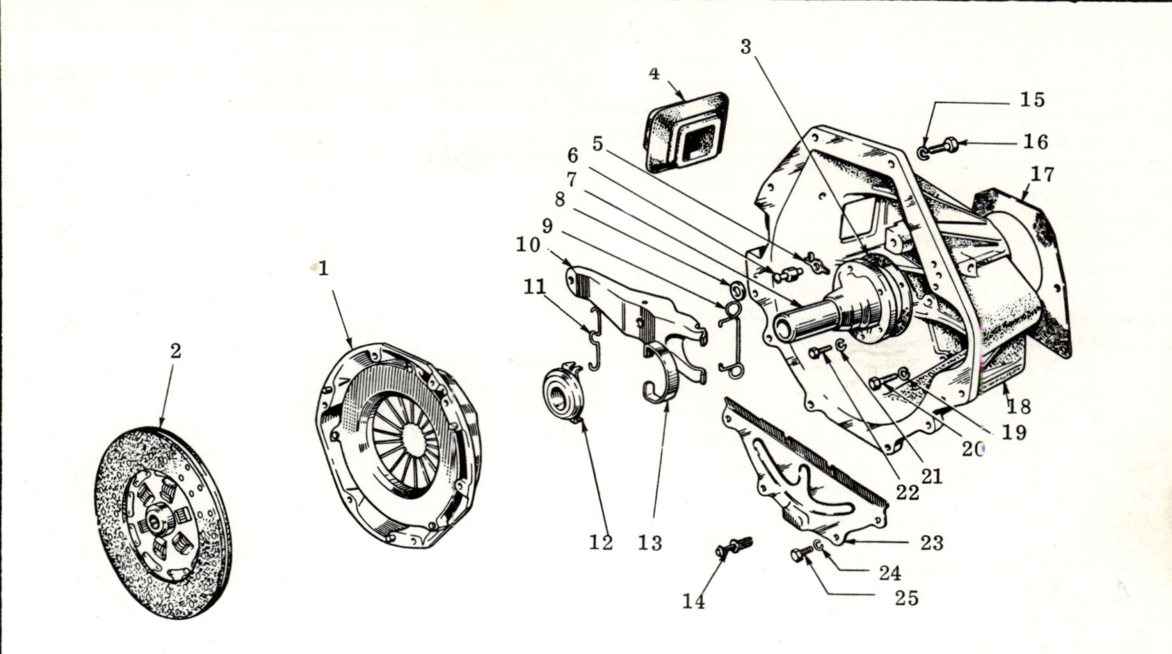

Fig. 5.5. CLUTCH ASSEMBLY AND ACTUATING MECHANISM — EXPLODED DRAWING

1 Cover and pressure plate	8 Bearing
2 Friction disc	9 Retaining spring
3 Gasket	10 Clutch actuating lever
4 Dust cover	11 Retaining clip
5 Pivot	12 Release thrust bearing
6 Lever pin	13 Pivot clip
7 Input shaft bearing retainer	14 Retainer

15 Washer	22 Bolt - bearing retainer
16 Bellhousing bolt	23 Inspection cover
17 Gasket	24 Washer
18 Clutch bellhousing	25 Inspection cover bolt
19 Washers	
20 Bolt - inspection cover	
21 Washer	

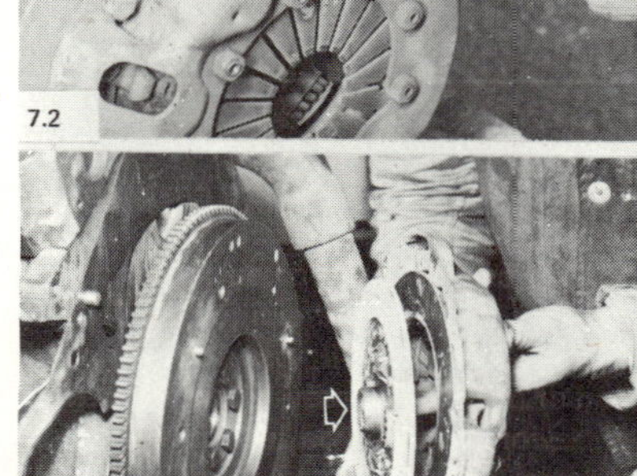

7.2

7.3

7.4

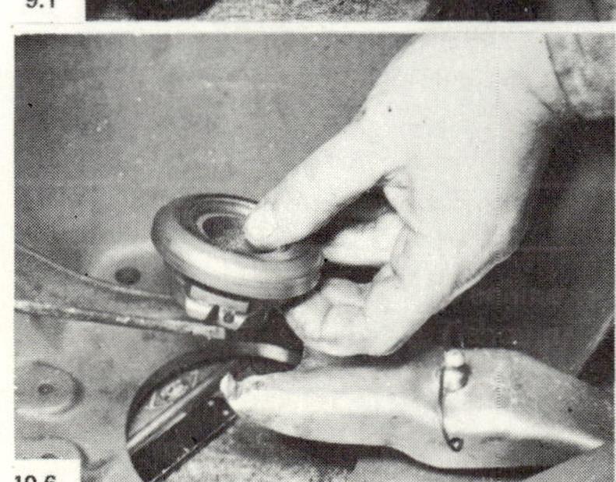

9.1

9.3A

9.3B

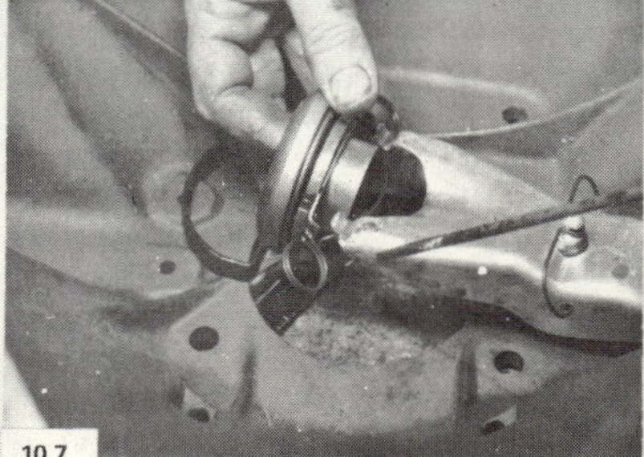

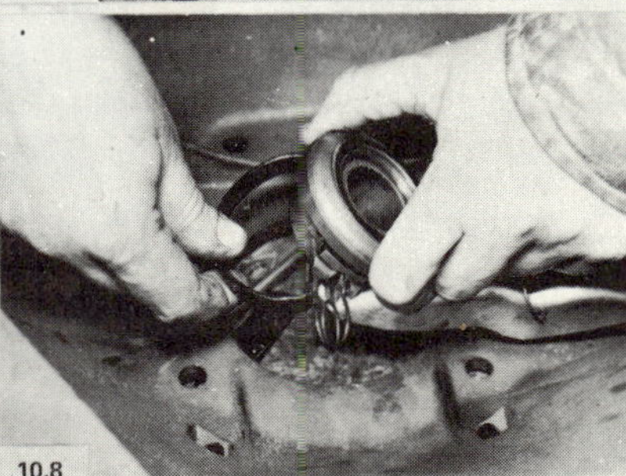

10.6

10.7

10.8

run in the proper plane and consequently the diaphragm centre will not be depressed evenly.

2. To replace the release bearing it will first be necessary to remove the gearbox as described in Section 6.

3. Remove the rubber gaiter from the clutch housing round the release lever.

4. The release arm and bearing assembly may then be removed by taking off the spring holding the arm to the pivot pin and taking the whole assembly away. Do not lose the washer behind the release arm on the pivot pin.

5. The special spring can then be unhooked from the arm and the bearing which also releases the 'D' link.

6. On replacing the bearing ensure the spring holes in the bearing hub face towards the release arm fulcrum pin (photo). (Note that in the photograph the clutch housing is detached from the gearbox and the release lever is in position on the pivot pin. If the gearbox and bellhousing are assembled the release arm would be fitted to the pivot pin last of all when the bearing had been reassembled.)

7. Fix the ends of the bearing spring into the bearing holes and hook the loop of the spring into the notches of the release arm (photo).

8. Lift up the bearing against the tension of the spring and place the 'D' link between the bearing and the arm so that the ends locate in the 'V' grooves in both arm and bearing (photo).

9. The purpose of this ingenious fitting is to ensure that the bearing moves in a straight line fore and aft even though the end of the release lever moves in an arc. The bearing thus remains centred on the diaphragm spring throughout the range of its travel.

10 Refit the release arm so that the bearing locates over the gearbox input shaft and the arm locates over the pivot, not forgetting the backing washer. Refit the securing spring over the pivot and place the rubber boot into the housing over the release arm.

11 Replace the gearbox as described in Chapter 6 and bleed the hydraulic system as described in Section 3 of this Chapter.

11. Clutch Faults - Diagnosis and Remedies

1. Provided the clutch is not intentionally slipped excessively, or the pedal used as a footrest, which may possibly keep the release bearing spinning due to permanent contact with the diaphragm spring, the only malfunction of the clutch one may expect would be due to wear of the friction plate. This normal wear will become obvious when the clutch starts to slip, that is the engine turns normally but the car fails to accelerate properly or slows down on hills.

In such cases the clutch must be examined and repaired immediately. Delay could be costly. For this job the gearbox will need removal.

2. Squealing noises from the clutch (and make sure the squeals ARE from the clutch and not the fan belt or water pump) are most likely to come from a worn out clutch release bearing. The actual efficiency of the clutch may not be immediately affected but if the bearing is not repaired in good time the wear will increase and result in the diaphragm spring being operated unevenly. This will lead to excessive and uneven wear of the clutch disc. Another cause of squealing could be due to the friction plate being worn out or contaminated. In either case the inspection and repair will involve removal of the gearbox.

3. Clutch spin, or failure to disengage completely when the pedal is fully depressed, can be caused by one or more of several reasons. The symptoms are that it is either impossible or the gearbox makes a very noisy 'crunch' when trying to engage bottom gear in the usual manner. First of all check the hydraulic system operation and condition to ensure that the clutch release lever is moving as necessary. If this is satisfactory then the clutch disc is sticking to the pressure plate or flywheel, or the release bearing is so badly worn that it is incapable of moving the diaphragm spring evenly or adequately. This will almost invariably be indicated by squeals and noises when the clutch pedal is operated. Check by stopping the engine, engaging a gear, depressing the clutch and putting on the handbrake. Then try starting the engine. If it refuses to turn the clutch is stuck solid and should be removed and examined. If the engine is started without difficulty try using the clutch in the normal manner. If the drive continues to 'creep' a little when the pedal is fully depressed carry on slipping the clutch for a few moments to try and rub off whatever may have been on the friction surfaces as a temporary measure. If no improvement of any kind results there must be a serious internal defect which will require gearbox removal and examination of the clutch.

4. The other fault which is associated with the clutch but not necessarily caused by any clutch defect is judder in the transmission system, particularly when moving away from rest. Check first that the two front engine mountings are secure and the gearbox mounting also. Then examine the propeller shaft universal joints and the back axle final drive for any signs of wear or excessive backlash as described in Chapters 7 and 8. Check also that the rear axle and suspension are securely attached to each other and the car body frame. If diagnosis indicates that the judder is due to a clutch fault it will be caused by 'snatching' between the friction surfaces - and possibly associated with concurring problems of clutch spin or clutch slip. In this case the gearbox will need removal for further inspection of the clutch.

Chapter 6/Gearbox

Contents

Specifications

No. of gears	4 forward, 1 reverse
Type of gears	Helical constant mesh
Synchromesh	On all forward gears

Main drive gear

No. of teeth	17 (1664 c.c.)
	19 (1996 c.c.)

Laygear

No. of teeth	1664 c.c.		1996 c.c.
	32		30
	28		26
	22		22
	19	Reverse	19
	17		17

Endfloat	.008 to .020 in. (.203 to .508 mm)
Thrust washer thickness	.061 to .063 in. (1.55 to 1.6 mm)
No. of rollers	40
Layshaft diameter	.6818 to .6823 in. (17.32 to 17.33 mm)

First gear

No. of teeth	32
End float	.005 to .010 in. (.127 to .254 mm)

Second gear

No. of teeth	28
End float	.005 to .010 in. (.127 to .254 mm)

Third gear

No. of teeth	21 (1664 c.c.)
	23 (1996 c.c.)
End float	.005 to .016 in. (.127 to .406 mm)

Reverse mainshaft gear (1st & 2nd synchro sleeve)

No. of teeth	40

Reverse idler gear

No. of teeth	22

Speedometer drive gears

Drive No. of teeth	7
Driven No. of teeth	23 (5.60 x 13 tyres 3.777 axle ratio)

Gearbox ratios

	1996 c.c.		1664 c.c.	
	Gearbox	Overall	Gearbox	Overall
1st	2.972:1	11.225:1	3.543:1	13.382:1
2nd	2.010:1	7.592:1	2.396:1	9.050:1
3rd	1.397:1	5.277:1	1.412:1	5.333:1
4th	1.000:1	3.777:1	1.000:1	3.777:1
Reverse	3.324:1	12.555:1	3.963:1	14.968:1

Oil capacity ... ...   1.75 Imp. pints (2.1 U.S. pints, 1 litre)

Torque Wrench Settings

Drain and filler plug ... ...   25 to 30 lbs.ft. (3.46 to 4.15 Kg.m)
Mainshaft assembly retaining nut ... ...   20 to 25 lbs.ft. (2.76 to 3.46 Kg.m)
Clutch bellhousing to gear case bolts ... ...   40 to 45 lbs.ft. (5.53 to 6.22 Kg.m)
Extension housing to gearcase bolts ... ...   20 to 25 lbs.ft (2.76 to 3.46 Kg.m)

1. General Description

The gearbox is a constant mesh four forward and one reverse speed unit with synchromesh fitted on all forward gears.

The input and mainshaft are mounted in the casing on ball bearings and locate with each other on caged needle rollers. The lay shaft is fixed and the lay gear rotates on needle rollers at each end with a thrust washer between the gear and the front and back of the gearbox casing.

With the exception of the reverse mainshaft gear and idler gear all gears are helically cut which gives quiet running.

Gear selection is by three forks on three separate rails and these vary slightly according to the type of selection used.

The design of the gearbox below the selection rails was changed very slightly in September, 1966 but sufficiently to make it very important as far as spare parts are concerned. Careful study of the exploded drawings will reveal a difference in the mainshaft and several shafts whose diameters were also changed.

2. Routine Maintenance

1. The manufacturers recommend that after the first 5,000 miles, when the oil should be drained and replenished, the only requirement is that the level be checked every 5,000 miles. However, in the author's opinion it is worthwhile draining and replenishing the oil every 30,000 miles. To check the oil level remove the square headed plug from the side of the casing. The oil level should be up to the lower edge of the hole so the easiest method of checking is to add oil until it runs out. Make sure the car is standing level when doing the check and do not overfill the gearbox. To drain the oil out run the car until the oil warms up and then remove the square headed plug at the bottom of the gear casing. Refill through the level/filler plug at the side with 1¾ pints of SAE 80 EP oil.

3. Gearbox - Removal and Replacement

1. If the gearbox is to be removed together with the engine the procedure as outlined in Chapter 1, Section 7 should be followed, after the remote control selection mechanism or steering column selection mechanism has been disconnected as described in this section.
2. Disconnect the selector mechanism in one of the three ways now described, according to whichever is fitted.

a) Pre-Sept. '66 models fitted with remote control gear change levers (Fig. 6.1.) will first require the carpets removing in the front of the car. The remote control housing is fitted above the floor of the car under a detachable cover and has to be detached from the gearbox before the gearbox can be lowered.
b) Unscrew the gear lever knob and remove the flexible cover from round the base of the lever. It is a press fit into the steel shroud (photo).
c) The plastic cover over the lever socket housing may be removed but it is not essential at this stage (photo).
d) Next remove the self tapping screws which hold the remote control cover plate to the floor and lift it off over the gear lever (photo).
e) Undo the screws holding the smaller plate and cover round the extension tube (photo).
f) Make sure the gear lever is set in neutral and with the cover slid back undo the four bolts holding the extension housing to the top of the gearbox (photo).
g) Lift off the gear change lever assembly (photo).

3. Remote control units on post-Sept. '66 models (Fig. 6.3) are different in that the mechanism runs directly in the gearbox mainshaft rear extension cover and is under the body floor. It is only therefore necessary to remove the gear lever. This is done by unscrewing the knob and removing the plate holding the rubber boot to the floor after taking away the surrounding carpet. Then unscrew the turret at the base of the lever and it can be lifted out complete.
4. Models fitted with steering column change levers (Fig. 6B and 6C) should have the linkage disconnected by removing the two locating clips which secure the two link rods to the levers on the top and side of the gearbox top cover. By removing the two bolts holding the selector lever relay linkage to the clutch housing the relay linkage can be moved away. Do this after the car has been jacked up as described in the following paragraphs.

5. If the gearbox is to be removed from the car without removing the engine as well the following procedure should be followed. Remote control floor change mechanism may be disconnected first but steering column change mechanisms will be easier to disconnect after the car is jacked up.
6. Drain the oil from the gearbox by removing the lower plug.
7. Disconnect the battery leads to prevent accidental starting of the engine.
8. Remove the carburettor throttle linkage so that any accidental excessive up or down movement of the engine

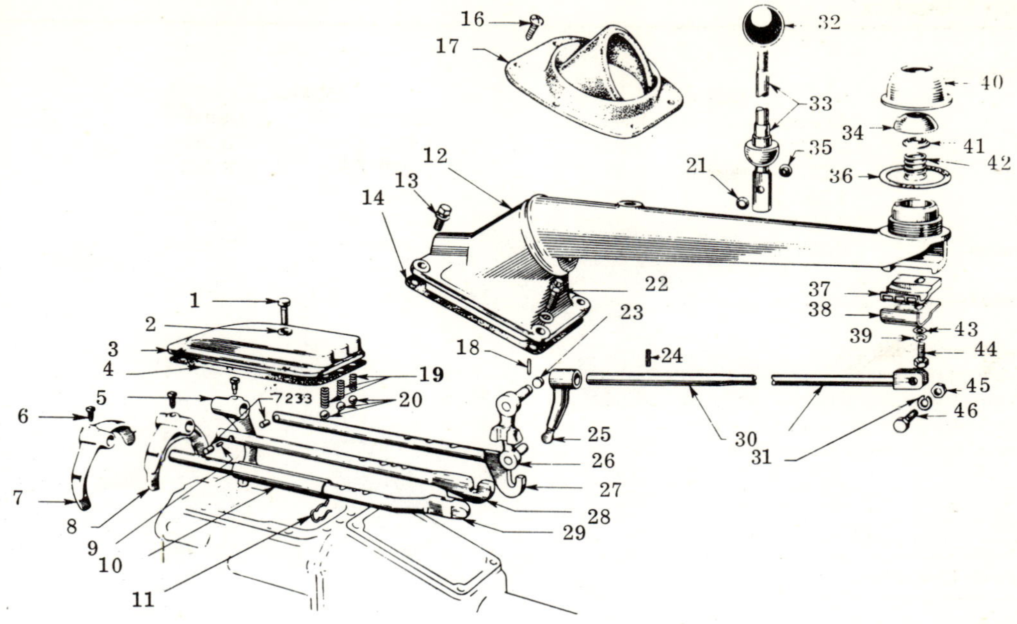

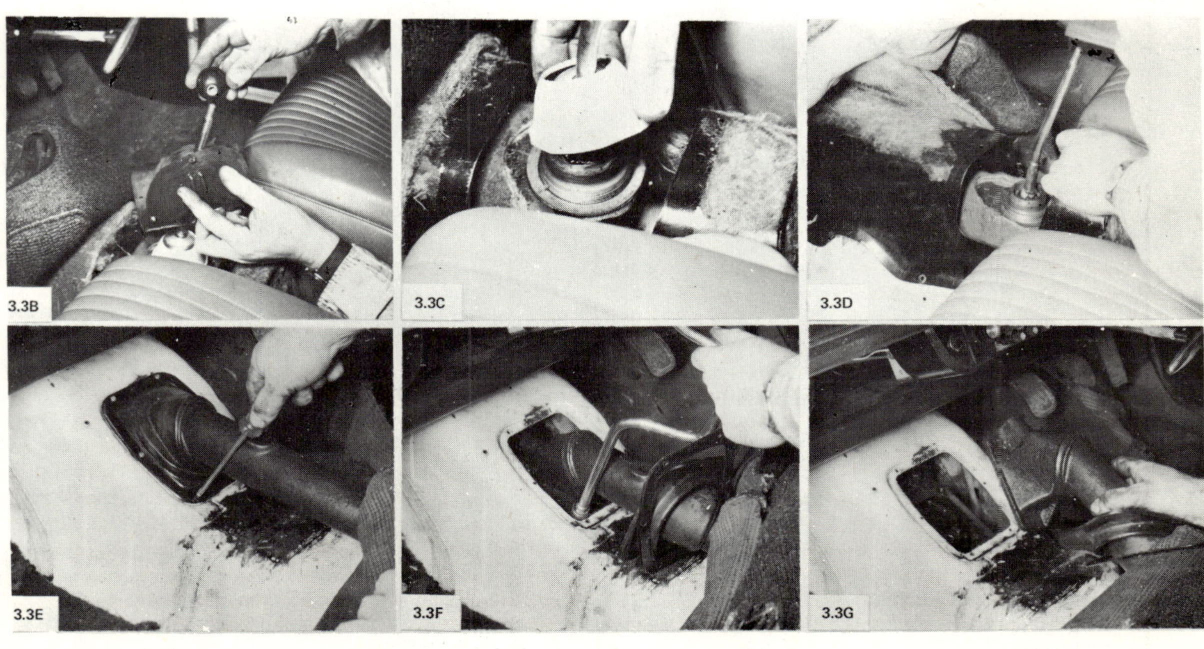

Fig. 6.1. REMOTE CONTROL CHANGE LEVER AND SELECTOR MECHANISM UP TILL SEPT. 1966 — EXPLODED VIEW

1 Top cover bolt	13 Bolt	25 Selector finger	37 Reverse stop plate
2 Washer	14 Gasket	26 Reverse selector lever	38 Clamp plate
3 Top cover	15 Interlock plungers	27 Selector fork rail - reverse	39 Washer
4 Gasket	16 Screw	28 Selector fork rail - 1st/2nd	40 Lever retaining cap
5 Selector fork - reverse	17 Shroud	29 Selector fork rail - 3rd/4th	41 Spring seat
6 Lock screws	18 Pin	30 Connecting rod	42 Spring
7 Selector fork 3rd/4th	19 Detent springs	31 Spring washer	43 Washer
8 Selector fork 1st/2nd	20 Detent balls	32 Lever grip	44 Clamp bolt
9 Interlock pin	21 Cup washers	33 Change lever	45 Nut
10 Sleeve	22 Vented bolt	34 Pressure cup washer	46 Bolt
11 Clip	23 Spacer	35 Cup washer	
12 Extension - change mechanism	24 Spring pin	36 Gasket	

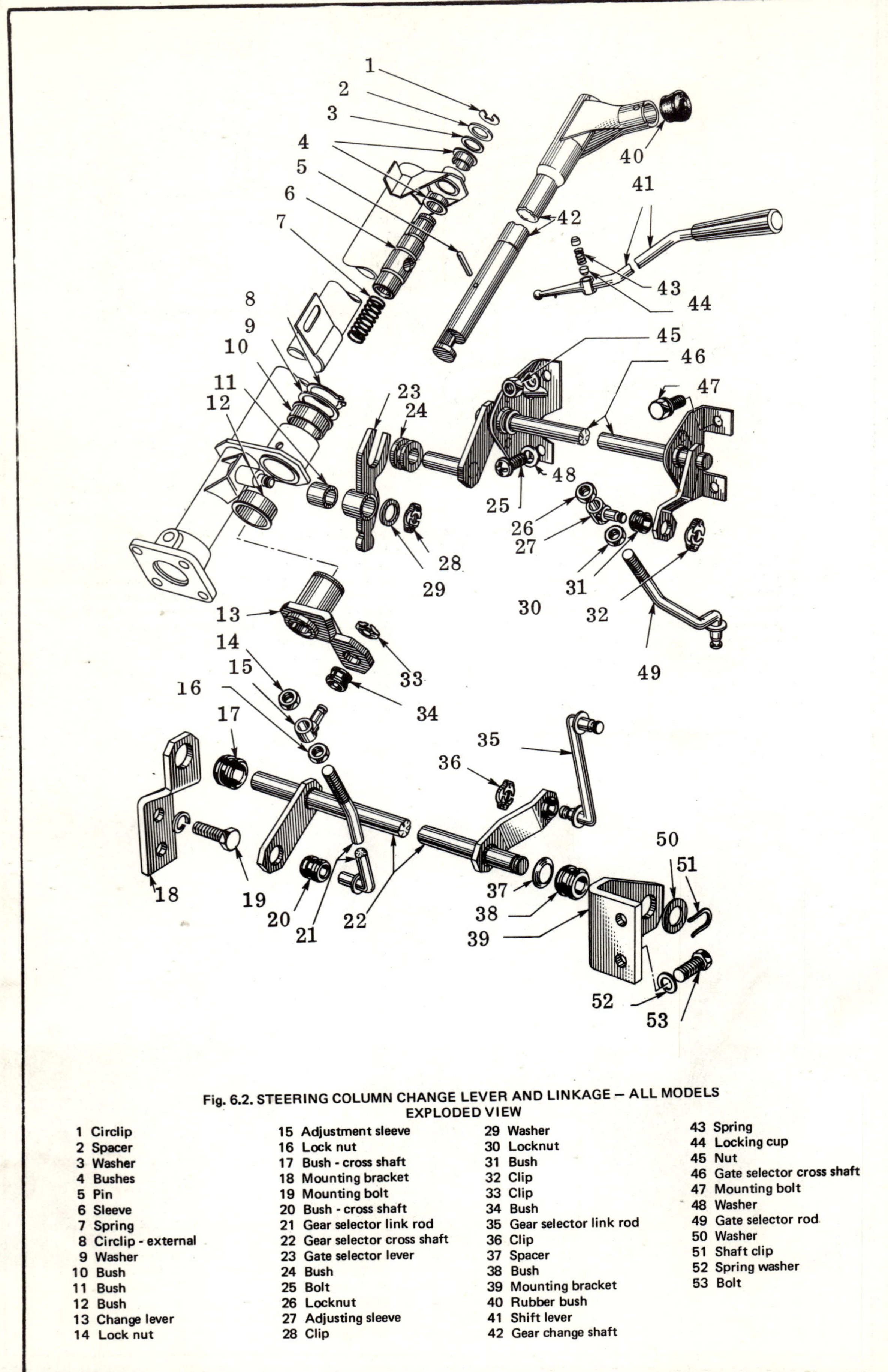

Fig. 6.2. STEERING COLUMN CHANGE LEVER AND LINKAGE — ALL MODELS
EXPLODED VIEW

1 Circlip	15 Adjustment sleeve	29 Washer	43 Spring
2 Spacer	16 Lock nut	30 Locknut	44 Locking cup
3 Washer	17 Bush - cross shaft	31 Bush	45 Nut
4 Bushes	18 Mounting bracket	32 Clip	46 Gate selector cross shaft
5 Pin	19 Mounting bolt	33 Clip	47 Mounting bolt
6 Sleeve	20 Bush - cross shaft	34 Bush	48 Washer
7 Spring	21 Gear selector link rod	35 Gear selector link rod	49 Gate selector rod
8 Circlip - external	22 Gear selector cross shaft	36 Clip	50 Washer
9 Washer	23 Gate selector lever	37 Spacer	51 Shaft clip
10 Bush	24 Bush	38 Bush	52 Spring washer
11 Bush	25 Bolt	39 Mounting bracket	53 Bolt
12 Bush	26 Locknut	40 Rubber bush	
13 Change lever	27 Adjusting sleeve	41 Shift lever	
14 Lock nut	28 Clip	42 Gear change shaft	

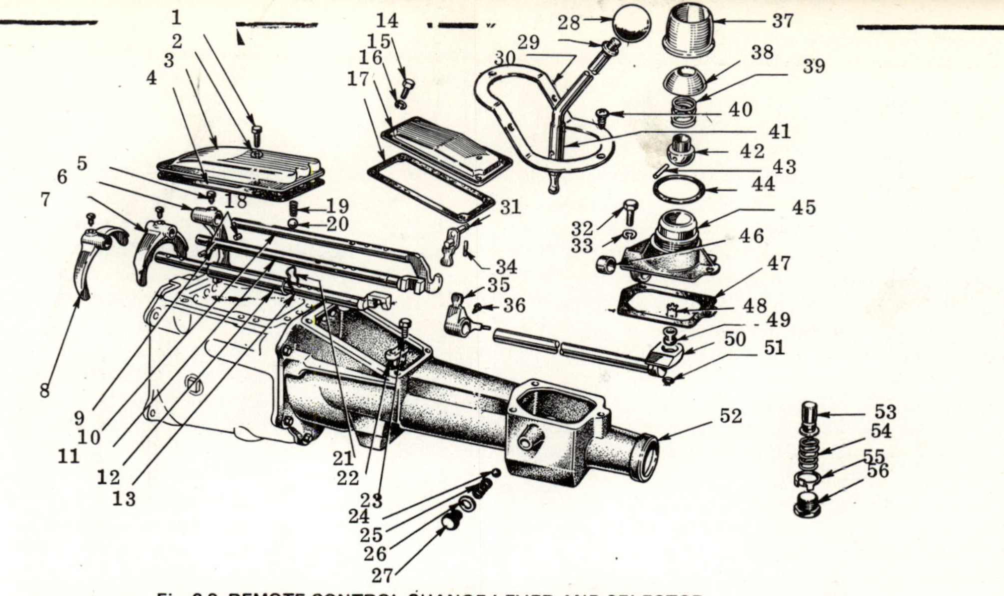

Fig. 6.3. REMOTE CONTROL CHANGE LEVER AND SELECTOR MECHANISM FROM SEPT. 1966 ON — EXPLODED VIEW

1 Top cover bolt	15 Spring washer	29 Locknut	43 Locking pin
2 Spring washer	16 Cover plate	30 Gasket	44 Sealing ring
3 Top cover	17 Gasket	31 Reverse selector finger	45 Lever turret
4 Gasket	18 Interlock plungers	32 Bolt	46 Connecting shaft bush
5 Lock screw	19 Detent spring	33 Spring washer	47 Gasket
6 Reverse selector fork	20 Detent ball	34 Spring pin	48 Bush retainer
7 Selector fork 1st/2nd	21 Clip	35 Forward selector finger	49 Lever bush
8 Selector fork 3rd/4th	22 Shaft bridge bearing	36 Lock screw	50 Connecting shaft
9 Interlock pin	23 Bolt	37 Turrett cover	51 Circlip
10 Selector fork rail reverse	24 Ball	38 Spring thrust cup	52 Extension housing
11 Selector fork rail 1st/2nd	25 Spring	39 Spring	53 Reverse stop plug
12 Sleeve	26 Washer	40 Screw	54 Spring
13 Selector fork rail 3rd/4th	27 Plug	41 Change lever	55 Tab washer
14 Extension housing cover bolt	28 Lever grip	42 Lever pivot ball	56 Plug

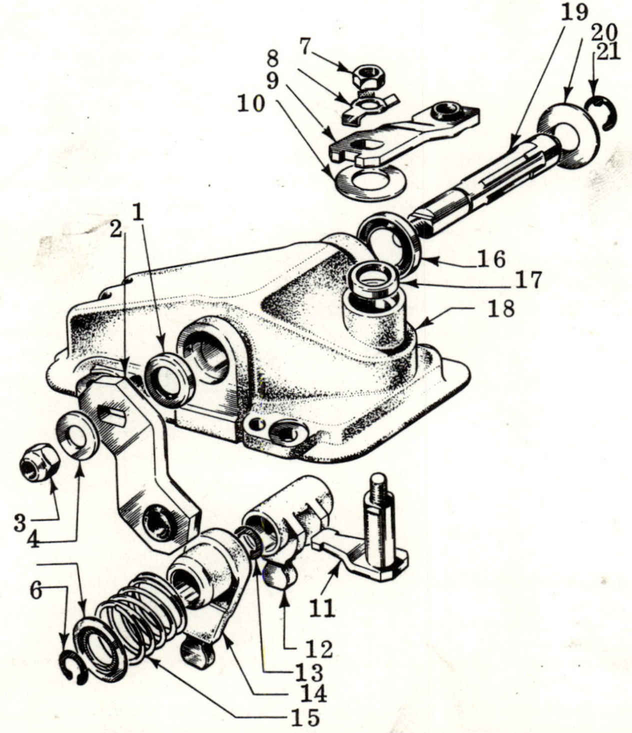

Fig. 6.4. GEARBOX TOP COVER FITTED TO MODELS WITH STEERING COLUMN GEARCHANGE UP UNTIL SEPT. 1966 — EXPLODED VIEW

1 Spacer	7 Nut	13 Circlip	19 Cross shaft
2 Actuating lever	8 Tab washer	14 Reverse gear shift finger	20 Washer
3 Locknut	9 Gate selector arm	15 Spring	21 Circlip
4 Washer	10 Washer	16 Oil seal	
5 Spring seat	11 Gate selector finger	17 Oil seal	
6 Circlip	12 Forward gear shift finger	18 Top cover	

will not strain it.

9. Remove the bolts holding the top (only) of the clutch housing to the engine (Chapter 1/7.).

10 Jack up the car and support it on stands under the side frame members all round. If only two stands are available support and raise the front only. As the gearbox is to be removed from under the car there must be sufficient clearance between the underside and the floor to draw it out. The bellhousing diameter is 18 inches approximately.

11 Remove the propeller shaft as described in Chapter 7/2.

12 Disconnect the steering column gear change linkage as described in paragraph 4.

13 Unhook the handbrake operating cables and return spring from the fulcrum arm which pivots on the cross-member under the gearbox on early models and on the back axle on later models.

14 Remove the clutch hydraulic cylinder as described in Chapter 5/4. It should not be necessary to disconnect the fluid pipe union and it may be left to hang out of the way. Make sure no one depresses the clutch pedal!

15 Disconnect the two branches of the exhaust pipe by slackening the clamps where they join the exhaust manifolds. Then slacken either the forward or rear exhaust pipe clamps so that the front section of the exhaust system may be removed (See Chapter 3/20).

16 Support the engine underneath the sump using a jack and/or blocks so that the load is supported over the area of the sump pan, otherwise it could become dented.

17 Remove the steel sheet dust cover held by four bolts to the lower half of the clutch bellhousing.

18 Remove the two bolts holding the starter motor in position and then move the starter motor forward far enough for the driveshaft to clear the bellhousing.

19 Remove the remaining bolts holding the bellhousing to the engine.

20 Place blocks under the gearbox casing to support it and then remove the four bolts holding the crossmember to the body frame and the single centre bolt holding the cross-member to the gearbox. Remove the crossmember.

21 Undo the bolt holding the speedometer cable clamping clip and withdraw the speedometer cable from the gearbox.

23 The gearbox is now supported on the blocks and its input shaft located into the clutch. It is necessary to draw it back about three inches to disengage the shaft, at the same time supporting its weight, and then lower it (not drop it!) to the ground. Although the unit is not exceptionally heavy (63 lbs. approximately) care should be taken to avoid any accidents. If possible avoid lying underneath it during the removal process.

23 Replacement of the gearbox is a straightforward reversal of the removal procedure. Make sure that:-

a) The clutch friction disc is centred if the clutch has been disturbed (See Chapter 5/9.).

b) The propeller shaft is correctly lined up on reassembly.

c) The speedometer cable is reconnected before the rear support crossmember is replaced.

d) The earthing strap is reconnected to one of the cross-member mounting bolts.

e) On pre-Sept. 1966 models with remote control change one of the four bolts holding the change lever assembly to the top of the gearbox extension housing is drilled to provide a breather orifice. Make sure the orifice is clear.

f) The gearbox is refilled with oil.

g) The gear change linkage connections for steering column lever models are adjusted after reconnection as described in Section 11.

4. Gearbox - Dismantling

1. Bracketed figures in the text refer to Fig. 6.1. until further notice. Before beginning the dismantling make sure that the exterior of the gearbox is thoroughly clean.

2. Remove the clutch release arm assembly as described in Chapter 5/10.

3. Unscrew the four bolts holding the clutch housing to the gearbox casing and remove it. For later models with remote control change turn now to Section 9.

4. Lay the gearbox on its side and remove the top cover (3) by unscrewing the securing bolts. Take care not to lose the three detent springs (19) and balls which locate in the recesses in the gear case.

5. The three selector rails may now be seen and the selector fork fitted to each of them. The selector forks are each held by a square headed screw (6). Cut and remove the locking wire and take out the three locking screws.

6. The three selector rails may now be drawn out through the aperture in the rear extension housing. Note that one rail has a sleeve (10) on it which should be held whilst the rail is being withdrawn. The centre rail has a hole at one end in which is located a floating pin (9). This should not be lost. On later models there is a clip also (11) on the rail with the sleeve.

7. When the three rails are out remove the other two locking plungers (15) from the internal recesses where the front ends of the outer selector rails are located.

8. The three selector forks (5, 7, 8) may next be lifted out.

9. Gearboxes fitted with steering column change have a completely different top cover plate and these are either of two types as shown in Figs. 6.4. and 6.5.

10 They are removed by unscrewing the four locating bolts and care should be taken not to lose the detent springs and balls which will be released as with the other type of cover.

11 The selector rails are also quite different and bracketed numbers in the text will refer from here on to Fig. 6.5. First remove the cover plate (55) on the mainshaft extension by removing the four bolts (53).

12 Locking wire holds the bolts which secure the selector forks to the rails and hollow dowel pins (51) locate the selector gates **(48 and 52)** to the rails. This wire should be cut and removed. The square headed bolts can be removed, and with a long nosed pin punch the dowel pins may be driven through the gear gates. If the gearbox is not being completely dismantled these must be kept from dropping into the gearbox by hooking them at the lower end on a piece of stiff wire before they are completely driven out.

13 The selector rails may now be drawn out to the rear and care should be taken to note how the gates, selector forks and sleeve are arranged on each one. The centre rail has a floating interlock pin at the front end which should be removed and kept safely and the reverse gear rail (right hand) has a flat machined at the front end.

14 There are interlock plungers located in the front recesses of the two outer rails and these should be shaken out for safe keeping.

15 Details of dismantling, reassembly and adjusting the gearbox top covers for the two types of steering column change mechanism are dealt with in Sections 10 and 11. The dismantling of the gearbox once the selectors have been removed is almost identical for all models.

16 Undo the bolts (29) securing the mainshaft extension housing (57) to the gear casing and draw it off. The speedometer driver gear may be tapped out of the casing from the inside at this point if necessary.

17 The bearing cover (19) over the input shaft bearing may

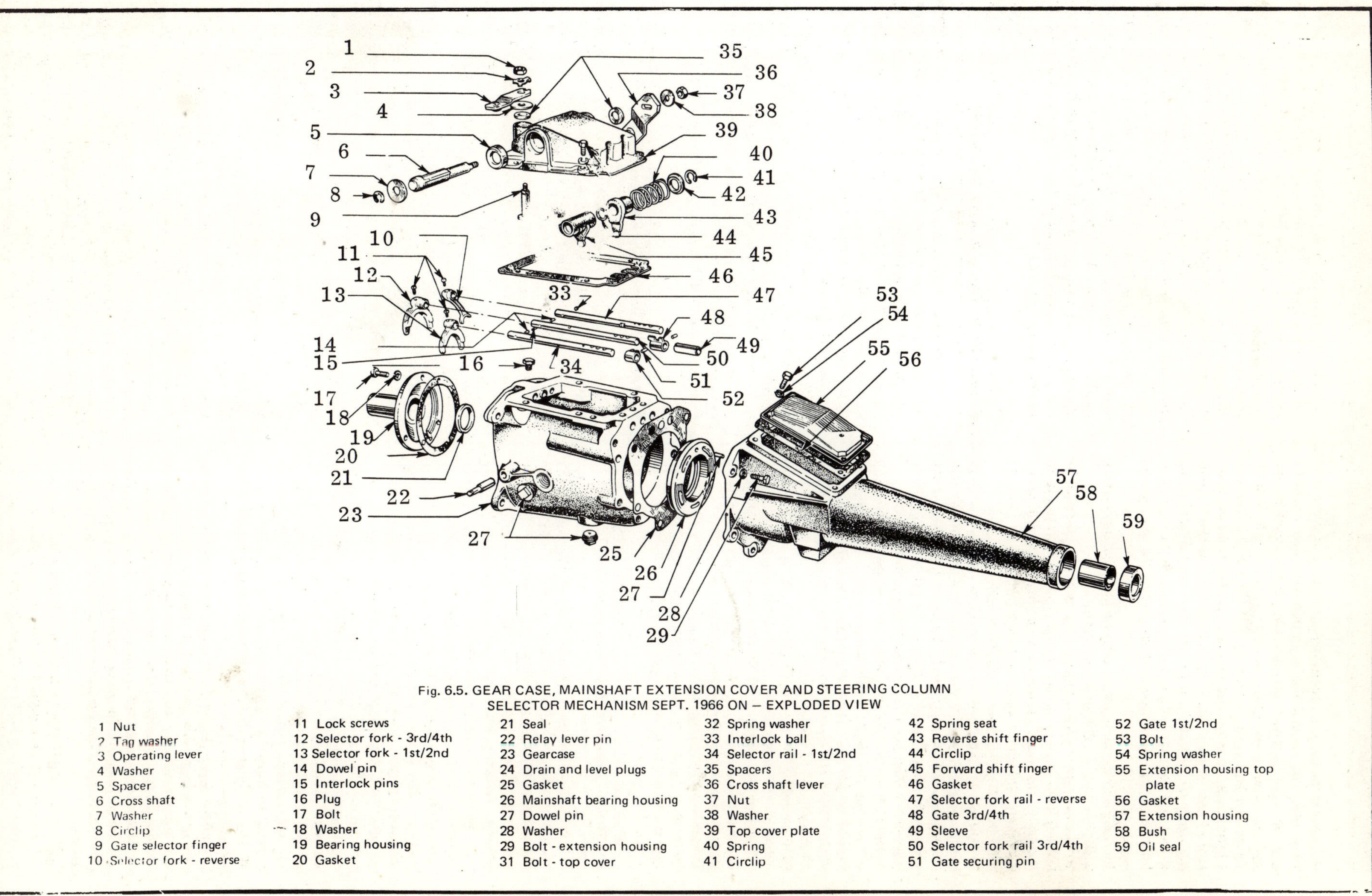

Fig. 6.5. GEAR CASE, MAINSHAFT EXTENSION COVER AND STEERING COLUMN
SELECTOR MECHANISM SEPT. 1966 ON — EXPLODED VIEW

1 Nut	11 Lock screws	21 Seal
2 Tag washer	12 Selector fork - 3rd/4th	22 Relay lever pin
3 Operating lever	13 Selector fork - 1st/2nd	23 Gearcase
4 Washer	14 Dowel pin	24 Drain and level plugs
5 Spacer	15 Interlock pins	25 Gasket
6 Cross shaft	16 Plug	26 Mainshaft bearing housing
7 Washer	17 Bolt	27 Dowel pin
8 Circlip	18 Washer	28 Washer
9 Gate selector finger	19 Bearing housing	29 Bolt - extension housing
10 Selector fork - reverse	20 Gasket	31 Bolt - top cover

32 Spring washer	42 Spring seat	52 Gate 1st/2nd
33 Interlock ball	43 Reverse shift finger	53 Bolt
34 Selector rail - 1st/2nd	44 Circlip	54 Spring washer
35 Spacers	45 Forward shift finger	55 Extension housing top
36 Cross shaft lever	46 Gasket	plate
37 Nut	47 Selector fork rail - reverse	56 Gasket
38 Washer	48 Gate 3rd/4th	57 Extension housing
39 Top cover plate	49 Sleeve	58 Bush
40 Spring	50 Selector fork rail 3rd/4th	59 Oil seal
41 Circlip	51 Gate securing pin	

also now be removed by removing the three securing bolts.

18 In order to remove the mainshaft assembly from the gearbox it is necessary to first lower the layshaft in the gearbox so that the gears on the mainshaft will clear it. To do this find a piece of rod about ¼ inch in diameter and a little longer than the gearbox casing. Then from the front face of the gearbox use a brass drift to drive the layshaft rearwards far enough for it to clear the casing. Then use the ¼ inch rod to push it right out so that when the layshaft is fully removed the laygear will drop onto the smaller rod now holding it.

19 There will possibly be a clatter of thrust washers falling when this occurs but it does not matter.

20 The mainshaft assembly may now be withdrawn with its bearing from the rear of the casing. Take care not to knock the gears. The caged needle roller bearing on the end of the mainshaft will either come out with it or can be removed from the connector bore in the input shaft.

21 Turning to the front of the gearbox remove the large circlip which locates in the external diameter of the ball bearing race of the input shaft. By tapping the end of the shaft with a soft headed hammer or block of wood the bearing and shaft can be removed from inside the casing.

22 Next lift up the lay gear from the bottom of the casing and retrieve the thrust washers and needle rollers from the ends of the lay gear. There should be a total of forty needle rollers. They are located by a washer on each side of the set at each end of the lay gear.

23 If necessary the reverse idler gear may be removed. To withdraw the shaft select a $^{5}/_{16}$ in. bolt and put a nut, flat washer and spacer on it (in that order), screw the bolt into the threaded hole in the end of the shaft and tighten down the nut to withdraw it.

24 The gearbox is now fully stripped. Examine the casing for signs of metallic deposits which could give a clue to any wear and then thoroughly clean it out.

5. Gearbox - Examination of Main Assemblies

1. The gearbox has been stripped, presumably, for reasons of wear resulting in ineffective synchromesh, excessive noise and vibration or failure to stay in some selected gear. The main cause of most gearbox ailments is failure of the ball bearings on the input or mainshaft and wear on the synchro rings, both the core surfaces and dogs. The nose of the mainshaft which runs in the needle roller bearing in the input shaft is also vulnerable and subject to wear on the pre-Sept. 1966 models. This can prove very expensive as the mainshaft would need replacement and this represents between 15% - 20% of the total cost of a new gearbox.

2. Examine the teeth of all gears for signs of uneven or excessive wear and of course chipping. If a gear on the mainshaft needs replacement check that the corresponding lay gear is not equally damaged. If it is the whole lay gear may need replacing also.

3. All gears should be a good running fit on the shaft with no signs of rocking. The hubs should not be a sloppy fit on the splines.

4. Selector forks should be examined for signs of wear or ridging on the faces which run in the hub grooves.

5. The ball bearings may not be very obviously worn but if one has gone to the trouble of dismantling the gearbox it would be short sighted not to renew them. The same applies to the four synchroniser rings although for these the mainshaft has to be completely dismantled for the new ones to be fitted.

6. The input shaft bearing retainer is fitted with an oil seal and this should be removed if there are any signs that oil has leaked past it into the clutch housing or, of course, if it

is obviously damaged. The mainshaft rear extension has an oil seal at the rear and a plain bush behind it in which the mainshaft runs. If either of these is worn oil will have leaked out. The bush requires careful fitting with special tools so it would be advisable to get both bush and seal renewed (never renew just one) by a local Ford agent.

7. Before finally deciding to dismantle the mainshaft and replace parts it is advisable to make enquiries regarding parts availability and cost and also to consider the acquisition of a new or used complete gearbox. There is a lot to be said for getting a unit from a breaker in the first place and fitting it. The box removed from the car can then be overhauled at leisure if necessary. Remember also that some Cortina models were fitted with identical gearboxes (below the selector mechanism) so it should not be very difficult to find what is required.

6. Input Shaft - Dismantling and Reassembly

1. All bracketed figures in the text in subsequent sections refer to Fig. 6.6 and 6.7. The only item to dismantle is the bearing if it needs replacement. On pre-1966 models it is simply a question of driving it off the shaft with a soft headed hammer (photo).

2. On later models a circlip round the shaft has to be removed first (photo).

3. When fitting a new bearing make sure that the circlip groove in the outer race faces away from the gear. This can be seen in the photo 6:1.

4. To drive the bearing on to the shaft support the INNER race on the jaws of a vice and tap the shaft with a soft hammer (photo).

5. Replace the small bearing circlip if there is one.

7. Mainshaft - Dismantling and Reassembly

1. Remove the caged roller bearing (3) and the synchro cone (14) from the nose of the mainshaft if not already off and then clamp the shaft horizontal between two wooden blocks in a vice.

2. Remove the circlip (13) which holds the 3rd/4th gear hub assembly (15) in position. The hub must then be drawn off the splines with care to prevent the whole hub assembly flying apart. If any leverage is required apply it behind the centre hub of the assembly.

3. Remove the 2nd synchro ring (17) and draw off third gear (18). All the rest has to come off the other end of the shaft because the shoulder has now been reached.

4. With the shaft still held as before in the vice bend back the tab on the large nut lockwasher and undo the nut. Then take the shaft out of the vice and remove the nut, washer, speedometer drive gear, drive gear locating ball and spacer collar (photo).

5. To remove the bearing housing and bearing, if it is particularly tight, grip the bearing retainer in the vice and tap the shaft out with a soft hammer.

6. Depending on whether the gearbox is an early or late model the next item to come off is either the splined thrust collar (37) or the separate hub boss (38) of first gear.

7. First gear (21) is then removed followed by the synchroniser ring (22).

8. On later models a circlip (36) has to be removed next and then the first/second gear synchroniser hub assembly (20) can be removed. The same care should be taken, if the centre hub is tight on the splines, to avoid pulling the whole assembly to pieces by applying any necessary leverage to the centre boss only. On mainshafts without a circlip fitted there is a steel ball in the shaft which locates the first gear

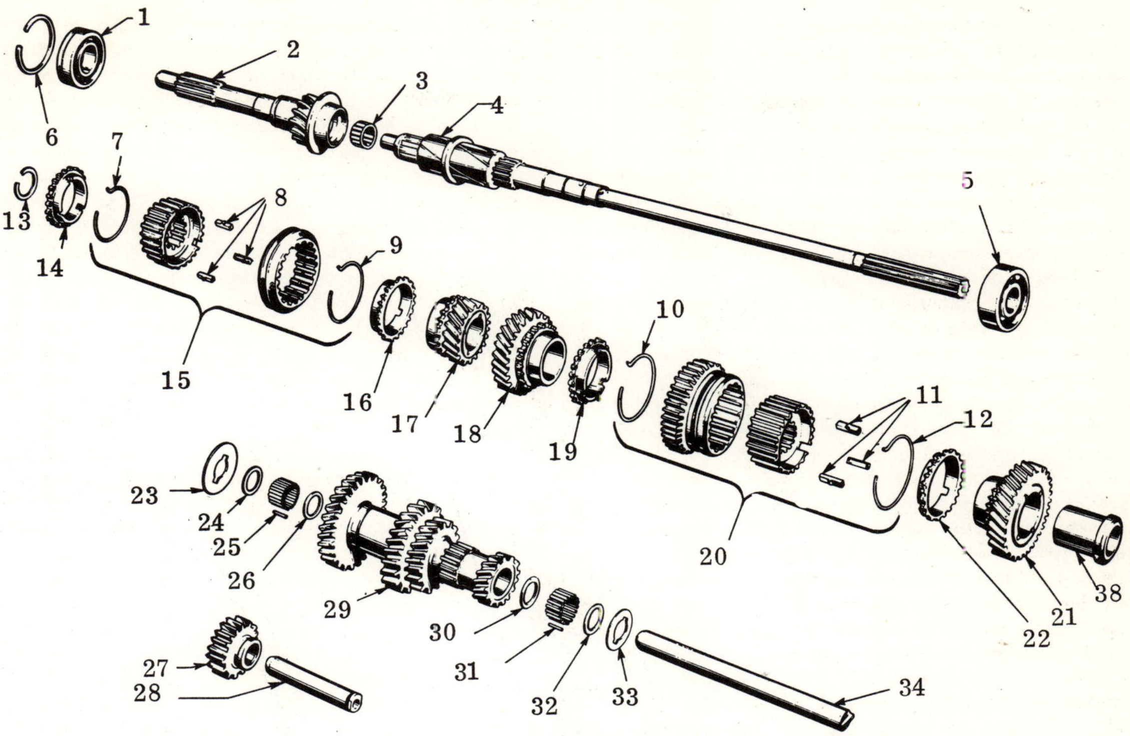

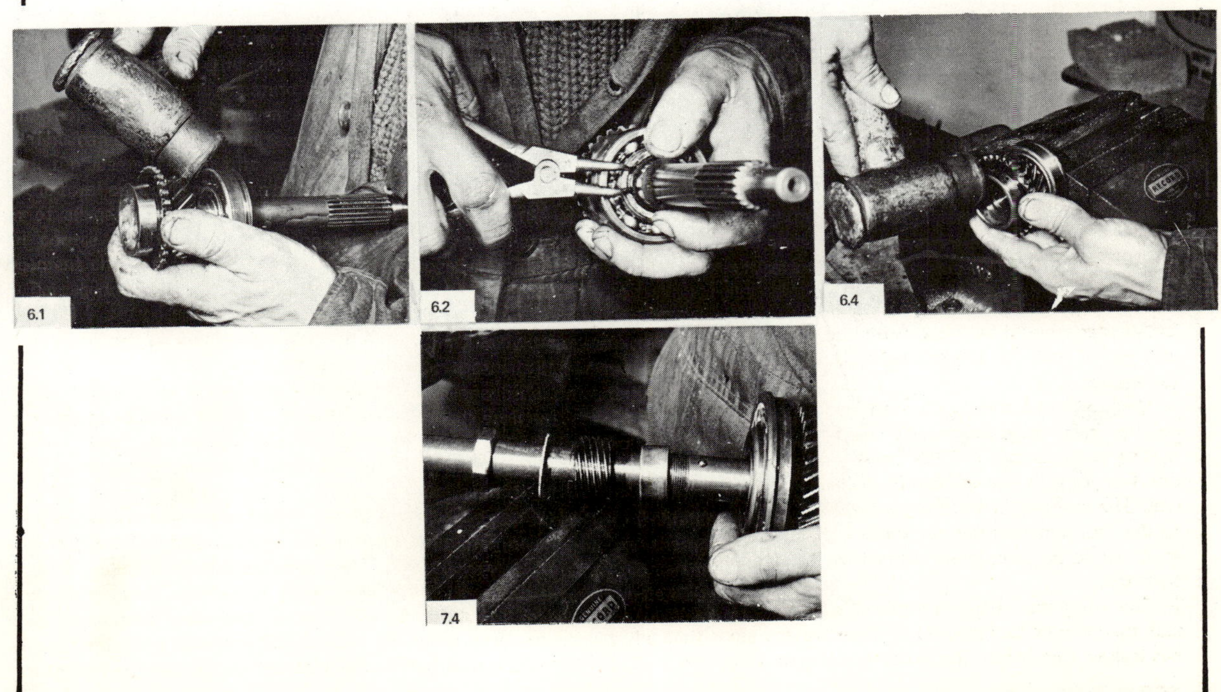

Fig. 6.6. GEARBOX — INPUT SHAFT, MAINSHAFT AND LAYGEAR ASSEMBLIES UP TO SEPT. 1966 — EXPLODED VIEW

1 Bearing - input shaft	10 Spring clip	19 Synchro cone	28 Idler pinion shaft
2 Input shaft	11 Blocker bars	20 Hub assembly 1st/2nd gears	29 Lay gear cluster
3 Roller bearing	12 Spring clip	21 1st gear	30 Spacer ring
4 Main shaft	13 Circlip	22 Synchro cone	31 Needle rollers
5 Bearing main shaft	14 Synchro cone	23 Thrust washer - front	32 Spacer ring
6 Circlip	15 Hub assembly 3rd/4th gears	24 Spacer ring	33 Thrust washer - rear
7 Spring clip	16 Synchro cone	25 Needle rollers	34 Lay shaft
8 Blocker bars	17 3rd gear	26 Spacer ring	38 1st gear boss
9 Spring clip	18 2nd gear	27 Reverse idler pinion	

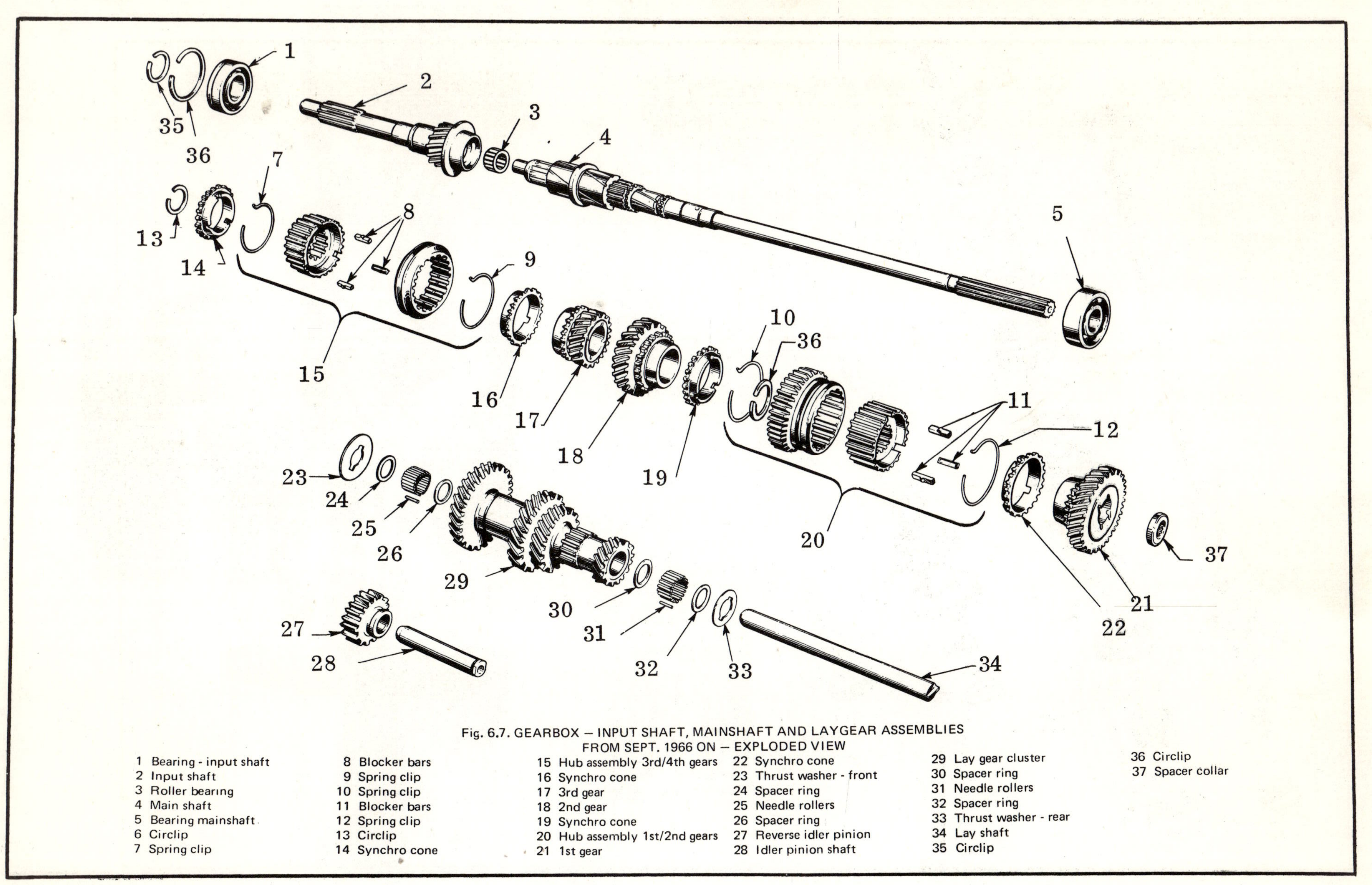

Fig. 6.7. GEARBOX — INPUT SHAFT, MAINSHAFT AND LAYGEAR ASSEMBLIES
FROM SEPT. 1966 ON — EXPLODED VIEW

1 Bearing - input shaft	8 Blocker bars	15 Hub assembly 3rd/4th gears	22 Synchro cone	29 Lay gear cluster	36 Circlip
2 Input shaft	9 Spring clip	16 Synchro cone	23 Thrust washer - front	30 Spacer ring	37 Spacer collar
3 Roller bearing	10 Spring clip	17 3rd gear	24 Spacer ring	31 Needle rollers	
4 Main shaft	11 Blocker bars	18 2nd gear	25 Needle rollers	32 Spacer ring	
5 Bearing mainshaft	12 Spring clip	19 Synchro cone	26 Spacer ring	33 Thrust washer - rear	
6 Circlip	13 Circlip	20 Hub assembly 1st/2nd gears	27 Reverse idler pinion	34 Lay shaft	
7 Spring clip	14 Synchro cone	21 1st gear	28 Idler pinion shaft	35 Circlip	

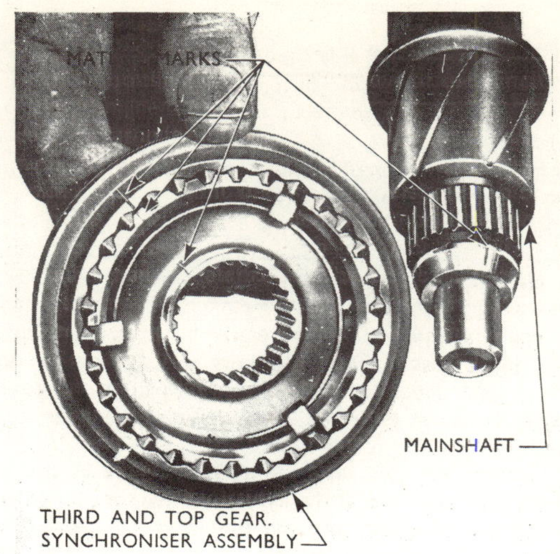

Fig. 6.8. Showing the mating marks on the inner and outer hub sections and the mainshaft

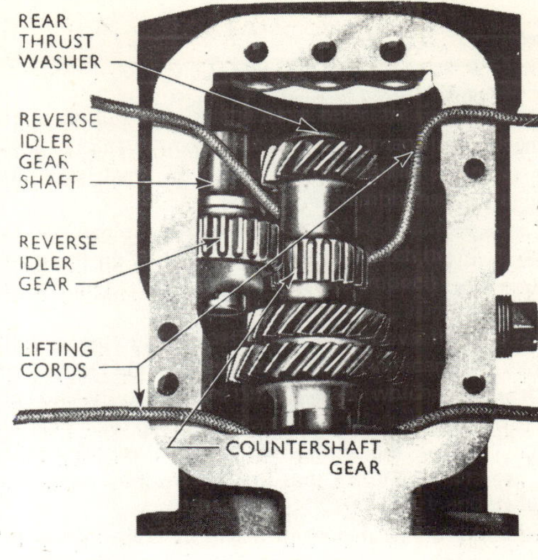

Fig. 6.9. Showing the gearbox with the laygear and reverse idler gear in position

Fig. 6.10. Replacing and locating the mainshaft with the input shaft

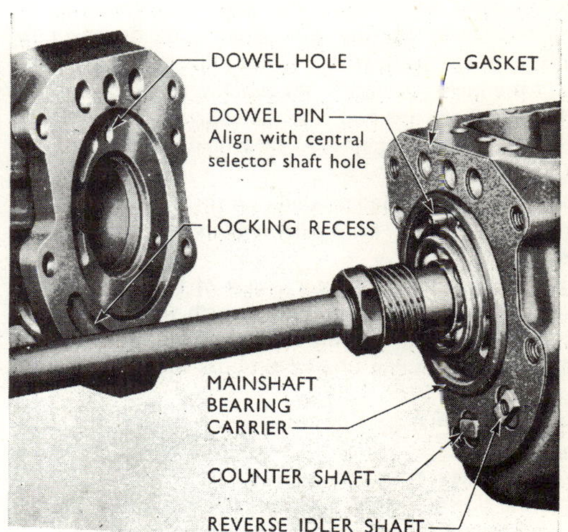

Fig.6.11. Line up the gearbox components for replacement of the rear extension housing

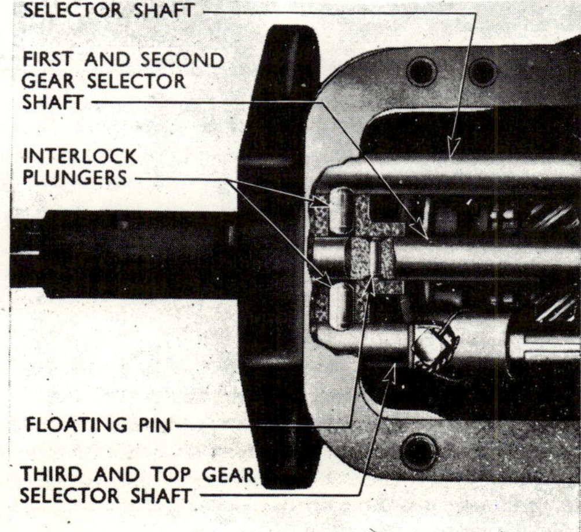

Fig. 6.12. Cutaway view of selector rail interlock plungers

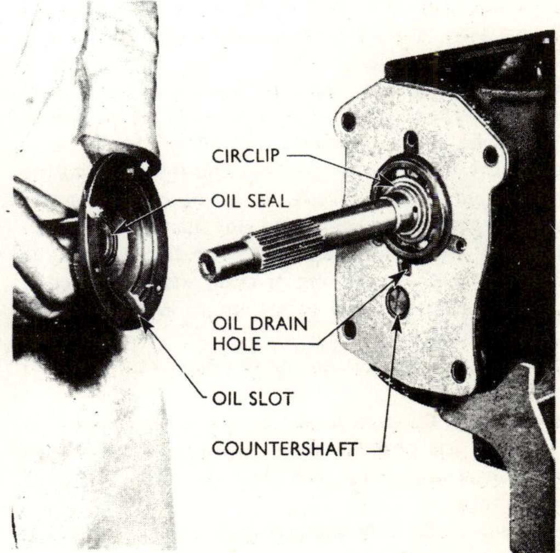

Fig. 6.13. Input shaft bearing retainer being fitted showing line up of oil drain hole and slot

hub sleeve

9. Second gear is removed last and the shaft is then completely dismantled.

10 If a new hub assembly is to be fitted it will need dismantling to clean all the preservative off. This is done simply by lifting out the wire circlip on each side and pushing out the centre hub.

11 To reassemble a hub fit the three blocker bars to the centre hub in the slots and line up the marks on the inner and outer sections of the hub before assembling them (Fig. 6.8.).

12 The two spring clips can only go in one way - that is with the hook facing inward into the locating hole. On one side of the hub therefore the spring runs clockwise to the end and on the other side anti-clockwise. This is worth remembering if by any chance the springs from two dismantled hubs should get mixed. Ensure that they fit securely under the three blocker bars.

13 Reassembly of the mainshaft begins by replacing second gear over the rear (the long clear end) of the shaft with the teeth towards the shoulder. Of the three helical cut gears on the mainshaft, second gear is the middle one of them in outside diameter size. Follow this with a synchro ring to fit over the taper on the gear. Then slide on the hub assembly with the teeth first. The hub blocker bars should engage in the three cut-outs in the synchro ring (photo).

14 Note that there are two sizes of synchro ring - two of each - in the box and they only fit snugly on their correct gears (photo).

15 After the hub is located properly on the shaft replace the circlip on later models. For earlier models fit the ball in the dimple (photo).

16 Next take up first gear (the largest of the three helical cut gears) and select a synchro ring which fits the tapered boss of the gear. Then put the synchro ring on to the shaft and into the hub, lining up the cut-outs with the blocker bars (photo).

17 Then replace first gear onto the shaft (photo) and into the synchro ring.

18 The hub is next fitted (on early models - photo). Make sure that the slot in the hub goes over the ball in the shaft.

19 On later models fit the splined spacer collar (photo).

20 The main bearing housing is next placed on the shaft (photo). The peripheral flange on the housing and the locating dowel pins are on the side away from the gear.

21 The bearing will be a tight fit so it may be supported against vice jaws and the shaft tapped home with a soft headed hammer (photo).

22 With the bearing fully home fit the spacer collar, ball and speedometer drive gear in that order, locating the groove in the speedometer drive gear over the ball (photo).

23 Replace the large washer and nut and tighten it to the specified torque of 20-25 lbs.ft. As a ring or open ended spanner will have to be used and not many owners will have a torque wrench for these the correct tightness will be obtained satisfactorily if a ring or open ended spanner of the correct size is tightened to maximum WITHOUT any additional leverage.

24 Finally lock the washer over on to a flat of the nut with a drift (photo).

25 The rear end of the shaft is now complete. Turning to the front, fit third gear onto the shaft. Third is the smallest of the three helical gears. The cone piece should face towards the front (photo).

26 Fit a synchro ring over the gear cone and then the hub assembly (photo).

27 The hub assembly should be replaced so that the mating marks on the shaft spline and hub centre are lined up (Fig. 6.8 refers). Also the longer boss of the centre hub faces the end of the shaft (photo).

28 The hub will probably be a tight fit on the splines so if it has to be driven on select a piece of pipe that will go over the shaft and use this to drive on the centre of the hub (photo).

29 Finally, fit the circlip into the groove in the shaft and the mainshaft assembly is complete.

8. Gearbox - Reassembly

1. The first thing to do on reassembly is prepare the lay gear. Put a spacer ring in the bore at each end and then smear thick grease in the bores and position the twenty needle rollers at each end. Then replace the outer spacer rings.

2. Position the two lay gear thrust washers in the gear casing, the larger one at the front. The two tongues on each washer should locate into the dimples in the casing. Then very carefully lower the lay gear into the gearbox and rest it at the bottom. The largest gear on the lay gear goes towards the front. The thrust washers must not be displaced while this is being done.

3. It is a good idea to lower the lay gear on two loops of string as this will enable it to be lifted into position easily when required.

4. Replace the reverse idler gear and shaft next so that the groove in the gear wheel is nearest the rear of the gearbox. The shaft should be tapped home with the plain end going in first.

5. The gearbox should now look as shown in Fig. 6.9.

6. The input shaft assembly should now be placed into position from the inside of the gearbox (photo). Tap the bearing into the casing and then refit the large circlip into the outside of the bearing against the front of the casing.

7. The mainshaft assembly may now be replaced from the rear of the gearbox. The caged needle roller bearing should be fitted over the nose of the mainshaft and then the nose located in the centre bore of the input shaft (Fig. 6.10.).

8. The lay gear is now lifted into position and the dummy shaft used in dismantling is put in to support it. If the shaft is only slightly smaller than the lay shaft proper so much the better. It should also be cut to exactly the same length as the lay shaft. Lift the lay gear on the strings and replace the dummy shaft, taking care not to disturb the thrust washers or needle rollers.

9. Using the lay shaft itself as a drift tap it in behind the dummy shaft from the rear end of the gearbox casing, plain end first. Do not let the dummy shaft get ahead of the lay shaft otherwise the needle rollers will drop out into the space between the two.

10 The gearbox rear extension may be fitted next. Position the dowel pin on the bearing housing in line with the centre selector rail hole and rotate the lay shaft and idler gear shaft so that the flats on the end line up with the locking recess in the extension housing (Fig. 6.11).

11 Fit a new gasket and replace the extension housing (photo A) locating the dowel pin in its recess, replacing the bolts and washers and tightening them to a torque of 20 to 25 lbs.ft. (photo B). Remember to fit the earthing strap to the bottom left hand bolt.

12 The input shaft bearing retainer cap should next be fitted. As the shaft splines are a larger diameter than the shaft on which the oil seal runs care must be taken to protect the seal from being sliced by the sharp edges of the splines when it is slid over them. This can be done by wrapping some cellulose tape round the splines first.

13 Make sure the oil drain hole in the casing matches up with the slot in the cover, fit a new gasket and replace the cover, tightening the bolts to 20 to 25 lbs/ft. These bolt threads should be smeared with a suitable sealing compound.

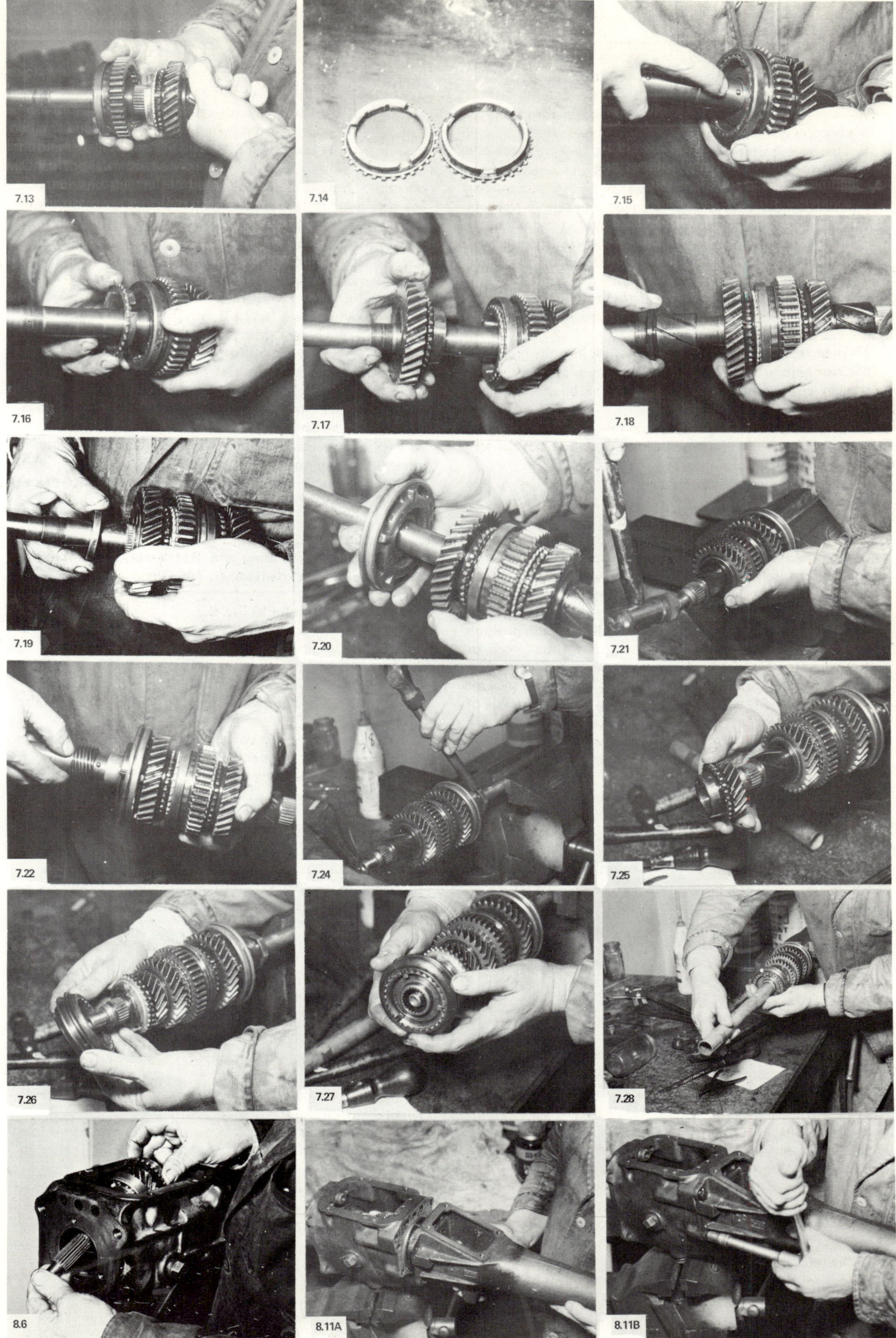

7.13

7.14

7.15

7.16

7.17

7.18

7.19

7.20

7.21

7.22

7.24

7.25

7.26

7.27

7.28

8.6

8.11A

8.11B

14 Revolve the input and main shafts to check that they rotate freely and make sure also that there are no indications of excessive end float which would indicate worn bearings or unproperly fitted circlips on the shaft.

15 The selector forks are replaced next together with the rails. On models fitted with remote control change levers these are practically identical although on the later models the ends of the selector rails are modified due to the fact that the remote lever link is accommodated in the extension housing rather than in a separate unit above the gearbox. The differences are quite clearly seen from a study of Figs. 6.1. and 6.3.

16 Replace the 3rd/4th fork so that it rests in the 3rd/4th hub groove. The fork boss should point towards the rear of the gearbox (photo).

17 Then replace the 1st/2nd selector fork into the groove in the rear side of the appropriate hub which also carries the straight cut reverse main shaft gear. The boss of the fork also points rearwards (photo).

18 Finally the reverse gear selector fork is fitted to engage with the groove in the reverse idler gear. The boss of this fork points forward (photo).

19 The forks in position should now appear as in the photograph (photo).

20 It is now time to make sure that the two interlock plungers are located in their holes in the front end of the casing. These engage with machined cutaways on the front end of the selector rails in such a way that only one selector rail at a time may move. If any one is moved the plunger is pushed across thus locking the other two in position. The two plungers can be a fiddle to get in position but it can be done with patience, using small rods or screwdrivers. Fig. 6.12. shows how they should be. The centre, smaller pin is positioned when the centre selector rail is replaced. If wished the expanding plug on the side of the casing may be removed to give easier access to the plunger drilling but it must be replaced with a new one.

21 Then replace the reverse gear selector rail through the gearbox casing and fork (photo).

22 The end will have to be rotated to clear the extension housing (photo) as it is slid forward.

23 When finally in position the end should point downwards as shown (photo).

24 Next replace the pin in the transverse hole in the end of the 1st/2nd gear selector rail (photo).

25 Replace the rail carefully (so as not to drop the pin into the gearbox) through the centre hole in the casing and the 1st/2nd gear selector fork (photo).

26 It is as well at this stage to replace the fork locking screws so that they engage in the rails, thus keeping everything in its correct relative position (photo).

27 The 3rd/4th gear selector rail is next positioned (photo).

28 This rail is fitted with a sleeve which must be replaced before the rail is put through the selector fork (photo). On some models there are spring clips also fitted to the rail.

29 The rail is finally positioned so that the cut-out in the end lines up with the one in the rail next to it (photo). It is important at this stage to ensure that the gearbox is in neutral. This can be verified by seeing that the selector hub outer sleeves are not engaged over the dogs of any gear wheels. On column change models refit the selector mechanism in the reverse order as described in Section 4: 9-14. The main differences are that the selector rails are moved by levers in the top cover rather than on extensions to the rear of the gear casing.

30 It is worthwhile at this stage to replace the change lever mechanism to ensure correct operation, even though it will need taking off before the gearbox is replaced.

31 The photo shows the change lever assembly of a pre-Sept. '66 model being temporarily replaced for this purpose.

32 On this same model there should be a clearance of .020 in. between the relay rod and reverse gear relay lever and thus can be checked with a feeler blade (photo). If it is incorrect it may be adjusted by moving the nylon stop at the base of the gear stick (Fig. 6.1., item 37).

33 Having ensured that the gear change selector mechanism operates freely and correctly tighten the selector fork securing bolts to the rails and then lock them with soft iron wire. Make sure the loops of wire go round the fork boss only and not in such a way as to catch anywhere when the fork is moved backwards and forwards. On early remote control models leave the box in neutral and remove the remote control lever assembly.

34 Replace the three steel balls into their recesses (photo).

35 Replace the detent springs over the balls (photo).

36 Replace the top cover of the gearbox so that the three springs locate in the recesses (photo) and refit the cover bolts.

37 Replace the clutch bellhousing (photo) to the gearbox and tighten the bolts to 40 to 45 lbs.ft.

38 Replace the clutch release arm to the clutch bearing, if removed, as described in Chapter 5/10.

39 The gearbox is now reassembled and ready for replacement in the car.

---

9. Gearbox Dismantling and Reassembly with Remote Floor Gear Change - September, 1966 on.

Figures in text refer to Fig. 6.3.

1. Having removed the gearbox from the car remove the mainshaft extension inspection cover (16).

2. Undo the bolts holding the bridge piece (22) and lift it out.

3. Remove the locking wire from the gearchange selector bolt (36) (photo).

4. Undo the selector arm bolt (photo) and when the selector rail is removed the arm will slide off.

5. Continue dismantling as described in Section 4 from paragraph 4 onwards. When reassembling the gearbox reverse this procedure when reassembly (as described in Section 8) has got as far as paragraph 29.

---

10. Column Gearchange - Gearbox Top Cover - Dismantling, Reassembly and Replacement

---

1. On steering column change models the operation of the selector rails and forks is actuated by a mechanism in the top cover of the gearbox and the gearbox selector rails and gates themselves are different as pointed out in the previous sections. Figure 6.14 shows the assembled view of the selector mechanism prior to replacement of the top cover. Figures in text now refer to Figure 6.4.

2. To dismantle the top cover first remove the gate selector arm locating nut (7) by bending back the locking tab on the washer (8) and unscrewing it.

3. Remove the arm (9) and washer (10) and draw the selector finger (11) out of the top cover. Do not damage the oil seal (17).

4. Unscrew the locknut (3) and remove the flat washer (xx) holding the selector lever (4) to the cross-shaft (2). Remove the circlip (21) and flat washer (20) at the other end.

5. In order to remove the circlip (6) it will be necessary to compress the spring (15) sufficiently to take the pressure off the washer (5).

6. By levering apart the selector fingers (12) and (14), the second circlip (13) may now be removed. The shaft can then be drawn out of the top cover. Take care not to

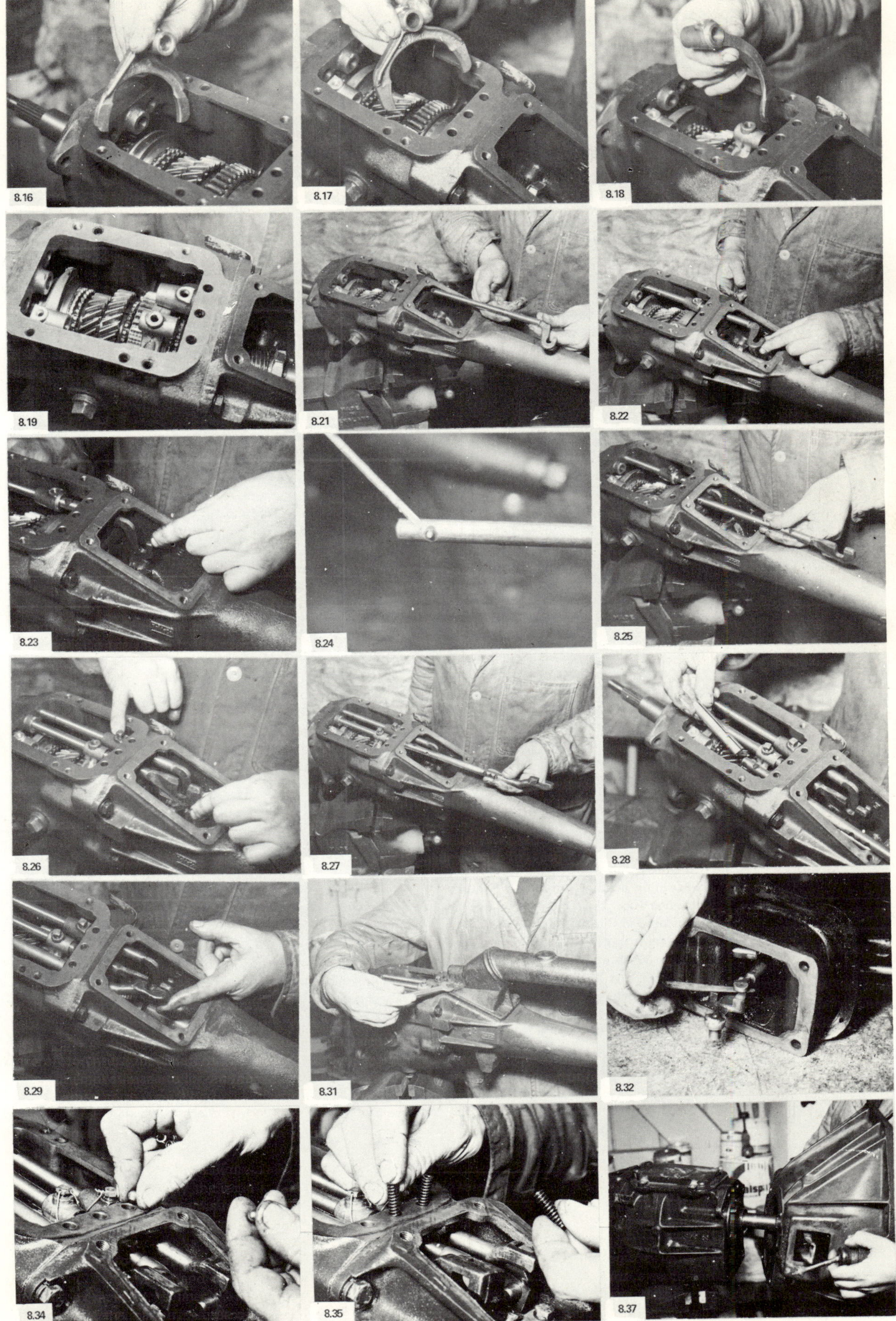

damage the oil seals (1) and (16) at each end of the shaft.

7. If the oil seals need replacement make sure new ones are available before driving them out, which cannot be done without damaging them.

8. Reassembly is a reversal of the dismantling procedure and care should be taken to protect the oil seals when refitting the cross shaft. Make sure the fingers are fitted the right way round on the cross shaft and that the two flats on the threaded end of the cross shaft are at right angles to them when assembled.

9. When replacing the top cover to the gearbox put the gears in neutral and centralize the selector fingers in the top cover. The same precautions should be taken for the detent balls and springs as for those of the top cover of other types as described in Section 8, paragraph 36.

11. Steering Column Change Lever Mechanism - Maintenance, Adjustment and Renovation

All bracketed figures in the text refer to Fig. 6.2.

1. Apart from the gate selector lever (23) all bushes are made from nylon and need no lubrication although a lithium based grease can assist ease of movement and reduce noise.

2. If difficulty is experienced with the change mechanism, such as excessive sloppiness in the linkage, or jamming in one or other of the gears the first thing to check, before attempting any adjustments, is the condition of all the nylon bushes in the linkage. There are eight of them and the combined lost motion if all are a little too slack can be sufficient to cause constant trouble. They can all be easily and cheaply replaced - although some are difficult to get at and are located by circlips or spring clips. It is well worthwhile changing the whole set when general wear is apparent. Change the bronze bush (11) of the selector arm also.

3. Provided all the bushes are in good condition and none of the linkage has been strained or bent, adjustment will only be required when a new gearbox is fitted, or if it is not possible to engage gear correctly.

4. To set up the linkage adjustment first slacken off the locknuts (26) on the gate selector rod adjustment sleeve (30).

5. Place the gear lever in the neutral position opposite the 3rd/4th gear selector position.

6. Push a $^3/_{16}$ inch diameter rod through the hole in the bottom of the steering column bracket and the corresponding hole in the gear change rod (42). The top of the pin should be inclined as indicated in Fig. 6.15.

7. Push down the gate selector rod (49) until the resistance of the spring in the top cover cross shaft can be felt. Then screw up the lower lock nut (30) on the rod until it just contacts the sleeve and then tighten the upper one. Make sure the rod does not twist whilst tightening the nuts.

8. Remove the pin and the gear change should operate correctly. If the column lever moves freely up and down in the neutral position but there is a lot of lost motion when trying to engage one or more gears it will be due to wear in the top cover selector mechanism (provided of course the change lever linkage is all in order).

12. Gearbox - Fault Finding

Faults in the gearbox can range from small noises and minor deficiencies in engagement of gears and operation of synchromesh, to serious faults consisting of loud whines, serious vibrations or inability to engage or remain in one or more gears. For serious faults there is no alternative other than removing the gearbox and either overhauling it completely or fitting another. For minor faults, other than those which can be detected in the change mechanism rather than the gearbox, it is more a question of how long can the fault be tolerated before taking action. Once something starts to wear to a degree which is noticeable, things usually start to deteriorate rapidly. Unfortunately, the amount of trouble to rectify a minor fault will be the same as for a major one - removal and dismantling of the gearbox. One may save something on spare parts but even this is problematical as it is not until the gearbox is stripped that many faults can be diagnosed accurately. Some faults can go on for thousands of miles without further deterioration to the whole unit - a worn synchro cone for example. Failure of the mainshaft bearing could, however, completely ruin the whole assembly in a few hundreds of miles.

The following list is intended as a guide to aid decisions on WHEN to take action.

Fault	Cause
Ineffective synchromesh on one or more gears.	Worn synchro cones.
	Worn blocker bars.
Jumps out of one or more gears	Worn selector forks.
	Weak detent springs.
	Worn gear engagement dogs.
	Worn selector hub fork groove.
	Selector fork loose on rail (rare).
Noisy - rough - whining, vibration	Worn bearings and/or laygear thrust washers (initially) resulting in extended wear generally due to play and backlash.
Noisy and difficult engagement of gear.	Clutch not disengaging properly.
Difficult selecting forward or reverse gears and moving change lever out of gear.	Worn change lever linkage, particularly on steering column controls. General wear on remote control. Maladjusted reverse lever stop on early remote control.

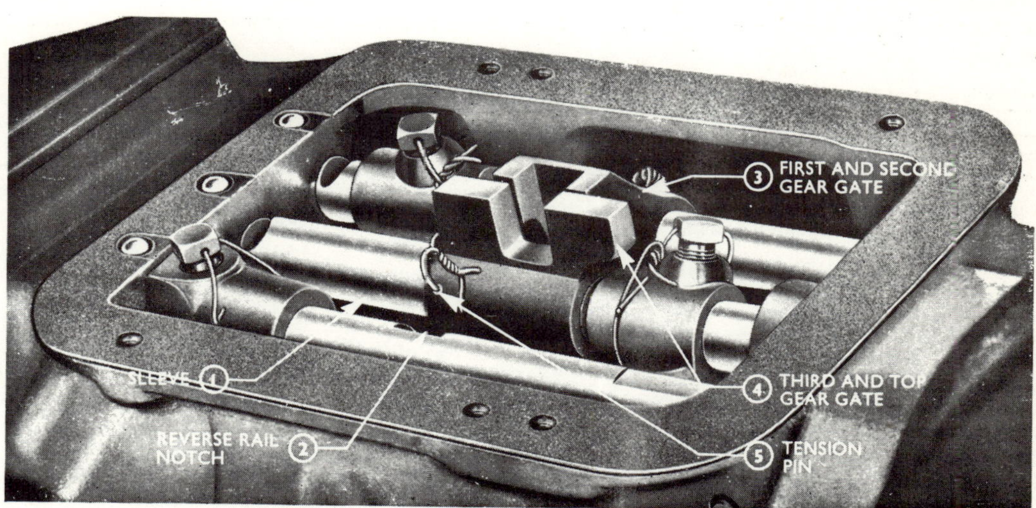

Fig. 6.14. Showing assembled selector rails, forks and gates of steering column change operated gearbox

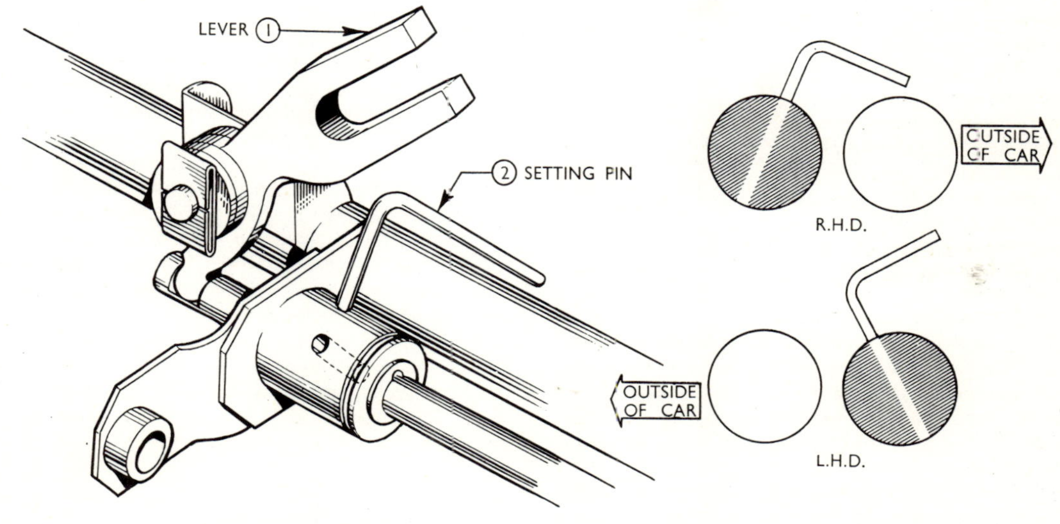

Fig. 6.15. Drawing to show position of setting pin to adjust steering column gearchange linkage

Chapter 7/Propeller Shaft and Universal Joints

Contents

Specifications

Torque Wrench Settings
Rear universal to rear axle pinion flange bolts ... ...   15 to 18 lbs.ft. (2.07 to 2.49 Kg.m.)

1. General Description

The engine power is transmitted through the gearbox, and from the gearbox mainshaft it is conveyed to the rear axle and driving wheels by means of a rotating shaft. Due to the vertical motion of the rear axle, the flexibility of the engine/gearbox assembly and the alteration in the distance between the rear of the gearbox and the final drive pinion flange, the propeller shaft has universal joints at both ends and a splined sleeve at one. The two universal joints permit the drive to be transmitted out of alignment and the splined sleeve which slides on the rear of the splined gearbox mainshaft takes up the variation in distance between gearbox and rear axle. The universal joints are lubricated and sealed on assembly and no maintenance is necessary. The splines are lubricated from the gearbox.

2. Propeller Shaft - Removal and Replacement

1. Jack up the rear of the car, or position the rear of the car over a pit or on a ramp.
2. If the rear of the car is jacked up supplement the jack with support blocks so that danger is minimised should the jack collapse.
3. If the rear wheels are off the ground place the car in gear or put the handbrake on to ensure that the propeller shaft does not turn when an attempt is made to loosen the four nuts securing the propeller shaft to the rear axle.
4. Unscrew and remove the four self-locking nuts and bolts which hold the flange on the propeller shaft to the flange on the rear axle.
5. The propeller shaft is carefully balanced to fine limits and it is important that it is replaced in exactly the same position it was in prior to its removal. Scratch a mark on the propeller shaft and rear axle flanges to ensure accurate mating when the time comes for reassembly.
6. Slightly push the shaft forward to separate the two flanges, and then lower the end of the shaft and pull it rearwards to disengage the gearbox mainshaft splines.
7. Place a large can or a tray under the rear of the gearbox extension to catch any oil which is likely to leak through the rear of the gearbox mainshaft extension housing, when the propeller shaft is removed.
8. Replacement of the propeller shaft is a reversal of the above procedure. Ensure that the mating marks scratched on the propeller shaft and rear axle flanges line up.

3. Universal Joints - Inspection and Repair

1. Wear in the needle roller bearings is characterised by vibration in the transmission, 'clonks' on taking up the drive, and in extreme cases of lack of lubrication, metallic squeaking, and ultimately grating and shrieking sounds as the bearings break up.
2. It is easy to check if the needle roller bearings are worn with the propeller shaft in position, by trying to turn the shaft with one hand, the other hand holding the rear axle flange when the rear universal is being checked, and the front half coupling when the front universal is being checked. Any movement between the propeller shaft and the front and the rear half couplings is indicative of considerable wear. If worn, the old bearings and spiders will have to be discarded and a repair kit, comprising new universal joint spiders, bearings, oil seals, and retainers purchased. Check also by trying to lift the shaft and noticing any movement in the joints.
3. Examine the propeller shaft splines for wear. If worn it will be necessary to purchase a new front half coupling, or if the yokes are badly worn, an exchange propeller shaft. It is not possible to fit oversize bearings and journals to the trunnion bearing holes.

4. Universal Joints - Dismantling

1. Clean away all traces of dirt and grease from the circlips located on the ends of the bearing cups, and remove the clips by pressing their open ends together with a pair of pliers (photo), and lever them out with a screwdriver. NOTE: If they are difficult to remove tap the bearing cup face resting on top of the spider with a mallet

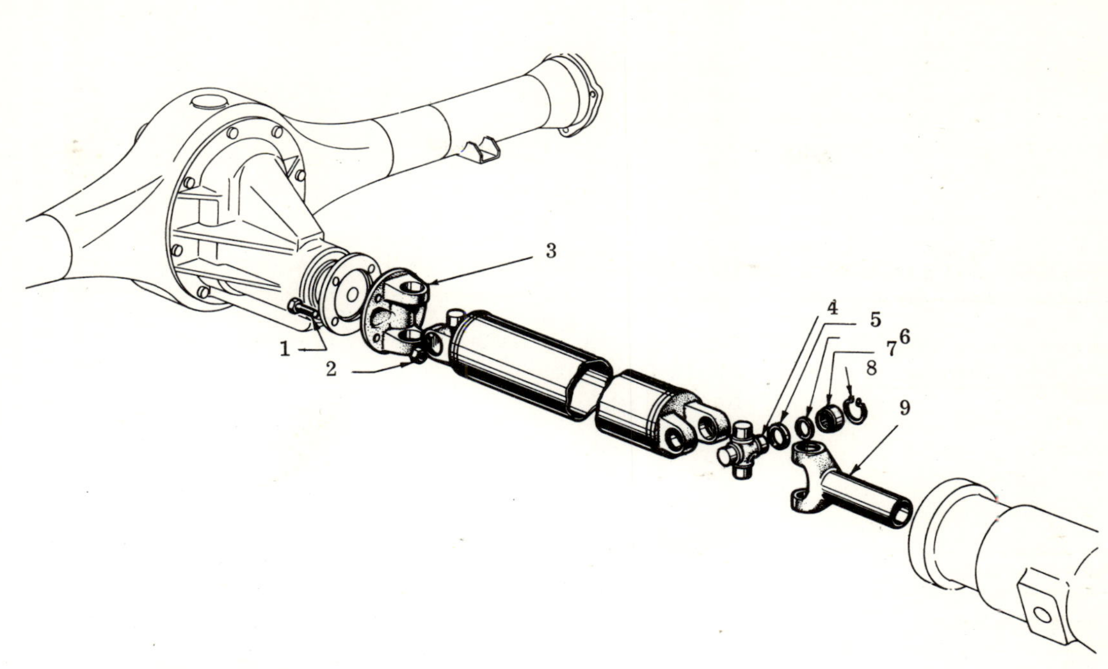

Fig. 7.1. PROPELLER SHAFT AND UNIVERSAL JOINTS — EXPLODED VIEW

1 Flange bolt
2 Flange nut
3 Flange yoke
4 Bearing trunnion
5 Seal
6 Spacer
7 Needle roller bearing assembly
8 Circlip
9 Sliding sleeve yoke

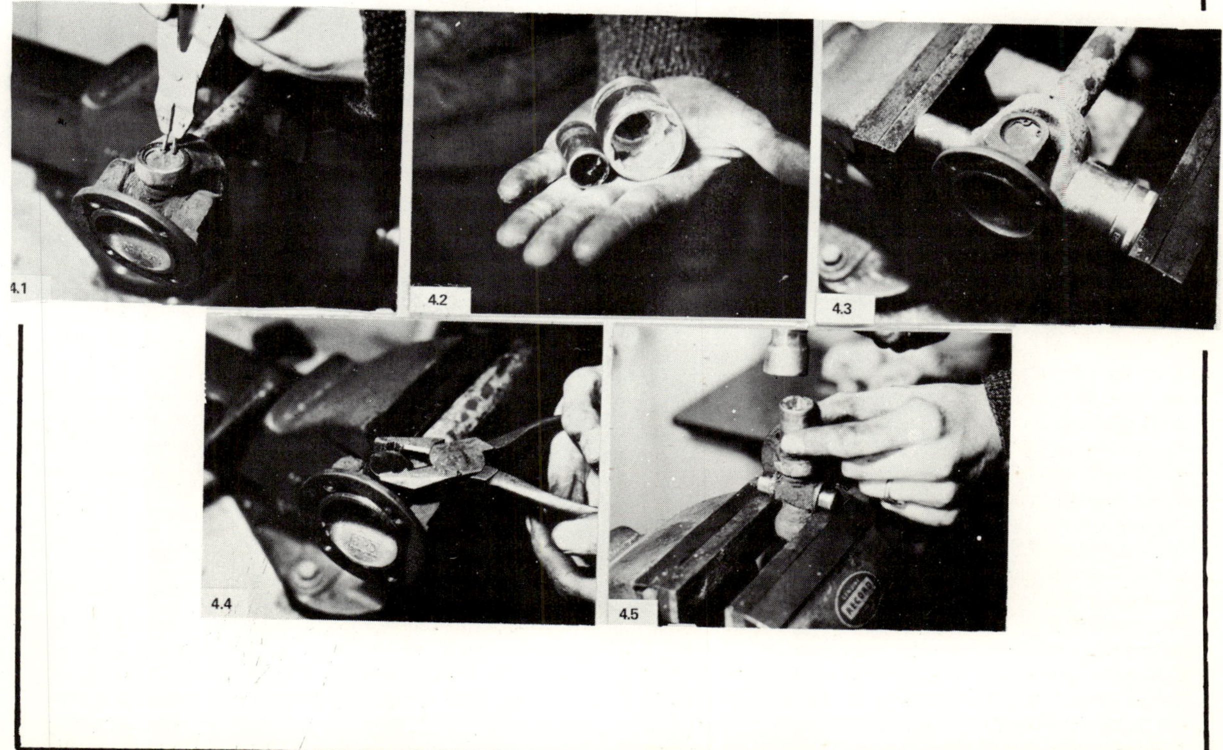

which will ease the pressure on the circlip.

2. Take off the bearing cups on the propeller shaft yoke. To do this select two sockets from a socket spanner set, one large enough to fit completely over the bearing cup and the other smaller than the bearing cup (photo).

3. Open the jaws of the vice and with the sockets opposite each other and the U.J. in between tighten the vice and so force the narrower socket to move the opposite cup partially out of the yoke (photo) into the larger socket.

4. Remove the cup with a pair of pliers (photo). Remove the opposite cup, and then free the yoke from the propeller shaft.

5. To remove the remaining two cups now repeat the instructions in paragraph 3, or use a socket and hammer

as illustrated (photo).

5. Universal Joints - Reassembly

1. Thoroughly clean out the yokes and journals.

2. Fit new oil seals and retainers on the spider journals, place the spider on the propeller shaft yoke, and assemble the needle rollers in the bearing races with the assistance of some thin grease. Fill each bearing about a third full with Castrolease LM or similar, and fill the grease holes in the journal spider making sure all air bubbles are eliminated.

3. Refit the bearing cups on the spider and tap the bearings home so they lie squarely in position. Replace the circlips.

Chapter 8/Rear Axle

Contents

Specifications

Type	Semi-floating hypoid
Ratio	3.777:1
Pinion/crown wheel No. of teeth	9:34
Pinion/crown wheel backlash	.005 to .007 in. (.127 to .178 mm)
Pinion bearing pre-load	9 to 11 lbs.ins. (.104 to .127 Kg.m) excluding oil seal
Differential bearing pre-load (cap spread)	.005 to .007 ins. (.127 to .178 mm)
Differential pinion thrust washer thickness	.030 to .032 ins. (.762 to .813 mm)

Oil capacity & type	2 Imp. pints (2.4 U.S. pints, 1.13 litres) S.A.E. 90 Hypoid

Torque Wrench Settings

Crown wheel to differential case bolts	50 to 60 lbs.ft. (6.93 to 7.60 Kg.m)
Differential carrier to axle housing nuts	15 to 18 lbs.ft. (2.07 to 2.49 Kg.m)
Differential bearing locking plate bolts	12 to 15 lbs.ft. (1.66 to 2.07 Kg.m)
Differential bearing cap bolts	45 to 50 lbs.ft. (6.22 to 6.91 Kg.m)
Axle shaft bearing retainer bolts	15 to 18 lbs.ft. (2.07 to 2.49 Kg.m)
Pinion to universal joint flange bolts	15 to 18 lbs.ft. (2.07 to 2.49 Kg.m)
Rear axle filler plug	25 to 30 lbs.ft. (3.46 to 4.15 Kg.m)

1. General Description

The rear axle, which is the same on all models, is of the semi-floating type, incorporating a hypoid crown wheel and pinion with a two pinion differential. The crown wheel and pinion are mounted in the differential carrier and this is bolted to the front of the banjo type axle housing. This means that all component parts may be repaired and pre-loads adjusted with the axle housing remaining on the car.

2. Routine Maintenance

The manufacturers recommend that other than periodic checks every 5,000 miles to ensure that the oil level is correct, nothing else is required. Thus no drain plug is provided. The author suggests however that every 30,000 miles the oil is drained when hot and replenished. This can be done by slackening the bolts holding the differential carrier to the axle casing. The oil will then drain out from the gap at the lowest point. Refill with two pints of SAE 90 Hypoid oil. The level plug should be replaced only after the oil level has settled as overfilling can cause leakage at the halfshaft oil seals with subsequent brake shoe contamination.

3. Half Shafts, Bearings and Oil Seals - Removal and Replacement

1. The halfshafts can be withdrawn without disturbing the differential gear. They are taken out when it is necessary to renew the bearings or oil seals or if the differential is being overhauled.
2. Jack up the car, support it on stands, remove the rear wheels, free the handbrake and remove the rear brake drums. Details of the latter may be found in Chapter 9.
3. The halfshafts are held in position by the bearing retainer which is bolted to the end of the axle casing. These four bolts are accessible through the two large holes in the axle shaft flange and may be removed with a socket spanner.
4. To draw out the halfshaft it is necessary to pull the bearing together with the shaft from the bearing housing in the axle casing. This normally requires impact as there is no way to draw it. There is a special tool (P.3072) which bolts to the wheel studs and into which a slide hammer bar is fitted. This makes the job easy if you are able to borrow one. Otherwise an old wheel rim fitted to the studs may be struck from the inside with something suitably heavy. It is because of this that the car must be very securely supported on stands. Once the bearing is drawn out of the axle housing

the halfshaft can be withdrawn.

5. The oil seal is fitted into the axle housing and this too is a press fit. Once again if you are able to borrow the special Ford tool (P.3072-3) and use the same type of sliding hammer bolt with it, extraction is easy. Otherwise it may be cut out with a small chisel but only, of course, if being renewed. Care must be taken when doing this as the seal housing must not be damaged. Otherwise the new seal will not fit properly.

6. A new seal must be carefully and squarely driven home. The lip of the seal should face into the axle casing.

7. The bearing and inner bearing retainer ring which remain on the axle shaft can only be removed and replaced with a proper press. A minimum pressure of 1,500 lbs. is required to fit the retainer. This is outside the scope of most owners so if the halfshaft is taken to a Ford garage they will be able to fit a new bearing and retainer as necessary.

8. Replacement of the halfshaft is the reversal of the removal procedure. Take care not to damage the oil seal whilst passing it into the axle casing. The bearing can be located into the casing by tapping the end of the halfshaft until the bolts of the retaining flange can pick up the threads. The bolts can then be used to draw the shaft into final position. Tighten the bolts to 15-18 lbs.ft.

9. Replace the brake drum, check the shoe adjustment and replace the road wheel.

4. Differential Carrier - Removal and Replacement

1. If a rear axle unit needs repairing or renewing it will require removing from the casing unless the whole axle is being replaced. If you have acquired a rear axle from a breaker it would be in order just to use this assembly in your existing casing. For enthusiasts who may like to try a different ratio of final drive there are some Cortina final drives which are interchangeable.

2. To remove the differential carrier assembly first partially withdraw the halfshafts, following the procedures described in Section 3.

3. Disconnect the propeller shaft flange as described in Chapter 7 and lower it to the ground. Do NOT remove the propeller shaft from the gearbox, otherwise the oil may leak out. In any case it is better not to disturb the oil seal.

4. Unscrew the eight nuts holding the differential to the axle and move it slightly forward and let the oil drain out.

5. Remove the whole unit from the axle.

6. Replacement is a reversal of the foregoing procedure, noting the following:-

a) Check the mating surfaces of the carrier and axle and remove all traces of gasket and any burrs.

b) Fit a new gasket locating it on the axle studs.

c) Install the carrier with the pinion at the bottom.

d) Tighten the nuts evenly to a torque of 15-18 lbs.ft.

e) Do not forget to replenish the oil.

5. Rear Axle - Removal and Replacement

1. Before removing the complete rear axle for any reason, check whether the operations referred to in previous sections will suffice.

2. Jack up the rear of the car and support it properly on stands. These stands should be placed under the rear jacking points.

3. Remove the road wheels and then place some form of support under the axle to take its weight when released.

4. Disconnect the propeller shaft from the pinion flange by undoing the four bolts. Mark the two flanges if the same differential carrier assembly is to be replaced.

5. Disconnect the handbrake cable (with the brake off) as described in detail in Chapter 9, according to the type fitted.

6. Remove the self locking nuts, washers and bolts which secure the lower ends of the shock absorbers to the spring seats and free the bottom end of the dampers from their locations.

7. Disconnect the brake hydraulic fluid pipe from the axle by undoing the union on the flexible pipe on the top of the axle casing. Plug the end of the pipe to prevent fluid loss.

8. Remove the nuts on the 'U' bolts which clamp the axle to the springs and lift away the clamping plates and 'U' bolts. If radius arms are fitted disconnect them from the axle. The axle is then free and may be lifted out.

9. Replacement of the axle is a reversal of the foregoing procedure. The 'U' bolt nuts should be tightened to a torque of 20 to 25 lbs.ft. Adjust and bleed the brakes as required when reconnected.

6. Differential Carrier - Overhaul

1. The overhaul of the crown wheel, pinion and differential gear assembly is a specialized job and any owner who decides to do an overhaul or replace the pinion oil seal himself is advised to consider carefully the relative economics - in time and new parts required - and the fact that an imperfect job may result in something far worse than the original state.

2. Specialized tools and measuring devices are essential. For these reasons this manual does not therefore detail the step by step procedures necessary to reassemble the unit. (Dismantling is easy!) Very few garages today would undertake to overhaul the differential assembly and if they did the cost (for a skilled and competent job) would be considerable.

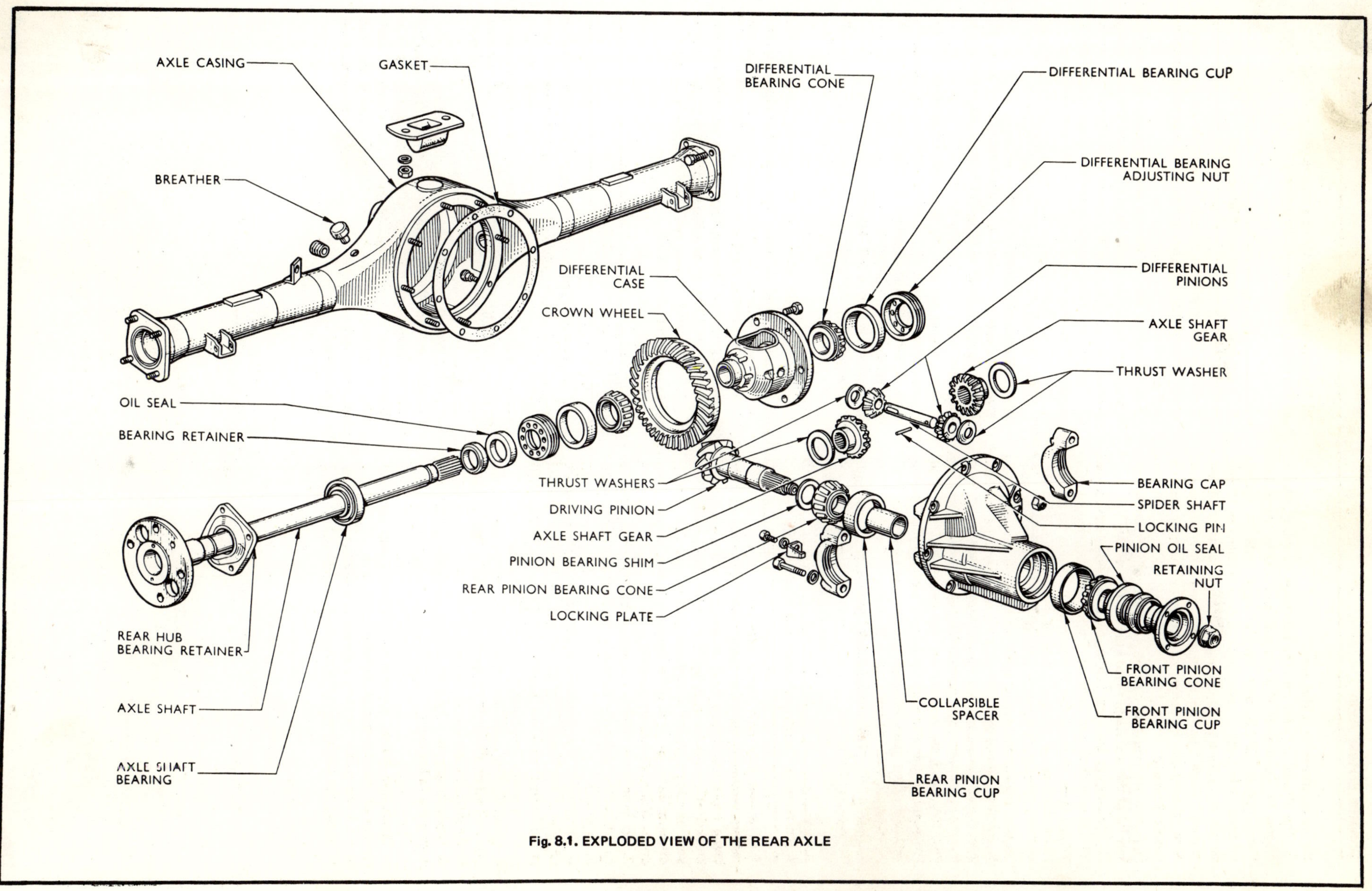

Fig. 8.1. EXPLODED VIEW OF THE REAR AXLE

Chapter 9/Braking System

Contents

Specifications

Type	Hydraulically operated discs at front and drums at rear, servo assisted on all 1996 c.c. engined models.
Hand brake	Mechanical to rear wheels only

Front brakes

Disc diameter	9.625 ins. (244.5 mm)
Disc run-out (max.)	.002 ins. (.051 mm)
Disc thickness	.5 ins. (12.7 mm)
Pad lining area (total)	20.64 in^2 (134.16 cm^2)
Pad identification - 1664 c.c. models	Red, green, red green, red spots
- 1996 c.c. models	Green paint spot
Calliper piston diameter	2.215 in. (53.97 mm)
Swept area (total)	189.5 in^2 (1,222.5 cm^2)

Rear brakes

Drum diameter	9.00 in. (22.86 cms.)
Lining size	7.00 x 1.70 in. (17.78 x 4.32 cms)
Total area	48 in.^{2} (312 cm^2)
Lining thickness	.195 in. (5 mm)
Wheel cylinder diameter - 1664 c.c. models	.98 in. (22.1 mm)
- 1996 c.c. models	.75 in. (19.1 mm)
Swept area (total)	96.1 in^2 (619.9 cm^2)

Master cylinder

Bore (maximum) - 1664 c.c. models	.70 in. (17.8 mm)
- 1996 c.c. models	.875 in. (22.2 mm)
Stroke (maximum)	1.375 in. (34.9 mm)

Servo (1996 c.c. models only)

Type	Suspended vacuum
Boost ratio	2.78:1

Torque Wrench Settings

Brake calliper to suspension bolts	45 to 50 lb.ft. (6.22 to 6.91 Kg.m)
Disc to hub bolts	30 to 34 lb.ft. (4.15 to 4.70 Kg.m)
Rear brake plate to axle tube bolts	15 to 18 lb.ft. (2.07 to 2.49 Kg.m)
Hydraulic unions	7 to 8 lb.ft. (.97 to 1.1 Kg.m)
Bleed valves	5 to 7½ lb.ft. (.7 to 1.0 Kg.m)

1. General Description

Disc brakes are fitted to the front wheels of all models together with single leading shoe drum brakes at the rear. The mechanically operated handbrake works on the rear wheels only.

The brakes fitted to the front wheels are of the rotating disc and static calliper type, with one calliper per disc, each calliper containing two piston operated friction pads, which on application of the footbrake pinch the disc rotating between them. The calliper is positioned on the leading edge of the disc.

Application of the footbrake creates hydraulic pressure in the master cylinder and fluid from the cylinder travels via steel and flexible pipes to the cylinders in each half of the callipers, thus pushing the pistons, to which are attached the friction pads, into contact with either side of the disc.

Two seals are fitted to the operating cylinders. The outer seal prevents moisture and dirt entering the cylinder, while the inner seal which is retained in a groove inside the cylinder, prevents fluid leakage.

As the friction pads wear so the pistons move further out of the cylinders and the level of the fluid in the hydraulic reservoir drops, Disc pad wear is therefore taken up automatically and eliminates the need for periodic adjustment by the owner.

On earlier models the handbrake lever is located under the fascia but on later models the lever is located between the front seats. A single cable runs from the lever to a compensator mechanism fitted either to the body frame halfway between the gearbox and rear axle or on the back of the rear axle casing. From the compensator a cable runs to the rear brake drums. As the rear brake shoes wear the handbrake cables operate a self adjusting mechanism in the rear brake drums thus doing away with the necessity for the owner to adjust the brakes on each rear wheel individually. The only adjustment required is on the handbrake compensator mechanism, due to wear in the linkage or stretching of the cables.

The 1996 cc engined cars are all fitted with a servo mechanism to provide additional boost to the hydraulic system by using the engine inlet manifold depression. This provides greater braking power with less pedal effort. In October, 1968, the system was modified on some of the 2000 series, providing a dual line so that either the front or rear brakes would continue to operate if a loss of hydraulic pressure occurred in any part of the system. Incorporated in this is a warning light indicating the failure of either circuit.

2. Routine Maintenance

1. Every week, clean the exterior of the brake fluid reservoir, remove the cap and check the level of the fluid which should be no more than ½ in. from the top. Make sure the vent hole is clear. Any need for regular topping up, regardless of the quantity involved, should be regarded with suspicion and the hydraulic system thoroughly checked for leaks as fluid is not normally consumed.

2. Every 30,000 miles it is worthwhile renewing all the hydraulic seals and the fluid, taking into account, of course, any repair work during the period under review.

3. The brakes are completely self-adjusting on all models. The only concern therefore is that the brake pads and linings should be replaced when they have worn down. Such inspections should be carried out every 5,000 miles.

4. Rear brake shoes should be replaced when the linings are worn nearly to the heads of the rivets - otherwise the rivets may eventually rub on the drums and damage them and reduce braking efficiency.

5. The absolute minimum thickness of disc brake pads is $1/16$ in. and in fact they should be changed at $1/8$ in. thickness for complete safety and efficiency.

6. Brakes wear out according to driving style and the type of country normally travelled, but it is unwise to expect any disc pads to last much more than 10,000 miles. The rear brake linings will last perhaps half as long again. The handbrake should be adjusted if necessary to hold the car adequately.

7. If you have just acquired a V4 Corsair it is strongly recommended that all brake drums, pads, shoes and discs are thoroughly inspected for condition and wear. Even though they may be working perfectly they could be nearing the end of their useful life and it is as well to know this straight away. Similarly, the hydraulic cylinders, pipes and connections should be carefully examined for signs of leaks or chafing. If any faults are apparent action should be taken immediately to rectify them. It should be remembered that V4 Corsairs which were in production from 1965 to 1970 have already become subject to the compulsory vehicle safety tests that pay particular attention not only to braking efficiency but the condition of the system. By 1973 all V4 Corsairs and 2,000's will be subject to these tests. Apart from the safety factor, which is paramount, regular brake inspection and servicing will avoid the inconvenience of the car being kept off the road if they are suspected of dangerous deterioration.

3. Disc Pads - Removal, Inspection and Replacement

1. If the brake pads have worn down to a thickness of $1/8$ in. (3.2 mm) they should be renewed as soon as possible. If they are as low as $1/16$ in. (1.6 mm) they are dangerous.

2. To check this dimension jack up the car, remove the wheel and measure the thickness of the material from the contact face against the disc to the pad support plate to which it is attached. Bracketed figures in the text refer to Fig. 9.1.

3. Unclip the dust cover if fitted.

4. Remove the clips (6) from the retaining pins (7) and withdraw the retaining pins.

5. Pull out the pads (16) and shims (3) using a pair of long nosed pliers if necessary.

6. Inspect the condition of the piston outer seals (12) and ensure that they are correctly located in the cylinder groove. If there are any signs of cracking or breaking up they will need replacement. (Section 9) Also there should be no trace whatsoever of hydraulic fluid.

7. Both pistons (11) should then be pushed back about ¼ in. (6.5 mm) to make way for the new pads. This will cause the fluid level in the master cylinder reservoir to rise so make sure that it will not overflow. Both pistons should require equal pressure to push back so if one should seem stiffer than the other compare the old brake pads to see if they are worn equally. If one should be worn more than the other it could indicate that one piston is not moving freely and will need overhaul (Section 9). Alternatively, it could mean that one side of the disc is worn more than the other side due to a bombardment of abrasive dirt thrown up by the front wheels.

8. New brake pads of correct specification should be fitted together with the shims so that the retaining pin holes line up correctly. Keep all traces of oil or grease away from the pads or pins.

9. Replace the pins. If they do not enter the hole freely find out why and rectify it. The pads must be free to slide

on the pins when installed.

10 Replace the pin retaining clips.

11 No bleeding of the brakes is necessary. Pump the pedal until they feel 'solid'. When the wheels are then spun the disc pads may touch the disc slightly but should not bind in any way.

4. Discs - Inspection, Removal and Replacement

1. The disc may have become distorted or damaged and be running out of true. This can be checked by jacking up the car, removing the road wheel and setting a backlash gauge against the face of the disc and spinning it. So that the whole unit can be held it will be necessary to detach the track rod. The hub can then be swung right over hard and held firm. The disc run out should not exceed a total of .004 in. If it does the wheel bearings are loose or worn or the disc is warped, or has worn unevenly.

2. The disc should be examined for signs of scoring also and if this is excessive renewal is necessary.

3. To remove the disc the hub assembly should be taken off as described in Chapter 11/14. The four bolts and two lockwashers are then undone and the disc tapped off the hub.

4. When refitting the disc new bolts and lockwashers should be used and tightened to a torque of 27 to 30 lbs.ft.

5. Replace the hub as described in Chapter 11, followed by the calliper and wheel.

5. Brake Drums and Shoes - Removal, Inspection and Replacement

1. The rear brake shoe linings will gradually wear and the periodic inspection requirements will call for the drum to be removed.

2. Jack up the car and remove the road wheel.

3. Remove the small screw holding the brake drum to the axle flange and then draw the drum off the four wheel studs. If the drum should bind at the roots of the studs it may be tapped with a soft hammer to assist. In some rare cases of extreme neglect it is possible that the linings and drums have scored and worn so badly that the automatic adjuster mechanism has moved the linings into the grooves in the drum to such an extent that the drum cannot be taken off. In such cases the hydraulic wheel cylinder must be disconnected and unclipped as described in Section 8 and freed into the drum so that it comes away from the ends of the brake shoes. The retractor spring will then pull the shoes inwards enough to allow the drum to be pulled off.

4. Bracketed figures in the text now refer to Fig. 9.2. Examine the interior of the brake drum where the friction surface should be smooth and bright. Remove any dust with a dry cloth and look for any score marks or other blemishes. Very light hairline scores around the drum are not serious but indicate that the shoes may be wearing out or heavy grit and dirt have got into the drum at some time. If there are signs of deep scoring the drum needs reconditioning or renewal. As reconditioning will probably cost as much as a new drum, and certainly more than a secondhand one (obtained from car breakers without difficulty) it is not recommended.

5. Examine the brake shoe friction linings (6) for signs of oil contamination, deep scoring or overall wear. Deep scoring will be immediately apparent and will relate to any scoring in the drum. Oil contamination is evident where there are hard, black shiny patches on the linings caused by the heat generated in braking which carbonises any oil which may have reached them. As a temporary measure

these may be rasped down but they must eventually be replaced. Normal wear may be judged from the depth of the rivet heads below the surface of the linings. If this is less than .025 in. (.65 mm) they should be renewed.

6. To remove the brake shoes make sure the handbrake is released and then turn the washer (11) through 90º so that it disengages from the head of the shoe retaining pin (1). Draw off the washers and springs and remove the pins from both shoes.

7. Pull the ends of the shoes away from the slave cylinder (9) to release them from the locating slots. Detach the two retractor springs (15) and (16) from the shoes.

8. Do not let the hydraulic piston come out of the cylinder. Take the automatic ratchet and adjuster screw from the other end of the cylinder and screw the ratchet down to the shoulder of the slotted screw head. This will assist the refitting of the shoes.

9. When new linings are needed it is simplest to get a set of replacement shoes. The linings themselves can be replaced but even if one has the riveting tool there is practically no advantage to be gained.

10 Shoes are replaced by first assembling the shoes and retractor springs as shown arranged in the exploded drawing. The hook ends of the springs go through the holes in the shoes from the outside. Also the shoes should be arranged so that the ends with the larger clear area is at the trailing end of the shoe in relation to the forward rotation of the drum. When the shoes are in position the springs should not bind against the backplate or slave cylinder. Refit the locating pins with their washers and springs.

11 Replace the brake drum. If it appears reluctant to go on it is because the shoes are not positioned centrally or because the brake adjuster mentioned in paragraph 8 has not been slackened off.

12 When the drum has been replaced and the locating screw tightened, operate the handbrake several times to adjust the shoes up to the drum.

13 Replace the wheel and road test at the first opportunity.

6. Handbrake - Adjustment, Removal and Replacement of Cables

1. On models up till Sept. 1966 the handbrake cable goes to a fulcrum arm mounted on the gearbox support cross-member and from there a secondary cable runs to the right hand rear wheel via an equalising bracket fitted to the right hand side of the rear axle. From this bracket, which is flexible, a rod runs to the left hand rear wheel. As tension is applied to the cable and the resistance of the brake comes on so the bracket flexes and applies equal tension on the rod to the other brake. After Sept. 1966 the fulcrum lever under the gearbox was taken away and the primary cable from the handbrake lever ran right back to a lever mounted on the rear axle banjo casing. This forced a pulley wheel on to a bowstring cable stretched between the two rear brake drums thus drawing on the brakes.

2. If the travel in the handbrake lever is excessive then it means that the cable(s) has stretched. To take up the slack adjust the locknuts on the equaliser bracket (early models). If necessary the left hand rod should also be adjusted at the equaliser bracket so that the bracket stands at 90º to the axle in the 'brake off' position.

3. On later bowstring types first release the handbrake and adjust the transverse cable at the right hand end so that it is as tight as possible without moving the operating links into the draw from the fully 'off' position. Then adjust the primary cable on the fulcrum lever until it is reasonably taut but does not move the brake levers.

4. To remove any secondary cables or rod is simply a

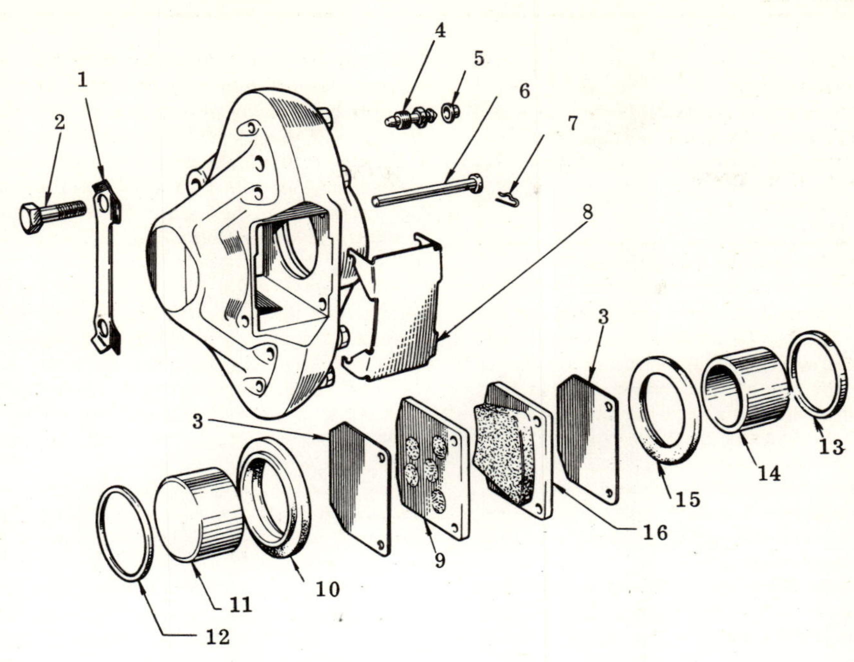

Fig. 9.1. DISC BRAKE CALLIPER AND PAD ASSEMBLY — EXPLODED VIEW

1 Locking plate	5 Dust cover	9 Pad	13 Piston seal
2 Mounting bolt	6 Retaining pin	10 Dust seal	14 Piston
3 Shim	7 Clip	11 Piston	15 Dust seal
4 Bleed nipple	8 Pad shield	12 Piston seal	16 Pad

Fig. 9.2. REAR BRAKE SHOES AND BACKPLATE ASSEMBLY — EXPLODED VIEW

1 Retaining pin	7 Shoe	13 Spring seat	19 Slotted washer
2 Dust cover	8 Parking brake lever	14 Support plate	20 Lining
3 Spring plate	9 Cylinder assembly	15 Retention spring	21 Rivet
4 Retaining plate	10 Backplate	16 Retention spring	
5 Rivet	11 Slotted washer	17 Spring seat	
6 Lining	12 Spring	18 Spring	

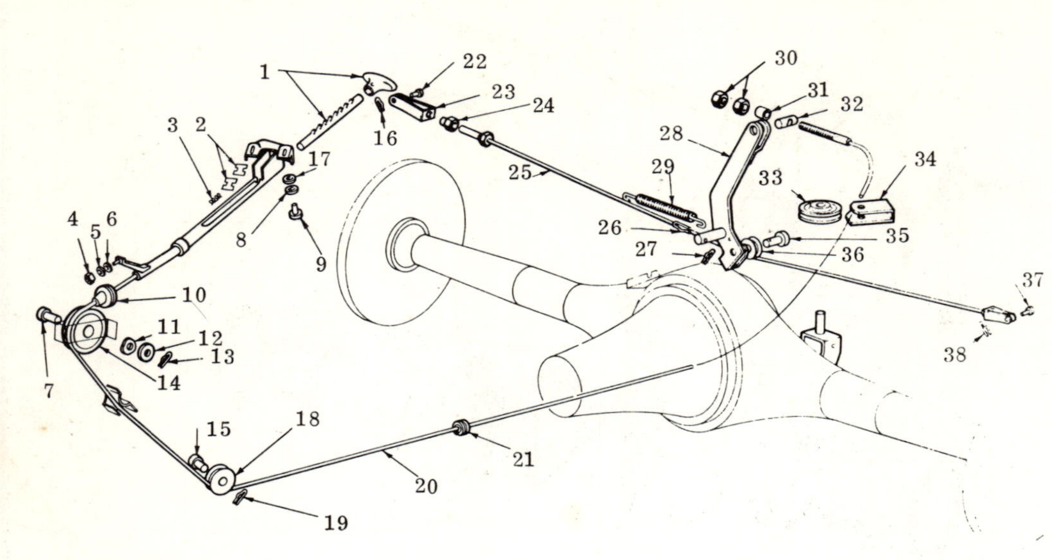

Fig. 9.3. PARKING BRAKE, DASH MOUNTED SEPT. 1966 ON — EXPLODED VIEW

1 Pull grip	11 Wave washer	21 Grommet	31 Sleeve
2 Pawls	12 Washer	22 Clevis pin	32 Anchor pin
3 Spring	13 Clip	23 Clevis	33 Pulley
4 Nut	14 Pulley	24 Cable anchor	34 Clevis
5 Washer	15 Spindle	25 Bowstring cable	35 Spindle
6 Insulation	16 Clip	26 Clip	36 Pulley
7 Spindle	17 Insulation	27 Clip	37 Clevis pin
8 Washer	18 Pulley	28 Fulcrum lever	38 Clip
9 Screw	19 Clip	29 Return spring	
10 Grommet	20 Cable	30 Locknut	

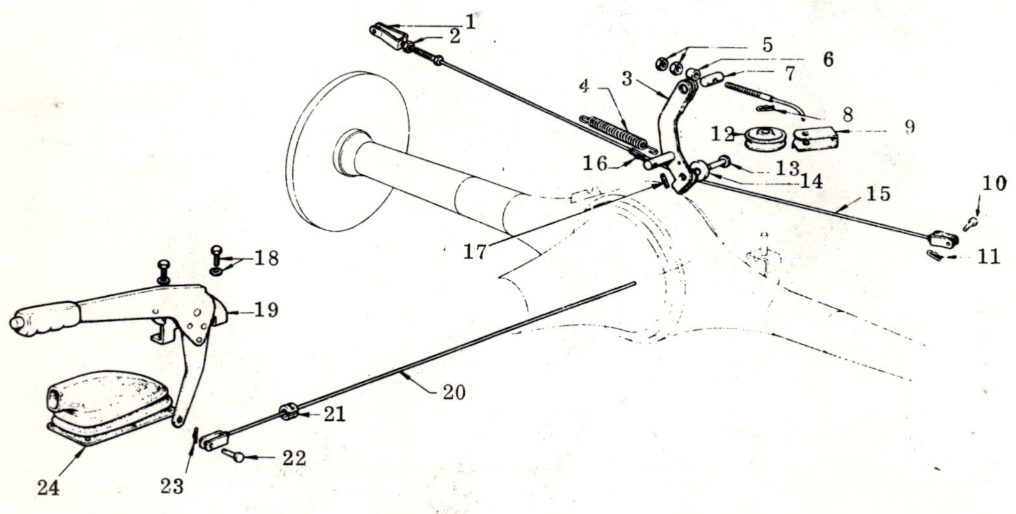

Fig. 9.4. PARKING BRAKE — FLOOR MOUNTED SEPT. 1966 ON — EXPLODED VIEW

1 Clevis	7 Anchor pin	13 Spindle	19 Hand lever
2 Cable anchor	8 Clip	14 Pulley	20 Main cable
3 Fulcrum lever	9 Clevis	15 Bowstring cable	21 Sleeve
4 Return spring	10 Clevis pin	16 Clip	22 Clevis pin
5 Locknuts	11 Clip	17 Clip	23 Clip
6 Sleeve	12 Pulley	18 Mounting bolt	24 Boot

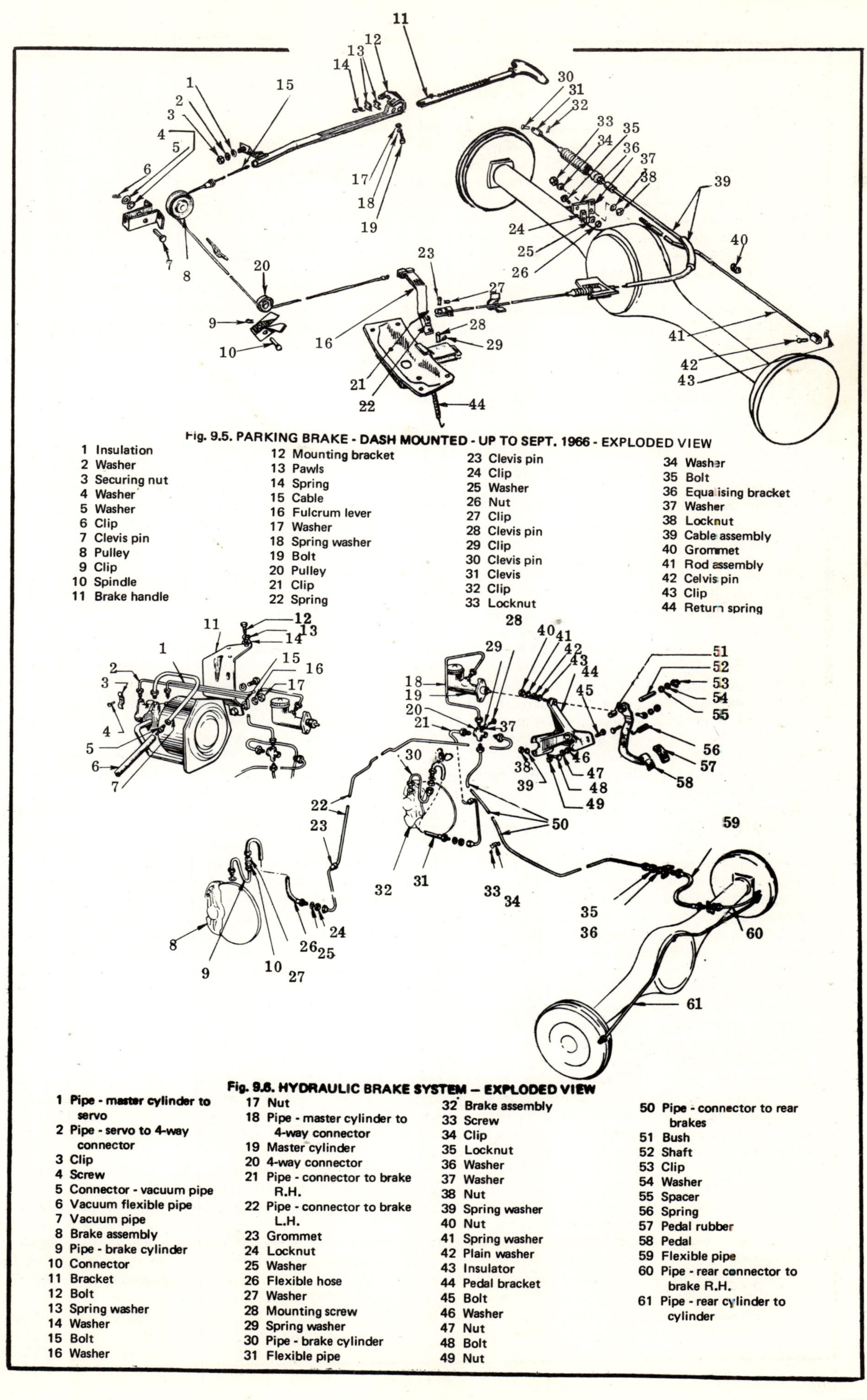

Fig. 9.5. PARKING BRAKE - DASH MOUNTED - UP TO SEPT. 1966 - EXPLODED VIEW

1	Insulation	12	Mounting bracket	23	Clevis pin	34	Washer
2	Washer	13	Pawls	24	Clip	35	Bolt
3	Securing nut	14	Spring	25	Washer	36	Equalising bracket
4	Washer	15	Cable	26	Nut	37	Washer
5	Washer	16	Fulcrum lever	27	Clip	38	Locknut
6	Clip	17	Washer	28	Clevis pin	39	Cable assembly
7	Clevis pin	18	Spring washer	29	Clip	40	Grommet
8	Pulley	19	Bolt	30	Clevis pin	41	Rod assembly
9	Clip	20	Pulley	31	Clevis	42	Clevis pin
10	Spindle	21	Clip	32	Clip	43	Clip
11	Brake handle	22	Spring	33	Locknut	44	Return spring

Fig. 9.6. HYDRAULIC BRAKE SYSTEM — EXPLODED VIEW

1	Pipe - master cylinder to servo	17	Nut	32	Brake assembly	50	Pipe - connector to rear brakes
2	Pipe - servo to 4-way connector	18	Pipe - master cylinder to 4-way connector	33	Screw	51	Bush
3	Clip	19	Master cylinder	34	Clip	52	Shaft
4	Screw	20	4-way connector	35	Locknut	53	Clip
5	Connector - vacuum pipe	21	Pipe - connector to brake R.H.	36	Washer	54	Washer
6	Vacuum flexible pipe	22	Pipe - connector to brake L.H.	37	Washer	55	Spacer
7	Vacuum pipe	23	Grommet	38	Nut	56	Spring
8	Brake assembly	24	Locknut	39	Spring washer	57	Pedal rubber
9	Pipe - brake cylinder	25	Washer	40	Nut	58	Pedal
10	Connector	26	Flexible hose	41	Spring washer	59	Flexible pipe
11	Bracket	27	Washer	42	Plain washer	60	Pipe - rear connector to brake R.H.
12	Bolt	28	Mounting screw	43	Insulator	61	Pipe - rear cylinder to cylinder
13	Spring washer	29	Spring washer	44	Pedal bracket		
14	Washer	30	Pipe - brake cylinder	45	Bolt		
15	Bolt	31	Flexible pipe	46	Washer		
16	Washer			47	Nut		
				48	Bolt		
				49	Nut		

question of undoing the clevis pin and/or adjuster nuts underneath the car.

5. The primary cable is also removed easily from the handbrake lever mounted on the floor by disconnecting the clevis from the lever at the front and the fulcrum arm at the rear. For models fitted with dash mounted umbrella handle levers, the cable should first be disconnected at the fulcrum lever. Then the handle assembly must be detached by removing the two mounting bolts under the dash and the nut securing the lower end to the bulkhead. The handbrake lever and cable are then all drawn out together from inside the car. The cable can then be removed from the handle. When threading the cable back make sure it goes round all the pulleys correctly and sits in the pulley grooves when all the adjustments are complete.

7. Hydraulic Fluid Pipes - Inspection, Removal and Replacement

1. Periodically and certainly well in advance of the M.O.T. test if due, all brake pipes, connections and unions should be completely and carefully examined. Figs. 9.6 and 9.7 show the composition of all such pipes and unions in the system.

2. Examine first all the unions for signs of leaks. Then look at the flexible hoses for signs of fraying and chafing (as well as for leaks). This is only a preliminary inspection of the flexible hoses as exterior condition does not necessarily indicate interior condition which will be considered later.

3. The steel pipes must be examined equally carefully. They must be thoroughly cleaned and examined for signs of dents or other percussive damage, rust and corrosion. Rust and corrosion should be scraped off and, if the depth of pitting in the pipes is significant, they will need replacement. This is most likely in those areas underneath the car body and along the rear axle where the pipes are exposed to the full force of road and weather conditions.

4. If any section of pipe is to be removed, first of all take off the fluid reservoir cap, line it with a piece of polythene film to make it airtight and screw it back on. This will minimise the amount of fluid dripping out of the system when the pipes are removed.

5. Rigid pipe removal is usually quite straightforward. The unions at each end are undone and the pipe drawn out of the connection. The clips which may hold it to the car body are bent back and it is then removed. Underneath the car exposed unions can be particularly stubborn, defying the efforts of an open ended spanner. As few people will have the special split ring spanner required, a self-grip wrench (Mole) is the only answer. If the pipe is being renewed new unions will be provided. If not then one will have to put up with the possibility of burring over the flats on the union and use a self-grip wrench for replacement also.

6. Flexible hoses are always fitted to a rigid support bracket where they join a rigid pipe, the bracket being fixed to the body frame and/or suspension unit. The rigid pipe unions must first be removed from the flexible union. Then the locknut securing the flexible pipe to the bracket must be unscrewed, releasing the end of the pipe from the bracket. As these connections are usually exposed they are more often than not rusted up and a penetrating fluid is virtually essential to aid removal (try 'Plus-Gas'). When undoing them, both halves must be supported as the bracket is not strong enough to support the torque required to undo the nut and can easily be snapped off.

7. Once the flexible hose is removed examine the internal bore. If clear of fluid it should be possible to see through it. Any specks of rubber which come out, or signs of restriction in the bore, mean that the inner lining is breaking up and the

pipe must be replaced.

8. Rigid pipes which need replacement can usually be purchased at any local garage where they have the pipe, unions and special tools to make them up. All that they need to know is the pipe length required and the type of flare used at the ends of the pipe. These may be different at each end of the same pipe.

9. Replacement of pipes is a straightforward reversal of the removal procedure. It is best to get all the sets (bends) in the pipe made preparatory to installation. Also any acute bends should be put in by the garage on a bending machine otherwise there is the possibility of kinking them and restricting the bore area and fluid flow.

10 With the pipes replaced, remove the polythene from the reservoir cap and bleed the system as described in Section 15.

8. Hydraulic Wheel Cylinders (Rear) - Inspection and Repair

1. If it is suspected that one or more of the wheel cylinders is malfunctioning, jack up the suspect wheel and remove the brake drum as described in Section 5.

2. Inspect for signs of fluid leakage around the wheel cylinder and if there are any, proceed as described in paragraph 5.

3. Next get someone to press the brake pedal very gently a small amount. Watch the wheel cylinder and see that the piston moves out a little. On no account let it come right out or it will need reassembly and bleeding. On releasing the pedal pressure make sure that the retraction springs on the shoes move the piston back into position without delay. If the piston moves satisfactorily make sure also that the cylinder body is free to slide endways in the slot in the backplate. If it should be seized it will mean that only one brake shoe is being applied.

4. If there is a leak, or the piston does not move (or only moves very slowly under excessive pressure) then the rubber piston seals will need renewal at least.

5. Seal the reservoir cap and remove the brake shoes as described in Section 5.

6. Disconnect the brake fluid pipes where they enter the cylinder - on the right hand wheel there are two of them - and plug the ends of the lines to minimise loss of fluid.

7. Remove the split pin and clevis pin from the handbrake operating link and the rubber dust cover.

8. The cylinder is retained by two U shaped clips and these can be drawn out by inserting a pointed instrument in the base of the U. The cylinder and operating link are now released. Make sure that the small pin on which the lever pivots is not lost out of its recess in the end of the cylinder.

9. Remove the clip from the boot over the piston and then pull out the piston, complete with seal and the spring. Examine the piston and cylinder for signs of wear or scoring and if there are any the whole assembly must be renewed. If they are in good condition only the seal needs renewal. Pull the old one off the piston and thoroughly clean the whole assembly using clean hydraulic fluid or methylated spirit.

10 Fit the new seal to the piston so that the lip faces away from the centre of the piston.

11 Lubricate the components in hydraulic fluid before reassembly which is carried out in the reverse order. Make sure the lip of the seal on the piston enters the cylinder first.

12 When refitting the cylinder to the backplate the handbrake link must be positioned correctly so that the pivot pin locates in the groove in the cylinder.

13 The cylinder securing clips should be replaced so that the curved spring clip goes on first with the base of the U

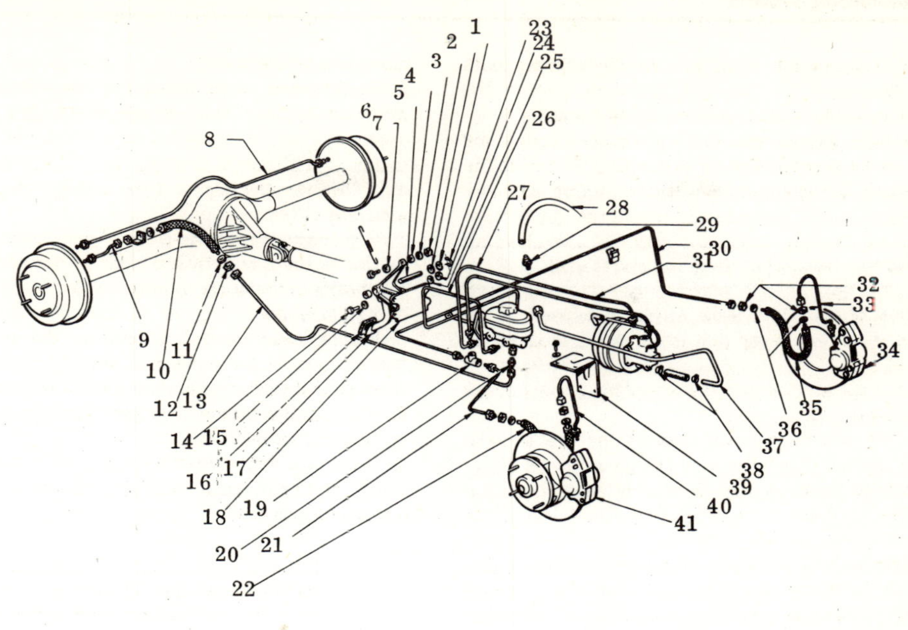

Fig. 9.7. HYDRAULIC BRAKE SYSTEM — DUAL LINE OCT. 1968 ON — EXPLODED VIEW

1 Washer	13 Pipe	24 Nut	33 Pipe - brake cylinder L.H.
2 Spacer	14 Bolt	25 Washer	34 Calliper assembly L.H.
3 Nut	15 Washer	26 Pipe - master cylinder to connector	35 Flexible pipe
4 Washer	16 Pedal rubber		36 Washer
5 Insulator	17 Pedal	27 Pipe - servo inlet	37 Pipe - servo vacuum
6 Shaft	18 Mounting	28 Hose - servo to inlet manifold	38 Clip
7 Washer	19 3-way connector		39 Bracket
8 Pipe - rear cylinders	20 Connector	29 Connector	40 Pipe - brake cylinder R.H.
9 Pipe - rear cylinder R.H.	21 Pipe - 3-way connector to front R.H.	30 Pipe - connector to front brake L.H.	41 Calliper assembly R.H.
10 Flexible pipe		31 Pipe - servo outlet	
11 Washer	22 Flexible pipe	32 Locknut	
12 Locknut	23 Clip		

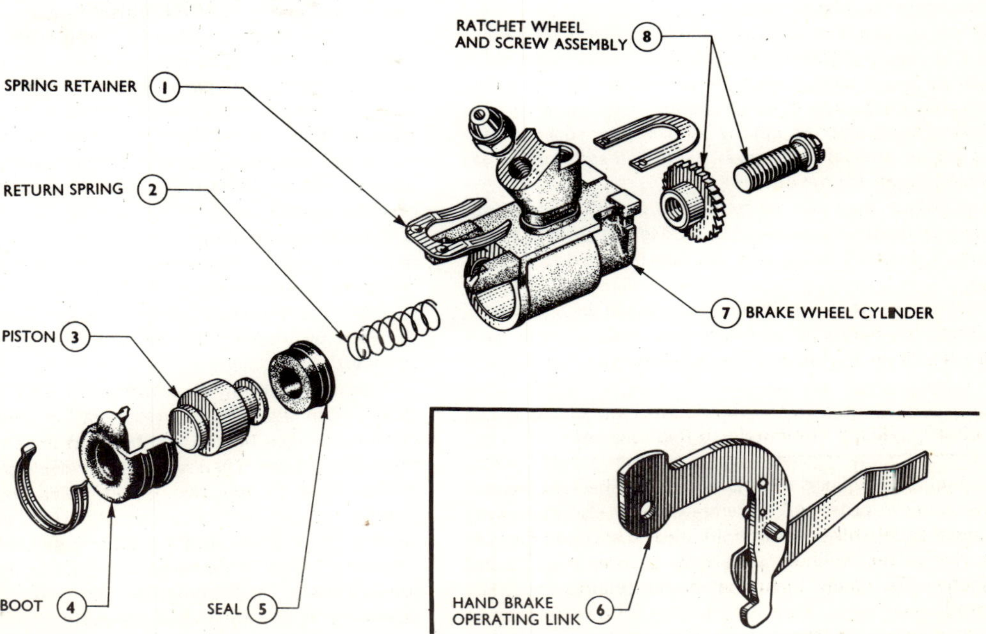

Fig. 9.8. REAR WHEEL BRAKE CYLINDER AND (INSET) PARKING BRAKE SHOE LEVER — EXPLODED VIEW

nearest the handbrake link. The two locating dimples should face upwards so that the two corresponding holes on the flat clip will locate over them when it is fitted above.

14 Reconnect the handbrake cable and hydraulic pipes and replace the brake shoes and drum as described in Section 5. Bleed the hydraulic system as described in Section 15.

9. Disc Callipers - Inspection, Removal and Repair

1. Any indications of fluid leaks or piston seizures in the front brake callipers will mean that they have to be removed for repair.
2. Jack up the car and remove the wheel and brake pads as described in Section 3.
3. To facilitate piston removal depress the brake pedal now to force them out as far as they can go up to the disc.
4. Seal the fluid reservoir cap with polythene sheet and disconnect the hydraulic pipe union from the body of the calliper.
5. The calliper is held to the stub axle by two bolts (see Fig. 9.9). Prise back the tabs of the lockwasher and remove them. Do not under any circumstances loosen the other four bolts as these hold the two halves of the calliper together. The calliper can then be lifted away.
6. Provided the pistons are not seized they can be drawn out by hand but in any case if some air pressure can be applied to the fluid inlet it will make things easier. If one piston is very tight try using methylated spirits to ease it. If drastic measures are necessary try and confine any damage to the piston rather than the calliper body.
7. Remove the bellows from the annular grooves in the cylinder bores and then pull out the piston fluid seals from their grooves.
8. Examine the pistons and bores for signs of wear and scores. If there are signs of wear the whole assembly will probably need replacement.
9. The cylinders and pistons should be thoroughly cleaned in fluid or methylated spirits and care taken to avoid contamination by dirt or mineral oils.
10 Before reassembly lubricate the parts with hydraulic fluid and begin by placing the piston seal in the cylinder in its groove and inserting next the bellows so that its outer lip engages in the top cylinder groove. The piston should then be carefully inserted and the bellows inner edge located in its piston groove. Then push the piston as far down as possible. Repeat for the other piston.
11 The calliper may now be refitted to the stub axle using a new locking plate behind the bolts. Tighten the bolts to a torque of 45 to 50 lbs.ft. and bend up the locking washer tabs.
12 Replace the pads and shims as described in Section 3, reconnect the hydraulic pipe and bleed the system as described in Section 15. Replace the wheel and road test the car.

10. Master Cylinder - Removal and Replacement

1. If the disc calliper pistons and rear wheel hydraulic cylinders are in order and there are no leaks elsewhere, yet the brake pedal still does not hold under sustained pressure then the master cylinder seals may be presumed to be ineffective. To renew them the master cylinder must be removed.
2. Disconnect the master cylinder pushrod from the brake pedal by removing the nut and concentric bolt.
3. Unscrew the hydraulic pipe union and push the pipe to one side.
4. Remove the two nuts and washers holding the master cylinder to the bulkhead and lift the unit away. Empty the

contents of the reservoir into a clean container.
5. Replacement is a reversal of the removal procedure, after which the braking system must be completely bled.

11. Master Cylinder - Dismantling, Overhaul and Reassembly

1. Unless there are obvious signs of leakage any defects in the master cylinder are usually the last to be detected in the hydraulic system.
2. Before assuming that a fault in the system is in the master cylinder the pipes and wheel cylinders should all be checked and examined as described in Sections 7 and 8.
3. Remove the master cylinder from the car as described in the previous Section.
4. Dismantle and reassemble the unit as described for the clutch master cylinder in Chapter 5, section 5, paragraphs 6 to 14 inclusive.

12. Dual Hydraulic System - Description

In the interest of additional safety some models were fitted with a dual system from October 1968 (see Fig.9.7). This was also servo-assisted but only to the front wheels. The main difference is in the master cylinder which has two outlets instead of one and these outlets are only interdependent insofar as they are both served by a common reservoir. One outlet goes to the servo where it is boosted and then operates the disc brakes of the front. The other outlet serves the rear brakes. Should a fault develop in either of the circuits the other will continue to operate.

13. Tandem Master Cylinder - Dismantling, Overhaul and Reassembly

1. The tandem master cylinder comprises two piston assemblies, one behind the other operating in a common bore. There are two outlets from the master cylinder, one to the front brake servo and one to the rear brakes.
2. To remove the tandem master cylinder disconnect the pushrod from the brake pedal, detach the two hydraulic pipes at their unions with the side of the master cylinder and undo the two nuts and spring washers holding the master cylinder to the bulkhead. Plug the loose pipes to prevent entry of dirt.
3. To dismantle the unit, pull off the rubber dust cover and remove the circlip and washer under the dust cover which holds the pushrod in place. Remove the pushrod.
4. Take the hydraulic fluid reservoir off the cylinder assembly by undoing the two screws on either side of the cylinder.
5. From the top of the cylinder remove the circlip and spring from the primary recuperating valve and with a suitable hexagon headed key take out the plug which holds this valve in place. Then remove the valve assembly.
6. Fit plugs to the two outlet holes and also to the primary recuperating valve aperture. Then, using a suitable air line, blow gently into the other hole on the top of the cylinder. This will remove from the cylinder bore the primary piston and spring, the secondary piston and the secondary recuperating valve assemblies.
7. Remove the piston seal from the primary piston. Lift the tab on the secondary piston spring retainer and remove the piston. Compress the secondary piston spring, move the retainer to one side and remove the secondary recuperating valve stem from the retainer. Then slide the valve spacer and shim from the valve stem, noting the way in which the

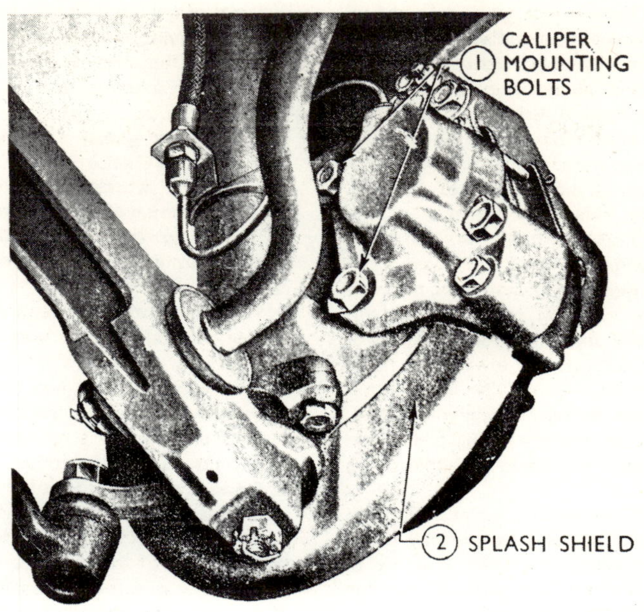

Fig. 9.9. Disc brake mounting bolts

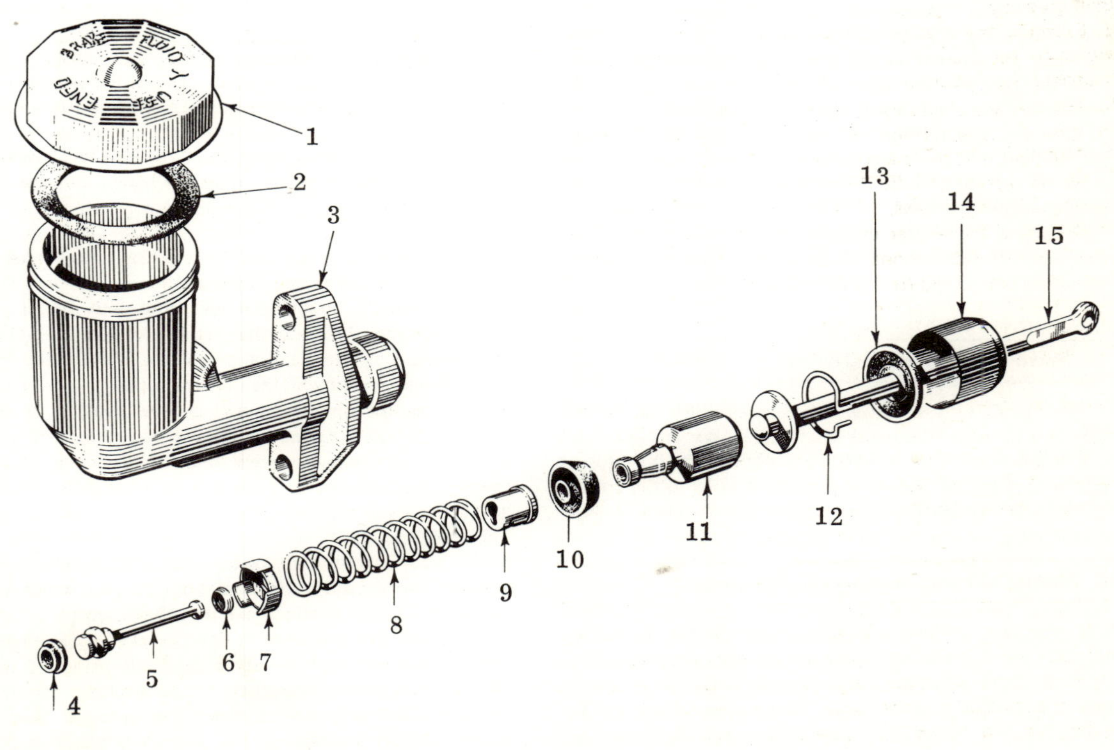

Fig. 9.10. BRAKE MASTER CYLINDER — EXPLODED VIEW

1 Reservoir cap	5 Valve stem	9 Spring seat	13 Dust seal
2 Seal ring	6 Spacer	10 Piston seal	14 Boot
3 Cylinder body	7 Retaining clip	11 Piston	15 Push rod
4 Valve seal	8 Spring	12 Circlip	

shim is fitted.

8. Remove the small rubber valve seal and also the secondary piston seal. Examine all the rubber seals for signs of loose fitting or swelling and renew as necessary. Also examine the state of the cylinder bore for signs of scoring or corrosion. If this is damaged in any way a replacement master cylinder must be fitted. It is also advisable to replace all rubber seals as a matter of course whether they are damaged or not.

9. Clean all parts with approved hydraulic fluid prior to reassembly in the cylinder bore.

10 Fit a new seal onto the secondary piston and a new seal to the valve stem. Replace the shim on the valve stem, making sure that the convex side faces towards the seal spacer which is fitted next, with its legs towards the valve seal.

11 Refit the secondary piston spring over the valve stem, insert the spring retainer, compress the spring and fit the boss in the valve stem into its location in the spring retainer.

12 Place the narrow end of the secondary piston into the spring retainer and secure it in place by pressing down the tab. Dip the now complete secondary assembly in approved hydraulic fluid and carefully slide it into the leading.

13 Place the primary piston spring into the cylinder, fit a new rubber seal to the primary piston, dip it in approved fluid and carefully slide it into the cylinder, drilled end first.

14 Fit the pushrod into the end of the primary piston and retain it with the washer and circlip.

15 Place the primary recuperating valve into its location in the top of the cylinder and check that it is properly located by moving the pushrod up and down a small amount. Screw the retaining plug into position and refit the spring and circlip to the valve plunger.

16 Move the pushrod in and out of the cylinder and check that the recuperating valve opens when the rod is fully withdrawn and closes again when it is pushed in.

17 Check the condition of the front and rear reservoir gaskets and if there is any doubt as to their condition they must be replaced. Refit the reservoir to the cylinder with its two retaining screws.

18 Refitting the master cylinder to the car is a reversal of the removal instructions. When replacement is complete bleed the brakes and road test the car.

---

14. Servo Unit - Removal, Overhaul and Replacement

1. The servo unit which is fitted to all 1996 cc engined cars and to those fitted with dual braking systems also, uses the depression in the engine inlet manifold as a source of power to boost the hydraulic pressure applied to the brakes.

2. Provided the air filter element is changed regularly every 5,000 miles - or more often in excessively dusty conditions - no other maintenance is necessary. Failure of the servo unit is indicated by a heavier than normal pressure required on the pedal. This can be verified by disconnecting the manifold connection pipe, blocking the manifold orifice so that the engine will run properly and trying the brakes. If the brakes are not working properly make sure that all other parts of the system are checked before deciding to dismantle the servo as it is a delicate mechanism and great care and cleanliness are essential.

3. Seal the hydraulic fluid reservoir cap, disconnect the vacuum hose from the top of the unit and the two hydraulic pipe connections. Block the ends of the hydraulic pipes.

4. Undo the mounting bolts and take the unit from the car.

5. Before starting dismantling clean the exterior thoroughly and prepare a clean surface (and clean hands!) to work on.

Dirt and grit must be kept out of the unit and every care must be taken to make sure of absolute cleanliness.

6. Remove the screws holding the power cylinder cover plate, releasing the cover gradually under pressure of the return spring.

7. Remove the gasket and take out the retainer, piston, wick, leather and return spring.

8. Inside the cylinder undo the three bolts holding the cylinder clamping plate to the servo body. The cylinder can then be detached from the body and the vacuum pipe detached from the rubber grommet in the cylinder end flange.

9. The slave piston and seals will now all be ejected from the cylinder body under pressure from the spring behind them.

10 Unscrew the suction pipe connector, which incorporates a non-return valve, from the top of the body.

11 Take out the four screws holding the cover to the valve chest on the side of the body.

12 Remove the two screws holding the retainer over the air valves and remove it together with the horseshoe spring.

13 By pressing in the plug on the end of the control piston the inner end of the tee piece is released and can be taken out together with the valves and springs.

14 By removing the plug from the control cylinder the control piston assembly may be taken out.

15 The control piston assembly may be dismantled by depressing the spring and removing the circlip. The two seals on the piston and plug can be pulled off.

16 The slave piston must be renewed, if necessary, as a complete assembly because the inner seal is an integral part of it.

17 Examine all the pistons and cylinders for any signs of wear and corrosion and if in doubt the parts as necessary must be renewed.

18 Thoroughly clean all parts in methylated spirits.

19 If the nylon air valves show signs of light ridging their faces may be lapped on a piece of glass using fine lapping paste.

20 Reassembly of the pistons and the unit is a reversal of the dismantling procedure. Renew all seals. Pay particular attention to:-

a) The lips of the seals on the control piston must face outwards from the centre of the piston.

b) Lubricate the control cylinder bore with rubber grease only and when inserting the piston take care that the seal lips are not turned back and that the hole in the piston lines up with the hole in the cylinder wall.

c) Replace the air valve rocking lever together with the valves with the locating lug for the horseshoe spring away from the retaining clip screw holes. Replace the horseshoe spring, clip, screws and cover but do not tighten the cover until the pipe has been located when the end cover is replaced.

d) Fit new gaskets and copper washers between the body and power cylinder and on the clamping bolts. When refitting the body to the cylinder make sure the power piston moves freely up and down in the cylinder before finally tightening the bolts.

e) The power piston leather should be renewed and the bore of the cylinder smeared with servo lubricant and the piston rod with rubber grease. The threads of the vacuum pipe plug should be treated with sealing compound before refitting.

21 Replace the unit in the car in the reverse order of removal and reconnect the vacuum and hydraulic pipes securely. Bleed the hydraulic system and road test the car. NOTE: On some later models and those fitted with dual

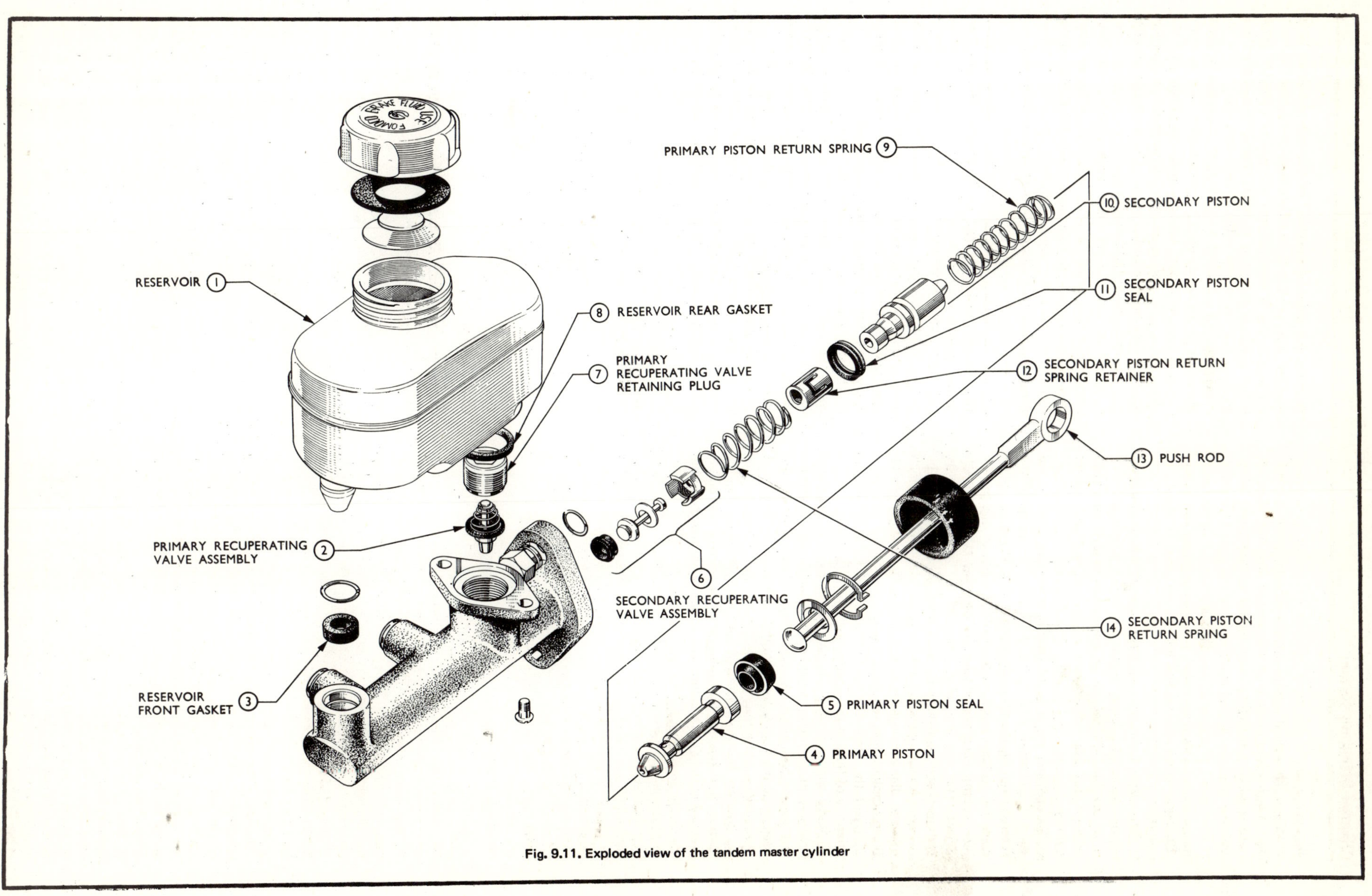

Fig. 9.11. Exploded view of the tandem master cylinder

braking systems the design of the servo unit is radically changed. These units are not normally serviced and in any case the average home owner normally will not have the special tools or facilities necessary for a proper overhaul to be made.

15. Hydraulic System - Bleeding

1. The system should need bleeding only when some part of the system has been dismantled which would allow air into the fluid circuit; or if the reservoir level has been allowed to drop so far that air has entered the master cylinder.

2. Ensure that a supply of clean non-aerated fluid of the correct specification is to hand in order to replenish the reservoir during the bleeding process. It is advisable, if not essential, to have someone available to help, as one person has to pump the brake pedal while the other attends to each wheel. The reservoir level has also to be continuously watched and replenished. Fluid bled out should not be re-used. A clean glass jar and a 9-12 inch length of $1/8$ inch internal diameter rubber tube that will fit tightly over the bleed nipples is also required.

3. Bleed the front brakes first as these hold the largest quantity of fluid in the system.

4. Make sure the bleed nipple is clean and put a small quantity of fluid in the bottom of the jar. Fit the tube onto the nipple and place the other end in the jar under the surface of the liquid. Keep it under the surface throughout the bleeding operation.

5. Unscrew the bleed screw ½ turn and get the assistant to depress and release the brake pedal in short sharp bursts when you direct him. Short sharp jabs are better than long slow ones because they will force any air bubbles along the line ahead of the fluid rather than pump the fluid past them. It is not essential to remove all the air the first time. If the whole system is being bled, attend to each wheel for three or four complete pedal strokes and then repeat the process. On the second time around operate the pedal sharply in the same way until no more bubbles are apparent. The bleed screw should be tightened and closed with the brake pedal fully depressed which ensures that no aerated fluid can get back into the system. Do not forget to keep the reservoir topped up throughout.

6. When all four wheels have been satisfactorily bled depress the foot pedal which should offer a firmer resistance with no trace of 'sponginess'. The pedal should not continue to go down under sustained pressure. If it does there is a leak or the master cylinder seals are worn out.

16. Brake Pedal and Stop Light Switch - Removal and Replacement

1. The brake pedal may need removing because wear in the pivot shaft may have caused it to become sloppy in its operation. Follow the procedures as described in Chapter 5, section 6, for removal of the clutch pedal.

2. The stop light switch is mounted on the pedal bracket above the shaft and is mechanically operated by a plunger from the pedal arm. The plunger setting is adjustable by two locknuts and should be such that the switch operates within a movement of $7/16$ in. depression of the pedal.

3. The removal of the switch is simply a matter of detaching the wire and unscrewing the mounting bolts. When fitting a new one, it should be positioned by means of the adjusting nuts so that it lines up with the operating plunger.

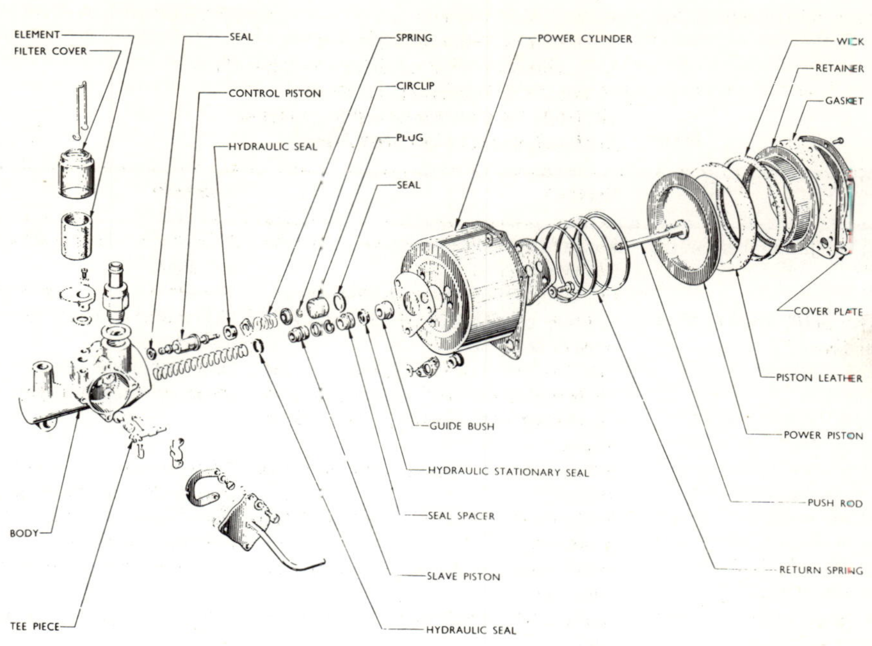

Fig. 9.12. Exploded view of the servo unit

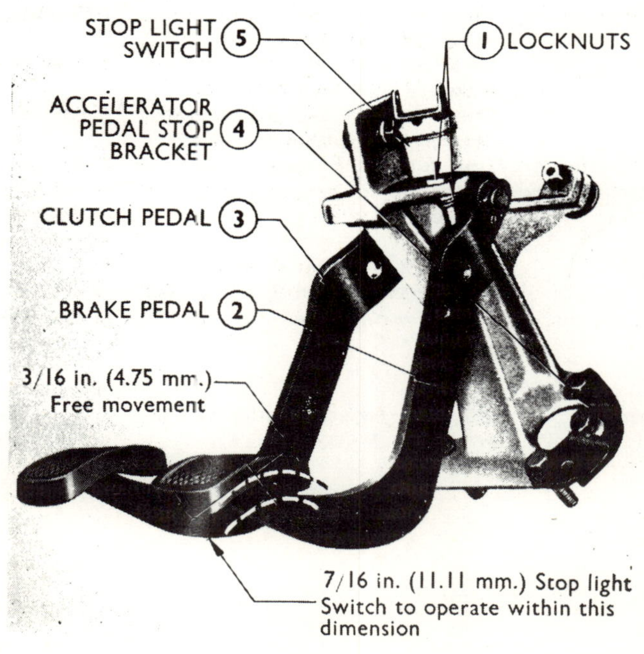

Fig. 9.13. Brake pedal bracket assembly

Before diagnosing faults from the following chart, check that any braking irregularities are not caused by:-

1. Uneven or incorrect tyre pressures
2. Incorrect 'mix' of radial and cross-ply tyres
3. Wear in the steering mechanism
4. Defects in the suspension and dampers
5. Misalignment of the body frame

Symptom	Reason	Remedy
Pedal travels a long way before the brakes operate	Automatic adjuster on rear shoes not functioning.	Check and repair rear brake automatic adjusters.
	Disc pads or linings excessively worn.	Inspect and renew as necessary.
Stopping ability poor, even though pedal pressure is firm	Linings, pads, discs or drums badly worn or scored.	Dismantle, inspect, and renew as required.
	One or more calliper piston or rear wheel cylinder seized, resulting in some pads/shoes not pressing against discs/drums.	Dismantle and inspect cylinders and repair or renew as necessary.
	Brake pads or linings contaminated with oil.	Renew pads or linings and repair source of oil contamination.
	Wrong type of pads or linings fitted (too hard)	Verify type of material which is correct for the car and fit it.
	Brake pads or shoes incorrectly assembled.	Check for correct assembly.
	Servo unit (where fitted) not functioning.	Check and repair as necessary.
Car veers to one side when brakes are	Brake pads on one side are contaminated with oil.	Renew pads and repair source of oil contamination.
	Hydraulic pistons in callipers are partially or wholly seized on one side.	Inspect calliper pistons for correct movement and repair as necessary.
	A mixture of pad materials used between sides.	Standardize on types of pads fitted.
	Unequal wear between sides caused by partially seized hydraulic pistons in brake callipers.	Check pistons and renew pads and discs as required.
Pedal feels spongy when the brakes are applied	Air is present in the hydraulic system.	Bleed the hydraulic system and check for any signs of leakage.
Pedal feels springy when the brakes are applied	Rear brake linings not beeded into the drums (after fitting new ones).	Allow time for new linings to bed in.
	Master cylinder, brake calliper or drum backplate mounting bolts loose.	Tighten mounting bolts as necessary.
	Severe wear in rear drums causing distortion when brakes are applied.	Renew drums and linings.
Pedal travels right down with little or no resistance and brakes are virtually non-operative.	Leak in hydraulic system resulting in lack of pressure for operation of wheel cylinders.	Examine the whole of the hydraulic system and locate and repair the source of the leak(s). Test after repairing each and every leak source.
	If no signs of leakage are apparent the master cylinder internal seals are failing to sustain pressure.	Overhaul the master cylinder. If indications are that seals have failed for reasons other than wear, all the wheel cylinder seals should be checked also and the system completely replenished with the correct fluid.
Binding, juddering, overheating	One, or a combination of causes given in the foregoing sections.	Complete and systematic inspection of the whole braking system.

Chapter 10/Electrical System

Contents

Specifications

Battery

Type	Lead acid 12 volt
Capacity (standard)	38 amp. hrs. at 20 hr. rate
(cold climate heavy duty)	57 amp. hrs. at 20 hr. rate
Plates per cell (standard)...	9
(heavy duty)	13
Specific gravity - charged	1.275 to 1.290
Electrolyte capacity (standard)	4.5 Imp. pints (5.4 U.S. pints, 2.5 litres)
(heavy duty)	6.4 Imp. pints (7.7 U.S. pints, 3.6 litres)
Earth lead	NEGATIVE

Generator

Type	Lucas C40/C40L - 12 v. 2 brush
Speed (ratio to engine)	1.8:1
Maximum charge	C40 22 amps. C40L 25 amps.
Brush length (new)	.72 ins. (18.24 mm)
Brush spring tension	18 to 24 ozs.
Field coil resistance	C40 6 ohms. C40L 5.9 ohms.
Cut in speed (engine r.p.m.)...	810 r.p.m. (Std.) 710 r.p.m. (Heavy Duty)

Starter Motor

Type	4 brush inertia pinion engagement
Gear ratio	13.44:1
Pinion/ring gear no. of teeth	9/121
Current load (zero r.p.m.)	340 amp at 7.4 volts
(1,000 r.p.m.)	245 amps at 8.7 volts

Regulator - Lucas RB340

Cut-out - cut-in voltage	12.6 to 13.4 volts
- Drop off voltage	9.3 to 11.2 volts
- Air gap - armature to core	.035 to .045 in. (.89 to 1.14 mm)
Current regulator - on - load setting	Generator output $\pm$ 1.5 amps.

132

- Air gap - armature to core	.045 to .049 in. (1.14 to 1.25 mm)
Voltage regulator - Open circuit setting	13.8 to 14.2 volts at 20ºC at 1500 r.p.m.
- Air gap - armature to core	.045 to .049 in. (1.14 to 1.25 mm)

Note:- Heavy duty generator (C40L) is matched by the appropriate heavy duty regulator (No. 37342 stamped on base).

Light Bulbs

Headlamps (seal beam units)	60/45 watts
Side lights	4 c.p.
Rear/stop lights	4/32 c.p.
Flasher lamps	32 c.p.
Number plate lamp	6 watt
Interior lamp	6 watt
Instrument panel and warning lights	2.2 watts

1. General Description

The electrical system is 12 volt and, excluding the ignition circuits (Chapter 4), the main items are:-

a) Battery - lead acid 12 v. Negative earthed.
b) Voltage and current regulator and cut-out.
c) D.C. dynamo driven by the fan belt.
d) Starter motor which engages into the flywheel starter ring with an inertia engagement pinion.

The battery provides starting power and also a reserve should the loading of the equipment exceed the output of the dynamo. When the dynamo is not fully loaded the extra power is used to recharge the battery. The battery and generator are protected by a cut-out and regulator system which ensures that when the battery is fully charged the dynamo output is reduced and controlled accordingly.

2. Battery - Removal and Replacement

1. The battery is positioned on a tray in the front of the engine compartment forward of the nearside suspension.
2. Disconnect the earthed negative lead (photo) and then the positive lead by slackening the retaining nuts and bolts.
3. Remove the battery clamp and carefully lift the battery off its tray (photo). Hold the battery vertical to ensure that no electrolyte is spilled.
4. Replacement is a direct reversal of this procedure. NOTE: Replace the positive lead and the earth (negative) lead, smearing the terminals with petroleum jelly (vaseline) to prevent corrosion. NEVER use an ordinary grease as applied to other parts of the car.

3. Battery - Maintenance and Inspection

1. Normal weekly battery maintenance consists of checking the electrolyte level of each cell to ensure that the separators are covered by ¼ in. of electrolyte. If the level has fallen top up the battery using distilled water only. Do not overfill. If a battery is overfilled or any electrolyte spilled, immediately wipe away the excess as electrolyte attacks and corrodes any metal it comes into contact with very rapidly.
2. As well as keeping the terminals clean and covered with petroleum jelly, the top of the battery, and especially the top of the cells, should be kept clean and dry. This helps prevent corrosion and ensures that the battery does not become partially discharged by leakage through dampness and dirt.

3. Once every three months remove the battery and inspect the battery securing bolts, the battery clamp plate, tray, and battery leads for corrosion (white fluffy deposits on the metal which are brittle to touch). If any corrosion is found, clean off the deposits with ammonia and paint over the clean metal with an anti-rust + anti-acid paint.
4. At the same time inspect the battery case for cracks. If a crack is found, clean and plug it with one of the proprietary compounds marketed by firms such as Holts for this purpose. If leakage through the crack has been excessive then it will be necessary to refill the appropriate cell with fresh electrolyte as detailed later. Cracks are frequently caused to the top of the battery cases by pouring in distilled water in the middle of winter AFTER instead of BEFORE a run. This gives the water no chance to mix with the electrolyte and so the former freezes and splits the battery case.
5. If topping up the batteries becomes excessive and the cases have been inspected for cracks that could cause leakage, but none are found, the batteries are being over-charged and the voltage regulator will have to be checked and reset.
6. With the batteries on the bench at the three monthly interval check, measure their specific gravity with a hydrometer to determine the state of charge and condition of the electrolyte. There should be very little variation between the different cells and if a variation in excess of 0.025 is present it will be due to either:-

a) Loss of electrolyte from the battery at some time caused by spillage or a leak resulting in a drop in the specific gravity of the electrolyte, when the deficiency was replaced with distilled water instead of fresh electrolyte.
b) An internal short circuit caused by buckling of the plates of a similar malady pointing to the likelihood of total battery failure in the near future.

7. The specific gravity of the electrolyte for fully charged conditions at the electrolyte temperature indicated, is listed in Table A. The specific gravity of a fully discharged battery at different temperatures of the electrolyte is given at Table B.

Table A

Specific Gravity - Battery Fully Charged

1.268 at 100ºF or 38ºC electrolyte temperature
1.272 at 90ºF or 32ºC electrolyte temperature
1.276 at 80ºF or 27ºC electrolyte temperature
1.280 at 70ºF or 21ºC electrolyte temperature
1.284 at 60ºF or 16ºC electrolyte temperature
1.288 at 50ºF or 10ºC electrolyte temperature

1.292 at 40°F or   4°C electrolyte temperature
1.296 at 30°F or -1.5°C electrolyte temperature

Table B

Specific Gravity - Battery Fully Discharged

1.098 at 100°F or 38°C electrolyte temperature
1.102 at   90°F or 32°C electrolyte temperature
1.106 at   80°F or 27°C electrolyte temperature
1.110 at   70°F or 21°C electrolyte temperature
1.114 at   60°F or 16°C electrolyte temperature
1.118 at   50°F or 10°C electrolyte temperature
1.122 at   40°F or   4°C electrolyte temperature
1.126 at   30°F or -1.5°C electrolyte temperature

4. Electrolyte Replenishment

1. If the battery is in a fully charged state and one of the cells maintains a specific gravity reading which is 0.025 or more lower than the others, and a check of each cell has been made with a voltage meter to check for short circuits (a four to seven second test should give a steady reading of between 1.2 to 1.8 volts), then it is likely that electrolyte has been lost from the cell with the low reading at some time.

2. Top up the cell with a solution of 1 part sulphuric acid to 2.5 parts of water. If the cell is already fully topped up draw some electrolyte out of it with a pipette. The total capacity of each cell is ¾ pint.

3. When mixing the sulphuric acid and water NEVER ADD WATER TO SULPHURIC ACID - always pour the acid slowly onto the water in a glass container. IF WATER IS ADDED TO SULPHURIC ACID IT WILL EXPLODE.

4. Continue to top up the cell with the freshly made electrolyte and then recharge the battery and check the hydrometer readings.

5. Battery Charging

1. In winter time when heavy demand is placed upon the battery, such as when starting from cold, and much electrical equipment is continually in use, it is a good idea to occasionally have the battery fully charged from an external source at the rate of 3.5 to 4 amps.

2. Continue to charge the battery at this rate until no further rise in specific gravity is noted over a four hour period.

3. Alternatively, a trickle charger charging at the rate of 1.5 amps can be safely used overnight.

4. Specially rapid 'boost' charges which are claimed to restore the power of the battery in 1 to 2 hours are most dangerous as they can cause serious damage to the battery plates through over-heating.

5. While charging the battery, note that the temperature of the electrolyte should never exceed 100°F.

6. Dynamo - Routine Maintenance

1. Routine maintenance consists of checking the tension of the fan belt, and lubricating the dynamo rear bearing once every 5,000 miles.

2. The fan belt should be tight enough to ensure no slip between the belt and the dynamo pulley. If a shrieking noise comes from the engine when the unit is accelerated rapidly, it is likely that it is the fan belt slipping. On the other hand, the belt must not be too taut or the bearings will wear rapidly and cause dynamo failure or bearing seizure. Ideally ½ in. of total free movement should be available at the fan belt midway between the fan and the dynamo pulley.

3. To adjust the fan belt tension slightly slacken the three dynamo retaining bolts, and swing the dynamo on the upper two bolts outwards to increase the tension, and inwards to lower it.

4. It is best to leave the bolts fairly tight so that considerable effort has to be used to move the dynamo; otherwise it is difficult to get the correct setting. If the dynamo is being moved outwards to increase the tension and the bolts have only been slackened a little, a long spanner acting as a lever placed behind the dynamo with the lower end resting against the block works very well in moving the dynamo outwards. Retighten the dynamo bolts and check that the dynamo pulley is correctly aligned with the fan belt.

5. Lubrication on the dynamo consists of inserting three drops of S.A.E. 30 engine oil in the small oil hole in the centre of the commutator end bracket. This lubricates the rear bearing. The front bearing is pre-packed with grease and requires no attention.

7. Dynamo - Testing in Position

1. If, with the engine running no charge comes from the dynamo, or the charge is very low, first check that the fan belt is in place and is not slipping. Then check that the leads from the control box to the dynamo are firmly attached and that one has not come loose from its terminal.

2. The lead from the 'D' terminal on the dynamo should be connected to the 'D' terminal on the control box, and similarly the 'F' terminals on the dynamo and control box should also be connected together. Check that this is so and that the leads have not been incorrectly fitted.

3. Make sure none of the electrical equipment (such as the lights or radio) is on and then pull the leads off the dynamo terminals together with a short length of wire.

4. Attach to the centre of this length of wire the positive clip of a 0-20 volts voltmeter and run the other clip to earth on the dynamo yoke. Start the engine and allow it to idle at approximately 750 r.p.m. At this speed the dynamo should give a reading of about 15 volts on the voltmeter. There is no point in raising the engine speed above a fast idle as the reading will then be inaccurate.

5. If no reading is recorded then check the brushes and brush connections. If a very low reading of approximately 1 volt is observed then the field winding may be suspect.

6. If a reading of between 4 to 6 amps is recorded it is likely that the armature winding is at fault.

7. On early dynamos it was possible to remove the dynamo cover band and check the dynamo and brushes in position. With the Lucas C40-1 windowless yoke dynamo it must be removed and dismantled before the brushes and commutator can be attended to.

8. If the voltmeter shows a good reading then with the temporary link still in position connect both leads from the control box to 'D' and 'F' on the dynamo ('D' to 'D' and 'F' to 'F'). Release the lead from the 'D' terminal at the control box end and clip one lead from the voltmeter to the end of the cable, and the other lead to a good earth. With the engine running at the same speed as previously, an identical voltage to that recorded at the dynamo should be noted on the voltmeter. If no voltage is recorded then there is a break in the wire. If the voltage is the same as recorded at the dynamo then check the 'F' lead in similar fashion. If both readings are the same as at the dynamo then it will be necessary to test the control box.

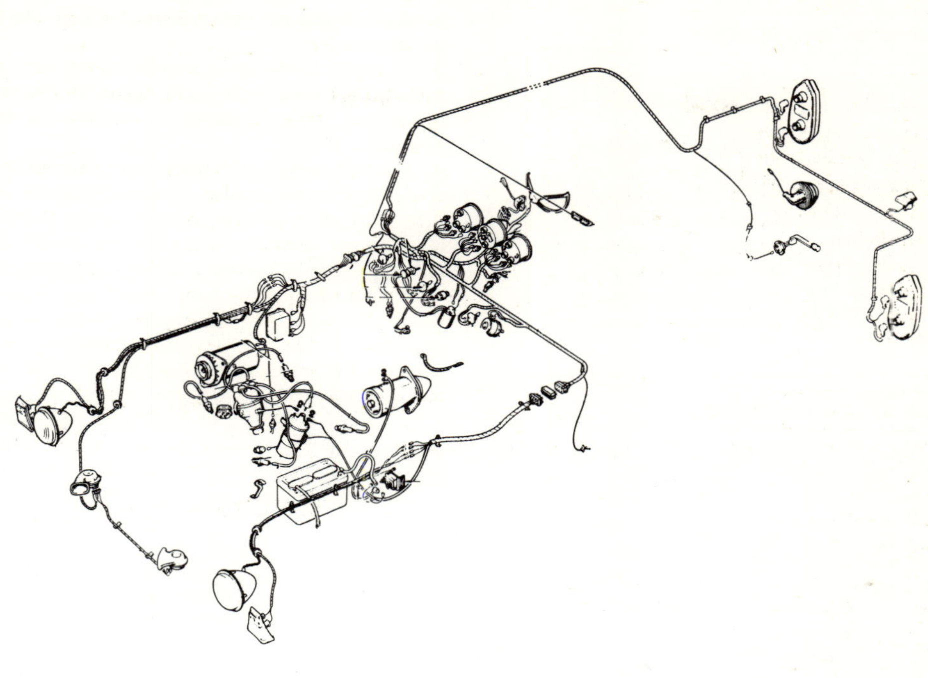

Fig. 10.1. General layout of the Electrical System

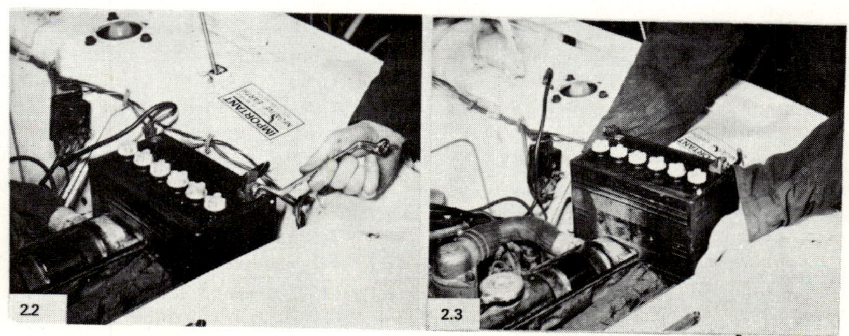

8. Dynamo - Removal and Replacement

1. Slacken the two dynamo retaining bolts, and the nut on the sliding link, and move the dynamo in towards the engine so that the fan belt can be removed.
2. Disconnect the two leads from the dynamo terminals.
3. Remove the nut from the sliding link bolt, and remove the two upper bolts. The dynamo is then free to be lifted away from the engine.
4. Replacement is a reversal of the above procedure. Do not finally tighten the retaining bolts and the nut on the sliding link until the fan belt has been tensioned correctly. See 10/6.2 for details.

9. Dynamo - Dismantling and Repair

1. Mount the dynamo in a vice and unscrew and remove the two through bolts from the commutator end bracket (photo).
2. Mark the commutator end bracket and the dynamo casing so the end bracket can be replaced in its original position. Pull the end bracket off the armature shaft. NOTE some versions of the dynamo may have a raised pip on the end bracket which locates in a recess on the edge of the casing. If so, marking the end bracket and casing is not necessary. A pip may also be found on the drive end bracket at the opposite end of the casing (see photo).
3. Lift the two brush springs and draw the brushes out of the brush holders (arrowed).
4. Measure the brushes and, if worn down to 9/32 in. or less, unscrew the screws holding the brush leads to the end bracket. Take off the brushes complete with leads. Old and new brushes are compared in the photograph.
5. If no locating pip can be found, mark the drive end bracket and the dynamo casing so the drive end bracket can be replaced in its original position. Then pull the drive end bracket, complete with armature, out of the casing (photo).
6. Check the condition of the ball bearing in the drive end plate by firmly holding the plate and noting if there is visible side movement of the armature shaft in relation to the end plate. If play is present the armature assembly must be separated from the end plate. If the bearing is sound there is no need to carry out the work described in the following two paragraphs.
7. Hold the armature in one hand (mount if carefully in a vice if preferred) and undo the nut holding the pulley wheel and fan in place. Pull off the pulley wheel and fan.
8. Next remove the woodruff key (arrowed) from its slot in the armature shaft and also the bearing locating ring.
9. Place the drive end bracket across the open jaws of a vice with the armature downwards and gently tap the armature shaft from the bearing (photo) in the end plate with the aid of a suitable drift.
10 Carefully inspect the armature and check it for open or short circuited windings. It is a good indication of an open circuited armature when the commutator segments are burnt. If the armature has short circuited the commutator segments will be very badly burnt, and the overheated armature windings badly discoloured. If open or short circuits are suspected then test by substituting the suspect armature for a new one (photo)
11 Check the resistance of the field coils. To do this, connect an ohmmeter between the field terminal and the yoke and note the reading on the ohmmeter which should be about 6 ohms. If the ohmmeter reading is infinity this indicates an open circuit in the field winding. If the ohmmeter reading is below 5 ohms this indicates that one of the field coils is faulty and must be replaced.

12 Field coil replacement involves the use of a wheel operated screwdriver, a soldering iron, caulking and riveting and this operation is considered to be beyond the scope of most owners. Therefore, if the field coils are at fault either purchase a rebuilt dynamo, or take the casing to a Ford dealer or electrical engineering works for new field coils to be fitted.
13 Next check the condition of the commutator (arrowed). If it is dirty and blackened, as shown, clean it with a petrol dampened rag. If the commutator is in good condition the surface will be smooth and quite free from pits or burnt areas, and the insulated segments clearly defined.
14 If, after the commutator has been cleaned, pits and burnt spots are still present, wrap a strip of glass paper round the commutator taking great care to move the commutator ¼ of a turn every ten turns till it is thoroughly clean (photo).
15 In extreme cases of wear the commutator can be mounted in a lathe and with the lathe turning at high speed, a very fine cut may be taken off the commutator. Then polish the commutator with glass paper. If the commutator has worn so that the insulators between the segments are level with the top of the segments, then undercut the insulators to a depth of $1/32$ in. (.8 mm). The best tool to use for this purpose is half a hacksaw blade ground to a thickness of the insulator, and with the handle end of the blade covered in insulating tape to make it comfortable to hold. This is the sort of finish the surface of the commutator should have when finished. (photo).
16 Check the bush bearing (arrowed) in the commutator end bracket for wear by noting if the armature spindle rocks when placed in it. If worn it must be renewed.
17 The bush bearing can be removed by a suitable extractor or by screwing a $5/8$ in. tap four or five times into the bush. The tap complete with bush is then pulled out of the end bracket.
18 NOTE before fitting the new bush bearing that it is of the porous bronze type, and it is essential that it is allowed to stand in S.A.E. 30 engine oil for at least 24 hours before fitment. In an emergency the bush can be immersed in hot oil (100°C) for 2 hours.
19 Carefully fit the new bush into the end plate, pressing it in until the end of the bearing is flush with the inner side of the end plate. If available, press the bush in with a smooth shouldered mandrel the same diameter as the armature shaft.

10. Dynamo - Repair and Reassembly

1. To renew the ball bearing fitted to the drive end bracket drill out the rivets which hold the bearing retainer plate to the end bracket and lift off the plate.
2. Press out the bearing from the end bracket and remove the corrugated and felt washers from the bearing housing.
3. Thoroughly clean the bearing housing, and the new bearing and pack with high melting-point grease.
4. Place the felt washer and corrugated washer in that order in the end bracket bearing housing.
5. Then fit the new bearing as shown.
6. Gently tap the bearing into place with the aid of a suitable drift.
7. Replace the bearing plate and fit three new rivets.
8. Open up the rivets with the aid of a suitable cold chisel.
9. Finally peen over the open end of the rivets with the aid of a ball hammer as illustrated.
10 Refit the drive end bracket to the armature shaft. Do not try and force the bracket on but with the aid of a suitable socket abuting the bearing tap the bearing on gently, so pulling the end bracket down with it.
11 Slide the spacer up the shaft and refit the woodruff

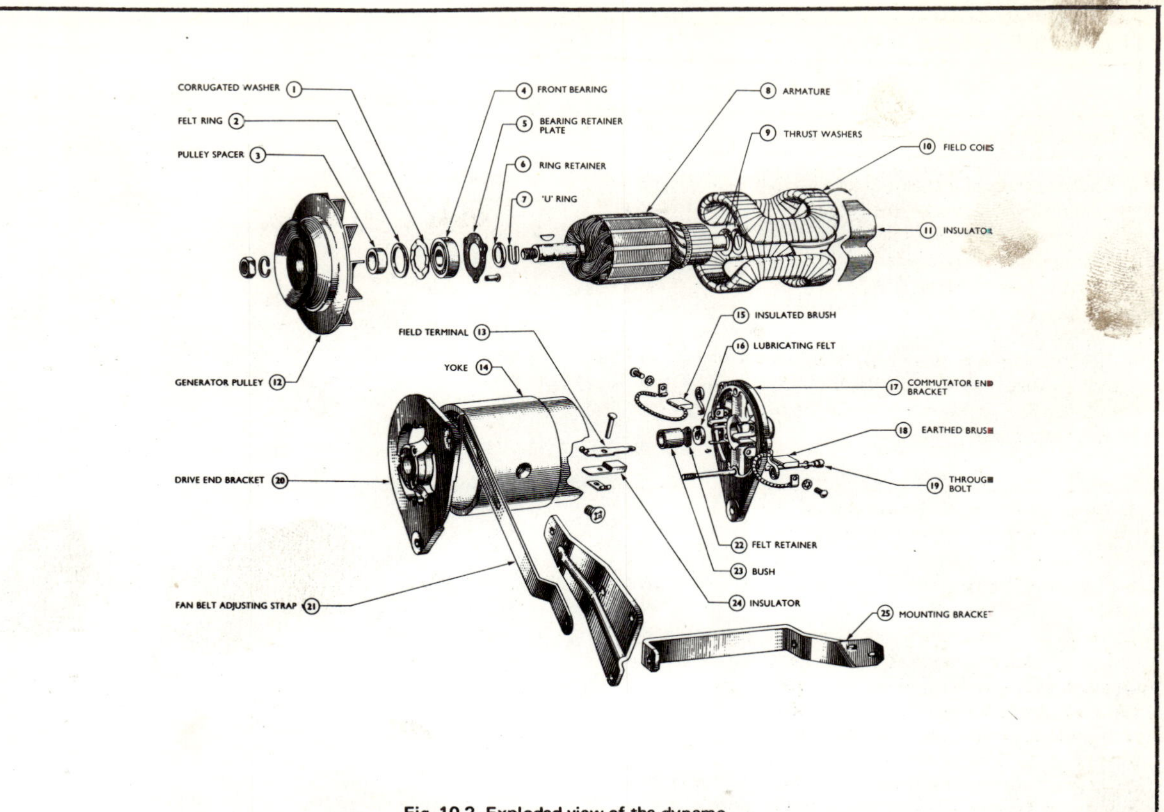

Fig. 10.2. Exploded view of the dynamo

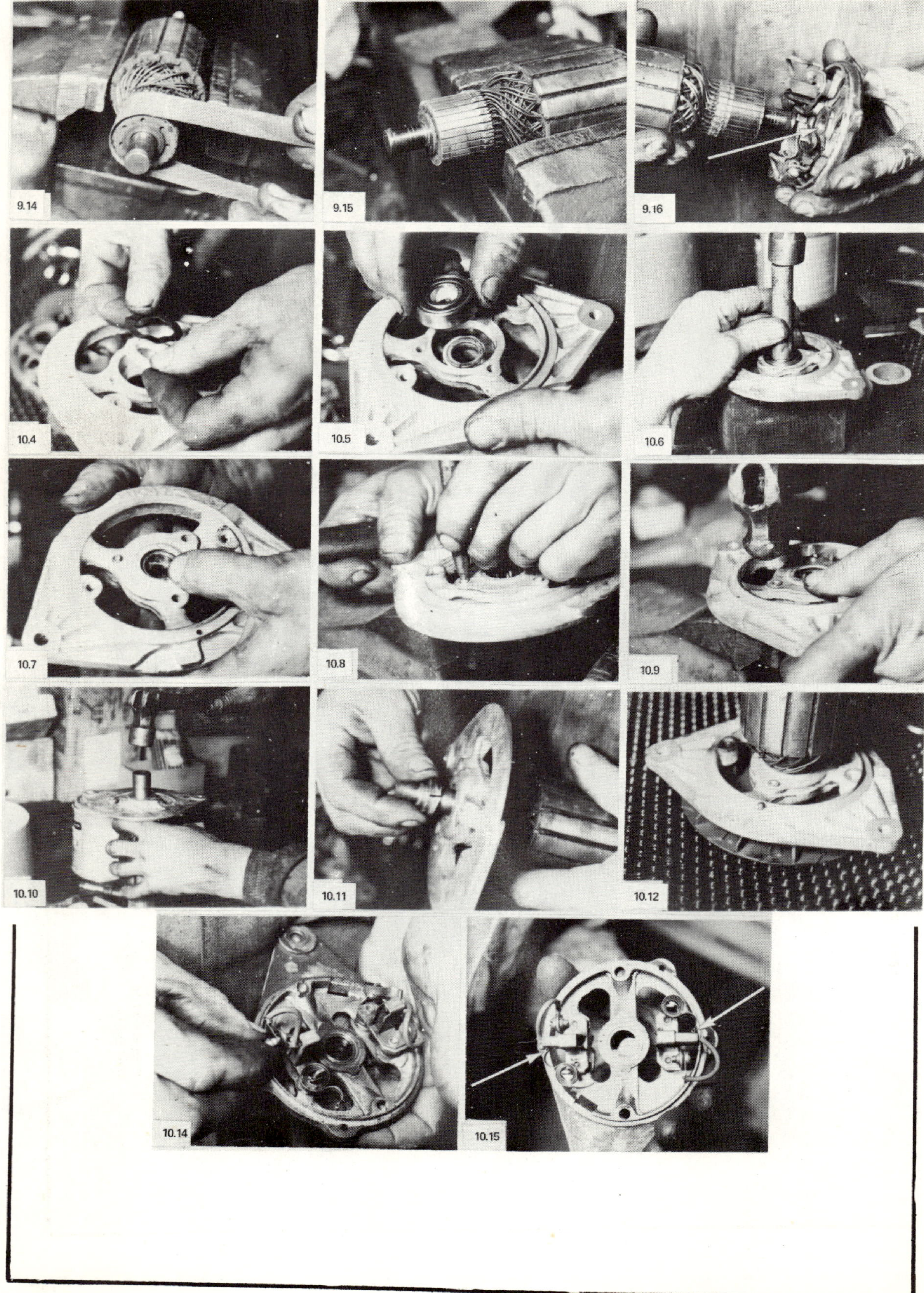

9.14
9.15
9.16
10.4
10.5
10.6
10.7
10.8
10.9
10.10
10.11
10.12
10.14
10.15

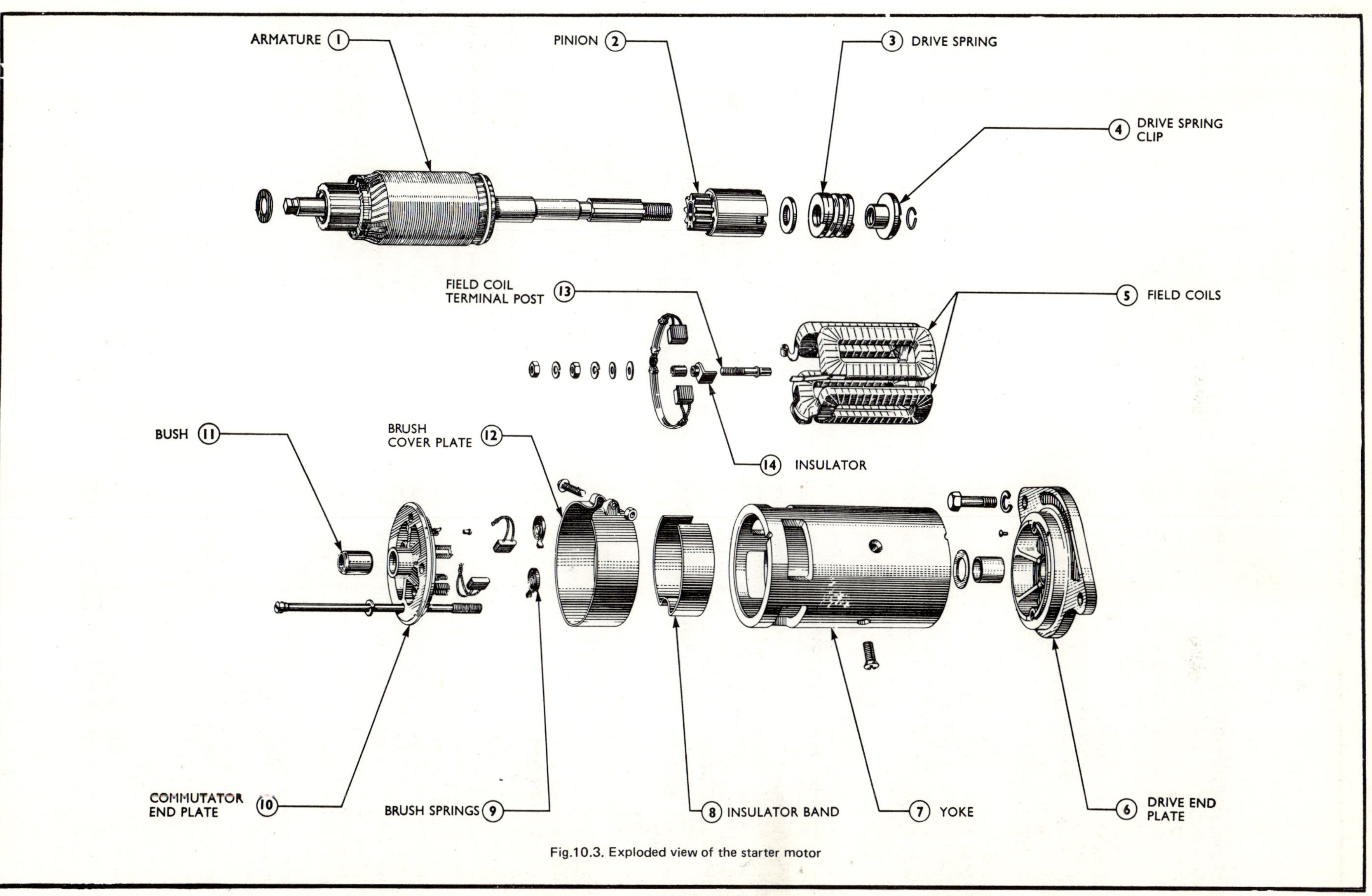

Fig.10.3. Exploded view of the starter motor

key.

12 Replace the fan and pulley wheel and then fit the spring washer and nut and tighten the latter. The drive bracket end of the dynamo is now fully assembled as shown.

13 If the brushes are little worn and are to be used again then ensure that they are placed in the same holders from which they were removed. When refitting brushes, either new or old, check that they move freely in their holders. If either brush sticks, clean with a petrol moistened rag and if still stiff, lightly polish the sides of the brush with a very fine file until the brush moves quite freely in its holder.

14 Tighten the two retaining screws and washers which hold the wire leads to the brushes in place.

15 It is far easier to slip the end piece with brushes over the commutator if the brushes are raised in their holders as shown and held in this position by the pressure of the springs resting against their flanks (arrowed).

16 Refit the armature to the casing and then the commutator end plate and screw up the two through bolts.

17 Finally, hook the ends of the two springs off the flanks of the brushes and onto their heads so the brushes are forced down into contact with the armature.

---

11. Starter Motor - General Description

The starter motor is mounted on the left hand lower side of the engine end plate, and is held in position by two bolts which also clamp the bellhousing flange. The motor is of the four field coil, four pole piece type, and utilises four spring-loaded commutator brushes. Two of these brushes are earthed, and the other two are insulated and attached to the field coil ends.

---

12. Starter Motor - Testing in Engine

1. If the starter motor fails to operate then check the condition of the battery by turning on the headlamps. If they glow brightly for several seconds and then gradually dim, the battery is in an uncharged condition.

2. If the headlamps glow brightly and it is obvious that the battery is in good condition then check the tightness of the battery wiring connections (and in particular the earth lead from the battery terminal to its connection on the body-frame). Check the tightness of the connections at the relay switch and at the starter motor. Check the wiring with a voltmeter for breaks or shorts.

3. If the wiring is in order then check that the starter motor solenoid switch is operating. On early models this can be done by pressing the central rubber covered plunger. If the starter now operates it means that the solenoid coil in the switch is not functioning. This can be due to the starter wires from the ignition switch to the solenoid terminals being broken. Otherwise the solenoid is burnt out and will need renewal. On later models no button is available so the only way to check is by shorting across the two main terminals with something very heavy. Do not prolong this as the load is anything up to 300 amps and burning the contacts may occur.

4. If the battery is fully charged, the wiring in order, and the switch working and the starter motor fails to operate then it will have to be removed from the car for examination. Before this is done, however, ensure that the starter pinion has not jammed in mesh with the flywheel. Check by turning the square end of armature shaft with a spanner. This will free the pinion if it is stuck in engagement with the flywheel teeth.

---

13. Starter Motor - Removal and Replacement

1. Disconnect the battery earth lead from the negative terminal.

2. Disconnect the starter motor cable from the terminal on the starter motor end plate.

3. Working under the car loosen, and then remove, the two starter motor securing bolts taking care to support the motor so as to prevent damage to the drive components.

4. Lift the starter motor out of engagement with the flywheel ring and lower it out of the car.

5. Replacement is a straightforward reversal of the removal procedure.

---

14. Starter Motor - Dismantling, Repair and Reassembly

1. With the starter motor on the bench, loosen the screw on the cover band and slip the cover band off. With a piece of wire bent into the shape of a hook, lift back each of the brush springs in turn and check the movement of the brushes in their holders by pulling on the flexible connectors. If the brushes are so worn that their faces do not rest against the commutator, or if the ends of the brush leads are exposed on their working face, they must be renewed.

2. If any of the brushes tend to stick in their holders then wash them with a petrol moistened cloth and, if necessary, lightly polish the sides of the brush with a very fine file, until the brushes move quite freely in their holders.

3. If the surface of the commutator is dirty or blackened, clean it with a petrol dampened rag. Secure the starter motor in a vice and check it by connecting a heavy gauge cable between the starter motor terminal and a 12 volt battery.

4. Connect the cable from the other battery terminal to earth in the starter motor body. If the motor turns at high speed it is in good order.

5. If the starter motor still fails to function, or if it is wished to renew the brushes, it is necessary to further dismantle the motor.

6. Lift the brush springs with the wire hook and lift all four brushes out of their holders one at a time.

7. Remove the terminal nuts and washers from the terminal post on the commutator end bracket.

8. Unscrew the two through bolts which hold the end plates together and pull off the commutator end bracket. Also remove the driving end bracket which will come away complete with the armature.

9. At this stage, if the brushes are to be renewed, their flexible connectors must be unsoldered and the connectors of new brushes soldered in their place. Check that the new brushes move freely in their holders as detailed above. If cleaning the commutator with petrol fails to remove all the burnt areas and spots, then wrap a piece of glass paper round the commutator and rotate the armature. If the commutator is very badly worn, remove the drive gear as detailed in the following section. Then mount the armature in a lathe and with the lathe turning at high speed, take a very fine cut-out of the commutator and finish the surface by polishing with glass paper. DO NOT UNDERCUT THE MICA INSULATORS BETWEEN THE COMMUTATOR SEGMENTS.

10 With the starter motor dismantled, test the four field coils for an open circuit. Connect a 12-volt battery with a 12-volt bulb in one of the leads between the field terminal post and the tapping point of the field coils to which the brushes are connected. An open circuit is proved by the bulb not lighting.

11 If the bulb lights, it does not necessarily mean that

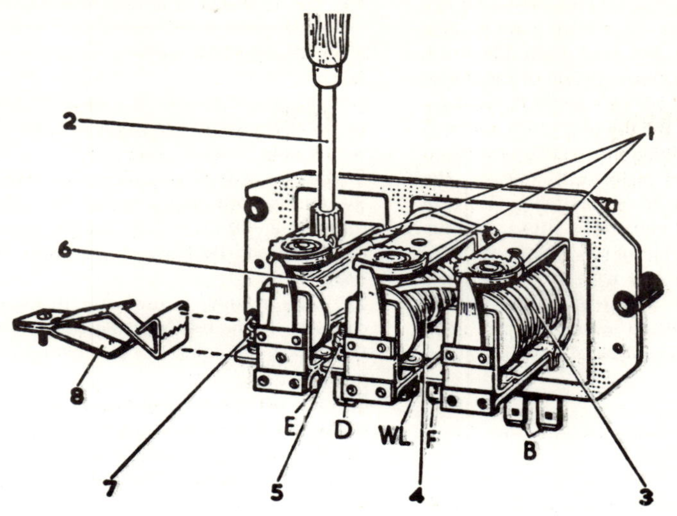

Fig. 10.4. THE CONTROL BOX (COVER REMOVED)

1 Adjustment cams   3 Cut-out relay   5 Current regulator contacts   7 Voltage regulator contacts
1 Setting tool   4 Current regulator   6 Voltage regulator   8 Clip

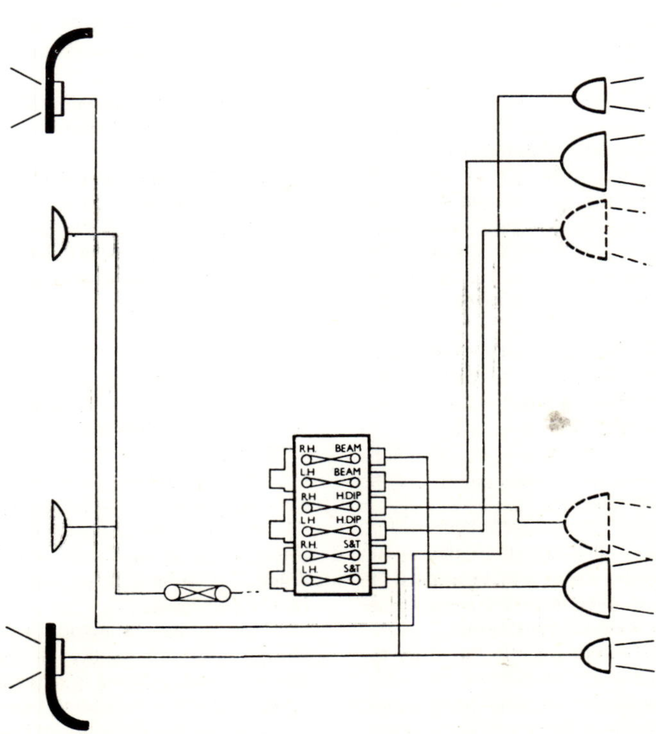

Fig. 10.5. Diagram of circuits protected by fuses

the field coils are in order, as there is a possibility that one of the coils will be earthing to the starter yoke or pole shoes. To check this, remove the lead from the brush connector and place it against a clean portion of the starter yoke. If the bulb lights the field coils are earthing. Replacement of the field coils calls for the use of a wheel operated screwdriver, a soldering iron, caulking and riveting operations and is beyond the scope of the majority of owners. The starter yoke should be taken to a reputable electrical engineering works for new field coils to be fitted. Alternatively, purchase an exchange starter motor.

12 If the armature is damaged this will be evident after visual inspection. Look for signs of burning, discoloration, and for conductors that have lifted away from the commutator. Reassembly is a straight reversal of the dismantling procedure.

15. Control Box - General Description

1. The control box is positioned on the right hand wing valance and comprises three units; two separate vibrating armature-type single contact regulators and a cut-out relay. One of the regulators is sensitive to changes in current and the other to changes in voltage.
2. Adjustments can only be made with a special tool which resembles a screwdriver with a multi-toothed blade. This can be obtained through Lucas agents.
3. The regulators control the output from the dynamo depending on the state of the battery and the demands of the electrical equipment, and ensures that the battery is not overcharged. The cut-out is really an automatic switch and connects the dynamo to the battery when the dynamo is turning fast enough to produce a charge. Similarly it disconnects the battery from the dynamo when the engine is idling or stationary so that the battery does not discharge through the dynamo.

16. Cut-Out and Regulator Contacts - Maintenance

1. Every 10,000 miles check the cut-out and regulator contacts. If they are dirty or rough or burnt place a piece of fine glass paper (DO NOT USE EMERY PAPER OR CARBORUNDUM PAPER) between the cut-out contacts, close them manually and draw the glass paper through several times.
2. Clean the regulator contacts in exactly the same way, but use emery or carborundum paper and not glass paper. Carefully clean both sets of contacts from all traces of dust with a rag moistened in methylated spirits.

17. Voltage Regulator Adjustment

1. The regulator requires very little attention during its service life, and should there be any reason to suspect its correct functioning, tests of all circuits should be made to ensure that they are not the reason for the trouble.
2. These checks include the tension of the fan belt, to make sure that it is not slipping and so providing only a very low charge rate. The battery should be carefully checked for possible low charge rate due to a faulty cell, or corroded battery connections.
3. The leads from the generator may have been crossed during replacement, and if this is the case then the regulator points will have stuck together as soon as the generator starts to charge. Check for loose or broken leads from the generator to the regulator.
4. If after a thorough check it is considered advisable to test the regulator, this should only be carried out by an electrician who is well acquainted with the correct method, using test bench equipment.
5. Pull off the Lucar connections from the two adjacent control box terminals 'B'. To start the engine it will now be necessary to join together the ignition and battery leads with a suitable wire.
6. Connect a 0-30 volt voltmeter between terminal 'D' on the control box and terminal 'WL'. Start the engine and run it at 2,000 r.p.m. The reading on the voltmeter should be steady and lie between the limits detailed in the specification.
7. If the reading is unsteady this may be due to dirty contacts. If the reading is outside the specified limits stop the engine and adjust the voltage regulator in the following manner.
8. Take off the control box cover and start and run the engine at 2,000 r.p.m. Using the correct tool turn the voltage adjustment cam anti-clockwise to raise the setting and clockwise to lower it. To check that the setting is correct, stop the engine, and then start it and run it at 2,000 r.p.m. noting the reading. Refit the cover and the connections to the 'WL' and 'D' terminals.

18. Current Regulator Adjustment

1. The output from the current regulator should equal the maximum output from the dynamo which is 22 amps. To test this it is necessary to bypass the cut-out by holding the contacts together.
2. Remove the cover from the control box and with a bulldog clip hold the cut-out contacts together.
3. Pull off the wires from the adjacent terminals 'B' and connect a 0-40 moving coil ammeter to one of the terminals and to the leads.
4. All the other load connections including the ignition must be made to the battery.
5. Turn on all the lights and other electrical accessories and run the engine at 2,000 r.p.m. The ammeter should give a steady reading between 19 and 22 amps. If the needle flickers it is likely that the points are dirty. If the reading is too low turn the special Lucas tool clockwise to raise the setting and anti-clockwise to lower it.

19. Cut-Out Adjustment

1. Check the voltage required to operate the cut-out by connecting a voltmeter between the control box terminals 'D' and 'WL'. Remove the control box cover, start the engine and gradually increase its speed until the cut-outs close. This should occur when the reading is between 12.6 to 13.4 volts.
2. If the reading is outside these limits turn the cut-out adjusting cam (1 in the illustration) by means of the adjusting tool, a fraction at a time clockwise to raise the voltage and anti-clockwise to lower it.
3. To adjust the drop off voltage bend the fixed contact blade carefully. The adjustment to the cut-out should be completed within 30 seconds of starting the engine as otherwise heat build-up from the shunt coil will affect the readings.
4. If the cut-out fails to work, clean the contacts, and, if there is still no response, renew the cut-out and regulator unit.

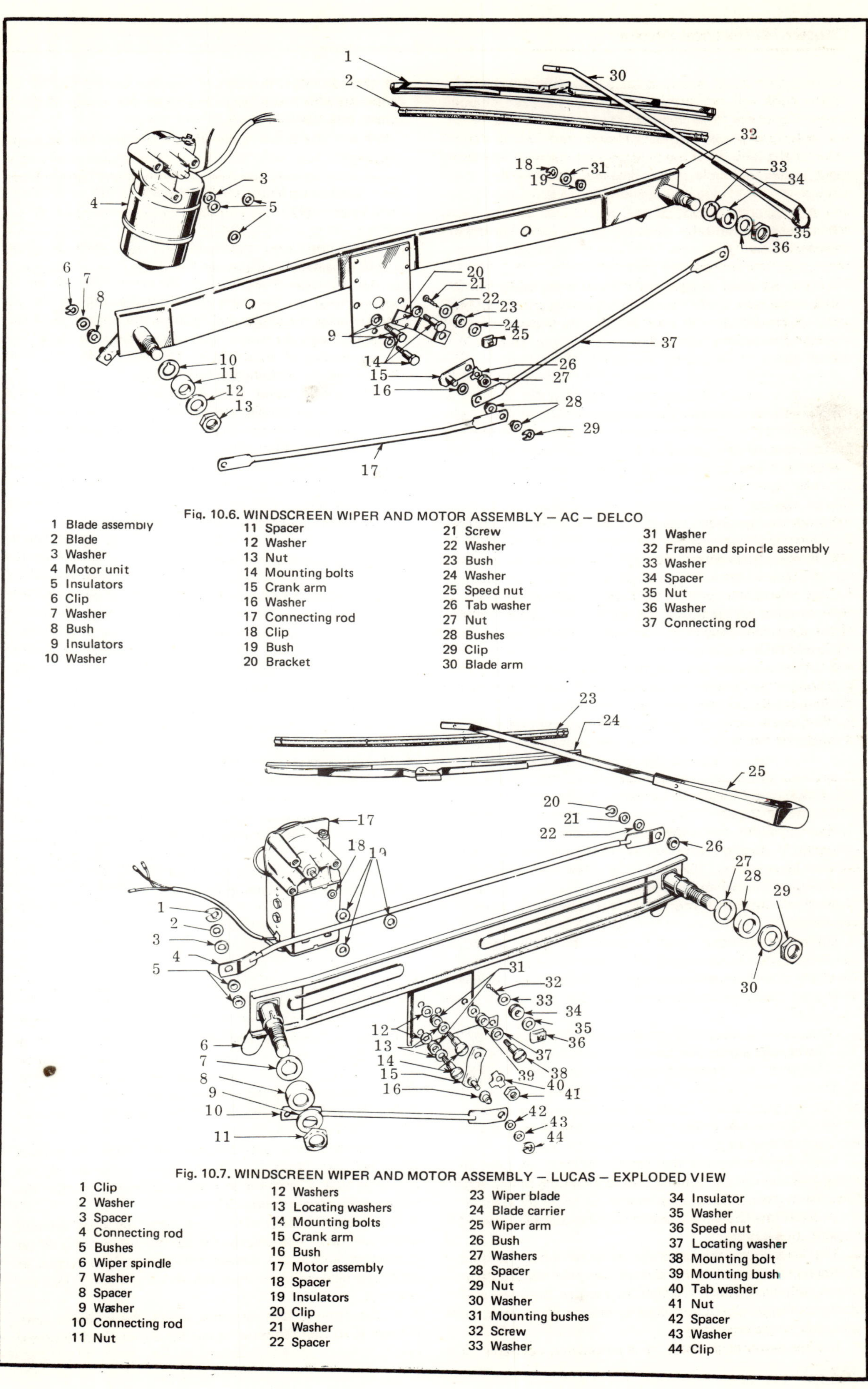

Fig. 10.6. WINDSCREEN WIPER AND MOTOR ASSEMBLY — AC — DELCO

1	Blade assembly	11	Spacer	21	Screw	31	Washer
2	Blade	12	Washer	22	Washer	32	Frame and spincle assembly
3	Washer	13	Nut	23	Bush	33	Washer
4	Motor unit	14	Mounting bolts	24	Washer	34	Spacer
5	Insulators	15	Crank arm	25	Speed nut	35	Nut
6	Clip	16	Washer	26	Tab washer	36	Washer
7	Washer	17	Connecting rod	27	Nut	37	Connecting rod
8	Bush	18	Clip	28	Bushes		
9	Insulators	19	Bush	29	Clip		
10	Washer	20	Bracket	30	Blade arm		

Fig. 10.7. WINDSCREEN WIPER AND MOTOR ASSEMBLY — LUCAS — EXPLODED VIEW

1	Clip	12	Washers	23	Wiper blade	34	Insulator
2	Washer	13	Locating washers	24	Blade carrier	35	Washer
3	Spacer	14	Mounting bolts	25	Wiper arm	36	Speed nut
4	Connecting rod	15	Crank arm	26	Bush	37	Locating washer
5	Bushes	16	Bush	27	Washers	38	Mounting bolt
6	Wiper spindle	17	Motor assembly	28	Spacer	39	Mounting bush
7	Washer	18	Spacer	29	Nut	40	Tab washer
8	Spacer	19	Insulators	30	Washer	41	Nut
9	Washer	20	Clip	31	Mounting bushes	42	Spacer
10	Connecting rod	21	Washer	32	Screw	43	Washer
11	Nut	22	Spacer	33	Washer	44	Clip

20. Fuses

1. A fuse circuit was introduced in October 1968 to protect the head, side and tail lamps. A six fuse carrier is located on the top of the wing inside the engine compartment.

21. Direction Indicator Flasher Circuit - Fault Tracing and Rectification

1. The unit which flashes the lights intermittently is a small cylindrical container about three inches long, located under the dashboard on the steering column brace with three Lucar connectors at one end.
2. If any fault occurs in the system check that all bulbs are working and that the wiring is all connected and intact.
3. If it is proved that current is reaching the '+' terminal of the flasher unit and still there is total failure on one side or both of the indicator bulbs, join the remaining two flasher terminals together. If all the lamps operate, or none, then the flasher unit is faulty and must be renewed.

22. Windscreen Wipers and Drive Motor - Fault Diagnosis

1. If the wipers fail to operate first check that current is reaching the motor. This can be done by switching on and using a voltmeter or 12 v bulb and two wires between the '+' terminal on the motor and earth. On two speed motors there are three leads from the motor and there should be a reading from two of them.
2. If no current is reaching the motor check whether there is any at the switch. If there is then a break has occurred in the wiring between switch and motor.
3. If there is no current at the switch go back to the ignition switch and so isolate the area of the fault.
4. If current is reaching the motor but the wipers do not operate, switch on and give the wiper arms a push - they or the motor could be jammed. Switch off immediately if nothing happens otherwise further damage to the motor may occur. If the wipers now run the reason for them jamming must be found. It will almost certainly be due to wear in either the linkage of the wiper mechanism or the mechanism in the motor gearbox.
5. If the wipers run too slowly it will be due to something restricting the free operation of the linkage or a fault in the motor. In such cases it is well to check the current being used by connecting an ammeter in the circuit. If it exceeds three amps something is restricting free movement. If less, then the commutator and brush gear in the motor are suspect.
6. If wear is obviously causing malfunction or there is a fault in the motor it is best to remove the motor or wiper mechanism for further examination and repairs.

23. Windscreen Wiper Mechanism and Motor - Removal and Replacement

1. Disconnect the battery terminals and then the motor wires from their snap connections.
2. Pull off the wiper arms from the splined ends of the drive spindles.
3. Undo the large locking nuts on the two spindles and remove the spacers and lockwashers, noting the order in which they came off. The whole assembly can now be taken out from within. Care should be taken not to wrench other wires off their terminals on the back of all the instruments when this is being done. Replacement is a reversal of the removal procedure. When refitting the spacers over the wiper spindles make sure that they are put on in the correct order and that the bevel follows the contour of the bodywork so that the whole assembly lines up properly.

24. Windscreen Wiper Mechanism and Motor - Dismantling and Reassembly

1. There are three types of unit that may be fitted, namely, Lucas, A C-Delco, or Autolite.
2. The exploded drawings show the various layouts and any serious wear on the crank spindle bushes can be rectified by removing the circlip and fitting a new bush. If the model is an AC Delco the motor must be renewed if faulty as there is no means of repairing it. Detach it from the wiper mechanism by undoing the three bolts.
3. The Lucas motor (Fig. 10.9) and the Autolite motor (Fig. 10.10) can be dismantled and examined if not working correctly. Remove the through bolts holding the end cover and body together. This will expose the armature and brush gear which is the most likely cause of malfunctioning. Brushes and brush assemblies may be renewed as required. The commutator should be inspected and may be cleaned up with glass paper (not emery) if necessary.
4. If there are signs of serious wear on any of the spindles or spindle bearings it is up to the owner to decide whether it is worthwhile to go to the trouble of renewing them or replacing the whole motor assembly. It must be remembered that one fault can cause another and although the bearings may seem to be the only fault it can be discovered on reassembly that the gears are all worn unevenly and do not run smoothly or that the commutator has worn off centre. To replace all the items individually will cost as much as a new assembly.
5. The Lucas motor has an adjustment screw for the endfloat of the commutator shaft. With the locknut slackened the screw should be tightened so that the spindle turns freely with negligible endfloat.

25. Horn - Fault Finding and Repair

If the horns fail to operate pull out the horn button escutcheon and check that proper contact is being made between the ring contact and the column. This can also be done without removing the operating button by putting a continuity test through the purple/black lead at both horns in turn with the horn button depressed. Then check that current is being fed from the brown wire. If current and earth circuits are intact the horn(s) must be at fault and will need renewal. To remove the horns, the radiator grille or radiator will need removal to gain access to them.

26. Headlamps - Adjustment, Removal and Replacement

1. The headlamps are sealed beam units consisting of lens, bulb and reflector and if any one is broken the whole unit must be replaced.
2. To ensure that the headlamp beams are set so that full illumination is achieved, without dazzling other road users, there are adjustment screws to set the complete unit in correct alignment. Set the car on level ground ten feet away from and facing a vertical surface which is marked as in Fig. 10.12. The distance 'H' is that measured from the ground to the centre of the lamps. The headlamp bezels should be removed by undoing the screws and bolts at the bottom and top and lifting them off. Then the adjusting screws (Fig. 10.11) are turned as necessary so that the centre of brightest

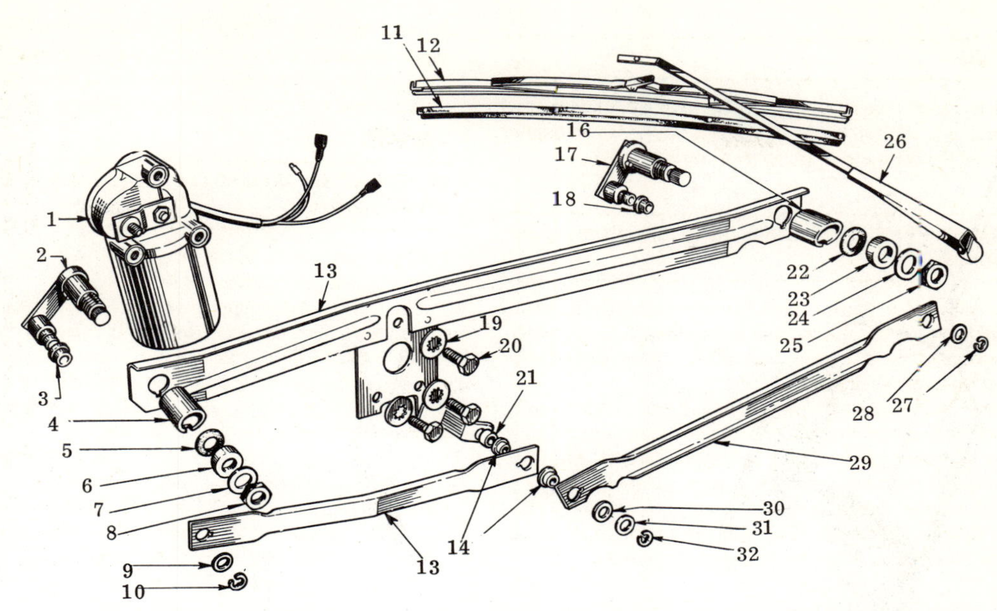

Fig. 10.8. WINDSCREEN WIPER AND MOTOR ASSEMBLY — AUTOLITE (2 SPEED) — EXPLODED VIEW

1 Wiper motor assembly	9 Washer	17 Crank assembly	25 Nut
2 Crank assembly	10 Clip	18 Bush	26 Wiper arm
3 Bush	11 Wiper blade	19 Stem washer	27 Circlip
4 Spacer collar	12 Blade carrier	20 Bolt	28 Washer
5 Washer	13 Frame	21 Bush	29 Connecting arm
6 Spacer	14 Bushes	22 Washer	30 Spacer
7 Washer	15 Connecting arm	23 Spacer	31 Washer
8 Nut	16 Spacer collar	24 Washer	32 Circlip

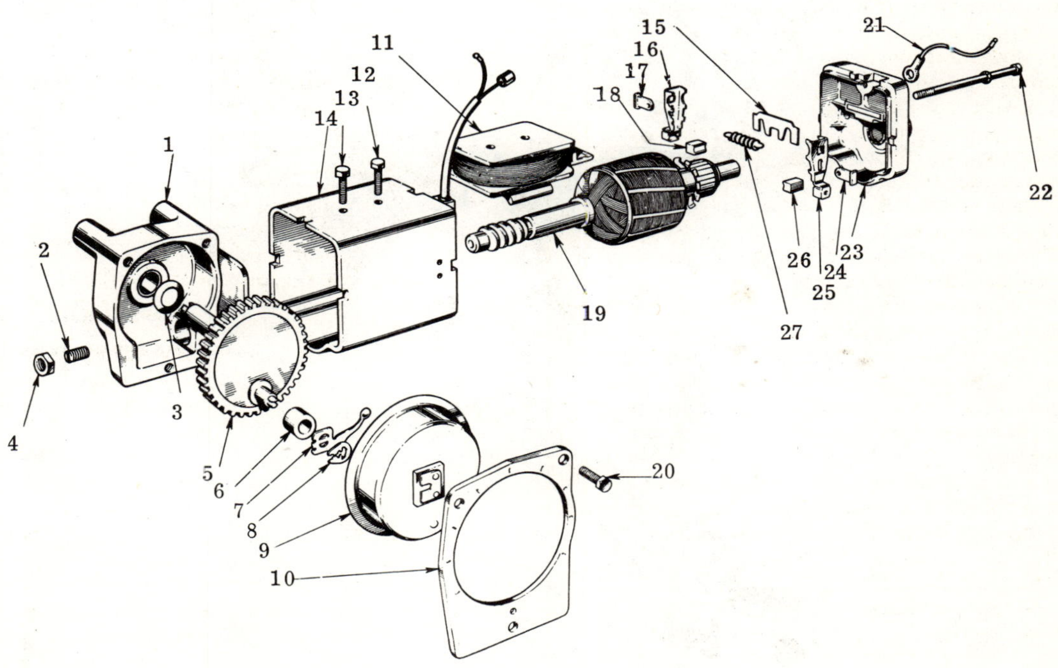

Fig. 10.9. WINDSCREEN WIPER MOTOR — LUCAS — EXPLODED VIEW

1 Crank wheel housing	8 Circlip	15 Pivot plate	22 Through bolt
2 Shaft end float adjuster	9 Park switch plate	16 Brush holder	23 End cover
3 Thrust washer	10 Cover plate	17 Clip	24 Clip
4 Lock nut	11 Field coil	18 Brush	25 Brush holder
5 Crank wheel	12 Screw	19 Armature	26 Brush
6 Bush	13 Screw	20 Screw	27 Spring
7 Park switch contact	14 Housing	21 Wire	

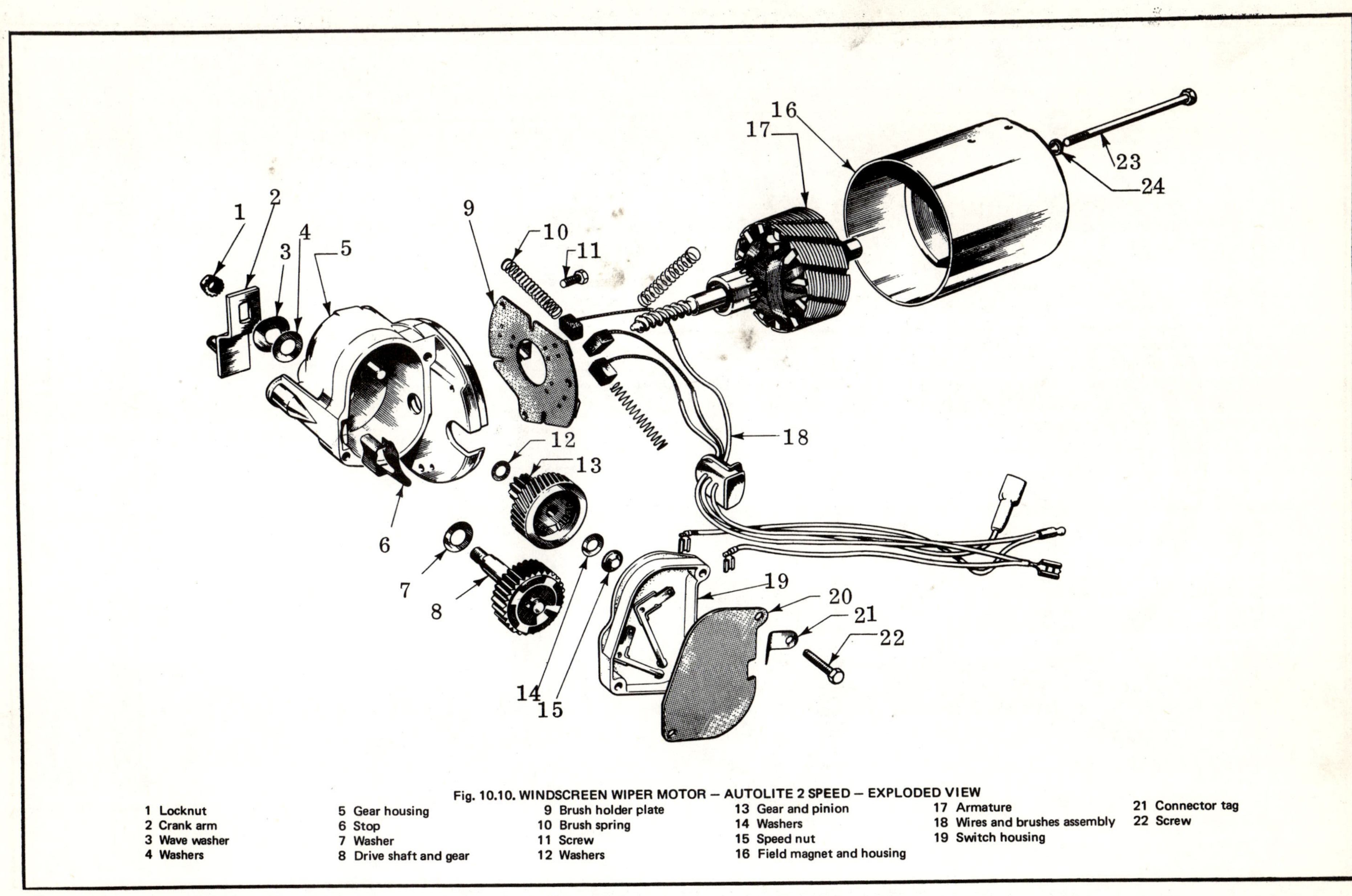

Fig. 10.10. WINDSCREEN WIPER MOTOR – AUTOLITE 2 SPEED – EXPLODED VIEW

1 Locknut	5 Gear housing	9 Brush holder plate	13 Gear and pinion	17 Armature	21 Connector tag
2 Crank arm	6 Stop	10 Brush spring	14 Washers	18 Wires and brushes assembly	22 Screw
3 Wave washer	7 Washer	11 Screw	15 Speed nut	19 Switch housing	
4 Washers	8 Drive shaft and gear	12 Washers	16 Field magnet and housing		

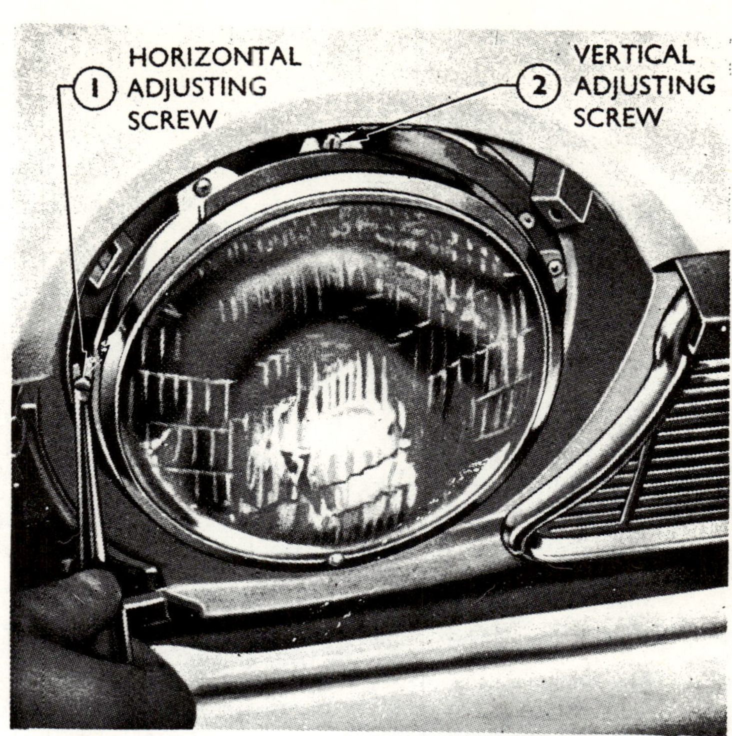

Fig. 10.11. Headlamp beam adjustment screws

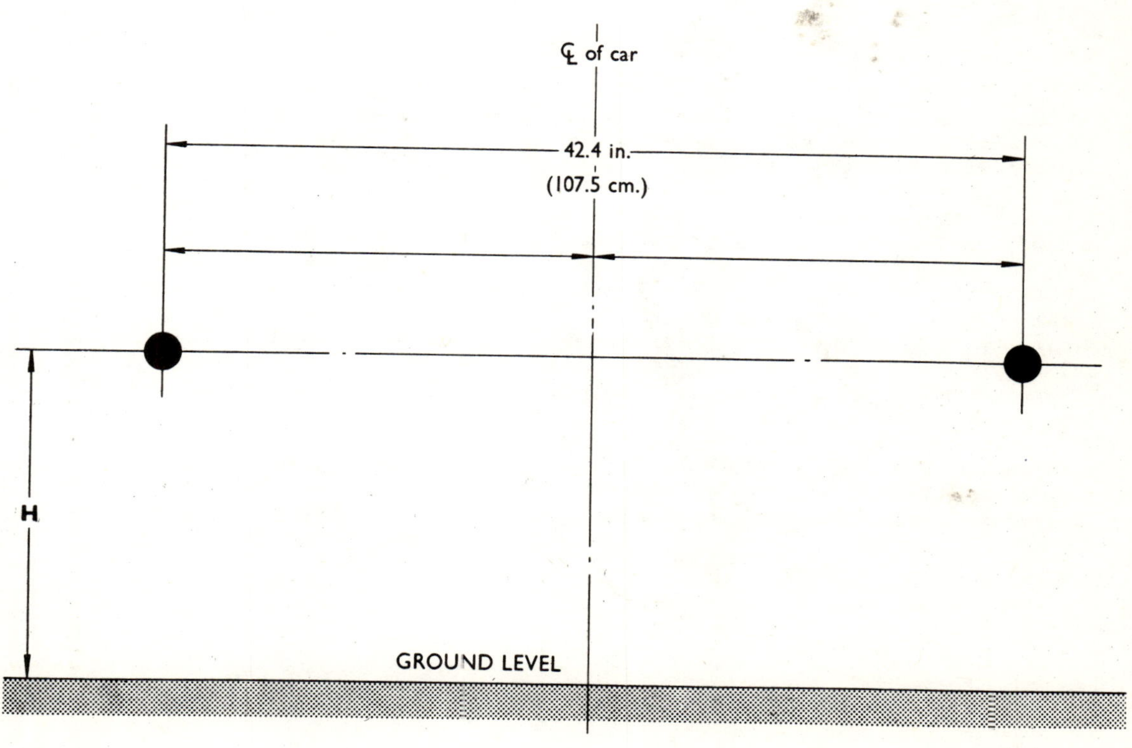

Fig. 10.12. Headlamp beam alignment chart

illumination is at the black spot marks with the lamps in the undipped position. It is easier if each lamp is covered whilst the other is being adjusted.

3. To remove the sealed beam unit remove the bezel as described and the sealing ring behind it as well.

4. Then remove the three crosshead screws holding the inner bezel - do NOT disturb the adjusting screws. The sealed beam unit may then be lifted out and the connector plug pulled from the rear.

5. Replacement is a reversal of the procedure and no adjustment should be necessary.

27. Side Lamp and Front Direction Indicator - Removal and Replacement

The unit is a single assembly with separate lenses and bulbs which may be replaced as required by removing the lens securing screws as necessary and replacing the bayonet bulb.

28. Rear Lamp, Stop Lamp and Direction Indicator - Removal and Replacement

The rear lamp assembly has bulb holders which are a push fit into the lamp body from inside the boot of the car. They are held in position by a number of spring tongues round the edge. A locating lug in the body ensures that the holder can only go in position in one way. To replace a bulb, therefore, the holder is pulled out of the body and the bulb taken from the holder in the usual way. The centre section of the lamp cluster is fitted with a reflector and lens which deflects light from the rear lamp bulb into the boot for illumination.

29. Headlamp Flasher, Direction Indicator and Dipswitch Assembly - Removal and Replacement

1. Should the combined switch unit fail for any reason on any one of its functions it can only be renewed complete as its construction is such that dismantling and repair is not feasible.

2. Disconnect the battery and remove the four crosshead screws holding the two halves of the shroud round the switch.

3. Disconnect the seven snap connectors behind the fascia panel.

4. Remove the two crosshead screws holding the switch to the steering column and remove the switch.

5. Replacement is a simple reversal of the removal procedure. Make sure that the connections are correctly remade, colour to colour.

30. Instrument Panel - Checking, Removal and Replacement of Instruments and Switches

1. Each instrument unit is removable independently from the fascia. This is done by rotating the instrument anti-clockwise by a tool pressing on the chrome bezel rim (NOT the glass). A suitable device for this can be made from a circular piece of wood $4^{1}/10$ in. diameter (10.1 cm) covered with some rubber sheet. If the speedometer head is to be removed it is first of all necessary to remove the instrument next to it so that the speedometer drive cable can be unscrewed from the back of it first. On models fitted with an oil pressure gauge it will also be necessary to remove the adjacent instrument to get at the oil pipe connector on the rear of the oil pressure gauge.

2. When the unit is released from the panel the connector can be pulled off the terminals but careful note should be made of the connections for reassembly.

3. The fuel and temperature gauges work on the variable voltage principle dependent on the resistance in the circuit induced by their respective sender units. Consequently, the standard line voltage in the circuits must not vary for other reasons such as a low charged battery. There is a regulator fitted into the system which keeps it at 10 volts. This unit is mounted on the back of the speedometer.

4. Should either of the gauges not work correctly the first action to take is to check the circuit as described in the relevant section of Chapter 2 (Cooling System) or Chapter 3 (Fuel System). If, as a result of the test described in these chapters, it is proved that the gauge is at fault it will have to be detached from its unit and replaced.

5. If both fuel and temperature units should go wrong at the same time it is most likely that the fault lies in the instrument regulator. This may be checked by bridging a voltmeter from the 'I' (Instrument) terminal to earth with all normal connections made and the ignition switched on. The voltage should be 10 v. If not the unit will need replacement.

6. The instrument illuminating bulbs may be replaced by withdrawing the holders from the back of the units.

7. Ignition warning light bulbs and direction indicator bulbs fail on occasions but when this happens it is as well to check the charging and flasher circuits at the same time to make sure that there is no fault which may have caused the bulb to blow.

8. Should the tachometer (where fitted) fail and the engine running is not affected the fault must lie in the instrument. Any failure in the wiring to and from the instrument would interrupt the engine ignition circuit as it is wired into this circuit.

9. Switches are held in position on the fascia by a chrome ring with two notches in it which fits the barrel of the switch to disconnect the battery first to prevent accidental short circuits. Then remove the chrome ring and push the switch out BEFORE pulling wires off the connectors at the rear. It will then be easier to see for sure which wires are attached to which terminals.

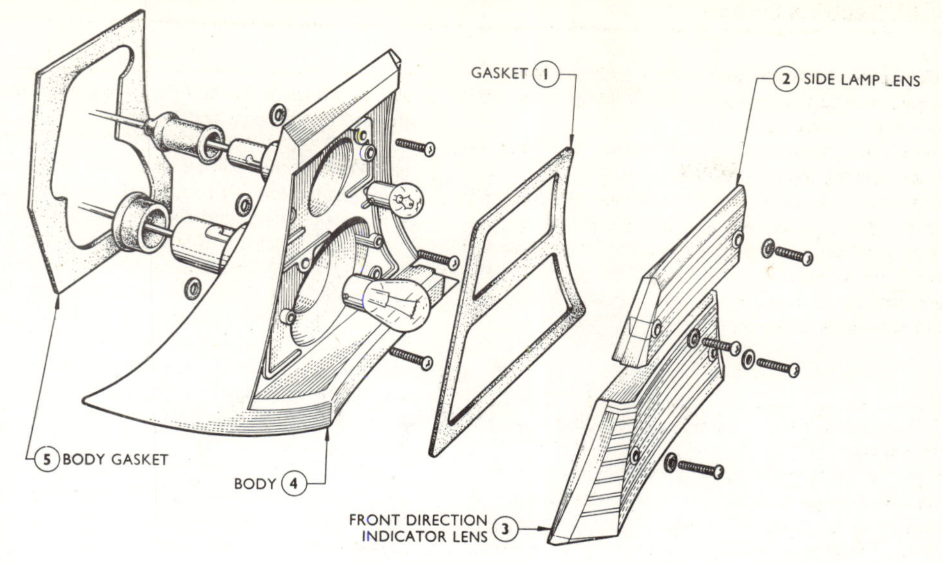

Fig. 10.13. Exploded view of the side lamp and front direction indicator

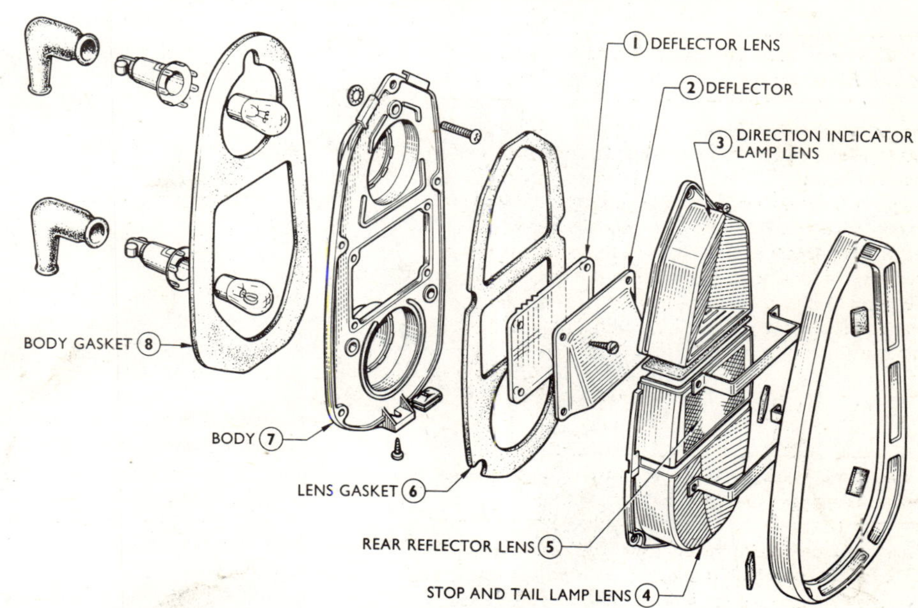

Fig. 10.14. Exploded view of the rear lamp, stop lamp and rear direction indicator

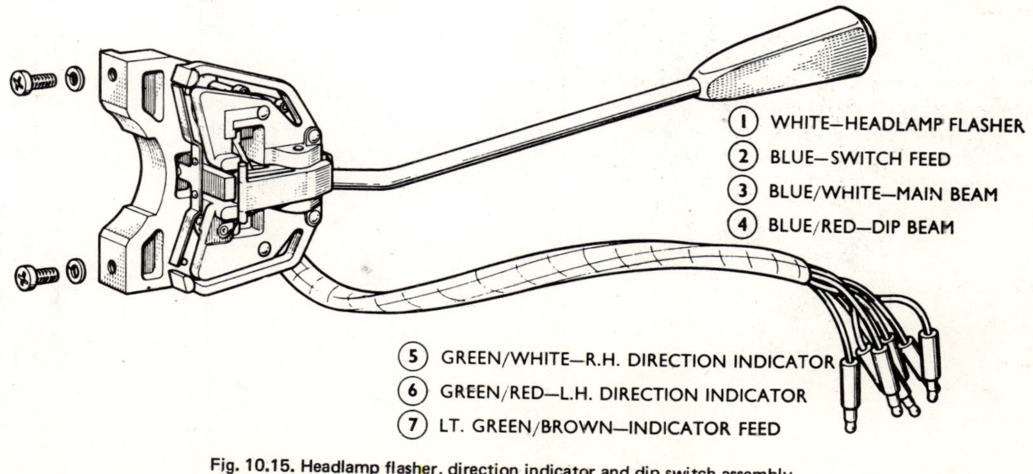

Fig. 10.15. Headlamp flasher, direction indicator and dip switch assembly

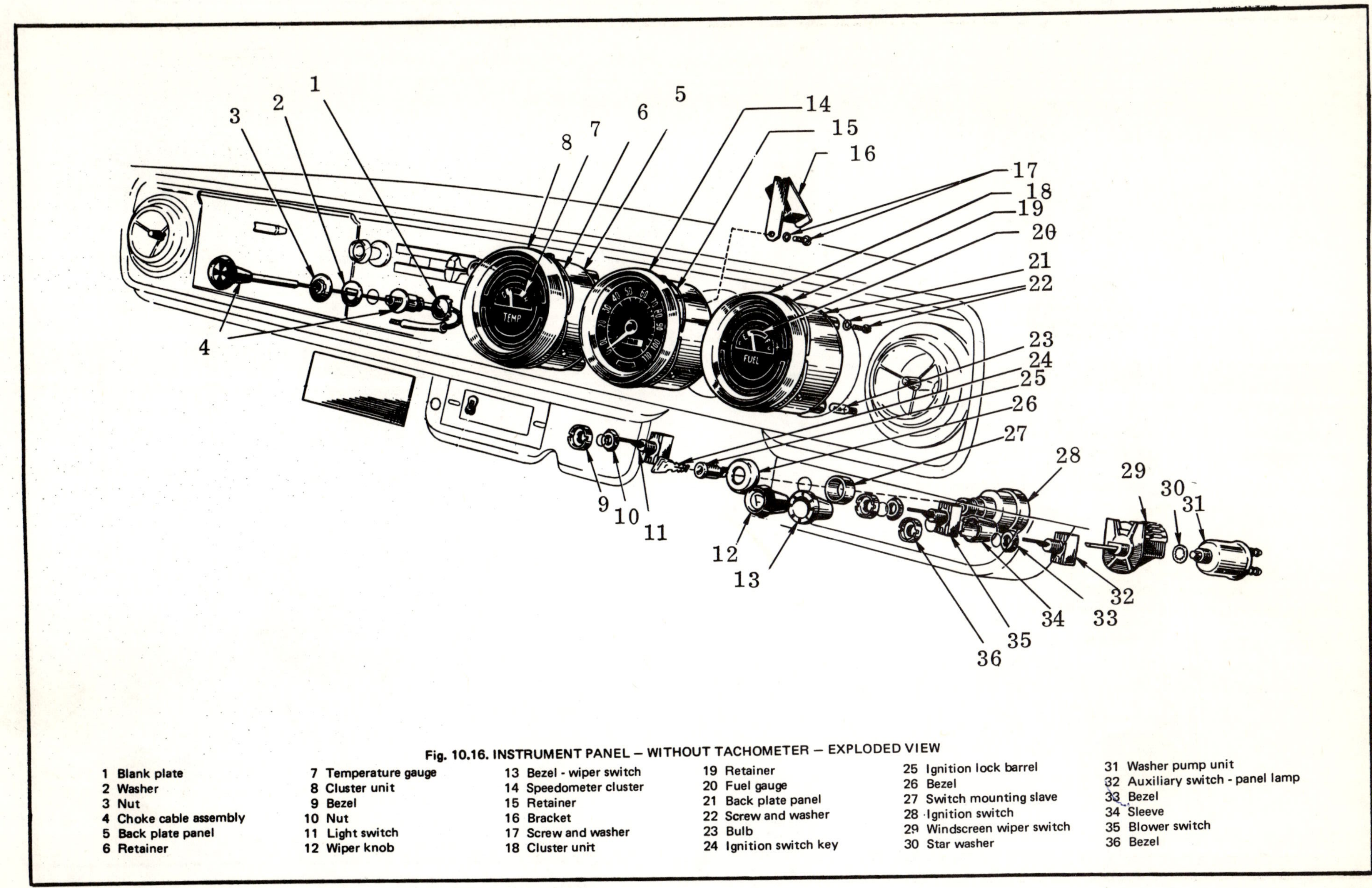

Fig. 10.16. INSTRUMENT PANEL — WITHOUT TACHOMETER — EXPLODED VIEW

1 Blank plate	7 Temperature gauge	13 Bezel - wiper switch	19 Retainer	25 Ignition lock barrel	31 Washer pump unit
2 Washer	8 Cluster unit	14 Speedometer cluster	20 Fuel gauge	26 Bezel	32 Auxiliary switch - panel lamp
3 Nut	9 Bezel	15 Retainer	21 Back plate panel	27 Switch mounting slave	33 Bezel
4 Choke cable assembly	10 Nut	16 Bracket	22 Screw and washer	28 Ignition switch	34 Sleeve
5 Back plate panel	11 Light switch	17 Screw and washer	23 Bulb	29 Windscreen wiper switch	35 Blower switch
6 Retainer	12 Wiper knob	18 Cluster unit	24 Ignition switch key	30 Star washer	36 Bezel

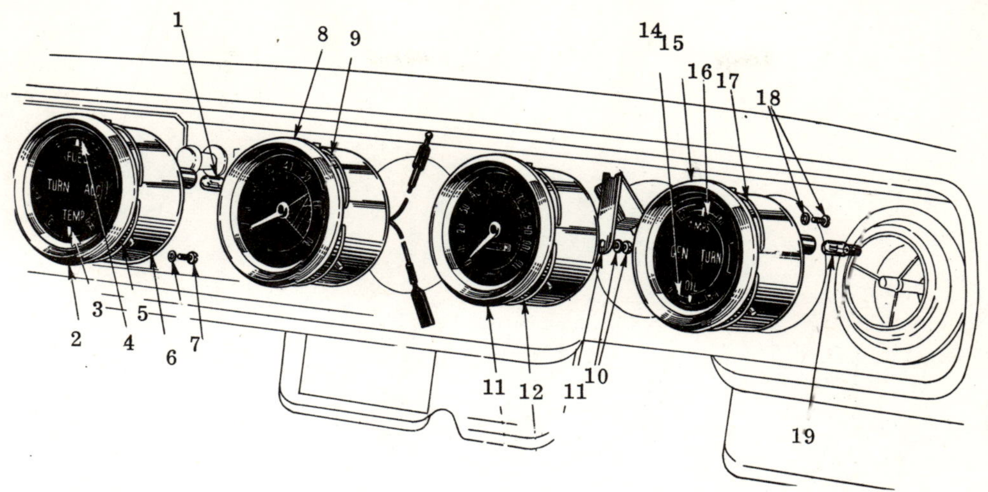

Fig. 10.17. INSTRUMENT PANEL — WITH TACHOMETER — EXPLODED VIEW

1 Bulb
2 Cluster unit
3 Temperature gauge
4 Fuel gauge
5 Retainer
6 Back panel plate
7 Screw and washer
8 Tachometer unit
9 Retainer
10 Screw and washer
11 Bracket
12 Retainer
13 Speedometer head
14 Oil pressure gauge
15 Cluster unit
16 Ammeter
17 Retainer
18 Screw and washer
19 Bulb

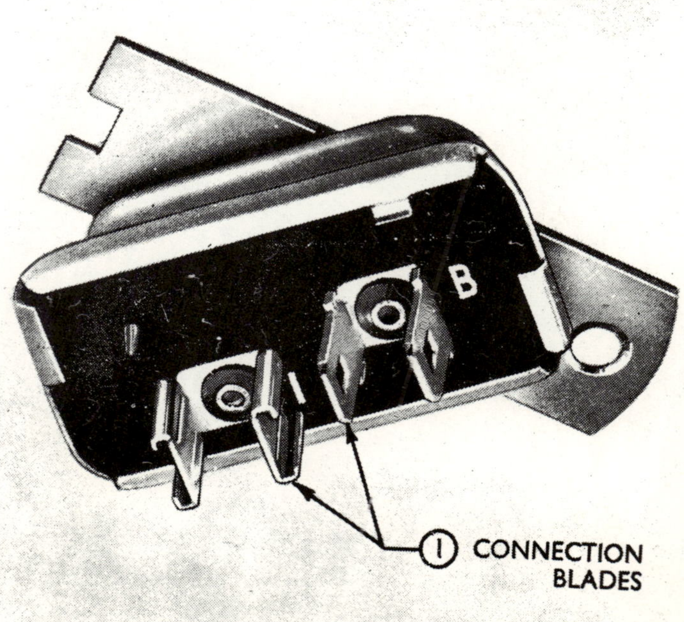

Fig. 10.18. Instrument voltage regulator

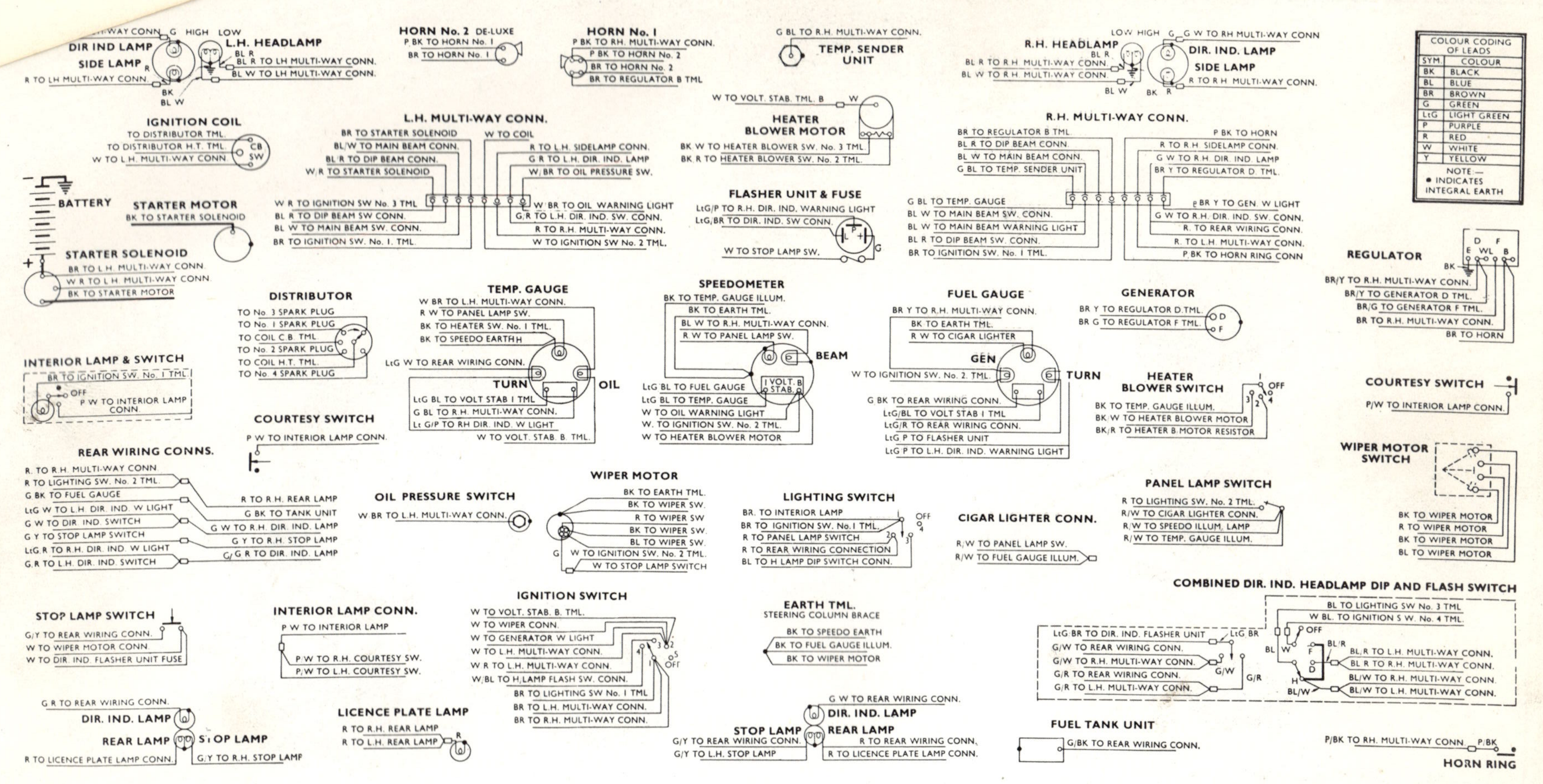

WIRING DIAGRAM

COLOUR CODING OF LEADS
SYM — COLOUR
BK — BLACK
BL — BLUE
BR — BROWN
G — GREEN
LtG — LIGHT GREEN
P — PURPLE
R — RED
W — WHITE
Y — YELLOW
NOTE —
• INDICATES INTEGRAL EARTH

DIR IND LAMP
SIDE LAMP
L.H. HEADLAMP
HORN No. 2 DE-LUXE
HORN No. 1
TEMP. SENDER UNIT
R.H. HEADLAMP
DIR. IND. LAMP
SIDE LAMP
REGULATOR
IGNITION COIL
L.H. MULTI-WAY CONN.
HEATER BLOWER MOTOR
R.H. MULTI-WAY CONN.
BATTERY
STARTER MOTOR
STARTER SOLENOID
FLASHER UNIT & FUSE
DISTRIBUTOR
TEMP. GAUGE
SPEEDOMETER
FUEL GAUGE
GENERATOR
INTERIOR LAMP & SWITCH
TURN
OIL
BEAM
GEN
TURN
HEATER BLOWER SWITCH
COURTESY SWITCH
COURTESY SWITCH
WIPER MOTOR SWITCH
REAR WIRING CONNS.
OIL PRESSURE SWITCH
WIPER MOTOR
LIGHTING SWITCH
CIGAR LIGHTER CONN.
PANEL LAMP SWITCH
STOP LAMP SWITCH
INTERIOR LAMP CONN.
IGNITION SWITCH
EARTH TML. STEERING COLUMN BRACE
COMBINED DIR. IND. HEADLAMP DIP AND FLASH SWITCH
DIR. IND. LAMP
REAR LAMP
STOP LAMP
LICENCE PLATE LAMP
DIR. IND. LAMP
REAR LAMP
STOP LAMP
FUEL TANK UNIT
HORN RING

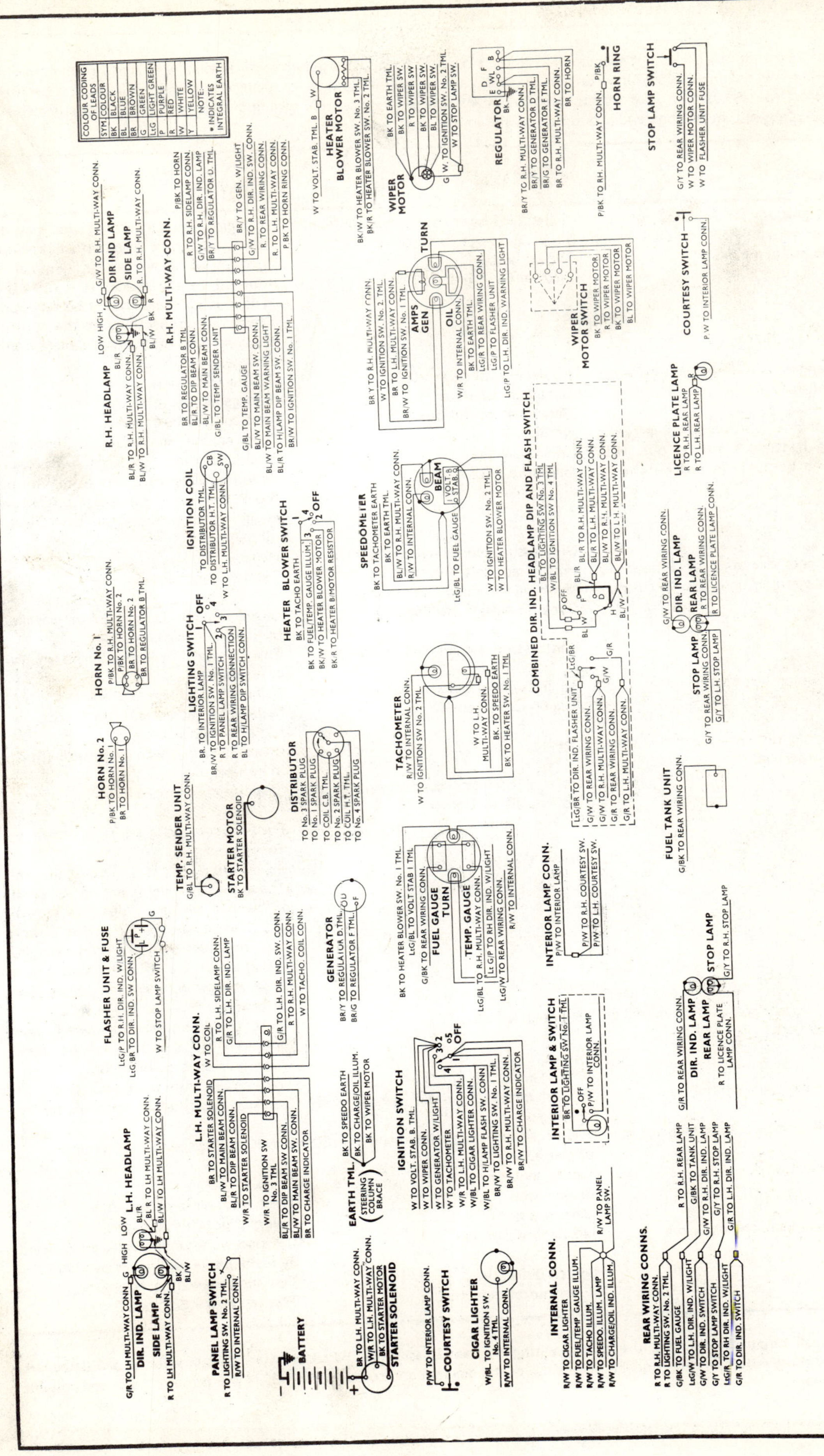

WIRING DIAGRAM – Models fitted with tachometer

The following chart does not include fault finding in connection with the failure of the engine to start or run correctly. These are covered in Chapter One (Engine) and Chapter Four (Ignition). It is assumed that a **good** battery is properly connected into the system. Also that the earth connecting strap between the engine and body frame is properly fixed in position (between the gearbox and supporting crossmember).

Symptom	Cause	Remedy
When ignition is switched on the ignition warning light or oil warning light do not come on.	Defective fuse or connection. Defective oil pressure sender switch. Blown bulbs. Broken feed wire.	If engine starts anyway bulbs may be defective. Check whether oil pressure light glows when sender terminal is touched to the block. If it does the sender is U/S and should be renewed. Check all connections at the control box and fuse block for cleanliness and tightness.
When engine is running ignition warning light does not go out.	Loose or broken fan belt. Defective generator. Defective control box.	Tighten or renew. Test generator in car. Test control box in car.
When engine is running oil pressure warning light does not go out. N.B. checks to be made in order shown.	No oil Severe oil leak Oil pump drive sheared.	Stop engine immediately. Check oil level and look for signs of leakage. Unscrew filter cartridge from side of block and see if oil spurts out when engine is cranked. If not investigate oil pump.
	Oil pressure sender switch defective.	Renew.
Battery goes flat after a few days yet dynamo warning light goes out normally.	Loose fan belt resulting in dynamo revolving too slowly due to slip. Dynamo output inadequate.	Tighten fan belt. Check dynamo output in the car and overhaul if necessary.
	Control box not controlling properly.	Test control box and adjust or renew as necessary.
No lights at all when switched on.	Broken wire or defective switch (blown fuse on later models).	Using wiring diagram check feed from battery to switch and from switch to relevant connectors.
Some lights do not come on when switch is operated.	Defective bulb(s).	Check bulb in another location known to be working.
	Dirty or corroded connections at the individual bulb holder. Broken circuit.	Clean up connections. Trace circuit using wiring diagram to isolate break.
	Blown fuse (later models)	Renew fuse. If it blows again immediately when lights are all switched on remove all light bulbs, renew fuse and then replace bulbs one at a time until fuse blows again. Then examine relevant circuit to find the fault. Use a piece of light wire as a temporary fuse for testing.
Stop lights do not come on when brake pedal depressed.	Defective switch.	Short out terminals on switch and replace it if lights still do not work when ignition is switched on.
Fuel gauge registers incorrectly.	Broken wire. Faulty voltage regulator, sender unit or gauge.	Trace circuit from wiring diagram. Check as described in this Chapter.
Water temperature gauge registers incorrectly.	Faulty voltage regulator, sender unit or gauge.	Check as described in this Chapter.
Horn does not work	Faulty switch. Broken lead Defective horn.	Check. Trace from wiring diagram. Adjust if possible or renew.
Windscreen wipers doe not work	Mechanism jammed.	If wipers work when blades are assisted by hand whole unit needs overhaul.
	Switch defective. Wiper motor defective.	Test and renew if necessary. Test and repair or renew.

NOTE: In all circuit tracing the use of the wiring diagram is essential. When switches or connections are detached, particularly those with multiple connections the use of the diagram and colour coding chart will prevent faults and possible further damage.

Chapter 11/Suspension - Dampers - Steering

Contents

Specifications

Front Suspension ... ...   Independent. McPherson strut and coil

Front springs:

	1664 c.c.	1996 c.c.	1664 c.c. H.D.	1996 c.c. H.D.
Free length	13.49 ins.	11.61 ins.	14.81 ins.	12.77 ins.
—	34.26 cms.	29.48 cms.	37.61 cms.	32.43 cms.
Loaded length	7.07 ins.	7.00 ins.	8.26 ins.	8.16 ins.
577 lbs (261.7 Kg.)	17.95 cms.	17.78 cms.	20.98 cms.	20.72 cms.
No. of coils	7½	7	8½	7¾
Wire diameter	.48 in. (1.21 cm)	.51 in. (1.29 cm)	.49 in. (1.24 cm)	.53 in. (1.34 cm)
Mean diameter of coils	5 in. (1.27 cm)	5 in. (1.27 cm)	5 in. (1.27 cm)	5 in. (1.27 cm)

Shock absorber type ... ...   Telescopic, hydraulic double acting.
Fluid capacity ... ...   330 c.c.

Rear suspension ... ...   Semi elliptic leaf springs
Springs - length (eye centres) ... ...   47 in. (119.4 cm)
     - width ... ...   2 in. (5.1 cm)
Leaf thickness:
  1664 c.c. ... ...   1 @ .235 to .245 in. (5.96 to 6.22 cms)
      4 @ .191 to .201 in. (4.84 to 5.11 cms)

  1996 c.c. ... ...   1 @ .300 to .310 in. (7.62 to 7.87 cms)
      2 @ .235 to .245 in. (5.96 to 6.22 cms)
      2 @ .220 to .230 in. (5.58 to 5.84 cms)

  1996 c.c. H.D. ... ...   1 @ .235 to .245 in. (5.96 to 6.22 cms)
      2 @ .220 to .230 in. (5.58 to 5.84 cms)
      1 @ .191 to .201 in. (4.84 to 5.11 cms)

Spring eye diameter:
  Front - 1664 c.c. ... ...   1.834 to 1.841 in. (4.66 to 4.68 cms)
        1996 c.c. ... ...   1.215 to 1.225 in. (3.09 to 3.11 cms)
    Rear ... ...   .795 to .805 (2.02 to 2.04 cms)
Rear dampers ... ...   Telescopic, incorporating bump stop. Sealed

Steering gear
  Type ... ...   Recirculatory ball
  Lubricant ... ...   S.A.E. 80 E.P.
  Capacity (approx.) ... ...   ¾ Imp. pint (.9 U.S. pint, .42 litre)
  Steering ratio ... ...   17.75 to 1
  Steering shaft bearing adjustment ... ...   Shims
  Steering shaft bearing pre-load ... ...   .003 in. (.076 mm)

Shim thickness and type...	.004 in. (.102 mm) steel .010 in. (.254 mm) steel .00025 in. (.063 mm) paper .010 in. (.254 mm) paper Shims
Rocker shaft bearing adjustment	
Rocker shaft pre-load (measured at steering wheel rim)	1¼ to 1½ lb. (.57 to .69 Kg)
Rocker shaft pre-load (at rocker shaft with thrust button and springs removed)	0-.003 in. (.076 mm)
Rocker shaft shim thickness and type	.002 (.051 mm) paper .010 (.254 mm) paper .005 (.127 mm) steel .010 (.254 mm) steel
Rocker shaft bush diameter	.9855 to .8765 (22.23 to 22.26 mm)
Number of balls in nut	38 of $7/32$ in. (5.56 mm) diameter
Number of balls in upper and lower bearing...	10 (each) of $9/32$ in. (7.14 mm) diameter

Wheel alignment (unladen)

Caster angle	1° 15' to 2° 45'
Camber angle	1° 11' to 2° 4'
Toe-in (straight ahead)	1/8 to $3/16$ in. (3.2 to 4.8 mm)
King pin inclination	3° 53' to 5° 23'
Toe-out (20° turn of outer wheel)...	1° 42' to 3° 12'
Track - front	50.5 ins. (128.2 cms)
- Rear	49.5 ins. (125.8 cms)

Torque wrench settings

Drop arm retaining nut	60 to 70 lb.ft. (8.3 to 9.7 Kg.m)
Steering wheel nut	20 to 25 lb.ft. (2.8 to 3.4 Kg.m)
Steering ball joints	18 to 22 lb.ft. (2.5 to 3.0 Kg.m)
Steering bore top cover to housing	12 to 15 lb.ft. (1.7 to 2.1 Kg.m)
Stabiliser bar attachment clamp bushing	15 to 18 lb.ft. (2.1 to 2.5 Kg.m)
Stabiliser to front track control arm nut	25 to 30 lb.ft. (3.5 to 4.1 Kg.m)
Front suspension thrust bearing retaining nut	45 to 55 lb.ft. (6.2 to 7.6 Kg.m)
Front suspension unit upper support	15 to 18 lb.ft. (2.1 to 2.5 Kg.m)
Front track control arm ball stud	30 to 35 lb.ft. (4.1 to 4.8 Kg.m)
Front track control arm inner bushing	22 to 27 lb.ft. (3.0 to 3.7 Kg.m)
Shock absorber to body	25 to 30 lb.ft. (3.5 to 4.1 Kg.m)
Rear spring 'U' bolts	20 to 25 lb.ft. (2.8 to 3.4 Kg.m)
Rear spring front hangar...	25 to 30 lb.ft. (3.5 to 4.1 Kg.m)
Rear spring shackle stud	12 to 15 lb.ft. (1.7 to 2.1 Kg.m)
Shock absorber to rear axle	40 to 45 lb.ft. (5.5 to 6.2 Kg.m)

Wheels and tyres

Wheel type	Pressed steel with wide based rims
Tyres	5.60 x 13

1. General Description

The independent front suspension consists of the well-tried Macpherson strut system which has been used on most Ford models since the early 1950's. This system comprises a single telescopic damper unit, the foot so designed to carry the wheel hub and brake assembly. A coil spring surrounds the damper. The top of the unit is located into a rubber mounted thrust bush in a reinforced section of the wing. The lower end is located by a track control arm which is fixed in a rubber bush to the frame crossmember; and to the bottom of the suspension unit by a ball joint which permits the whole unit to turn for steering. A stabiliser bar links the outer ends of each track control arm and is also attached to the body frame in its centre section in rubber insulated brackets. This provides fore and aft location of the struts also.

The rear suspension consists of conventional semi-elliptical leaf springs mounted on hangers and shackles. The springs are clamped to the axle tube by 'U' bolts. On G.T. and '2000' models the rear suspension is further aided by the fitting of radius arms from mountings welded on the axle to the underside of the body. The ends of the radius arms are located in rubber bushes. The rear suspension is damped by double acting telescopic hydraulic dampers.

The steering action is transferred from the column to the wheels via a worm and recirculating ball form of unit. The longitudinal movement of the nut on the worm is relayed via the steering shaft and drop arm to the idler arm and track rods. The extremity of the steering lock is controlled by adjustable stops fitted to the front crossmember.

2. Routine Maintenance

1. Lubrication is required only on the front wheel bearings and the steering box as all bushings and ball joints are either bonded rubber or are pre-packed and sealed with grease.
2. The front wheel hub bearings should be removed, cleaned and regreased every 10,000 miles.
3. Every 5,000 miles the steering box filler plug should be cleaned and removed to examine the oil level. If necessary top up to the bottom of the hole with S.A.E. 90 E.P. gear oil.
4. Every 5,000 miles all the suspension assemblies should

be examined for signs of deterioration in the mounting bushes and steering connections. Particularly important are those at the inner end of each track control arm. Any play in these will throw the wheels out of alignment and cause serious vibration at certain speeds.

5. The track rod end ball joints and track control arm ball joints at the bottom of each suspension leg also need checking every 5,000 miles for signs of excessive play.

3. Springs and Dampers - Inspection

1. The safety of a car depends more on the steering and suspension than anything else and this is the reason why the compulsory tests made for vehicles over three years old pay attention to the condition of all the steering and suspension components.

2. The rear suspension should be examined for broken spring leaves. This will usually be obvious as the car will be down on the side affected. Such broken leaves must be renewed.

3. The spring hangar and shackle pin bushes may be checked by jacking up the body and at the same time watching to see if there is any movement between the shackle pins and the frame when the weight is gradually shifted. As mud normally collects round these mounting points a badly worn bush is usually immediately apparent because the movement prevents the mud from caking.

4. Check for any signs of movement also in the 'U' bolts clamping the springs to the axle tube. If any one is loose check first that the axle is correctly located in the spring seat before tightening the 'U' bolt.

5. The top and bottom anchorage points of the hydraulic damper should be firm. If there are signs of oil on the outside of the lower cylinder section it indicates that the seals have gone and the damper must be renewed. The damper may also have failed internally and this is more difficult to detect. It is usually indicated by excessive bounce at the rear end and axle patter or 'tramp' on uneven surfaces. When this occurs remove the shock absorber in order to check its damping power in both directions.

6. The front suspension should be checked by first jacking the car up so that the wheel is clear of the ground. Then place another jack under the track control arm near the outer end. When the arm is raised by the jack any movement in the suspension strut ball stud will be apparent. So also will any wear in the inner track control arm bush. The ball joint endfloat should not exceed .060 in. (1.5 mm). However, it is not possible to gauge this movement very accurately without removing the joint so if there is some doubt it is better to be on the safe side and dismantle it. There should be no play of any sort in the track control arm bush.

7. The top end of the suspension unit should have no discernible movement and to check it grip the strut at the lower spring seat and try pushing it from side to side. There should be no detectable movement either between the outer cylinder and inner piston rod or at the top of the piston rod near the upper mounting.

4. Stabiliser Bar - Removal and Replacement

1. The stabiliser bar may get bent or the locating bushes into the track control arms can break up and as well as this the centre mounting bushes may become worn. These conditions would require removal of the whole assembly.

2. Jack up the car with clips previously fitted to hold the front coils if possible. If not possible block the car under the track control arms sufficiently high to give working clearance.

3. Remove the splash tray under the front grille and then undo the four bolts holding the stabiliser bar attaching clamps. These bolts are locked by tab washers.

4. Remove the split pins and castellated nuts from each end of the bar and then pull the bar out of its location in the track control arms.

5. Remove the conical rubber bushes, flat washers, and sleeve from each mounting point.

6. Replacement is a reversal of the removal procedure. Make sure the sweep of the stabiliser bar goes upwards when in position and that the rubber bushes are fitted one each side of the control arm so that their narrow ends go into the hole in the arm each side. The castellated nuts must be tightened to a final torque of 25 to 30 lbs.ft.

7. Refit the attachment clamps and rubber bushes and tighten the bolts to 15 to 18 lbs.ft. Bend back the lock washer tabs.

5. Track Control Arm Ball Joint - Removal and Replacement

1. If the track control arm (see Fig.11.1) ball joint shows signs of excessive play it will have to be removed in order to adjust or renew it.

2. It will be necessary to fit spring clips to prevent the coil spring from expanding when the car is jacked up. There is a Ford tool (P5030) for this purpose but they can be made from suitable lengths of ½ in. diameter mild steel bar with their ends bent over to form hooks. Three such hooks are desirable and to prevent them slipping round the coils of the spring they can be stitched into a canvas belt, to be held tight round the coil of the spring when they are in position.

3. With the spring clips in position jack up the car, support it on stands, and remove the front wheels.

4. Remove the track rod from the steering arm by undoing the split pin and castellated nut on the track rod end ball joint pin. If this pin is stubborn it will need a special puller to break the taper fit. Alternatively, the car can be lowered to the ground and a hard support put under the end of the pin so that by smartly striking the steering arm the pin will be released.

5. By removing the split pin and castellated nut from the bottom of the strut where the joint pin goes through the track control arm the steering arm and ball joint nut can be released in the same way. Here again a puller may be required or alternatively the track control arm could be detached from the crossmember.

6. Finally remove the two bolts holding the steering arm to the bottom of the strut and release it - watching out for the ball stud spring.

7. To dismantle the ball joint first remove the rubber 'O' ring from the upper face of the steering arm and then the gaiter retaining ring. Then pull out the snap ring, spring seat and any shims. Remove the upper bearing, ball stud and lower bearing and examine them, after cleaning, for any signs of unusual wear in the form of flats, scoring or ridging. If such wear is apparent it is advisable to replace the whole assembly but certainly the ball stud and bearing cups.

8. Reassembly is a reversal of the dismantling procedure, after having thoroughly cleaned all parts and lubricated them with a molybdenum sulphide lithium based grease. Line up the lugs on the bearings so that they fit correctly to the arm and each other. Make sure the top bearing and spring plate are driven fully home without shims and then measure the gap between the cover and the underside of the lip in the top of the arm. Fit one or two shims depending

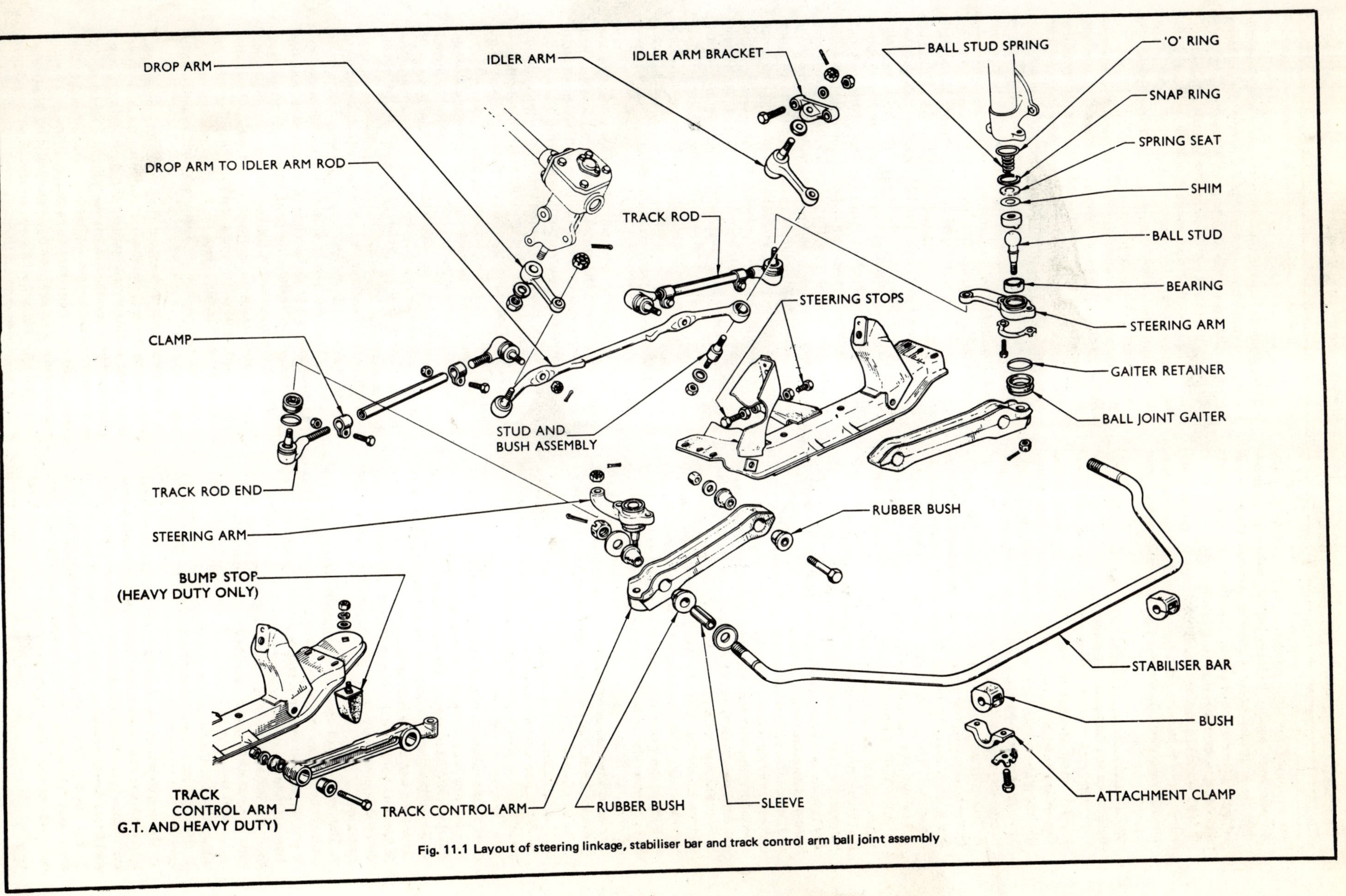

Fig. 11.1 Layout of steering linkage, stabiliser bar and track control arm ball joint assembly

on whether the gap is between .060 in. and .072 in. or over .072 in. If the clearance is overshimmed there will not be enough clearance to fit the snap ring back. Any shims should be fitted under the spring seat.

9. The rubber gaiter should be packed 2/3 full with the same sort of molybdenum disulphide grease and a new retainer ring fitted. Make sure the retainer is not twisted when in position.

10 To replace the nut to the suspension strut fit the spring over the raised section of the spring seat and secure it to the strut with a semi-circular locking plate and the two bolts. Make sure the spring is properly located in the strut and tighten the bolts to a torque of 30 to 35 lbs.ft. after which the lock tabs must be bent up.

11 Refit the ball stud taper into the track control arm and tighten the nut to 30 to 35 lbs.ft. torque. Fit a new split pin.

12 Then reconnect the track rod ball joint pin and tighten that nut to 18 to 22 lbs.ft. with a new split pin to lock it.

13 Replace the wheels, lower the car to the ground and remove the clips from the springs.

6. Track Control Arm - Removal and Replacement

1. Fit coil spring retaining clips and jack up the front of the car as described in Section 5.
2. Detach the ball stud pin from the end of the control arm as described in Section 5.
3. Remove the nut from the pivot bolt at the other end of the arm, draw out the bolt and lower the end of the arm from the crossmember.
4. Remove the castellated nut from the end of the stabiliser bar and draw off the flat washer and rubber bush.
5. Pull the track control arm off the stabiliser rod.
6. If necessary drive out the old pivot bush and press in a new one.
7. Replacement is a direct reversal of the removal procedure. Make sure all the nuts are tightened to the correct torques.

7. Front Suspension Units - Removal, Repair and Replacement

1. If the damping part of the suspension unit is not working properly, or the spring is broken and needs renewal it will be necessart first to remove the whole unit from the car.
2. Fit spring clamps, jack up the car and support it on stands and remove the road wheels.
3. Detach the brake calliper as described in Chapter 9/9 but do NOT undo any hydraulic unions as this is not necessary.
5. Remove the two bolts which hold the steering arm and ball joint assembly to the foot of the strut and then push the track control arm downwards so moving the assembly away from the suspension unit.
5. From inside the bonnet remove the plastic dust cover over the top of the upper bearing and then undo the three bolts with spring and plain washers which hold the upper support unit to the wing apron flange.
6. The unit may then be withdrawn from underneath the car.
7. If the spring is being renewed the next item to take off is the piston rod locking nut. To do this a heavy screwdriver should be held in the end slot at the top of the piston and the locknut undone.
8. The upper thrust race and ball bearing can then be lifted out followed by the mounting assembly. The old spring - in its clips still - can be taken off.
9. When fitting a new spring it is a good idea to take your

spring clamps to the parts store where the spring is bought and get it compressed on a special tool so that you can take it away clamped ready to assembly. Make sure you buy a spring of the correct colour code - the same as before.

10 Reassembly of the spring is a reversal of the removal procedure. At the same time the upper ball races can be renewed if worn. Pack them with lithium based grease on reassembly.

11 If the unit has been removed from the car because of failure of the hydraulic damping part of the assembly it is strongly recommended that the whole hydraulic unit is renewed. Even if the component parts can be obtained they cost cumulatively as much as the assembly. Check first whether you can use the original spring and upper bearing retainer as it is pointless buying these as well if they are in good condition. The wheel hub and bearing assembly, together with the brake disc should be removed from the old unit of course, as the new damper section will incorporate a new stub axle as well to which they will be fitted.

12 When the upper spring seat is replaced make sure that the flat in the piston rod matches the flat in the seat hole; and when replacing the ball bearings, thrust races and upper mounting make sure that everything is fitted square and goes completely into position before tightening up. The locknut must be tightened to 45 to 55 lbs.ft. torque and care will be required to make sure that the piston is held securely when this is being done. If in difficulty take the unit to a Ford garage and ask them to do the final tightening with their special tool No. P.5025.

13 Refit the track control arm, brake calliper and wheel and lower the car to the ground. Remove the spring clamps.

8. Rear Springs and Dampers - Removal and Replacement

1. To renew the rear dampers jack up the car under the axle and remove the wheel for ease of access. Then remove the lower anchor bolt, nut and lockwasher and pull the bottom of the damper from its location.
2. From inside the boot remove the locknut from the top mounting spindle and then grip the flats on the spindle with a suitable spanner so that the second nut can be undone and removed.
3. The damper may then be taken out from underneath. When refitting make sure first that all the rubber mountings and steel bushes are in good condition. Renew them if necessary. New bushes may come with the damper. The lower mounting bolt should be tightened to 40 to 45 lbs.ft. on reassembly.
4. The rear springs must be detached either to renew a broken leaf or to renew the mounting bushes at the front or rear. Jack up the car and support it on stands at the rear and then support the axle on a jack at a point away from the spring mountings. Remove the road wheel.
5. Detach the lower end of the damper from the mounting.
6. Thoroughly clean off all the dirt from the 'U' bolts and shackle pins and soak the nuts and threads with a suitable easing fluid such as 'Plus-Gas'.
7. Remove the 'U' bolt nuts and jack up the axle a little way to separate it from the springs.
8. Remove the nut and washer from the front hanger bolt. This may prove very stubborn and if it needs driving out replace the nut to try and protect the threads. In any case one should be prepared to renew the bolt.
9. When removing the shackle plates at the rear end of the spring both nuts must first be removed as the two halves each comprise one shackle pin and plate and need separating. Here again the pins may be very difficult to shift and it is not unknown to have to cut them off.

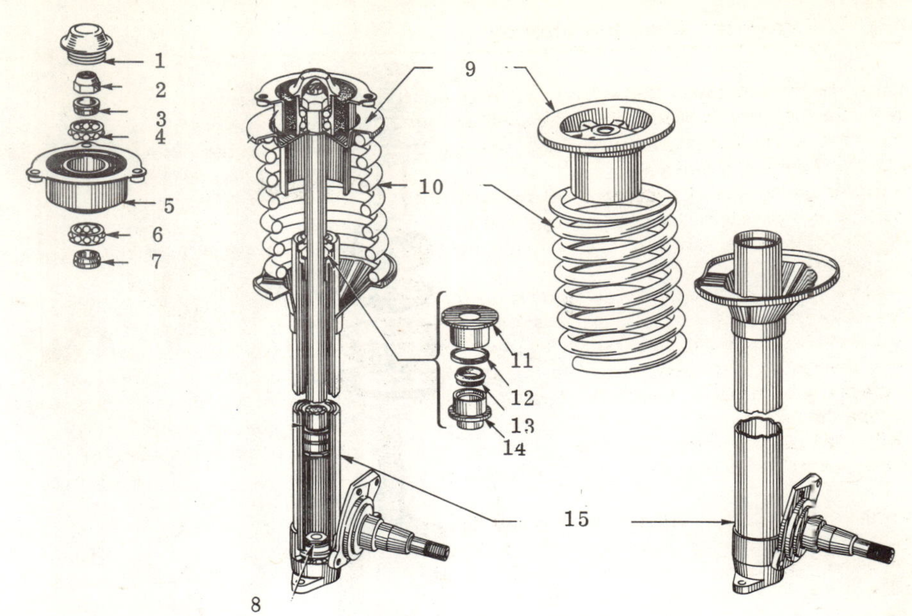

Fig. 11.2. FRONT SUSPENSION UNIT GIVING EXPLODED VIEWS OF INTERNAL SEALS AND UPPER BEARINGS

1 Cap	5 Mounting bush	9 Spring seat	13 Gland
2 Locknut	6 Caged balls	10 Spring	14 Guide
3 Bearing race	7 Bearing race	11 Gland cap	15 Tube and spindle
4 Caged balls	8 Cap	12 Piston rod guide	assembly

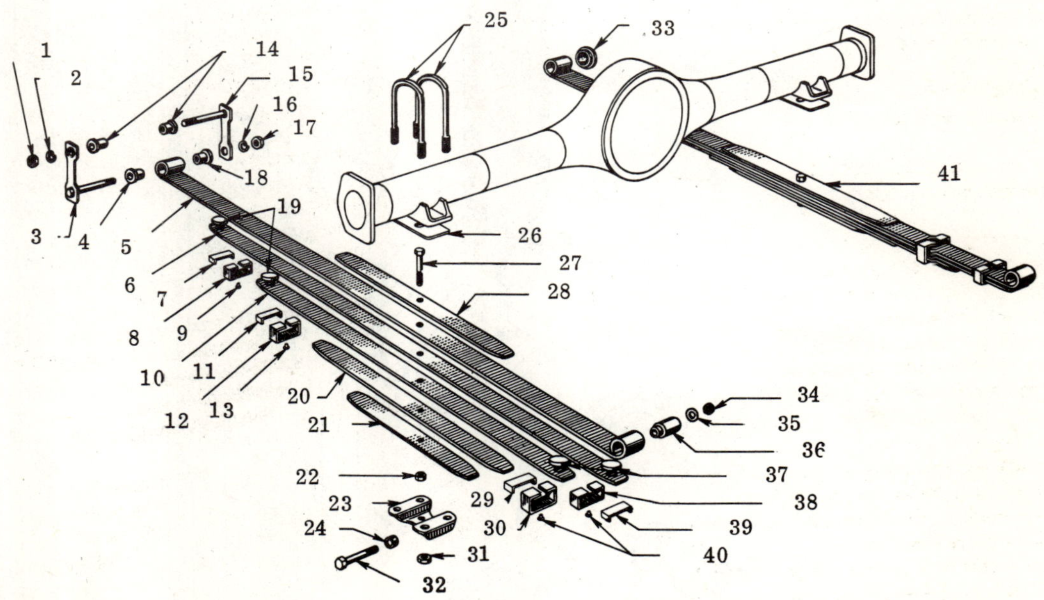

Fig. 11.3. REAR SPRINGS AND MOUNTINGS — EXPLODED VIEW

1 Nut	12 Clamp	23 Clamp plate	34 Nut
2 Spring washer	13 Rivet	24 Spacer	35 Washer
3 Shackle plate	14 Bush	25 'U' bolts	36 Bush
4 Bush	15 Shackle plate	26 Insulator	37 Insert
5 Main leaf	16 Spring washer	27 Tie bolt	38 Clamp
6 Leaf No. 2	17 Nut	28 Rebound leaf	39 Clip
7 Clip	18 Bush	29 Clip	40 Rivet
8 Clamp	19 Insert	30 Clamp	41 Spring assembly
9 Rivet	20 Leaf No. 4	31 Nut	
10 Leaf No. 3	21 Leaf No. 5	32 Bolt	
11 Clip	22 Nut	33 Plug	

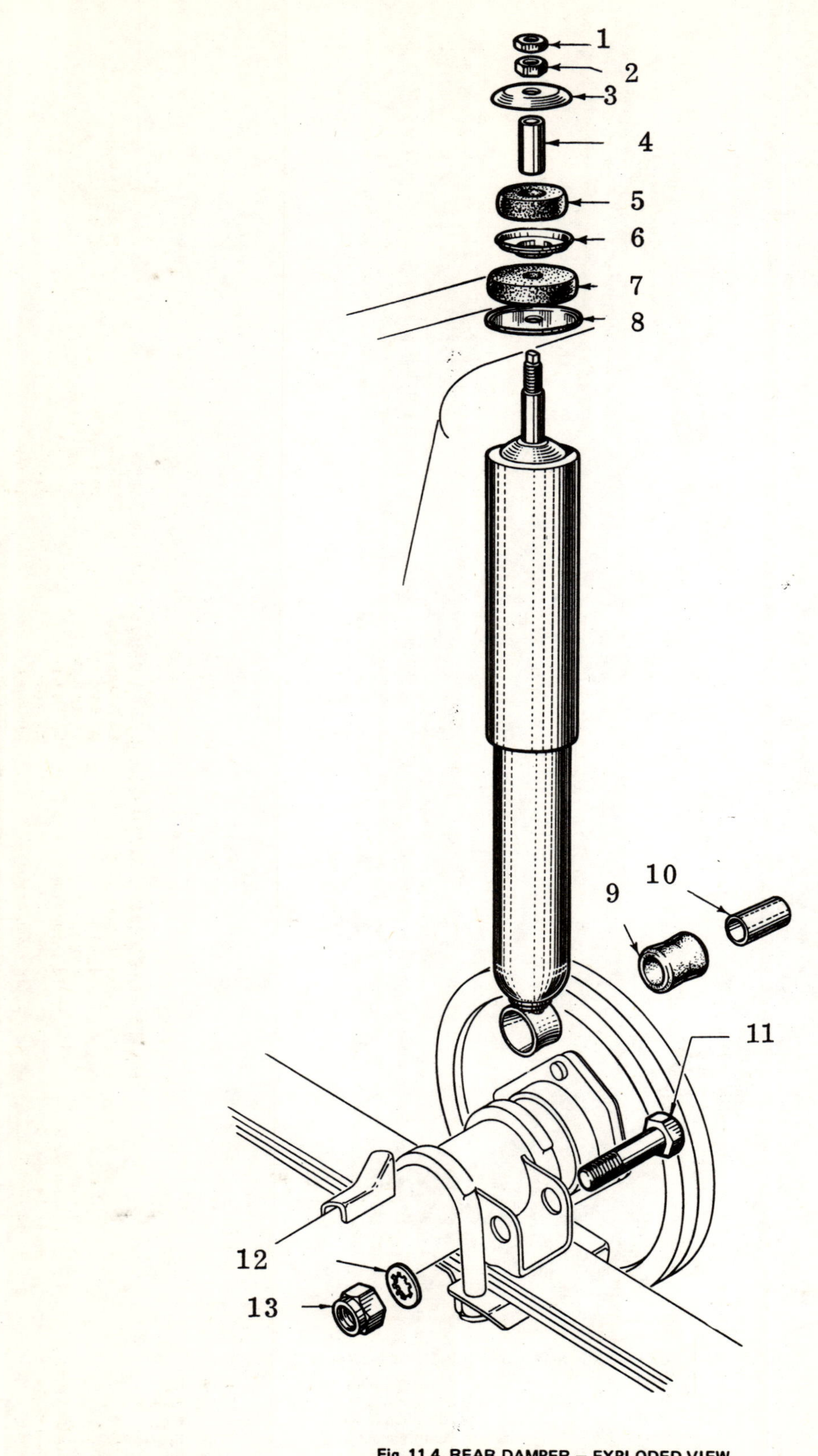

Fig. 11.4. REAR DAMPER — EXPLODED VIEW

1 Locknut	5 Insulator	8 Seat washer	11 Bolt
2 Securing nut	6 Seat washer	9 Bush	12 Stem washer
3 Seat washers	7 Insulator	10 Sleeve	13 Locking nut
4 Sleeve			

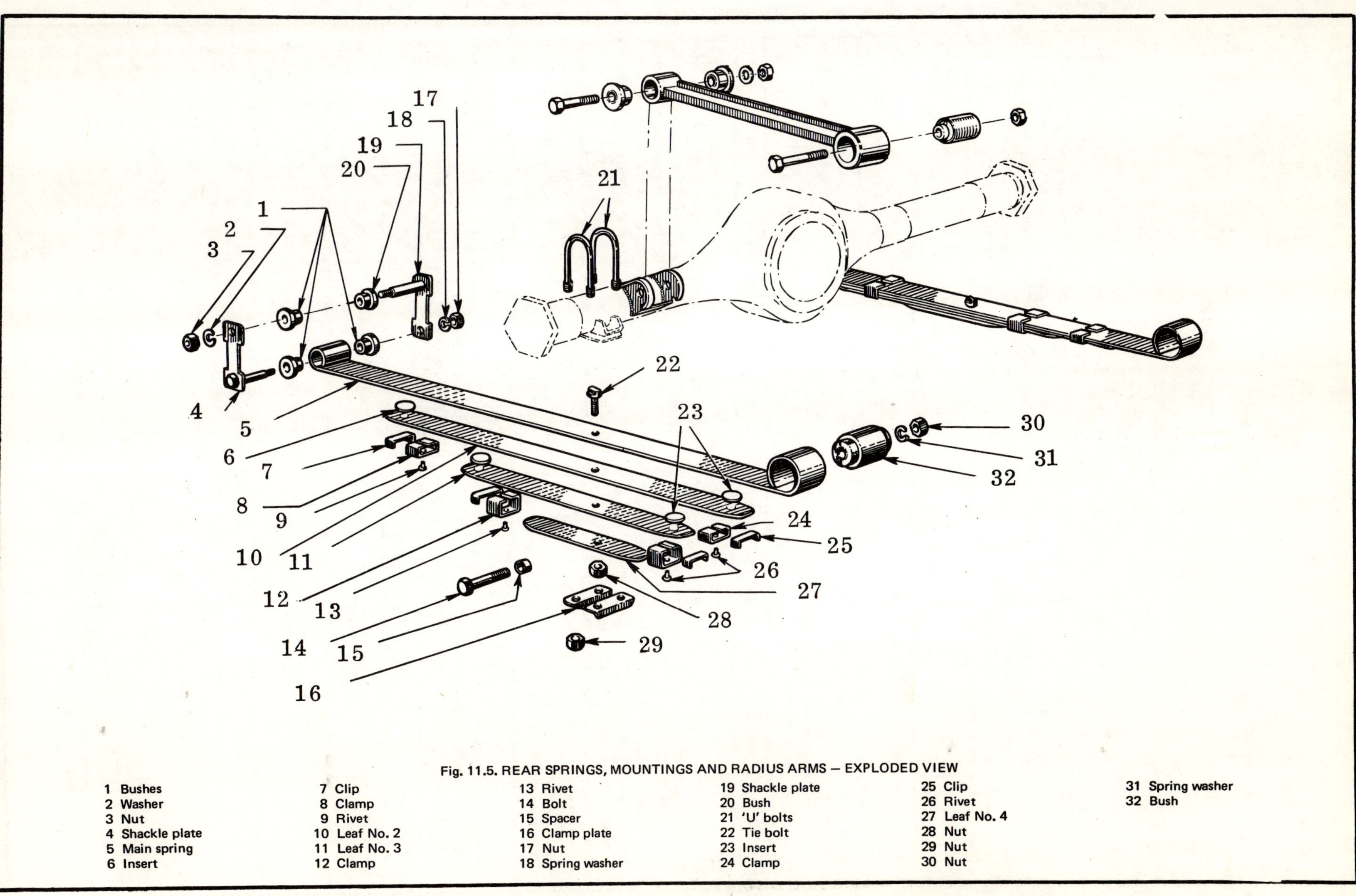

Fig. 11.5. REAR SPRINGS, MOUNTINGS AND RADIUS ARMS — EXPLODED VIEW

1 Bushes	7 Clip	13 Rivet	19 Shackle plate	25 Clip	31 Spring washer
2 Washer	8 Clamp	14 Bolt	20 Bush	26 Rivet	32 Bush
3 Nut	9 Rivet	15 Spacer	21 'U' bolts	27 Leaf No. 4	
4 Shackle plate	10 Leaf No. 2	16 Clamp plate	22 Tie bolt	28 Nut	
5 Main spring	11 Leaf No. 3	17 Nut	23 Insert	29 Nut	
6 Insert	12 Clamp	18 Spring washer	24 Clamp	30 Nut	

10 A broken spring can be replaced as a complete unit or the individual leaf can be renewed. If the leaf only is being replaced new spring clips, rivets and inserts will be required to reassemble the leaves. A replacement unit can usually be found at a breaker's and this is the simplest and cheapest way to go about it.

11 When reassembling the rubber bushes for the shackles use some soapy water to lubricate them. The front spring hanger bush is a press fit unit into the spring. It will have to be driven out and a new one pressed in if it needs renewal.

12 When refitting the spring to the body, fix the front hanger pin first as it will be easier to line up the shackles to replace the pins rather than the other way round.

13 Use the axle jack to get the spring seats and 'U' bolts correctly positioned before tightening up the nuts. The hangar bolt nuts, 'U' bolt nuts and shackle stud nuts should all be tightened moderately and the damper lower mounting bolt replaced. Lower the car to the ground and bounce it a few times to settle the spring bushes and then tighten the nuts finally to the specified torque.

9. Steering Gear and Linkage - Inspection

1. Wear in the steering gear and linkage is indicated when there is excessive movement in the steering wheel without corresponding movement at the road wheels, and also when there is a tendency for the car to 'wander' off the line in which one is intending to steer it. This latter fault is due to misalignment of the wheels caused by wear, maladjustment or possibly damage to the steering linkage.

2. To check the steering, first jack up the front of the car and support it on stands so that both the front wheels are clear of the ground. With someone to help grip one front wheel and rock it the way in which it would move in steering and look at, in turn, the seven moving linkage points which may be worn (see Fig. 11.5). Do not consider the steering gear at this stage.

3. The seven points subject to wear are the ball joints at the ends of each track rod, the bonded bushes at each end of the rod linking the drop arm to the idler arm, and the idler arm joint itself.

4. Any sign of play in any of the foregoing joints means that it is worn and should be renewed. Each item is an assembly and can be removed and replaced as a unit. The idler arm bush is integral with the arm so in case of failure the idler arm assembly needs renewal.

5. Having established that the steering linkage (and of course the track control arm as dealt with in Section 5) is in order any play between the steering wheel and road wheels is due to wear in the steering gear. This could be rectified by adjustment but dismantling and renovation may be necessary.

6. Remember that badly worn steering is most dangerous in a vehicle and must not be left unrepaired.

10. Steering Linkage - Removal and Replacement

1. The seven moving joints are all located by a taper pin secured by a castellated nut and split pin. It is always a simple matter to remove the split pin and nut but getting the taper pin out of the hole is often a source of frustration. If you are unable to get hold of a claw clamp which will get them out easily the only other way is to support the pin in question with something very solid and hard and striking the arm into which it fits. Alternatively, one may support the arm and strike the pin but this is not usually so effect-ive. One thing is certain - unless the support is really solid and the strike can be made cleanly and smartly there is no

point in battling away. Save your time and temper by going out and borrowing a proper clamp or something like a sledge hammer head to provide the firm base to strike against.

2. Track rod end ball joints may be unscrewed from the track rod once they have been removed from their pin locations and the track rod clamping bolt slackened. Note that they are either right or left hand threaded. It is a good idea also to count how many threads on the shank are showing before taking them off the track rod as this will give a guide to the approximate position on replacement.

3. If either of the rubber bushes in the ends of the drop arm/idler arm link rod need replacement the rod itself must be removed. This entails disconnecting the inner ends of both track rods and then the connections to the idler arm and drop arm. When removed the bushes may be driven out and replaced as required.

4. The idler arm bush is renewable by detaching the idler arm from the bracket and the link rod. It must be replaced complete.

5. If any track rod end joint is replaced the steering should be re-aligned (see Section 15). Provided the track rod ends are not disturbed in relation to the track rods it is not necessary to re-align the wheels after replacing any of the other three joints. However, in view of the fact that the steering may have been re-aligned previously in a misguided attempt to compensate for wear, it would be worthwhile to have it checked any way.

11. Steering Gear - Adjustments

1. Adjustments may be made to the steering gear to take up steering shaft endfloat or rocker shaft adjustment when the unit is in the car. Signs of excessive backlash or move-ment, however, indicate abnormal wear and although these may be alleviated to some extent by adjustments it is unlikely that the benefits achieved will be either satisfactory or long-lasting.

2. Wear in the gearbox occurs in the rocker shaft bush, which, if serious will probably result in an oil leak. It can also be seen when the steering wheel is turned, as a sideways movement of the shaft as well as a rotary one.

3. The steering shaft ball bearings which are positioned at each end of the worm, can also wear and this wear can be detected by any up and down movement of the steering shaft when there should be none.

4. The other area of wear, which cannot be adjusted, is in the worm itself and also between the nut and the rocker arm.

5. To determine the amount of steering shaft end float accurately is difficult with the gear mounted in the car. By removing the steering wheel centre motif the end of the shaft is exposed, and theoretically, one can mount a dial gauge micrometer against the end and pull the steering wheel upwards and measure the amount of movement. In practice this is not so simple, so one can only proceed by trial and error. Ideally the bearing pre-load would be .003 in.

6. First remove the steering wheel by taking out the centre motif and bending back the lockwasher tab behind the shaft nut. Mark the wheel in relation to the shaft, undo the nut and pull the wheel off.

7. Remove the steering column shroud and indicator switch assembly (see Chapter 10) and then slacken the bolts hold-ing the steering column clamp and mounting bracket.

8. Inside the engine compartment undo the four bolts holding the steering column flange to the top of the steering box. The column may then be drawn upwards a small way from the box.

9. The shims under the flange will now be apparent and

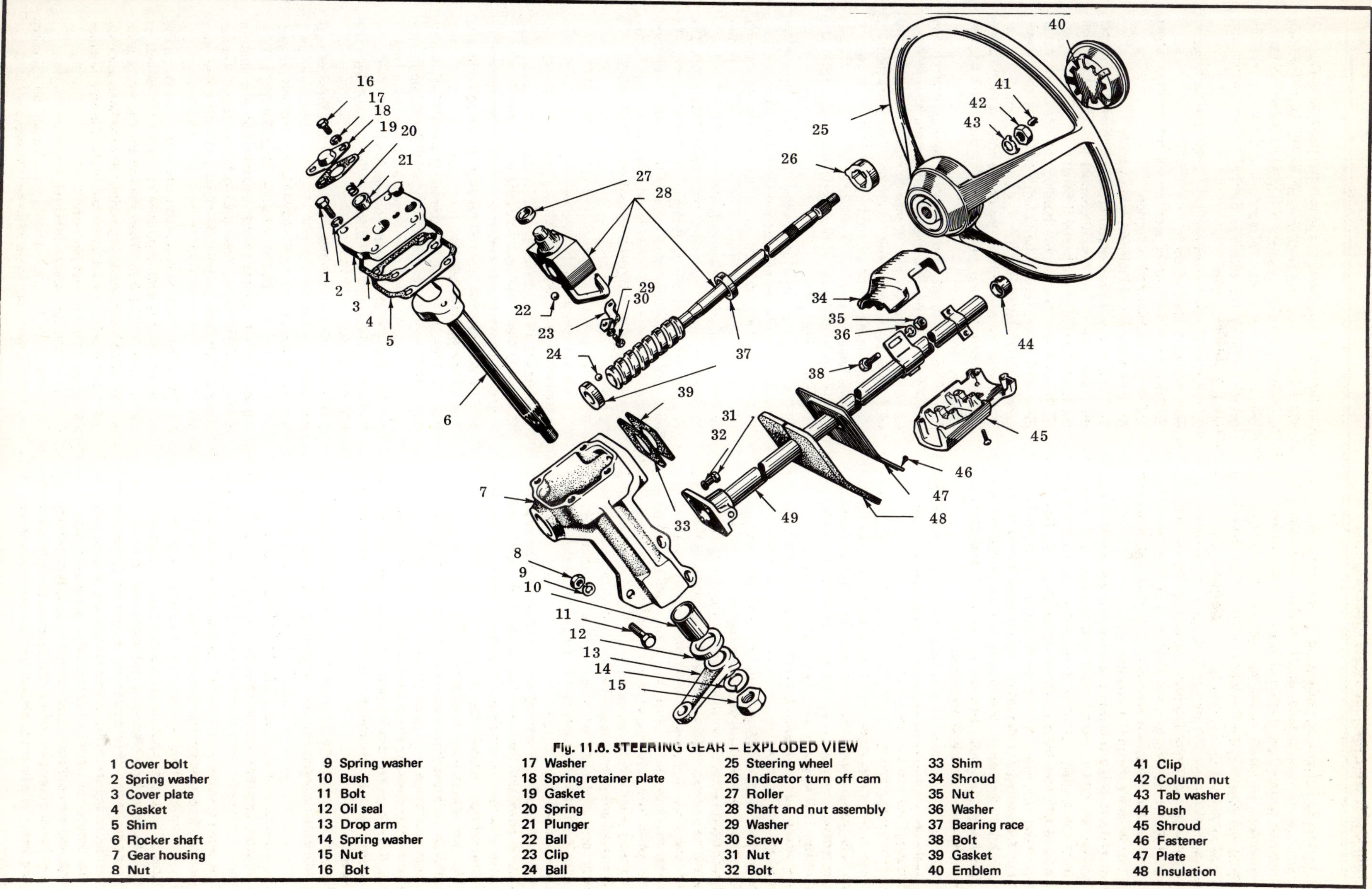

Fig. 11.8. STEERING GEAR — EXPLODED VIEW

1 Cover bolt	9 Spring washer	17 Washer	25 Steering wheel	33 Shim	41 Clip
2 Spring washer	10 Bush	18 Spring retainer plate	26 Indicator turn off cam	34 Shroud	42 Column nut
3 Cover plate	11 Bolt	19 Gasket	27 Roller	35 Nut	43 Tab washer
4 Gasket	12 Oil seal	20 Spring	28 Shaft and nut assembly	36 Washer	44 Bush
5 Shim	13 Drop arm	21 Plunger	29 Washer	37 Bearing race	45 Shroud
6 Rocker shaft	14 Spring washer	22 Ball	30 Screw	38 Bolt	46 Fastener
7 Gear housing	15 Nut	23 Clip	31 Nut	39 Gasket	47 Plate
8 Nut	16 Bolt	24 Ball	32 Bolt	40 Emblem	48 Insulation

the purpose is to reduce the thickness of this shim pack so that when the flange is bolted down it will bear more closely on the bearing cups and take up the play. If play is detectable then one knows that at least .003 in. thickness plus the play may be removed. In such a case it would be safe to remove up to .005 in. of shims. This can only be done of course by cutting the shim to remove it from round the shaft. Tighten back the column flange bolts and if there is no longer any play do not alter the shims any further. If there is still detectable play remove another .003 in. at a time until it disappears.

10 Unfortunately the shims normally fitted came in thicknesses of .004 in. or .010 in. (metal) and .010 in. and .025 in. (paper). Thus it is necessary to calculate the necessary combinations of thicknesses to achieve the required reduction. Strictly speaking, once a shim has been cut and removed it should not be replaced. As the repair is essentially of a short term nature however it may be done provided care is taken to ensure that the cut edges of the shim cannot overlap when replaced.

11 The four flange mounting bolts should be coated with sealer on replacement to prevent oil seepage through the threads.

12 The rocker shaft setting is decided by the degree of force which it is necessary to apply at the periphery of the steering wheel to turn it with the wheel linkage disconnected.

13 Disconnect the linkage from the drop arm, after setting the steering in the straight ahead position, by removing the split pin and castellated nut and pressing or driving out the stud.

14 The straight ahead position should result in the steering arm lying parallel with the steering column. To measure the pull required to turn the wheel attach a spring balance to one of the steering wheel spokes at the rim and pull it in a direction at right angles to the spoke. The pull required should be from 1¼ to 1½ lbs. (.6 to .7 Kgs.). If the pull required is less than specified then the end loading on the rocker shaft can be increased by reducing the shim thickness under the top cover.

15 Remove the four bolts holding the cover to the box and lift if off carefully with the shims, gaskets and the two coil springs and thrust button.

16 In this adjustment the amount of shim thickness to be removed cannot be pre-calculated, so by trial and error remove shims and replace the cover until the required degree of pull is obtained.

17 Throughout this adjustment procedure the steering wheel should be moved from lock to lock at each stage to make sure that there is no trace of stiffness and binding. If there is any binding anywhere especially in the central position and the required turning pull is still not reached, then the worm must be excessively worn and the unit will need overhaul.

18 Although it is most unlikely, there may be a need to REDUCE the pull by increasing the number of shims and the same procedure will apply. Make sure that the stiffness is properly diagnosed before doing this adjustment.

19 When adjustments are complete reconnect the steering linkage, tighten the column clamp bolts as necessary and replace the steering wheel. Tighten the bolts and nuts to the torques as detailed in the specifications.

12. Steering Gear - Removal and Replacement

1. If the adjustments outlined in the previous section are ineffective, or wear is such that it is obvious that mere adjustments will not rectify the situation, the steering gear will need renovation. For this it must be removed from the car. For the owner to rebuild the unit is not advised as the cost of the components would be little less than the whole. Furthermore, the rocker shaft bush would need broaching or reaming if renewed and this requires a degree of fitting skill and special tools. We recommend therefore that the owner confines his activities to the actual removal and replacement of the unit.

2. The steering gear is removed from under the car together with the whole steering shaft.

3. Disconnect the battery and remove the steering wheel and shroud as described in Section 11/6.

4. Detach the dip and horn switch assembly.

5. Remove the screws securing the ends of the parcel shelf and take it out. Also disconnect the bracket bolt on the left hand side of the heater if fitted.

6. Remove the two screws holding the toe-board cover plate and gasket round the column and bring them back away from the bulkhead.

7. Remove the two bolts clamping the column to the panel and the bolt holding the column to the pedal bracket assembly.

8. For models fitted with a steering column gear change the pin securing the gear change tube to the housing must be removed. Also the gear change tube and lever assembly must then be removed and finally the two bolts securing the gear change housing to the steering box must be undone and the linkage supported to one side.

9. Next jack up the car as high as possible and support the front on stands.

10 Disconnect the steering linkage from the drop arm by removing the split pin and nut and separating the stud.

11 Unscrew the three nuts and bolts holding the steering box to the body side member and then manoeuvre the whole unit and shaft downwards out of the car.

12 Replacement is a reversal of the removal procedure. Do not tighten any of the mounting or clamping bolts finally until the whole assembly is correctly located; and then tighten first the three bolts mounting the steering box to the body member. Do not forget to refill the unit with oil.

13. Front Wheel Bearings - Adjustment

1. To check that the front wheel bearings are correctly set, jack up the front wheels and, by gripping the wheel at the top and bottom, rock it to ascertain if there is any movement. If there is, it is most likely that the bearing needs adjustment. Make sure nevertheless that the movement is not due to any slackness in the suspension joints.

2. Remove the wheels and prise out the dust cap from the hub flange boss.

3. Remove the split pin from the spindle and then take off the bearing nut retainer.

4. If a torque wrench is available tighten the bearing nut, whilst turning the hub, to a torque of 27/28 lbs.ft. Then replace the nut retainer so that a castellation slot lines up with the split pin hole. Then back off the nut and retainer together 90º (two castellation slots) and refit a new split pin.

5. If no torque wrench is available use a box spanner on the nut and tighten it until a positive resistance can be felt to the rotation of the hub. Then slacken the spanner a little and retighten it as much as is possible with the hand gripping the spanner without a tommy-bar. Refit the nut retainer and new split pin in that position.

6. Replace the dust cover and wheel.

7. If, when adjusted, the bearing feels 'rough' on spinning the hub it is worn out and should be renewed.

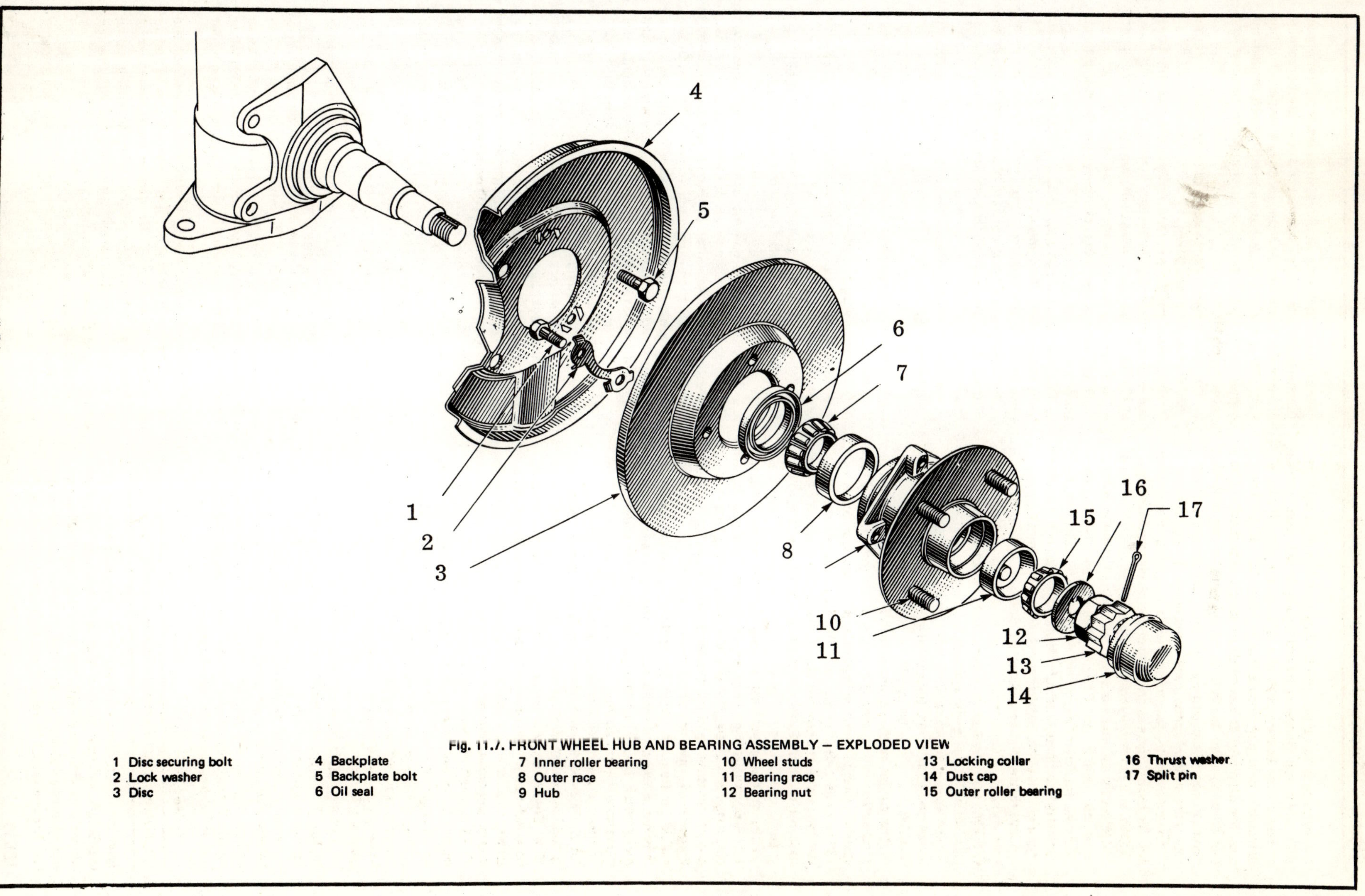

Fig. 11.7. FRONT WHEEL HUB AND BEARING ASSEMBLY – EXPLODED VIEW

1 Disc securing bolt	4 Backplate	7 Inner roller bearing	10 Wheel studs
2 Lock washer	5 Backplate bolt	8 Outer race	11 Bearing race
3 Disc	6 Oil seal	9 Hub	12 Bearing nut

13 Locking collar	16 Thrust washer
14 Dust cap	17 Split pin
15 Outer roller bearing	

14. Front Wheel Bearings and Hubs - Removal and Replacement

1. When the scheduled 15,000 mile grease repacking of the bearings is due - or when a bearing needs renewal, it is necessary to remove the complete hub assembly.
2. Jack up the car and remove the wheel.
3. Remove the brake calliper unit as described in Chapter 9/9. It is not necessary to remove the pads for this. Neither need the hydraulic pipe be disconnected provided it is detached from the suspension unit. The calliper should be supported on one side so that no strain is imposed on the hydraulic line.
4. Remove the hub dust cap and take out the split pin from the spindle. Then remove the nut retainer and bearing nut.
5. Take the thrust washer off the spindle and the outer roller bearing.
6. The hub disc may now be taken off the stub axle.
7. Remove the grease retainer ring from the inner end of the hub by levering it out.
8. Remove the inner bearing race.
9. Wash out the hub interior with paraffin and examine the surfaces of the bearing races for signs of wear. They should be shiny bright in appearance with no signs of ridging or pitting. If they are worn they must be renewed together with new roller bearings.
10 If the bearing races are to be removed it is best to use a special tool (Ford No. P.1024-7a). If a drift is used carelessly damage could be caused to the hub which would prevent the cups from seating properly when replaced. However, if this method is adopted use only a brass drift and tap out the cups from the inside of the hub, making sure that they came out perfectly square by striking evenly round the periphery of the race.
11 When the new races are ready for insertion make sure that the hub bore recesses are perfectly clean and free from snags and burrs. Replace the races with the wide aperture facing outwards and tap them in carefully and evenly. Make sure they are driven completely home.
12 Pack the space between the two bearing races with lithium based wheel bearing grease leaving some air space for expansion.
13 Whether or not the roller bearings are new or old they should be thoroughly washed in spirit, dried off and packed between rollers and cage with the same lithium based grease.

14 Replace the inner hub bearing and fit a new grease retainer behind it with the lip facing the bearing. Make sure the seal is also driven in square and fully home.
15 Reposition the hub on the spindle and fit the hub outer bearing into position having greased it in the same way as the other.
16 Refit the thrust washer and bearing nut.
17 Adjust the bearings as described in Section 13.
18 Replace the calliper to the hub, tightening the bolts as specified and bend back the lock washer tabs.
19 Refit the hydraulic pipe to the bracket on the suspension leg.
20 Replace the road wheel and lower the car to the ground.

15. Front Wheel Alignment

To obtain true and accurate steering the correct alignment of the front wheels is essential. Also the rate of tyre wear, if the front wheels are misaligned, is excessive. There are several factors which can contribute to misalignment and these are:-

a) Tyre pressure incorrect.
b) Buckled wheels.
c) Loose or worn out wheel bearings.
d) Loose clamps at the centre of the stabiliser bar.
e) Incorrectly seated coil springs.
f) Worn ball joints or bushes in the steering linkage.
g) Incorrectly adjusted track rods.

Wheel alignment consists of four factors, namely, the castor angle, the camber angle, the king pin inclination and the toe-in. Any or all of these may be affected by the faults listed. As there is only one feature in the layout which is adjustable, namely, the track rods (which only alter the toe-in) it will be obvious that this adjustment by itself is futile if any of the other six faults are also apparent.

Having repaired the obvious faults it is essential that the alignment is then checked on a proper gauge. There is no other way of doing this accurately. Provided the toe-in is the only incorrect part of the alignment, adjustment of the track rods can rectify the fault. It must also be remembered that even though all the linkage joints and bushes are in good order distortion of any of the components due to impact damage can cause misalignment.

Before diagnosing faults from the following chart, check that any irregularities are not caused by:-
1. Binding brakes
2. Incorrect 'mix' of radial and cross-ply tyres
3. Incorrect tyre pressures
4. Misalignment of the body frame

Symptom	Reason	Remedy
Steering wheel can be moved considerably before any sign of movement of the wheels is apparent.	Wear in the steering linkage, gear and column coupling.	Check movement in all joints and steering gear and overhaul and renew as required.
Vehicle difficult to steer in a consistent straight line - wandering.	As above.	As above.
	Wheel alignment incorrect (indicated by excessive or uneven tyre wear)	Check wheel alignment.
	Front wheel hub bearings loose or worn	Adjust or renew as necessary.
	Worn suspension unit swivel joints.	Renew as necessary.
Steering stiff and heavy	Incorrect wheel alignment (indicated by excessive or uneven tyre wear).	Check wheel alignment.
	Excessive wear or seizure in one or more of the joints in the steering linkage or suspension unit ball joints.	Renew as necessary or grease the suspension unit ball joints.
	Excessive wear in the steering gear unit	Adjust if possible or renew.
Wheel wobble and vibration	Road wheels out of balance.	Balance wheels.
	Road wheels buckled.	Check for damage.
	Wheel alignment incorrect.	Check wheel alignment.
	Wear in the steering linkage, suspension unit bearings or track control arm bushes.	Check and renew as necessary.
	Broken front spring.	Check and renew as necessary.
Excessive pitching and rolling on corners and during braking.	Defective dampers and/or broken spring	Check and renew as necessary.

Chapter 12/Bodywork and Underframe

Contents

1. General Description

The combined body and underframe is an all-welded unitary structure of sheet steel. Openings in it provide for the engine compartment, luggage compartment, doors and windows. The rear suspension is bolted directly to it at the side members. The front of the body under the engine compartment is braced by a crossmember which also supports the lower part of the suspension. Reinforced panels in the wing aprons support the upper ends of the suspension units.

The engine and gearbox assembly is supported at three points - forward by flexible mountings attached to the side members and at the rear by a detachable crossmember underneath the gearbox bolted to the floor panel.

The model was made in two, four and four door estate car versions. Front door windows are fitted with opening quarter lights. Air extraction vents are fitted in both the saloon and estate versions behind the rear side windows.

All except the standard models are fitted with heaters and windscreen washers. G.T. models have an oil pressure gauge and tachometer.

2. Maintenance - Body Exterior

1. The general condition of a car's body work is the one thing that significantly affects its value. Maintenance is easy but needs to be regular and particular. Neglect - particularly after minor damage - can quickly lead to further deterioration and costly repair bills. It is important also to keep watch on those parts of the bodywork not immediately visible, for example the underside, inside all the wheel arches and the lower part of the engine compartment.

2. The basic maintenance routine for the bodywork is washing - preferably with a lot of water from a hose. This will remove all the loose solids which may have stuck to the car. It is important to flush these off in such a way as to prevent grit from scratching the finish. The wheel arches and underbody need washing in the same way, to remove any accumulated mud which will retain moisture and tend to encourage rust. Paradoxically enough, the best time to clean the underbody and wheel arches is in wet weather when the mud is thoroughly wet and soft. In very wet weather the underbody is usually cleaned of large accumulations automatically and this is a good time for inspection.

3. Periodically, it is a good idea to have the whole of the underside of the car steam cleaned, engine compartment included, so that a thorough inspection can be carried out to see what minor repairs and renovations are necessary. Steam cleaning is available at many garages and is necessary for removal of accumulation of oily grime which sometimes collects thickly in areas near the engine, gearbox and back axle. If steam facilities are not available there are one or two excellent grease solvents available which can be brush applied. The dirt can then be simply hosed off.

4. After washing the paintwork wipe it off with a chamois leather to give a clear unspotted finish. A coat of clear wax polish will give added protection against chemical pollutants in the air and will survive several subsequent washings. If the paintwork sheen has dulled or oxidised use a cleaner/polisher combination to restore the brilliance of the shine. This requires a little more effort but is usually caused because regular washing has been neglected! Always check that door and ventilator drain holes and pipes are completely clear so that water can drain out. Brightwork should be treated the same way as paintwork. Windscreens and windows can be kept clear of the smeary film which often appears if a little ammonia is added to the water. If glasswork is scratched a good rub with a proprietary metal polish will often clean them. Never use any form of wax or other paint/chromium polish on glass.

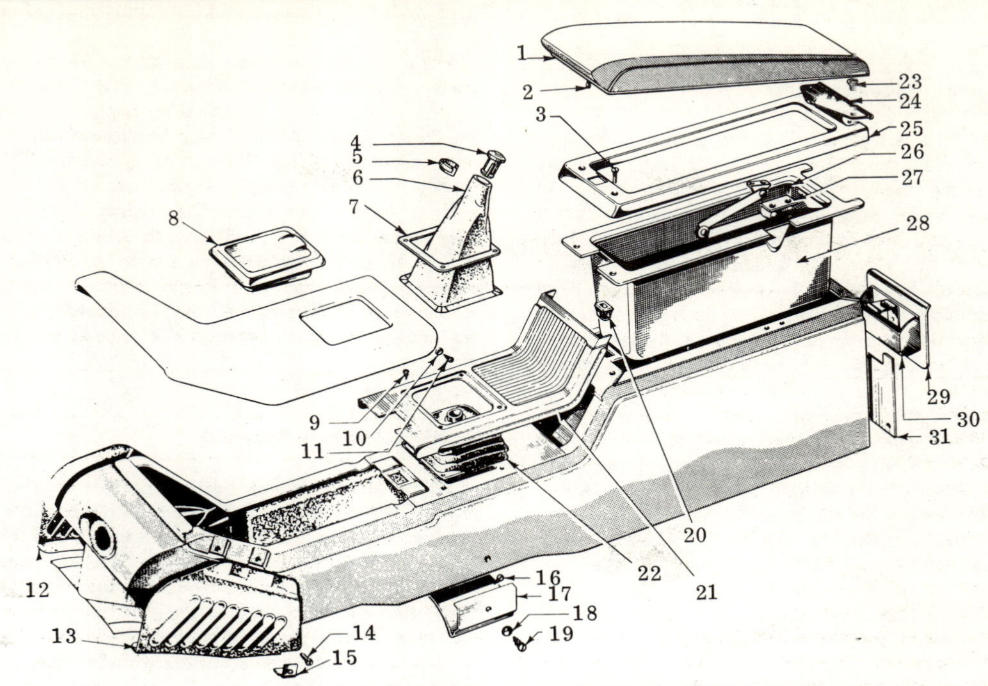

**Fig. 12.1. CENTRE FLOOR CONSOLE ASSEMBLY — REMOTE GEAR CHANGE
UP TILL SEPT. 1967 — EXPLODED VIEW**

1 Arm rest	9 Screw	17 Bracket	25 Surround
2 Catch	10 Cup washer	18 Washer	26 Screw
3 Screw	11 Screw	19 Screw	27 Check strap
4 Grommet	12 Louvre panel	20 Catch plate	28 Container
5 Clip	13 Louvre panel	21 Finisher trim	29 Ash tray finisher
6 Gaiter	14 Screw	22 Boot	30 Ash tray
7 Fixing plate	15 Bracket	23 Screw	31 Bracket
8 Ash tray	16 Screw	24 Hinge	

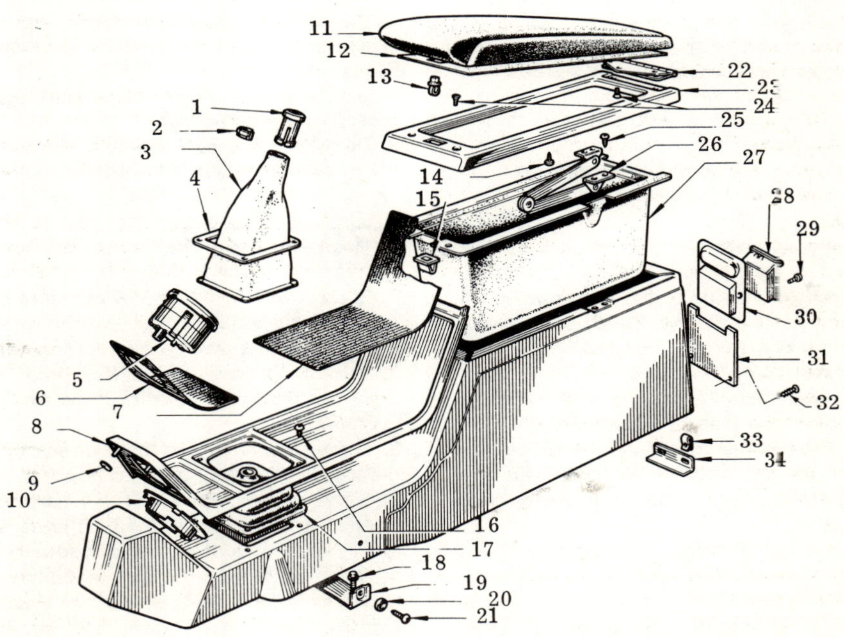

**Fig. 12.2. CENTRE FLOOR CONSOLE ASSEMBLY — REMOTE GEAR CHANGE —
SEPT. 1967 ON — EXPLODED VIEW**

1 Grommet	10 Clock support	19 Bracket	28 Ashtray
2 Clip	11 Arm rest	20 Cup washer	29 Screw
3 Gaiter	12 Panel	21 Screw	30 Escutcheon
4 Fixing plate	13 Catch	22 Hinge	31 Panel
5 Clock	14 Screw	23 Surround	32 Screw
6 Finisher	15 Catch plate	24 Screw	33 Clip
7 Finisher	16 Screw	25 Screw	34 Bracket
8 Cover plate	17 Boot	26 Check strap	
9 Clip	18 Bolt	27 Container	

3. Maintenance - Body Interior

Mats and carpets should be brushed or vacuum cleaned regularly to keep them free of grit. If they are badly stained, remove them from the car for scrubbing or sponging and make quite sure that they are dry before replacement. Seat and interior trim panels can be kept clean with a wipe over with a damp cloth. If they do become stained (which can be more apparent on light coloured upholstery) use a little liquid detergent and a soft nailbrush to scour the grime out of the grain of the material. Do not forget to keep the headlining clean in the same way as the upholstery. When using liquid cleaners inside the car do not over-wet the surfaces being cleaned. Excessive damp could get into the upholstery seams and padded interior, causing stains, offensive odours or even rot. If the inside of the car gets wet accidentally it is worthwhile taking some trouble to dry it out properly, particularly where carpets are involved. Do NOT leave oil or electric heaters inside the car for this purpose.

4. Minor Repairs to Bodywork

1. A car which does not suffer some minor damage to the bodywork from time to time is the exception rather than the rule. Even presuming the gate post is never scraped or the door opened against a wall or high kerb there is always the likelihood of gravel and grit being thrown up and chipping the surface, particularly at the lower edges of the doors and sills.
2. If the damage is merely a paint scrape which has not reached the metal base, delay is not critical but where bare metal is exposed action must be taken immediately before rust sets in.
3. The average owner will normally keep the following 'first aid' materials available which can give a professional finish for minor jobs:-

a) A resin based filler paste.
b) Matched paint either for spraying by gun or in an aerosol can.
c) Fine cutting paste.
d) Medium and fine grade wet and dry abrasive paper.

4. Where the damage is superficial (i.e. not down to the bare metal and not dented) fill the scratch or chip with sufficient filler to smooth the area, rub down with paper and apply the matching paint.
5. Where the bodywork is scratched down to the metal, but not dented, clean the metal surface thoroughly and apply a suitable metal primer first - such as red lead or zinc chromate. Fill up the scratch as necessary with filler and rub down with wet and dry paper. Apply the matching colour paint.
6. If more than one coat of colour is required rub down each coat with cutting paste before applying the next.
7. If the bodywork is dented, first beat out the dent to conform as near as possible to the original contour. Avoid using steel faced hammers - use hard wood mallets or similar and always support the panel being beaten with a hardwood or metal 'dolly'. In areas where severe creasing and buckling has occurred it will be virtually impossible to reform the metal to the original shape. In such instances a decision should be made whether or not to cut out the damaged piece or attempt to re-contour over it with filler paste. In large areas where the metal panel is seriously damaged or rusted the repair is to be considered major and it is often better to replace a panel or sill section with the

appropriate piece supplied as a spare. When using filler paste in largish quantities make sure that the directions are carefully followed. It is false economy to rush the job as the correct hardening time must be allowed between stages and before finishing. With thick applications the filler usually has to be applied in layers - allowing time for each layer to harden. Sometimes the original paint colour will have faded and it will be difficult to obtain an exact colour match. In such instances it is a good scheme to select a complete panel - such as a door or boot lid - and spray the whole panel. Differences will be less apparent where there are obvious divisions between the original and resprayed areas.

5. Major Repairs to Bodywork

Where serious damage has occurred or large areas need renewal due to neglect it means certainly that completely new sections or panels will need welding in and this is best left to professionals. If the damage is due to impact it will also be necessary to completely check the alignment of the body shell structure. Due to the principle of construction the strength and shape of the whole can be affected by damage to a part. In such instances the services of a Ford agent with specialist checking jigs are essential. If a body is left misaligned it is first of all dangerous as the car will not handle properly and secondly uneven stresses will be imposed on the steering, engine and transmission, causing abnormal wear or complete failure. Tyre wear may also be excessive.

6. Maintenance - Hinges, Door Catches and Locks

1. Oil the hinges of the bonnet, boot and doors with a drop or two of light oil periodically. A good time is after the car has been washed.
2. Oil the bonnet release catch pivot pin and the safety catch pivot pin periodically.
3. Do not over lubricate door latches and strikers. Normally a little oil on the rotary cam spindle alone is sufficient.

7. Doors - Tracing of Rattles and Rectification

1. Check first that the door is not loose at the hinges and that the latch is holding the door firmly in position. Check also that the door lines up with the aperture in the body.
2. If the hinges are loose or the door is out of alignment it will be necessary to reset the hinge positions, as described in Section 8.
3. If the latch is holding the door properly it should hold the door tightly when fully latched and the door should line up with the body. If it is out of alignment it needs adjustment as described in Section 9. If loose, some part of the lock mechanism must be worn out and requiring renewal.
4. Other rattles from the door would be caused by wear or looseness in the window winder, the glass channels and sill strips or the door buttons and interior latch release mechanism. All these are dealt with in Sections 11 and 15.

8. Door Alignment - Hinge Adjustment

1. The hinges are adjustable both on the door and on the pillar mountings. Access to the pillar mounting stud nuts will require the removal of the panel trim for both front and rear doors.
2. When re-aligning is necessary first slacken the bolts

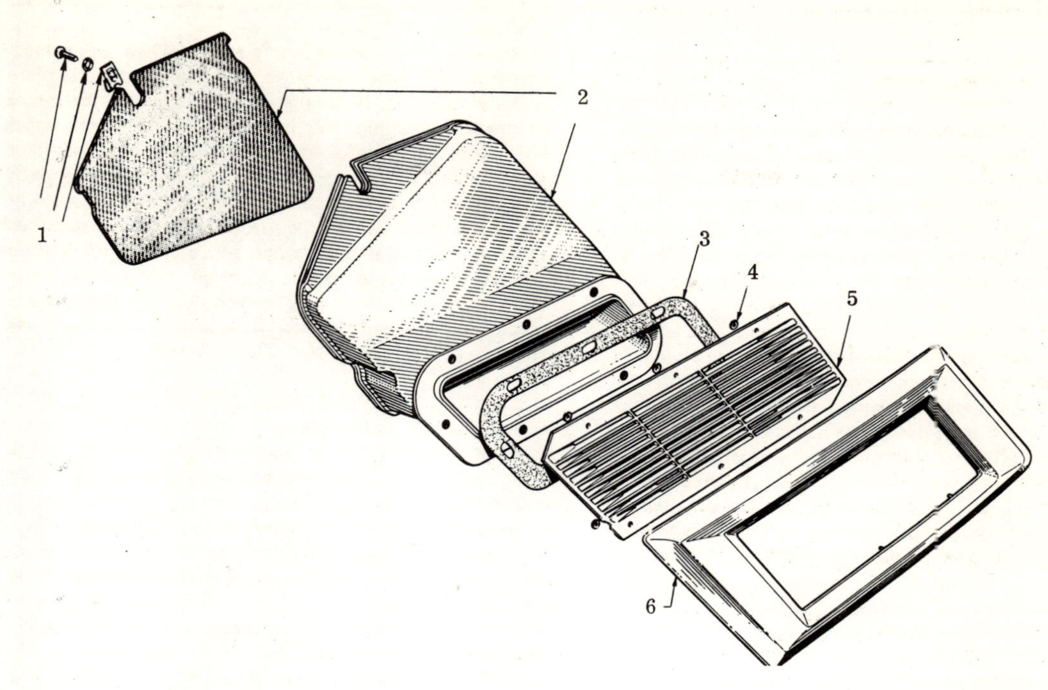

Fig. 12.3. REAR PANEL AIR EXTRACTION VENT — SALOON — EXPLODED VIEW

1 Securing screws and nut	3 Gasket	5 Louvre panel	6 Moulding
2 Panel and flap	4 Nut		

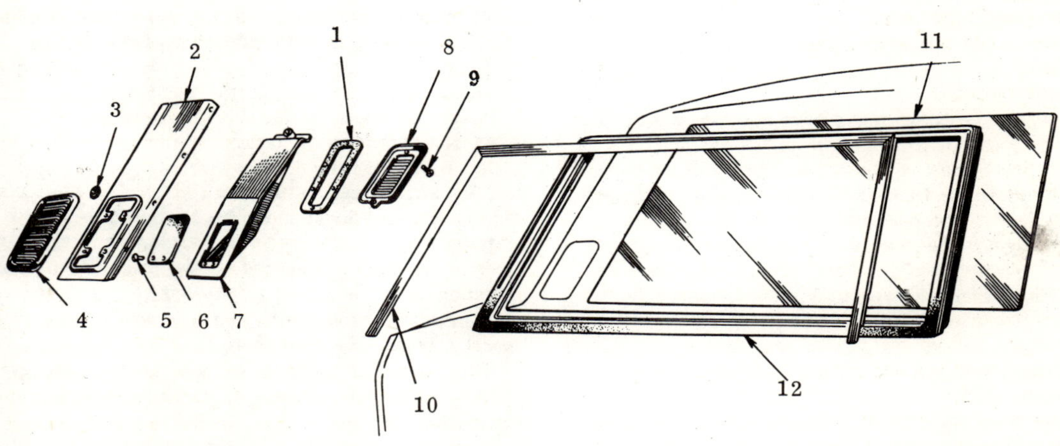

Fig. 12.4. ESTATE CAR — REAR SIDE WINDOW AND AIR EXTRACTION VENT — EXPLODED VIEW

1 Gasket	4 Outer louvre panel	7 Vent panel	10 Embellisher
2 Moulding	5 Screw	8 Inner louvre panel	11 Glass
3 Nut	6 Flap	9 Screw	12 Moulding strip

holding the hinge to the door and reposition the door as required and make sure the bolts are thoroughly tightened up again. If the amount of movement on the door half of the hinges is insufficient remove the trim as appropriate so that further movement can be obtained on the pillar mountings.

3. If the hinges themselves are worn at the hinge pin the door should be detached from the hinges, the hinges removed and new ones fitted.

9. Door Latch Striker - Adjustment

1. Assuming that the door hinges are correctly aligned but the trailing edge of the door is not flush with the body when the door is fully latched, then the striker plate needs adjustment.

2. Slacken the three crosshead screws holding the striker plate to the door pillar just enough to hold the striker plate in position and then push the plate to the inner limit of its position. Try and shut the door, moving the striker plate outwards until the latch is able to engage fully.

3. Without touching the release button pull the door outwards until it is flush with the bodywork. This will move the striker plate along with the latch.

4. Release the latch very carefully so as not to disturb the striker plate and open the door. Tighten down the striker plate securing screws.

10. Door Trim Panels - Removal and Replacement

1. Remove the handles from the inside of the door by unscrewing the crosshead screws holding them to the shaft. Pull off the handles and the escutcheon plates fitted behind them.

2. Remove the arm rest by undoing the two crosshead securing screws.

3. The door panel should be then pulled away from the door by detaching the loop clips from the holes in the door inner panel. If any leverage is necessary try to apply it at a point close to the clip. Otherwise there is a risk of pulling the clip out of the trim.

4. Once the trim is removed a piece of plastic sheet will be revealed, stuck to the inner panel of the door, which protects the inner surfaces of the door and the various mechanisms within from rain water. This should be pulled off and if torn a new piece obtained.

5. Replacement is a reversal of the removal procedure - a piece of plastic sheet first being stuck to the door panel with a suitable adhesive such as Bostick No. 3.

11. Window Regulators - Removal and Replacement

1. The window regulator is a single arm lever with a roller mounted at one end which runs in a channel at the base of the window. The movement of the arm is spring assisted and operated by a toothed quadrant from the winder handle shaft.

2. Remove the interior trim panel and plastic sheet as described in Section 10.

3. Remove the screws which hold the lower window stop bracket to the inner door panel and remove the stop.

4. On front doors replace the winder handle temporarily and lower the window as far as it will go until it is possible to support it and disengage the arm from the bottom channel.

5. Lower the glass to the bottom of the door.

6. Undo the four screws securing the regulator unit to the door and lift it out.

7. Replacement is a straightforward reversal of the removal procedure.

8. On rear doors CLOSE the window before detaching the lower stop and then undo the four regulator screws and disengage the lever from the channel whilst supporting the window in the raised position. Then lower the glass to the bottom of the door and remove the regulator. Replace the regulator in the reverse order.

12. Front Window Quarter Light - Removal and Replacement

1. The quarter light glass and frame position may be adjusted if necessary by altering the lower pivot stud or setting the top pivot. In any case the whole assembly should be removed.

2. Remove the door trim panel as described in Section 10.

3. Wind the main window right down and then remove the three screws which hold the quarter light outer frame to the door.

4. Pull out the channel from the top of the door frame next to the vertical dividing strip.

5. Remove the screw securing the lower end of the vertical dividing strip to the door inner panel.

6. Lever out the inner and outer weather strips from the window sill and remove the two clips next to the vertical dividing strip.

7. Pull the quarter light and strip together towards the rear of the door, clear the dividing channel from the main window and lift out the assembly.

8. Replace the unit in the reverse order.

13. Front Door Windows - Removal and Replacement

1. Remove the quarter light assembly as described in Section 12.

2. Remove the window lower stop bracket by taking out the two screws holding it to the inner panel.

3. Wind the window down sufficiently to disengage the regulator handle whilst supporting the window.

4. Lift the glass up and out.

5. Replace in the reverse order.

14. Rear Door Windows - Removal and Replacement

1. The rear door has a fixed quarter panel which must be removed before the opening main window can be taken out.

2. Wind the window right down and remove the door trim panel as described in Section 10.

3. Prise out the weather strips from the window sill retaining clips and remove the two clips next to the vertical dividing channel.

4. Lever out the channel in the top of the door next to the vertical channel.

5. Drill out the pop rivet at the top of the vertical channel and remove the screw at the bottom.

6. The channel and fixed window can then be eased out. It may be necessary to spread the two halves of the window sill to get the dividing channel and fixing bracket out.

7. Remove the main window lower stop bracket and wind the window down so that the regulator arm may be disengaged. Turn the window through 90° and lift it out of the door.

8. Replacement is a reversal of the removal procedure. There will be need for a pop rivet gun to secure the upper end of the vertical dividing channel.

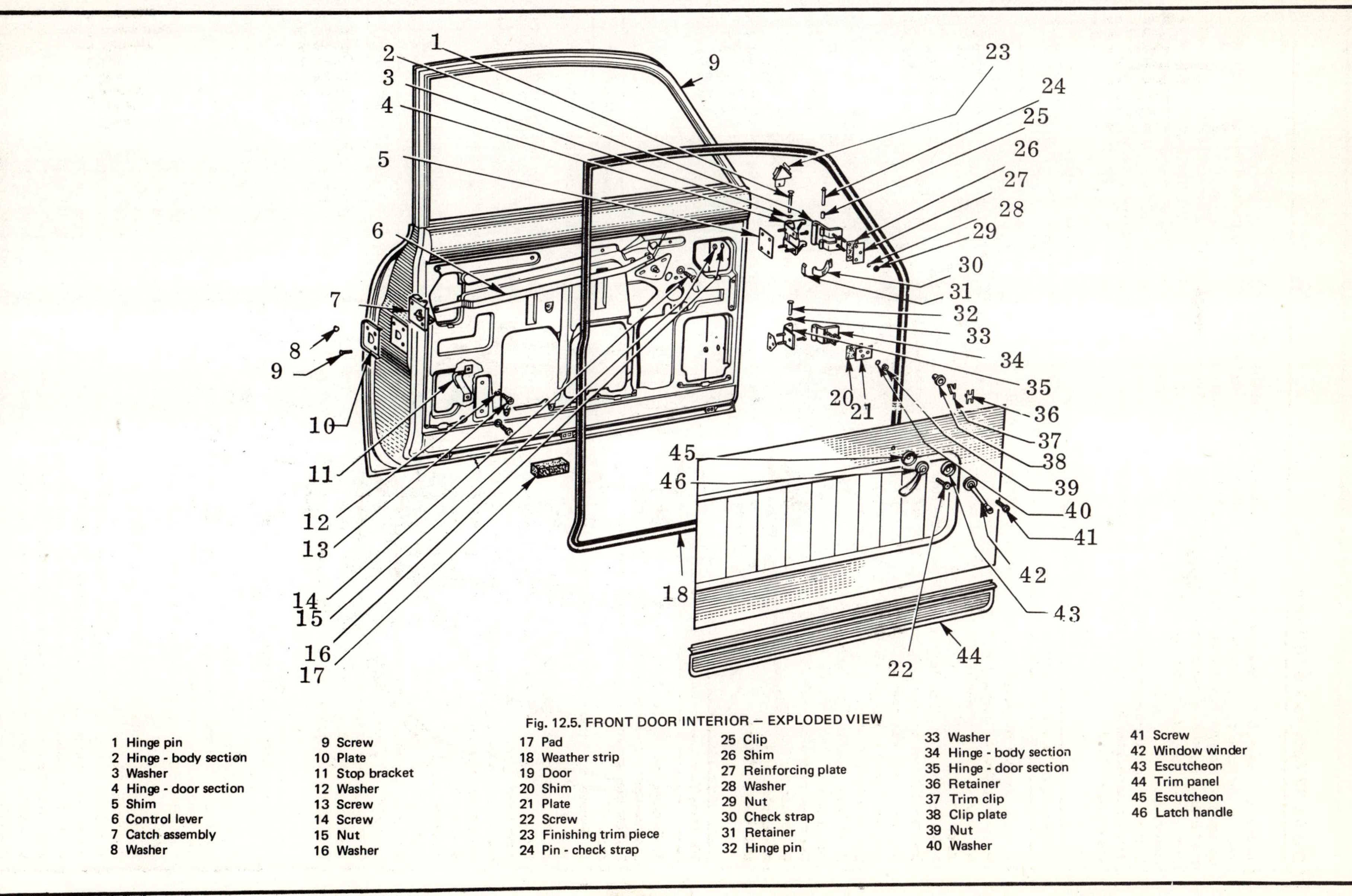

Fig. 12.5. FRONT DOOR INTERIOR – EXPLODED VIEW

1 Hinge pin	9 Screw	17 Pad	25 Clip	33 Washer	41 Screw
2 Hinge - body section	10 Plate	18 Weather strip	26 Shim	34 Hinge - body section	42 Window winder
3 Washer	11 Stop bracket	19 Door	27 Reinforcing plate	35 Hinge - door section	43 Escutcheon
4 Hinge - door section	12 Washer	20 Shim	28 Washer	36 Retainer	44 Trim panel
5 Shim	13 Screw	21 Plate	29 Nut	37 Trim clip	45 Escutcheon
6 Control lever	14 Screw	22 Screw	30 Check strap	38 Clip plate	46 Latch handle
7 Catch assembly	15 Nut	23 Finishing trim piece	31 Retainer	39 Nut	
8 Washer	16 Washer	24 Pin - check strap	32 Hinge pin	40 Washer	

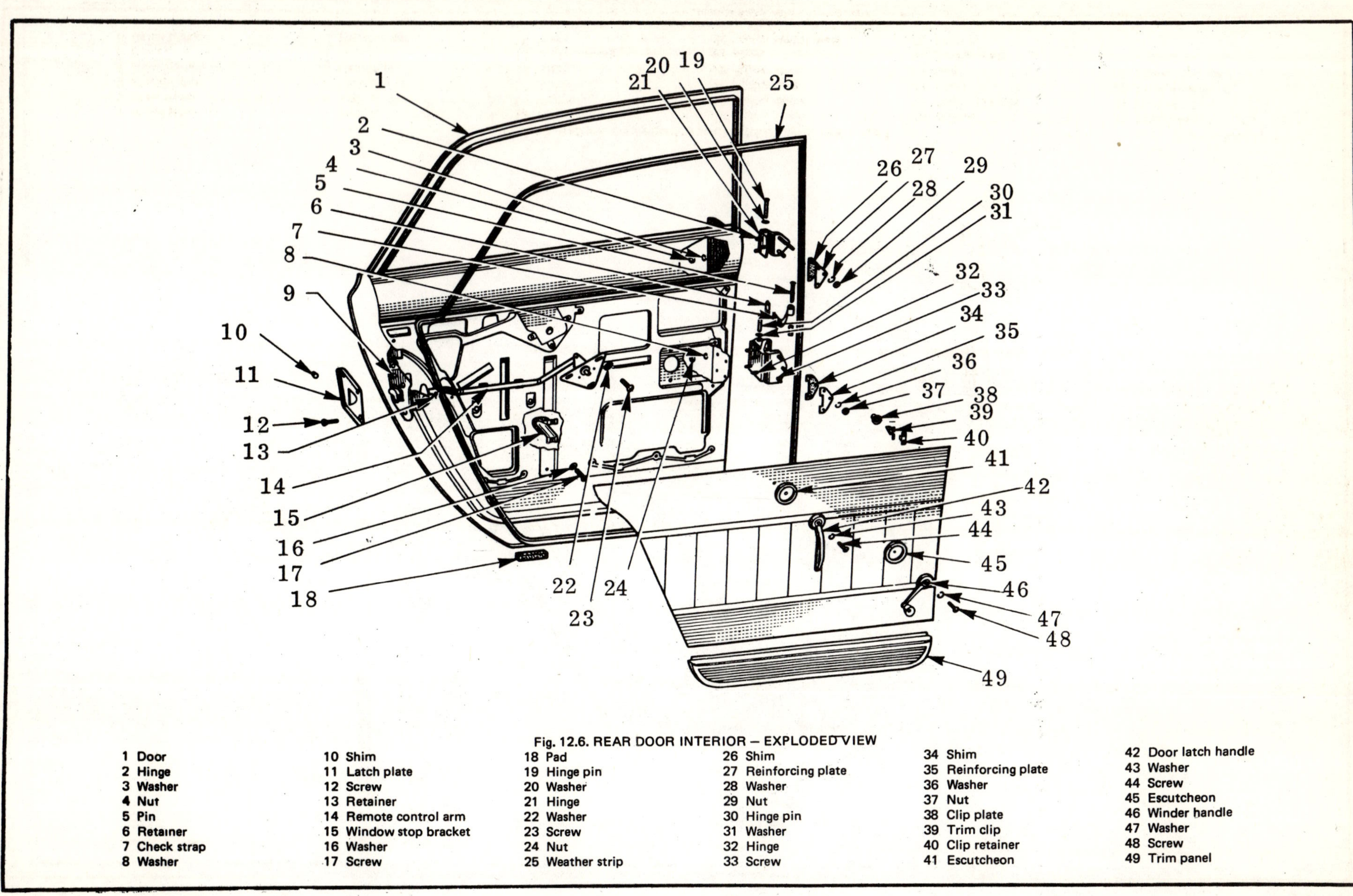

Fig. 12.6. REAR DOOR INTERIOR – EXPLODED VIEW

1 Door	10 Shim	18 Pad	26 Shim	34 Shim	42 Door latch handle
2 Hinge	11 Latch plate	19 Hinge pin	27 Reinforcing plate	35 Reinforcing plate	43 Washer
3 Washer	12 Screw	20 Washer	28 Washer	36 Washer	44 Screw
4 Nut	13 Retainer	21 Hinge	29 Nut	37 Nut	45 Escutcheon
5 Pin	14 Remote control arm	22 Washer	30 Hinge pin	38 Clip plate	46 Winder handle
6 Retainer	15 Window stop bracket	23 Screw	31 Washer	39 Trim clip	47 Washer
7 Check strap	16 Washer	24 Nut	32 Hinge	40 Clip retainer	48 Screw
8 Washer	17 Screw	25 Weather strip	33 Screw	41 Escutcheon	49 Trim panel

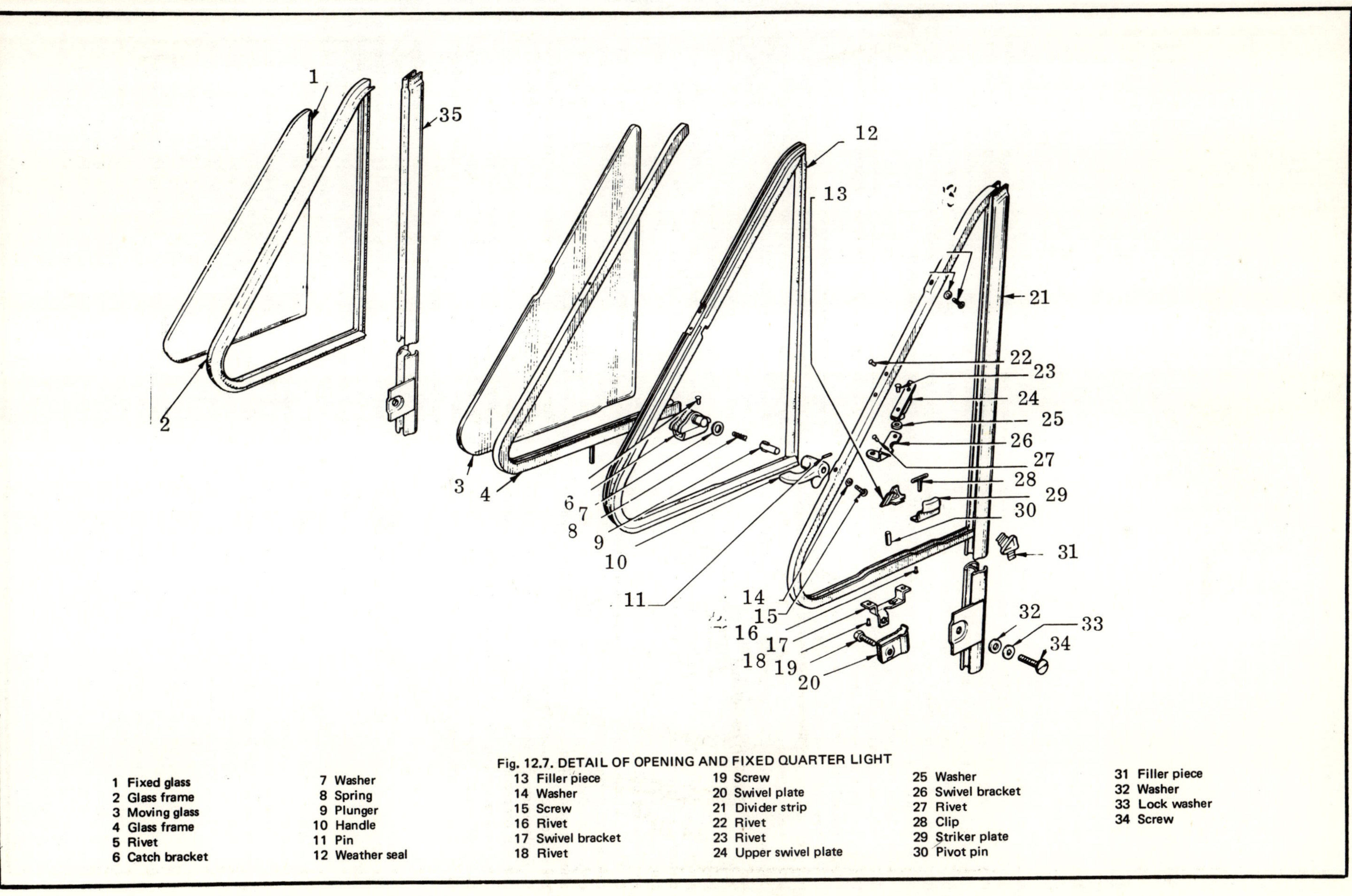

Fig. 12.7. DETAIL OF OPENING AND FIXED QUARTER LIGHT

9. On two door models the rear side windows are hinged at the front edge. To remove the window first remove the two crosshead screws holding the toggle fastener to the body frame at the rear of the window. Then remove the two lower screws in each of the hinges. Slacken the upper two screws (do not remove) and the window may be lifted out as the top hinge holes are slotted.

15. Door Locks and Controls - Removal and Replacement

1. On both front and rear doors the locks are removed in the same manner.
2. Close the windows and remove the interior door trim and plastic sheet as described in Section 10.
3. Temporarily replace the inner lock handle and operate it so as to reveal the wire spring clip which holds the remote operating lever to the lock stud. Detach the clip and arm.
4. Take out the screw securing the rear window channel lower end and push it to one side. Then remove the three screws holding the lock dovetail plate (Fig. 12.10) on the outside edge of the door.
5. From inside the door press the lock release lever, detach the latch from the key lock shaft (on front doors only) and remove the assembly through the door panel interior.
6. The key lock unit fitted to both front doors may be removed after detaching the main latch unit by compressing the twin legged retaining clip (Fig. 12.9) from inside the door with a pair of pliers. Whilst the two halves of the clip are compressed the lock can be withdrawn from the door.
7. The push button control which operates the door lock lever is a separate unit (Fig. 12.11) which is held to the door panel by a locking ring on the inside of the door panel. The distance the button travels may be adjusted by moving the stud in the back of the button. Simply undo the locknut and move the threaded bolt in or out as required.
8. The rear door latches are fitted with child proof safety catches which are visible below the dovetail plates on the edge of the door when it is open (Fig. 12.10). This does not affect removal of the unit which is as described earlier in the section for the front doors.
9. Replacement of all latches and locks is a reversal of the removal procedure. The key lock unit on the front doors should be located on the lock operating rod lugs (Fig. 12.9) and then driven smartly home with a soft faced mallet when it will automatically lock into place.

16. Bonnet (Hood) - Adjustment, Removal and Replacement

1. The bonnet when closed should be located centrally in the aperture which means that the width of the gap all round it should be equal.
2. The bonnet position may be adjusted by slackening some or all of the hinge mounting bolts as necessary to move it vertically, laterally or fore and aft (photo).
3. The bonnet catch post is also adjustable to ensure that the front edge lies flush with the bodywork. Slacken the locknut and screw the post in or out at the top end to set the height.
4. To remove the bonnet (photo) it is only necessary to remove two nuts and bolts from the top or bottom section of each hinge. Whichever is moved, make sure that the position of the hinge is marked so that it can be easily lined up on replacement.
5. To prevent accidental paint scratches cover the adjacent areas of paintwork with protective material before lifting it off.

17. Boot Lid - Adjustment, Removal and Replacement

1. Both vertical and lateral position of the boot lid can be effected by slackening either set of hinge mounting bolts as required and simply moving the lid.
2. To adjust the closing level, the height of the catch may be altered by slackening the bolts holding the striker catch loop and moving it up or down as required.
3. To remove the boot lid protect the surrounding paintwork and then remove the bolts attaching the hinge to the lid and lift it off.
4. The weight of the boot lid is counteracted by a torsion bar running across the car between the lid hinges. The degree of tension may be altered by pulling one end of the torsion bar from the securing bracket and relocating it in the catch. To do this needs considerable force. One way of moving it is to attach a length of strong wire about four feet long to the end of the bar. Then run it over the rear bumper and lever it down with a suitable article to pull the torsion bar from the bracket.

18. Windscreen and Rear Window - Removal and Replacement

1. Unless the glass has been broken it is assumed that it is being removed because the sealing strip is leaking seriously or that there is nearby body damage which calls for its removal before repairs can be effected. If you are buying a secondhand screen from a breakers yard ask them to remove it from the car, if still fitted, before paying for it. If the screen has already been removed check the edges very carefully for signs of chipping. The screen should be smoothly ground all round the edges. Any chips are potential starting points for cracks.
2. Cover the bonnet with protective material and pull the wiper blades off their spindles. The bright metal mouldings on the weather strip should also be prised out, having first removed the joint cover clips.
3. Remove the rear view mirror by undoing the two securing screws inside the car.
4. Remove the windscreen pillar mouldings also on each side of the screen held by further crosshead screws.
5. Determine what sort of glass the screen is made from. It will be toughened or laminated and a mark on the screen in the lower centre edge will indicate which.
6. Find an old screwdriver and file off its sharp edges and corners. Use this as a means of pushing the outer edge of the weather strip under the window aperture flange from inside the car. When about 2/3 of the strip has been pushed under in this way the whole screen may be pushed out together with the weather strip from the inside. Ensure that only a steady pressure is used, on laminated glass especially.
7. If difficulty is experienced, on toughened glass screens only, it is possible to use a thin flat lever on the outside of the screen. Get the end of the lever under the outside edge of the weather strip and behind the edge of the glass. Using a cloth pad as a fulcrum the lever may be moved until the inner lip of the weather strip is clear of the body flange. Move the lever around repeating this operation until the whole screen can be taken out.
8. When refitting a screen (or rear window) first make sure that all traces of sealer are removed from the glass and weather strip. Do not use solvents which could affect the rubber. It is generally better to pull and scrape off any such particles of adhesive.
9. Fit the weather strip to the glass and secure it temporarily with strips of adhesive tape over the rubber and to both

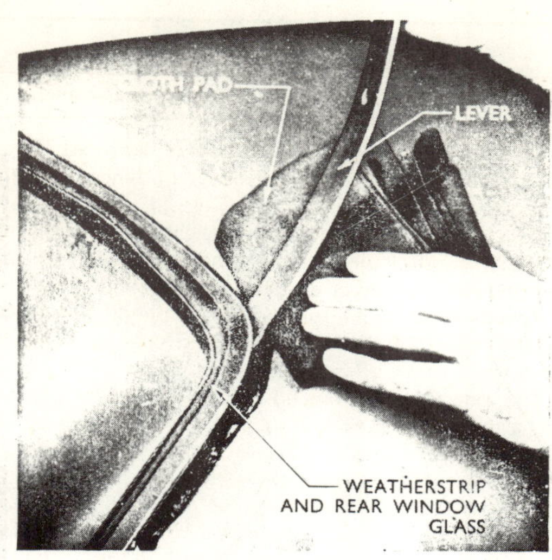

Fig. 12.8. Showing use of lever to assist removal of toughened glass screens

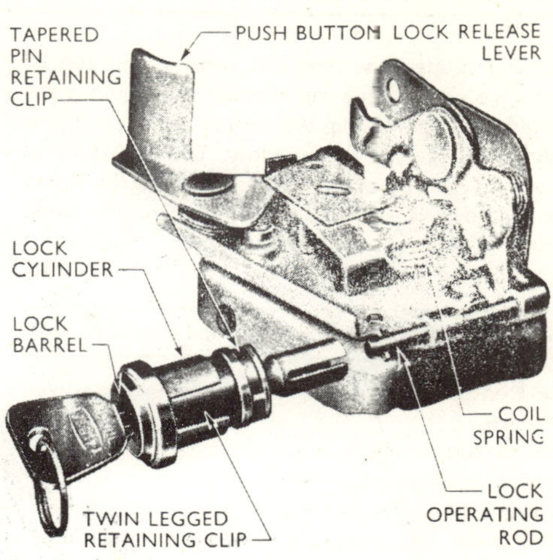

Fig. 12.9. Latch and key details

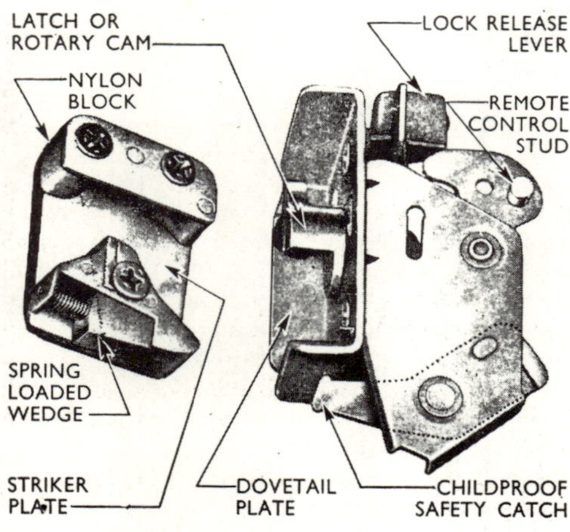

Fig. 12.10. Striker plate and latch cam details

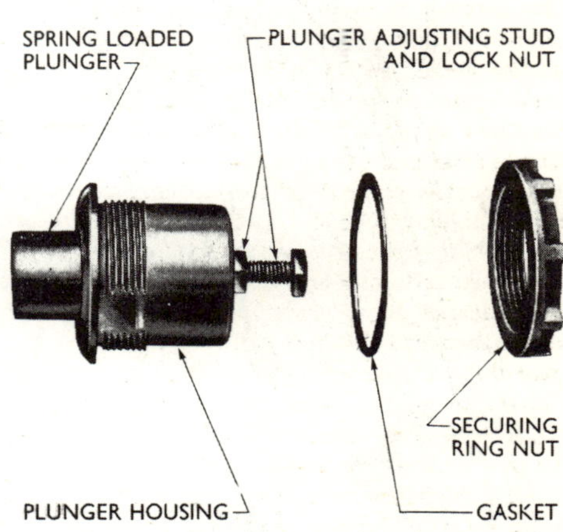

Fig. 12.11. Latch operating button details

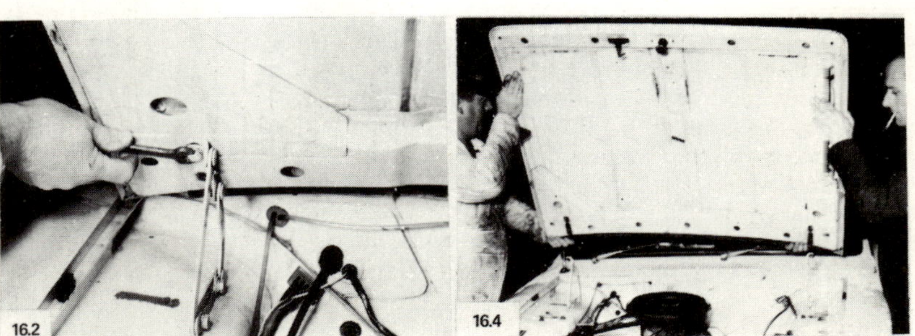

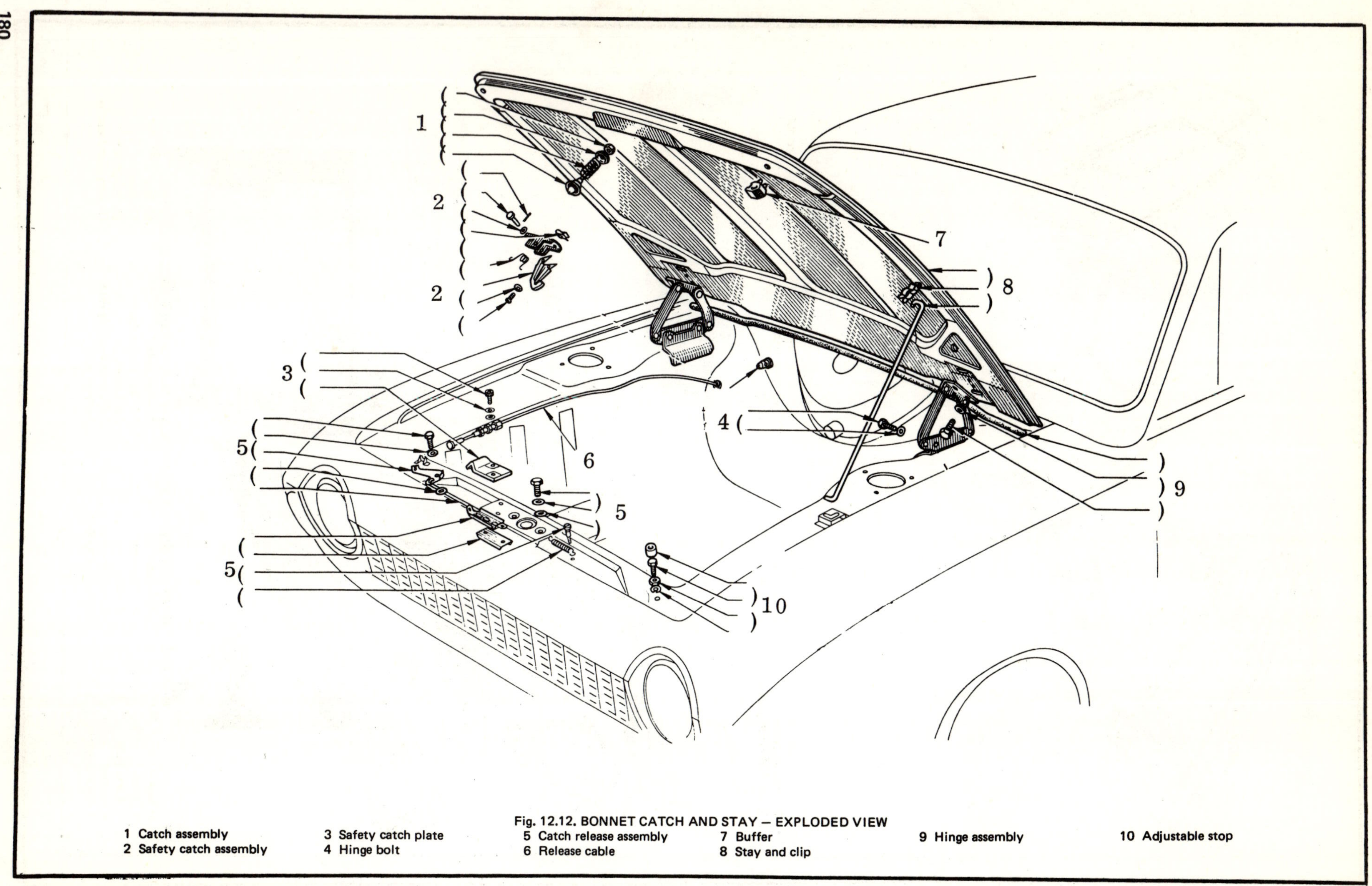

Fig. 12.12. BONNET CATCH AND STAY — EXPLODED VIEW

1 Catch assembly	3 Safety catch plate	5 Catch release assembly	7 Buffer	9 Hinge assembly	10 Adjustable stop
2 Safety catch assembly	4 Hinge bolt	6 Release cable	8 Stay and clip		

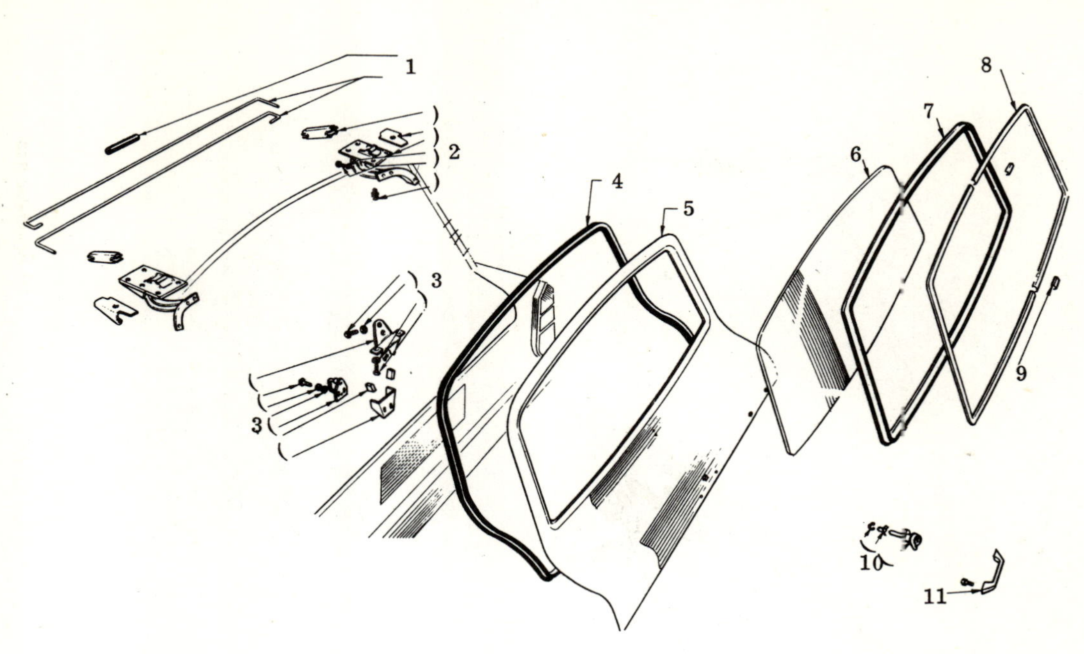

Fig. 12.13. ESTATE CAR TAIL GATE — EXPLODED VIEW

1 Torque springs	4 Weather strip	7 Weather strip moulding	10 Lock assembly
2 Hinge assembly	5 Tailgate	8 Chrome insert	11 Handle
3 Catch & catch plate assembly	6 Glass	9 Clip	

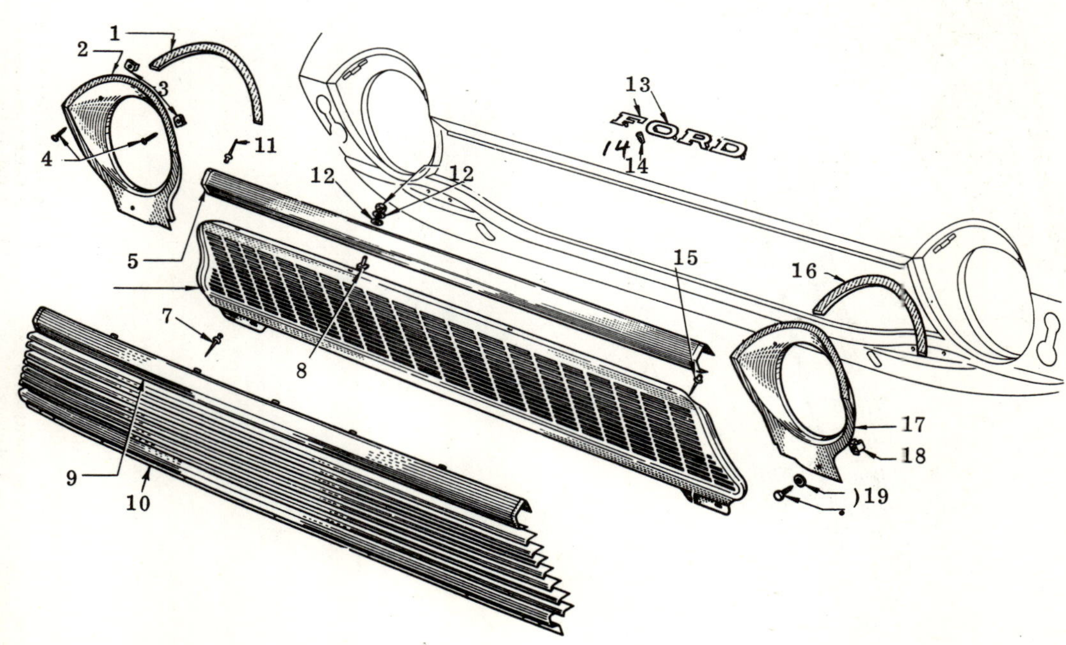

Fig. 12.14. RADIATOR GRILLE AND HEADLAMP SURROUNDS — EXPLODED VIEW

1 Seal	6 Grille	11 Pop rivet	16 Seal
2 Bezel	7 Pop rivets	12 Nut and washers	17 Bezel
3 Speed nuts	8 Clips	13 Letters	18 Speed nut
4 Screws	9 Fusing plate	14 Letter securing stud	19 Screw and washer
5 Finishing strip	10 Grille (2000E)	15 Pop rivet	

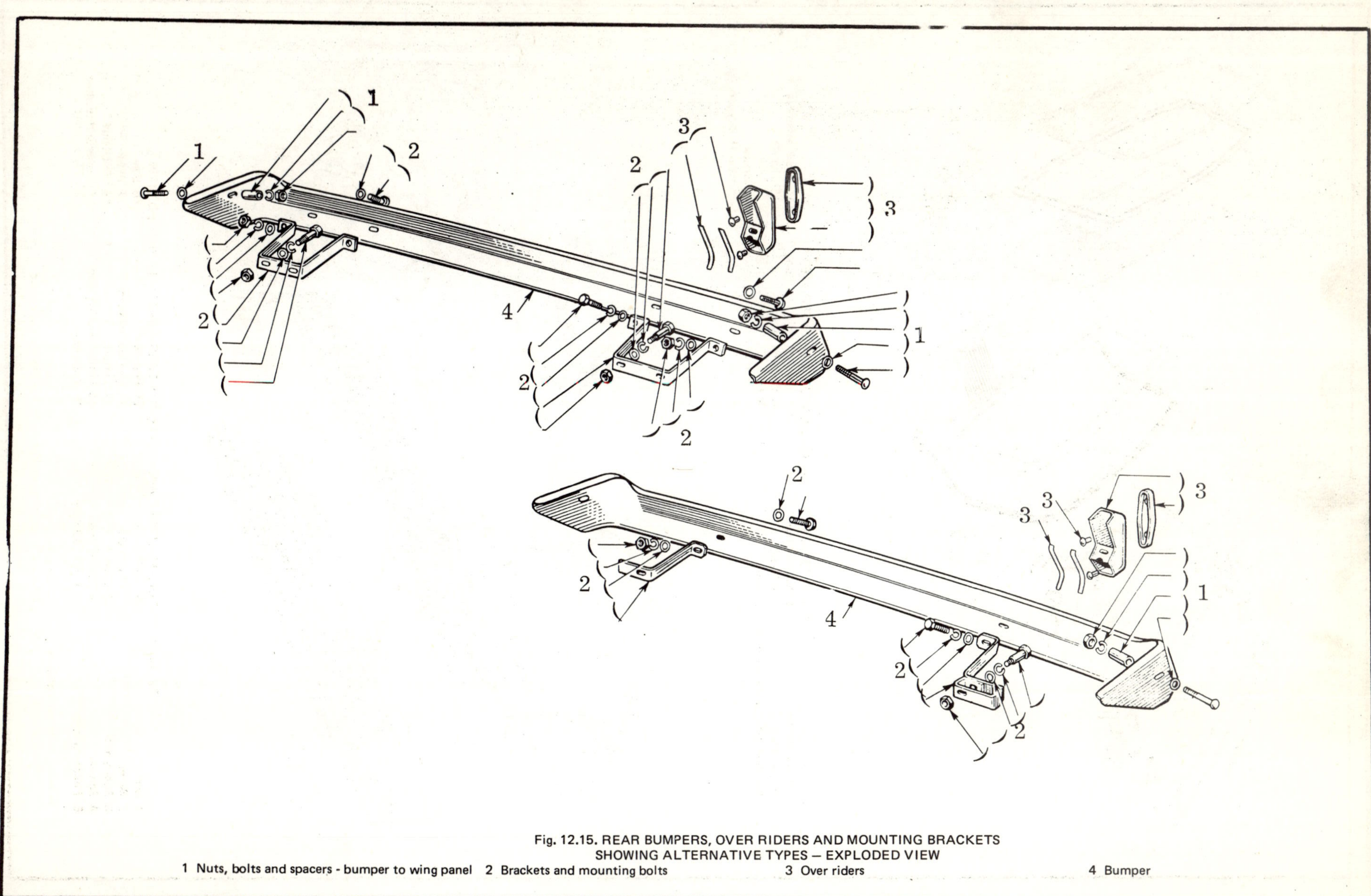

Fig. 12.15. REAR BUMPERS, OVER RIDERS AND MOUNTING BRACKETS
SHOWING ALTERNATIVE TYPES — EXPLODED VIEW

1 Nuts, bolts and spacers - bumper to wing panel   2 Brackets and mounting bolts   3 Over riders   4 Bumper

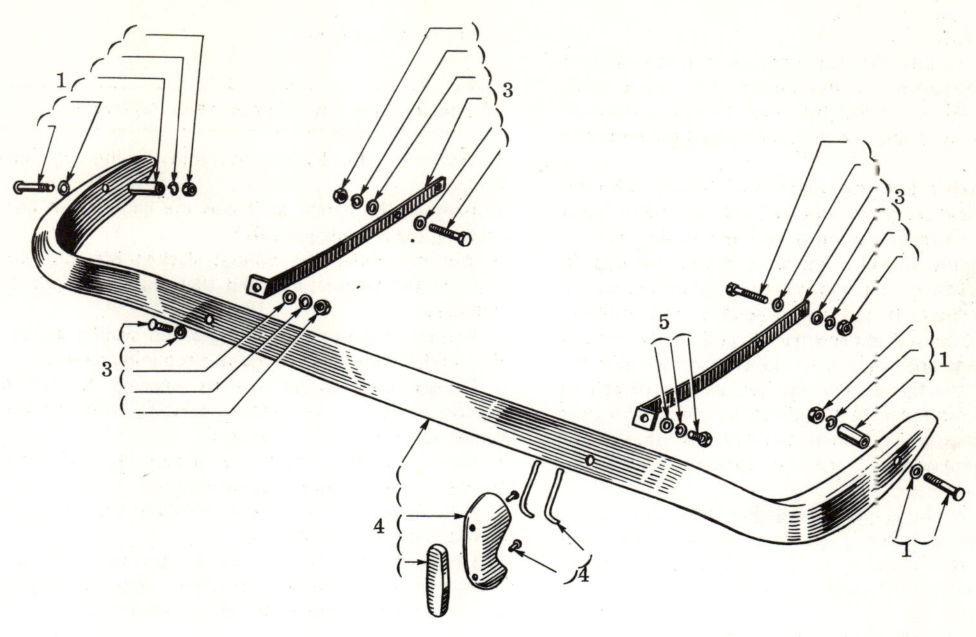

Fig. 12.16. FRONT BUMPER, OVER RIDER AND MOUNTING BRACKETS — EXPLODED VIEW

1 Nuts, bolts and spacers — bumper to wing panel
2 Nuts, bolts — bumper to bracket
3 Nuts and bolts — bracket to body frame
4 Over riders
5 Over rider fixing bolt

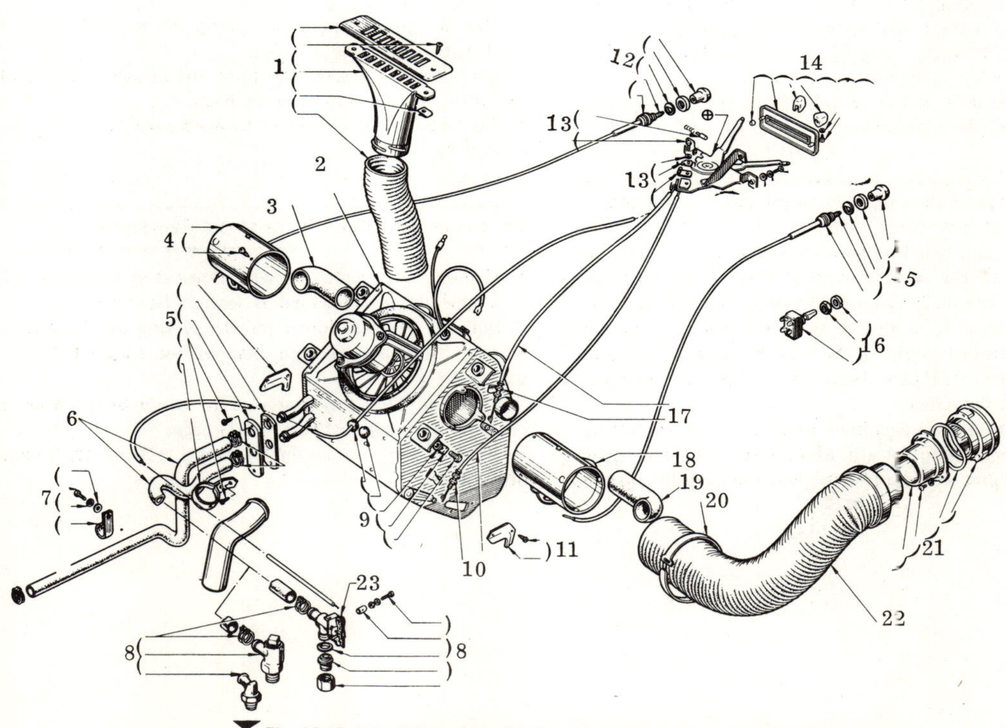

Fig. 12.17. HEATING AND VENTILATING SYSTEM — EXPLODED VIEW

1 Air intake and duct
2 Fan/heater assembly
3 Duct hose
4 Duct and air valve assembly
5 Water hose connections and brackets
6 Water hoses
7 Hose clip
8 Water valves and clips
9 Mounting bracket and grommets
10 Control cable
11 Bracket
12 Control cable assembly — air vent
13 Contro' lever assembly
14 Control lever escutcheon
15 Control cable assembly — air vent
16 Fan switch
17 Control cable
18 Duct and air valve assembly
19 Duct hose
20 Hose clip
21 Outlet vent
23 Water valve

sides of the glass.

10 Fit a drawcord into the flange groove so that there is at least a six inch crossover at the bottom. To make this job easy a good tip is to thread the cord through a piece of small bore rigid tube and use the tube to feed the cord into the grooves.

11 Using a suitable gun with a nozzle of $1/8$ in. (3.5 mm) in diameter (these are often supplied with the sealer) inject sealing liquid between the glass and the rubber on the outside. Also apply a bead of sealer on the section of strip which goes against the outside of the body mounting flange.

12 Offer up the screen and strip assembly into position, making sure it is centralized and start to pull out one end of the draw cord so that the lip of the strip comes over the inside edge of the flange. Try and get another person to apply a light pressure to the outside of the glass at the same time. When top centre is reached start with the other end of the cord. Remove the pieces of adhesive tape when suitable.

13 To refit the moulding into the weather strip lubricate the groove with soapy water or glycerine and then feed one edge into the slot. Then use the specially prepared screwdriver to lift the lip of the weather strip over the other side of the moulding.

14 Clean off all traces of adhesive and replace the interior fittings which have been removed.

19. Radiator Grille - Removal and Replacement

1. The grille is held by screws at the bottom and pop rivets at the top so ensure that pop rivets are available to refit it before taking it off.

2. Remove the four screws holding the headlamp bezels and then remove the lower screws securing the grille. Then drill out the pop rivets along the top edge and lift the grille out.

3. Replace the unit in the reverse order of removal using a pop rivet gun where required.

20. Front and Rear Bumpers - Removal and Replacement

1. Both front and rear bumpers are the wrap around type and the ends of the wrap around are bolted to the body in addition to the main support brackets. As bumper bolts tend to get rusty it is always best to detach the whole assembly by the bolts holding the main bracket to the body of the car. Over riders and brackets can then be detached more easily on the bench.

2. When refitting the assemblies replace all the mounting bolts before tightening any up. Make sure that the bumper is properly aligned and centralized and then tighten up the mounting bolts evenly.

21. Heater Assembly - Removal and Replacement

1. Disconnect the battery by removing the negative earth lead.

2. Remove the parcel shelf and the heater trim panel by undoing the retaining screws.

3. Working under the bonnet slacken off the two wire clips on the heater pipes and then pull the pipes off the bulkhead.

4. Remove the heater pipe plate and sealing gasket from the bulkhead by undoing the two retaining screws.

5. Release the two spring clips securing the two heater control cables to the heater operating arms and pull the cables out of the operating arms.

6. Make a careful note of wiring positions and disconnect the wires from the heater blower motor.

7. Pull off the face level vent pipes and the demister pipes from the heater assembly.

8. Undo the four bolts securing the heater to the bulkhead and withdraw the complete heater assembly. Replacement is a reversal of the above procedure.

22. Heater Motor - Removal and Replacement

1. Undo the thirteen small screws securing the blower motor to the heater and remove the blower motor and mounting plate as an assembly from the heater.

2. Remove the sealing gasket from the mounting plate. Then remove the rubber gasket and pull the motor wires through the mounting plate.

3. Remove the spring clip holding the blower motor fan in place and withdraw the fan.

4. Undo the three screws holding the blower motor to the mounting plate and remove the motor.

5. Replacement is a straight forward reversal of the above procedure.

23. Heater Radiator - Removal and Replacement

1. Remove the heater blower motor and mounting plate as an assembly as described in Section 19 above.

2. Pull off the rear lower panel covering the radiator and remove the foam packing that will be found behind the panel.

3. Carefully slide the heater radiator out of its recess and examine it for signs of leaks or damage.

4. Replacement is a straight forward reversal of the above procedure.

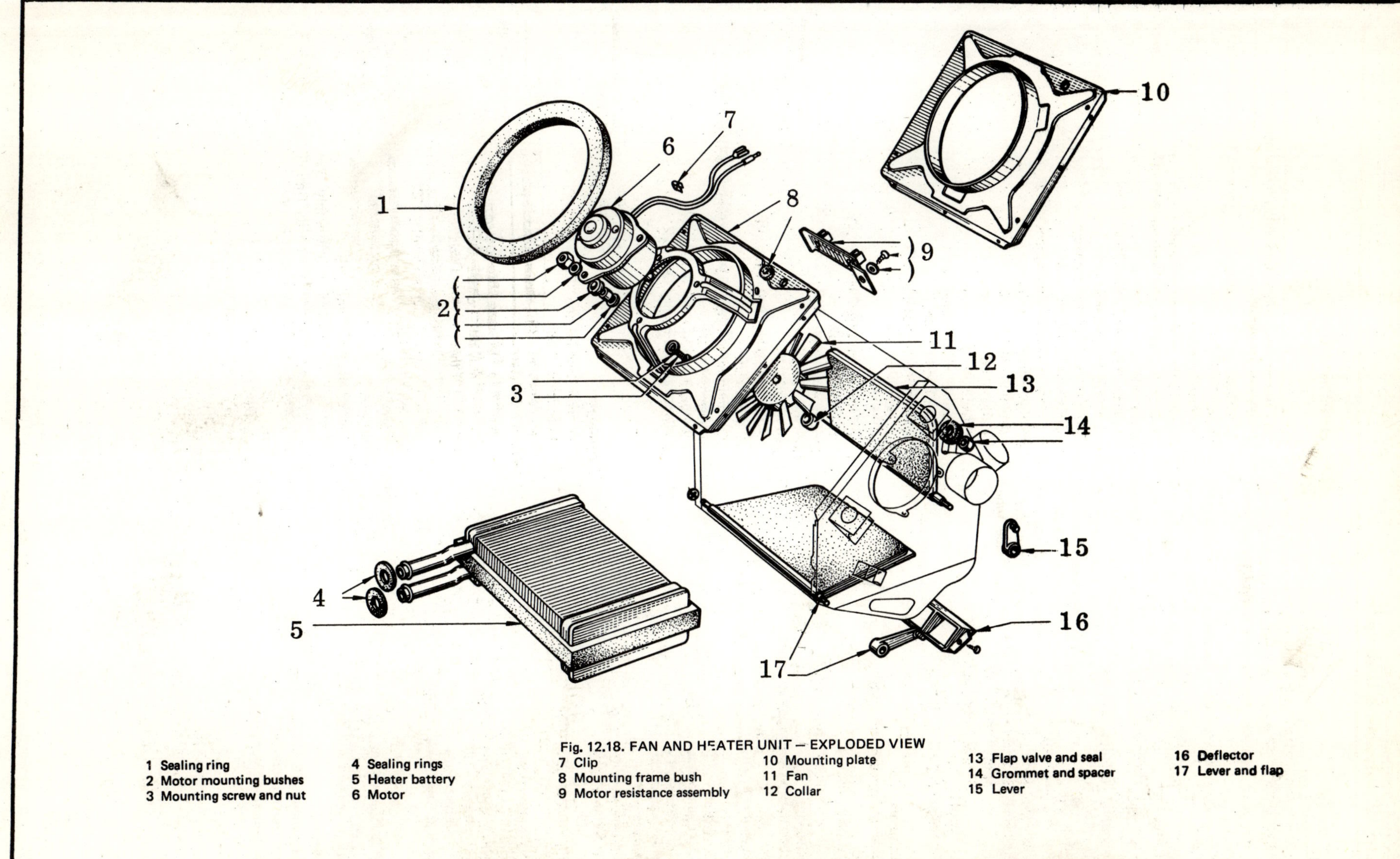

Fig. 12.18. FAN AND HEATER UNIT — EXPLODED VIEW

1 Sealing ring
2 Motor mounting bushes
3 Mounting screw and nut
4 Sealing rings
5 Heater battery
6 Motor
7 Clip
8 Mounting frame bush
9 Motor resistance assembly
10 Mounting plate
11 Fan
12 Collar
13 Flap valve and seal
14 Grommet and spacer
15 Lever
16 Deflector
17 Lever and flap

Index

PRINTED BY
ODCOMBE PRESS
WEST CAMEL, YEOVIL, SOMERSET